# Mortals with Tremendous Responsibilities

A History of the United States District Court for the Eastern District of Pennsylvania

# Mortals with Tremendous Responsibilities

A History of the United States District Court for the Eastern District of Pennsylvania

Harvey Bartle III

Saint Joseph's University Press
Philadelphia

This volume was supported by a generous gift from the
Historical Society of the United States District Court for the Eastern District of Pennsylvania.



Library of Congress Cataloging-in-Publication Data
Bartle, Harvey, 1941-
Mortals with tremendous responsibilities : a history of the United States District Court for the eastern district of Pennsylvania / Harvey Bartle III.
p. cm.
ISBN 978-0-916101-72-5
1. United States. District Court (Pennsylvania : Eastern District)--History. 2. District courts--United States--History. 3. District courts--Pennsylvania--Philadelphia--History. I. Title.
KF8755.P38B47 2011
347.73'2209748--dc23
2011021983

Saint Joseph's University Press
5600 City Avenue
Philadelphia, PA 19131
www.sjupress.com

Saint Joseph's University Press is a member of the Association of American University Presses and the Association of Jesuit University Presses.

# TABLE OF CONTENTS

# List of Illustrations

TO

MY JUDICIAL COLLEAGUES,

PAST AND PRESENT.

"I think there are a number of qualities that are essential [to be a good, effective trial judge]. One is a love of the law. Two, a fairly well balanced rather than a specialized experience in trial work . . . . Third, I would say patience, and that in my view is a very important ingredient . . . A sense of humor is a very helpful attribute and last but not least, a subordination of any tendency to egotism. . . . *You are a mortal charged with tremendous responsibilities. You're dealing with other people's rights, not your own*, and a good trial judge in my view should have those qualities plus of course a willingness to work hard and good basic knowledge of the law."

— C. William Kraft Jr.
Judge, United States District Court
for the Eastern District of Pennsylvania
(Interview given on February 28, 1995)

# PREFACE

In early 2006, shortly after becoming Chief Judge, I had lunch with Patrick Kittredge, a prominent Philadelphia lawyer who happened to be the President of the Historical Society of the United States District Court for the Eastern District of Pennsylvania. Pat and I have been friends for over forty years from our days when we served as law clerks in the mid-1960's. As we reminisced about the olden times, the idea arose that a Court history should be written before any more of its illustrious past fades from memory. A seven member History Committee to oversee the project was soon established consisting of: Judge J. William Ditter Jr.; Judge Eduardo C. Robreno; C. Clark Hodgson Jr., Esquire; Patrick W. Kittredge, Esquire; Seymour I. Toll, Esquire; the Clerk of Court Michael E. Kunz; and the undersigned.

Coordinating with the Committee, the Historical Society of the Court then engaged Dr. Jason S. Lantzer, an Adjunct Professor of History at the University of Indiana, to assist with this effort. He did much of the initial research without which it is unlikely that this history would have been written. He also provided helpful comments as the work progressed. We sincerely thank him for the many hours that he has devoted to this project.

This Court was one of the original thirteen federal district courts established in 1789 under the Judiciary Act signed by President Washington. Francis Hopkinson, a signer of the Declaration of Independence, was the Court's first judge. The story of the Court in large part is the story of its judges and the lawsuits over which they have presided. Any history spanning a period of over 220 years must necessarily be selective. Consequently, the cases that are highlighted here are those which, in the view of the History Committee, are historically or legally significant or are representative of the type of cases heard in this District during a particular era. Occasionally, a case made its way into this chronicle because of its interesting facts or its colorful personalities. The growth of the Court and the changes in its composition, its jurisdiction, its workload, and its administration over more than two centuries are also subjects which permeate the pages to follow. To complete the picture, a number of anecdotes about the judges and life at the Court are recounted. As Judge William Kraft aptly remarked many years ago, a judge is "a mortal charged with tremendous responsibilities."

This volume is intended not only to memorialize the story of this Court but also to serve as a reminder of the consequential role that this Court has played as part of the separate and coequal judicial branch of our constitutional system of government.

The preamble to the Constitution declares:

> We the People of the United States, in Order to form a more perfect Union, establish Justice, insure domestic Tranquility, provide for the common defence, promote the general Welfare, and secure the Blessings of Liberty to ourselves and our Posterity, do ordain and establish this Constitution for the United States of America.

The United States District Court for the Eastern District of Pennsylvania, like its sister courts, strives to carry out the goal of establishing justice and securing the blessings of liberty to ourselves and our posterity. It seeks to do so by resolving specific cases and controversies consistent with the rights and limitations incorporated into the Constitution and the relevant statutory and common law. As will be seen, implementing and safeguarding this rule of law is not always an easy or simple task.

Alexis de Tocqueville, a French aristocrat, wrote *Democracy in America* after his visit to the United States in the 1830's. In his book he observed, "Scarcely any political question arises in the United States that is not resolved, sooner or later, into a judicial question."[1] Time and time again, issues which begin as political questions in American history become enmeshed in lawsuits before the judges of this Court. The actions of the Court simply cannot be isolated from what is occurring beyond its courtrooms.

In addition to Jason Lantzer, I am grateful to my six colleagues on the History Committee for their invaluable suggestions and wise counsel. Each has made important contributions. Their congeniality and enthusiasm for this project have made my research and writing of this history a most pleasant experience.

Further, a special thanks goes to the Historical Society of the Court which has undertaken the sponsorship of this project. The Court is fortunate to have in its midst this vibrant organization, currently led by Pat Kittredge. It has done so much over the years to preserve and promote the history of this Court.

The Committee is likewise most appreciative that St. Joseph's University Press has agreed to serve as the book's publisher. We salute Father Joseph F. Chorpenning, its Editorial Director, as well as Carmen R. Croce, its Director, for their genuine interest and support of this effort.

A heartfelt thanks goes to my long-time secretary, Frances Porreca, not only for her patience and support but also for her invaluable help in typing and reviewing innumerable drafts of the manuscript and for keeping all my files and materials organized. Her attention to detail is nonpareil.

Many others have also contributed in various ways to this book. A number of judges and former judges as well as lawyers were interviewed or otherwise provided valuable input. My law clerks, Robert Fay, Jane Minerly, and Shelby Schwartz checked the citations. Michael Hayes, the Assistant Librarian of the Court of Appeals Library, was kept busy finding answers to my sundry inquiries and was gracious in doing so. Garth Herrick did a masterly job in making many of the photographs appearing within these pages. Members of the staff of the Clerk of Court Michael Kunz assisted him in gathering historical records. They were Stephen Bissell, Miriam Coco, Fred Druding, Diane Michalik, Shannon Ostien, and Susan Renz. I gratefully acknowledge the help of all of these individuals.

Finally, I thank my wife, Nathalie Akin Bartle, for her support, suggestions, and encouragement throughout this project. It could not have been done without her.

All members of the Committee hope that the reader enjoys this volume as much as all of us have enjoyed bringing it to fruition.

Harvey Bartle III
Philadelphia, Pennsylvania
September 2011

**Notes**

1. Tocqueville, Alexis de, *Democracy in America*, p. 280 (Alfred A. Knopf, Inc., 1972).

# I
# The Beginning: 1787-1792

The story of the United States District Court for the Eastern District of Pennsylvania and the federal judicial system of which it is a part begins with the Constitutional Convention of 1787. In the hot summer of that year, delegates from twelve states met in Philadelphia behind closed doors at the Pennsylvania State House, now known as Independence Hall, at a convention called to revise the flawed Articles of Confederation.[1] George Washington presided. The delegates, acting boldly and beyond their charge, decided to forego any revision and instead to draft a new Constitution of the United States.

Several plans for the structure of a new government soon emerged. While the modern focus is generally on the debates about the nature and power of the Executive and Legislative Branches, the Convention also wrestled with the question of a federal judiciary.[2] The Virginia Plan proposed that a "national judiciary" be established consisting of "one supreme tribunal to be chosen by the second branch of the national legislature" and that "the national legislature be empowered to appoint inferior tribunals." The New Jersey Plan suggested "a federal judiciary be established to consist of a supreme tribunal the judges of which to be appointed by the Executive." Both plans had judges holding office "during good Behaviour," that is, for life. Both favored judges to be paid "a fixed compensation" which should be neither increased nor diminished for any sitting judge.[3]

James Madison and James Wilson, two of the leading nationalists at the Convention, urged that the Constitution require the establishment of a system of federal courts below the Supreme Court and that the judiciary play a role along with the Executive in revising or vetoing laws passed by the national legislature.[4] There was strong opposition to these ideas. Although no real disagreement to a Supreme Court developed, a resolution that the Constitution mandate the establishment of lower federal courts was defeated. According to delegates such as John Rutledge, later the second Chief Justice of the United States, the existing state courts were adequate for the adjudication of all legal matters, and besides a federal judiciary would be an encroachment on the rights of the states. Roger Sherman of Connecticut expressed concern about the expense of an array of federal courts.[5] In the end, the delegates voted to establish a Supreme Court and to allow Congress to determine whether other federal courts should be created.

The Convention rejected the proposal to give the courts a role in revising the laws. The prevailing sentiment was against any amalgamation of the judicial and executive functions.[6]

It was decided that all federal judges would be appointed during good behavior. Alexander Hamilton, a delegate to the Constitutional Convention, later wrote in No. 78 of *The Federalist* that life tenure "is the best expedient which can be devised in any government, to secure a steady, upright, and impartial administration of the laws." He further observed that "nothing will contribute so much as this to that independent spirit in the judges which must be essential to the faithful performance of so arduous a duty."

The all-important issue of judicial compensation was also debated. Both the Virginia and New Jersey Plans, as noted, provided that salaries should never be increased or decreased. In a move for which federal judges will forever be grateful, the delegates voted down any rule prohibiting salary increases. They recognized the uncertainty and likely fluctuations in the economy during the tenure of judges appointed for life. On the other hand, the Convention wisely retained the provision against any diminution in their compensation in order to bolster judicial independence and to protect judges from retribution for handing down unpopular decisions.[7]

The Constitution, as finally drafted, provides in Article III, § 1:

> The judicial Power of the United States, shall be vested in one supreme Court, and in such inferior Courts as the Congress may from time to time ordain and establish. The Judges, both of the supreme and inferior Courts, shall hold their Offices during good Behaviour, and shall, at stated Times, receive for their Services, a Compensation, which shall not be diminished during their Continuance in Office.

The delegates struggled over the mode for the appointment of judges. During the debate over whether the executive or the national legislature should be invested with this authority, Benjamin Franklin injected "what he understood was practiced in Scotland." According to Madison's notes, "He then in a brief and entertaining manner related a Scotch mode, in which the nomination proceeded from the Lawyers, who always selected the ablest of the profession in order to get rid of him, and share his practice among themselves."[8] At one point the delegates decided to have the judges named by what was to become the Senate.[9] Ultimately, the Convention opted for the President to appoint the "judges" of the Supreme Court and all other officers of the United States "by and with the Advice and Consent of the Senate."[10]

In addition to judicial tenure and compensation and the method of appointment of judges, the Convention specified the jurisdictional boundaries of the Supreme Court and of other federal courts should they be established. The Constitution declares in Article III, § 2:

> The judicial Power shall extend to all Cases, in Law and Equity, arising under this Constitution, the Laws of the United States, and Treaties made, or which shall be made, under their Authority;
> – to all Cases affecting Ambassadors, other public Ministers and Consuls;
> – to all Cases of admiralty and maritime Jurisdiction;
> – to Controversies to which the United States shall be a Party;
> – to Controversies between two or more States;
> – between a State and Citizens of another State;
> – between Citizens of different States,
> – between Citizens of the same State claiming Lands under Grants of different States, and between a State, or the Citizens thereof;
> – and foreign States, Citizens or Subjects.[11]
>
> In all Cases affecting Ambassadors, other public Ministers and Consuls, and those in which a State shall be a Party, the supreme Court shall have original Jurisdiction. In all other Cases before mentioned, the supreme Court shall have appellate Jurisdiction, both as to Law and Fact, with such Exceptions, and under such Regulations as the Congress shall make.

The Convention completed its work and adjourned on September 17, 1787 after thirty-nine delegates from twelve states signed the Constitution and submitted it to the states for ratification. The Constitution took effect on June 21, 1788, when New Hampshire became the ninth state to give its assent.[12] Congress convened on March 4, 1789, and George Washington was inaugurated as President on April 30.

That first Congress voted to "ordain and establish" federal courts "inferior to the Supreme Court," by passing the Judiciary Act which President Washington signed on September 24, 1789.[13] The Act created thirteen District Courts including the United States District Court for the District of Pennsylvania. There was one court for each of the eleven states which by that time had ratified the Constitution as well as a court for Maine, which was then part of Massachusetts and one for Kentucky which was then part of Virginia.[14]

The Act authorized one District Judge for each court, although the salaries of the judges varied. The judge in tiny Delaware, for example, was to be paid at the low end of the scale at $800 per year whereas in Pennsylvania he was to receive twice that amount or $1,600. The Pennsylvania District Court was designated by the Act to be held alternatively at Philadelphia and "York Town," a hamlet approximately one-hundred miles west of Philadelphia in York County. It had served as the nation's temporary capital from September 1777 through late June 1778 when the Continental

Congress met there during the British occupation of Philadelphia. The Court has no record of any judicial business ever having been conducted at that location.[15]

President Washington, a proponent of a strong federal government, moved swiftly to submit to the Senate for its advice and consent the names of his nominees for lifetime appointments to the Supreme Court and the thirteen District Courts. In fact, he transmitted his list on September 24, 1789, the same day he signed the Judiciary Act into law, except for the District Court nominees for New Jersey and New York which came a day later.[16] All were leading citizens and supporters of the Constitution.

Most were prominent political figures.[17] Some had signed either the Declaration of Independence or the Constitution and one, Supreme Court Justice James Wilson of Pennsylvania, had signed both.[18]

Included among Washington's choices was Francis Hopkinson, a signer of the Declaration of Independence and a state Admiralty judge, to fill the seat on the District Court for the District of Pennsylvania. Hopkinson was well known to Washington. He had lobbied the President for a judgeship, and his selection came as no surprise.[19] The Senate confirmed Hopkinson two days later, on Saturday, September 26, and the President signed his Commission before the day had come to an end.[20] At least in regard to judicial appointments, events of the eighteenth century moved with greater alacrity than today. There were no lengthy questionnaires to fill out, no American Bar Association evaluations, no FBI or IRS background checks, no fingerprinting, no Judiciary Committee hearings, and no filibusters.

> Hopkinson's Commission read:
>
> George Washington, President of the United States of America.
>
> To All who shall see these Presents – Greeting.
>
> Know Ye, that reposing special Trust and Confidence in the Wisdom, Uprightness and Learning of Francis Hopkinson of Pennsylvania, Esquire, I have nominated, and by and with the Advice and Consent of the Senate, do appoint him Judge of the District Court in and for Pennsylvania District; and do authorize and empower him to execute and fulfil the Duties of that Office according to the Constitution and Laws of the said United States; and to have and to hold the said Office, with all the Powers, Privileges and Emoluments to the same of Right appertaining, unto him the said Francis Hopkinson during his good Behaviour. In Testimony whereof I have caused these Letters to be made patent, and the Seal of the United States to be hereunto

> affixed. Given under my Hand the twenty sixth Day of September in the Year of our Lord one thousand seven hundred and eighty nine.
>
> G. Washington

This wording for the Commission of a United States District Judge continues in use to the present time with only minor changes.

In a letter to Hopkinson enclosing his commission, Washington wrote:

> I have the pleasure to enclose to you a commission as Judge of the United States for the District of Pennsylvania, to which office I have nominated, and, by and with the advice and consent of the Senate, have appointed you.
>
> In my nomination of Persons to fill offices in the Judicial Department, I have been guided by the importance of the object-- considering it as of the first magnitude, and as the Pillar upon which our political fabric must rest. I have endeavored to bring into the office of its administration such Characters as will give stability and dignity to our national Government,--and I persuade myself that they will discover a due desire to promote the happiness of our Country by a ready acceptance of their several appointments.[21]

Francis Hopkinson was born into an eminent colonial family in Philadelphia in September 1737. His father, Thomas Hopkinson, who died when Francis was fourteen, was a close friend of Benjamin Franklin. The elder Hopkinson had sat as an admiralty judge and for a time was a member of the Council of the Pennsylvania Governor.[22]

A few years after his father's death, Hopkinson entered the College of Philadelphia (the forerunner of the University of Pennsylvania) and was graduated in its first class in 1757 at the age of nineteen. He proceeded thereafter to study law under Benjamin Chew, the Attorney General of Pennsylvania, and in due course was admitted to the Pennsylvania bar.[23]

In May 1766, he set sail for England where his mother's cousin, James Johnson, officiated as the Anglican Bishop of Worcester. In October 1767, after an extended stay at Hartlebury Castle, the country seat of the Bishop, he returned to Philadelphia[24] and, within a year, married Anne Borden of Bordentown, New Jersey. Her father was a leading citizen in Burlington County.[25]

In late 1773 or early 1774, as the storm clouds preceding the American Revolution were gathering, the Hopkinson family moved from Philadelphia to

Bordentown. At that time, William Franklin, son of Benjamin Franklin, was the Royal Governor of New Jersey. Hopkinson soon was named a Justice of the Peace for Burlington County and a member of the Governor's Council. He also joined the New Jersey Bar.[26]

By 1774, despite Hopkinson's ties with prominent loyalists, he had become an ardent patriot. In late June 1776, he was elected as a delegate from New Jersey to the Second Continental Congress sitting in Philadelphia. A few days later, on July 2, he voted for the resolution declaring the colonies free and independent states and thereafter signed the Declaration of Independence.[27] With the stroke of the pen, he joined that group of patriots about whom Benjamin Franklin purportedly remarked, "... we must indeed all hang together, or most assuredly we shall all hang separately."[28]

In August 1776, while serving in the Continental Congress, John Adams wrote a letter from Philadelphia to his wife Abigail in which he described Hopkinson after meeting him in the studio of the artist Charles Wilson Peale:

> At this shop [Peale's] I met Mr. Francis Hopkinson, ... now a member of the Continental Congress, who, it seems, is a native of Philadelphia, a son of a prothonotary of this county, who was a person much respected. The son was liberally educated, and is a painter and a poet. I have curiosity to penetrate a little deeper into the bosom of this curious gentleman, .... He is one of your pretty, little, curious, ingenious men. His head is not bigger than a large apple .... I have not met with anything in natural history more amusing and entertaining than his personal appearance; yet he is genteel and well-bred, and is very social.[29]

Hopkinson remained a member of the Continental Congress for only a few months. In November 1776, it named him to the three member Navy Board where he probably served as its Chair. The Board had responsibility during the Revolution for the oversight and operation of the American Navy.[30]

There is evidence that at this time he designed the American Flag, albeit with six rather than five pointed stars. Several years later, he attempted to obtain compensation from the Government for that effort but was unsuccessful. A committee responsible for looking into the matter decided that others were also involved with Hopkinson and that no payments should be made.[31]

During part of the time Hopkinson served on the Navy Board, the British occupied Philadelphia. In May 1778, as the British General William Howe was about to evacuate the City and return to New York, he decided to put the homes of a few selected patriots to the torch. He sent an expedition of Hessians to Bordentown who burned down the home of Joseph Borden, Hopkinson's father-in-law. Hopkinson's home, across the street, was spared. Legend has it that when the Hessian Captain entered the house, he saw Hopkinson's library filled with scientific apparatus and volumes of books. He purportedly commented that while Hopkinson may be a rebel, he must also be "a very learned man." The Captain could not bring himself to destroy Hopkinson's property and ordered the fires that were started to be extinguished.[32] This house in Bordentown can still be seen today.

A year later, in 1779, Hopkinson was back in Philadelphia. The Supreme Executive Council of Pennsylvania appointed him a Judge of Admiralty, a position his late father Thomas Hopkinson had held many years before. His time in that office, which continued until he was appointed a federal District Judge, was marked with distinction.[33]

He authored many significant pamphlets and poems, often satirical, supporting the colonists' struggle with Great Britain. In the mid-1780's, while on the state bench, Hopkinson did not shrink from the political thicket in advocating a new constitution to replace the ineffective Articles of Confederation. After the Constitutional Convention, he pushed hard for ratification through his writings.[34] On December 12, 1787, Pennsylvania became the second state, following Delaware, to ratify the Constitution and join the Union. In the summer of 1789, after the new Constitution took effect, Hopkinson provided suggestions to Congress for the Judiciary Act which it was then drafting. According to Robert Morris, one of Pennsylvania's first senators, the suggestions were received with "great effect."[35]

Hopkinson was a true renaissance man. He was a prolific poet and writer, not only on political and legal subjects but also an insightful writer on a wide range of topics, including education and science.[36] Furthermore, he composed a large amount of music both secular and religious, including hymns for the singing of the Psalms.[37]

The most famous of his many poems, which showed his mastery of satire, was called the *Battle of the Kegs* written in early 1778 to ridicule the British troops occupying Philadelphia. On January 1 of that year, the Continental forces, with the approval of General Washington and the Navy Board, floated kegs of gunpowder down the Delaware River from Bordentown, New Jersey. They were rudimentary mines designed to blow up the British ships anchored at Philadelphia if and when the kegs came into contact with the ships. No ships were ever destroyed or damaged by these devices, but the British were so concerned that their troops were ordered to shoot at the kegs to explode them as they appeared in the waters at Philadelphia. The popular poem was set to music and sung throughout the Revolution.[38]

While a state admiralty judge, he wrote a satire entitled "A Specimen of a Modern Law-Suit" about the mysteries of the legal profession and the public's need for a better understanding of the law. He bemoaned the fact that "the subject matter [was] concealed in technical jargon, and a cloud of artificial terms, to many of which professors themselves have not yet assigned a determinate meaning." To remedy this sad state of affairs, he recommended that "all trials and law proceedings" including the rendition of the "opinions of the judges" should be stated in "as few and plain words as may be" and "in *dramatic* form."[39]

In 1788, in support of the new Constitution, he penned a ballad called *The New Roof: A Song for Federal Mechanics* which included an encomium to judges:

> Our *King Posts* are judges — how upright they stand,
> Supporting the *Braces*, the Laws of the Land
> --
> The Laws of the Land, which divide right from wrong,
> And strengthen the weak, by weak'ning the strong.[40]

Hopkinson was active in the American Philosophical Society for most of his adult life where from time to time he presented scholarly papers. He was also an inventor. He made a significant improvement to the construction of the harpsichord which enhanced its sound. The Society presented him shortly before his death with a medal for his invention of a spring block to assist vessels in sailing.[41] His correspondence with Thomas Jefferson and Benjamin Franklin contained frequent discussions of scientific topics. Franklin held him in such high esteem that he wrote in his will: "The philosophical instruments I have in Philadelphia I give to my ingenious friend Francis Hopkinson." He designated Hopkinson as one of his executors.[42] In addition to all of Hopkinson's other achievements, it appears he was an amateur artist.[43]

Hopkinson served as a member of the Vestry and a Warden of Christ Church in Philadelphia as well as its organist for a number of years. In 1789, shortly after he was appointed a federal judge, he was named a deputy and secretary of the organizing convention which established the Protestant Episcopal Church of the United States with a form of governance with lay participation. He helped craft the Church's Book of Common Prayer.[44] Just as he played a prominent role in severing the political ties between Great Britain and the American Colonies in 1776, he was an important participant in severing the ecclesiastical ties between the Church of England and the Episcopal Churches in America.[45]

When Hopkinson assumed his duties as a federal District Judge in September 1789, the jurisdiction of the District Court was quite limited. Congress, bowing to Anti-Federalist sentiment, had not vested the lower federal courts with the full scope of jurisdiction allowed by the Constitution. The District Courts, for the most part, were created to hear admiralty and maritime claims, an area of the law in which Hopkinson had considerable expertise as a Pennsylvania Admiralty judge. Of all the areas of federal court jurisdiction, this was the one on which there was clearly a consensus for inclusion.[46] The Judiciary Act of 1789 also granted those courts cognizance of tort actions by aliens in violation of the law of nations or a treaty, suits by the United States where the amount in dispute did not exceed $100, certain suits against consuls and vice-consuls, and suits for penalties and forfeiture under United States law. It was not to be long after the passage of the Judiciary Act that Congress expanded the types of civil claims to be heard by the District Courts to include those under the patent and copyright laws as well as bankruptcy matters.[47]

The Court's criminal jurisdiction was restricted to those crimes "where no other punishment than whipping, not exceeding thirty stripes, a fine not exceeding one hundred dollars or a term of imprisonment not exceeding six months, is to be inflicted."[48]

The District Judges had additional responsibilities besides those within the jurisdiction of the District Court. The Judiciary Act established three Circuit Courts on which a District Judge sat along with two Supreme Court justices. The Middle Circuit consisted of Pennsylvania, New Jersey, Delaware, Maryland, and Virginia. The Circuit Courts had jurisdiction of "all suits of a civil nature at common law or in equity" where the amount in dispute exceeded $500, exclusive of interest and costs, and either the United States was a plaintiff or the parties were of diverse citizenship, that is, citizens of different states. Removal of diversity actions from the state court to the Circuit Court was authorized. The latter also heard appeals from certain cases assigned to the District Court.[49]

The Circuit Court was vested with "exclusive cognizance of all crimes and offenses cognizable under the authority of the United States" except as otherwise directed and with "concurrent jurisdiction with the District Court of the crimes and offenses cognizable therein."[50] In 1793, Congress reduced from two to one the number of Supreme Court justices needed to hear a matter with a District Judge in the Circuit Court.[51]

Significantly, the first Congress did not provide either the District Courts or the Circuit Courts with general jurisdiction over civil actions "arising under ... [the] Constitution, the laws of the United States and Treaties made, or which shall be made under their authority." Such authority was not to be granted until after the Civil War.[52] While federal courts would hear cases where the parties were of diverse citizenship or had admiralty or maritime claims, other cases in law and equity involving federal law were to be adjudicated in the state courts.

Congress recognized in the Judiciary Act the importance of the right to a jury trial in certain types of civil cases before the right was engrafted into the Seventh Amendment to the Constitution. The Act stated, "... the trial of issues in fact in the circuit courts shall, in all suits, except those of equity, and or admiralty, and maritime jurisdiction, be by jury."[53] In another important provision, the Act empowered all federal courts to issue writs of habeas corpus "agreeable to the principles and usages of law" and "to grant writs of habeas corpus for the purpose of an inquiry into the cause of commitment."[54]

To be able to function, courts always need to have rules of procedure. The Act allowed the courts of the United States "to make and establish all necessary rules for the orderly conducting business in said courts, provided such rules are not repugnant to the laws of the United States."[55]

Judge Hopkinson opened the first session of the District Court on November 10, 1789, in the Pennsylvania State House where thirteen years earlier, at the age of 38, he had courageously voted for separation from Great Britain as a delegate to the Second Continental Congress. At this first proceeding of the Court, the Mayor and Recorder of Philadelphia, as well as members of Congress attended along with a "number of respectable citizens." The commissions of Judge Hopkinson, the United States Attorney for the District of Pennsylvania William Lewis, and the Marshal for the District Clement Biddle were "proclaimed" and a number of "Gentlemen of the Bar" admitted.[56]

Judge Hopkinson on this occasion addressed the grand jury. In that early era, the grand jury address was more than legal instructions concerning the handing down of indictments. It served as an opportunity for the judge to endorse the new Constitution and federal government.[57] At the outset Hopkinson spoke of the importance of the courts:

> ... The institution of courts for the administration of justice is the conclusive criterion of an organized system of polity; in as much as it implies the security of all just rights and the redress of all real injuries to every individual of the community. Revolutions may take place, former systems of government may be done away, by the all powerful will of the people, and new constitutions proposed, and even agreed to; but until laws are enacted, and courts established for carrying those laws into effect, the business is not complete, nor can the people boast of a settled government or a national character.[58]

He then reviewed for those assembled the weakness of the Articles of Confederation and the subsequent formation of the Constitution with its judiciary article. He also outlined the jurisdiction of the District and Circuit Courts under the recently passed Judiciary Act. Thereafter, he brought his address to a close:

> Thus hath the Government of the United States been established on the broad basis of the will of the people; which is the only just and permanent foundation on which government can be built; for the people are the true source of power, and the object of government should be the good and prosperity of those from whom government is derived and for whom it is instituted.

> My hearers will, I am sure, rejoice with me in the prospect of the future glory of our new founded empire – a dominion extending to various climates – resources inexhaustible – the blessings of nature improved and heightened by the powers of art – endless population – commerce unlimited – and, above all, the wealth and strength of so many potent states, united and bound together by a liberal, and yet vigorous constitution, give us a reasonable hope that America will soon rise, like her own eagle, and soar above those clouds and storms which disturb and terrify birds of a weaker wing.[59]

Thus began the work of the District Court. Hopkinson had no law clerks and no secretary. His only staff consisted of the Court Clerk, Samuel Caldwell whom he had appointed on October 6, 1789, pursuant to authority granted him under the Judiciary Act.[60] In 1790, a court crier, Joseph Fox, was added.[61]

The Court's docket was sparse compared with the situation today. Admiralty matters, in which Hopkinson was well versed, seemed to have accounted for the bulk of his workload. One of his first cases in 1789 involved the attachment of the Sloop *Polly* in Philadelphia to secure the payment of wages to two seamen who had boarded the vessel in Halifax, Nova Scotia.[62] In another, he ruled in favor of seamen who sought their wages after leaving a brig in Lisbon because of cruel beatings by the ship's captain. While acknowledging that the master of a vessel must be given great discretion, he determined the relationship is properly dissolved "when the master is found to abuse his authority by undue severity and cruelty."[63]

In April 1790, Supreme Court Justice James Wilson and Judge Hopkinson presided in Independence Hall at the first session of the Circuit Court "in and for the Pennsylvania District of the Middle Circuit." A formal Rule for Admission of Attorneys was adopted and read into the record:

> Ordered, that it shall be requisite to the admission of Attorneys and Counsellors, to practice in this Court, that they shall have been such, for two years past, in the Supreme Court of the States to which they respectively belong, and that their private and professional characters shall appear to be fair. That they respectively take the following oath (or affirmation), vis:
>
> I, A.B. do solemnly swear (or affirm) that I will demean myself, as an Attorney of the Court, uprightly and according to law; and that I will support the Constitution of the United States.[64]

At this session of the Circuit Court, on the motion of William Lewis, the

Attorney for the United States in the District of Pennsylvania, twenty-six attorneys, including Lewis, were formally admitted. The minutes refer to them all as "gentlemen" and presumably the "private and professional characters" of all appeared to be "fair." With Pennsylvania having been founded by William Penn, a member of the Society of Friends (Quakers), and with a significant presence of coreligionists in Philadelphia, it was not surprising that six, including Lewis, "affirmed" according to Quaker practice rather than "swore" the required oath.[65]

Unfortunately, Hopkinson's days on the federal bench were short-lived. Sometime in 1790, it appears that he had a stroke, and while he continued to sit as a judge and participate in the life of the American Philosophical Society, he had to be assisted to and from the courtroom at least for a time. He died suddenly on May 9, 1791, at the age of fifty-three, less than two years after taking office.[66] A couplet lauding him read:

> And be this truth upon his marble writ
> He shone in virtue, science, taste and wit[67]

He was interred in the Christ Church burial ground at Fifth and Arch Streets, approximately two blocks from Independence Hall and the present federal courthouse.[68]

With the death of Judge Hopkinson, President Washington named William Lewis, the United States Attorney, as the new District Judge. After his appointment in July 1791 while the Senate was in recess, Supreme Court Justice James Wilson administered him the oath of office. As a Quaker, Lewis "solemnly affirmed."[69]

Lewis was born in Edgmont, Chester (now Delaware) County, Pennsylvania, on February 13, 1751, into a Welsh Quaker family, with roots in the area dating back to the time of William Penn. He studied at a local Friends School in Chester County and with the encouragement of his parents, became proficient in French, Latin, and German. Around his seventeenth birthday, he commenced study in a Friends School in Philadelphia and was entrusted to the care of his cousin, the successful Philadelphia merchant Mordecai Lewis, who further contributed to his knowledge in the fields of finance and business.[70]

Lewis, who did not attend college, thereafter decided to make the law his profession. Though his mother did not approve, perhaps showing a Quaker aversion to that vocation, his father aided Lewis' ambitions. In 1770, when he was just nineteen, Lewis began studying law with Nicholas Waln. Over the next six years, he became a leader of the Philadelphia Bar and kept many of Waln's clients when his mentor decided to retire from the profession.[71]

In contrast to Hopkinson, who was physically diminutive with, in John Adams' picturesque description, a head "not bigger than a large apple," Lewis stood over six feet tall though he eventually developed something of a stoop and was very thin. He had a rather prominent nose and a deep baritone voice with a penchant for cigars from which he was rarely separated either inside or outside the courtroom. With respect to his attire, he was his own man and wore knee britches long after they had gone out of fashion.[72]

In October 1775, he was disowned by the Philadelphia Monthly Meeting of Friends for "marrying contrary to the good order used among us; bearing arms; and keeping unprofitable company."[73] By 1776, Lewis had cast his lot with those advocating independence.[74] While his precise activities during the war remain somewhat shrouded, Lewis continued to practice law during the Revolution, outside the reach of the British. Despite the fact that he was no longer a member in good standing with the Friends, part of his practice during and after the war centered upon defending those charged with aiding the British, many of whom were Quakers.[75]

By the time the war ended, Lewis, like Hopkinson, favored an energetic national government. He worked for the ratification of the new United States Constitution as a delegate to the Pennsylvania Convention summoned to decide the issue. He was elected as a member of the unicameral Pennsylvania Assembly in 1787 and 1789. While in the State Assembly, he supported the successful effort to call a convention to amend the Commonwealth's 1776 Constitution and was chosen as a delegate to that convention which wrote the more conservative Constitution of 1790. Among the significant changes which were achieved were a bicameral legislature, a strong independent judiciary, and a Governor with extensive powers of appointment in place of a Supreme Executive Council.[76]

Lewis developed a friendship with George Washington and Alexander Hamilton with whom he shared similar political views.[77] In 1789, President Washington appointed Lewis as the first United States Attorney for the District of Pennsylvania.[78] His workload was minimal, and he continued to maintain his private practice as was then permitted. The one indictment he signed charged two defendants with murder on the high seas.[79] During this period, Hamilton, Washington's Secretary of the Treasury, consulted Lewis regularly and even requested him to review his 1791 opinion on the constitutionality of the First Bank of the United States.[80]

Like other members of the Bar, Lewis took an active role in promoting Philadelphia. He was one of the founders of the Pennsylvania Academy of the Fine Arts, along with William Rawle and Joseph Hopkinson.[81]

In 1790, he helped to forge the merger of the College of Philadelphia and the University of the State of Pennsylvania into what became the University of Pennsylvania after a long period of acrimony between the two educational institutions. The new entity had the benefit of his service as a trustee for the rest of his life. He was also one of the organizers of the Law Library Company of the City of Philadelphia, which was the forerunner of the Philadelphia Bar Association.[82] Other of his activities included advocating the construction of the Schuylkill Falls Bridge and serving as a counselor for the Bank of North America.[83]

Lewis, consistent with his Quaker heritage, was an early opponent of slavery. He was a longtime member and counselor of the Pennsylvania Abolition Society. One of his most praiseworthy accomplishments was as the principal draftsman of the Act for the Gradual Abolition of Slavery in the Commonwealth, enacted by the Pennsylvania Assembly on March 1, 1780. It was the first such law in any state. He further put his legal talents to work and thereafter successfully represented several slaves who sought their freedom under the Act.[84]

In August 1791, not long after Lewis was inducted as a District Judge, what is now known as Philadelphia's Old City Hall was completed and ready for occupancy. The handsome Georgian edifice, which still stands immediately east of Independence Hall at the southwest corner of Fifth and Chestnut Streets, became the home of the District Court. At that time, the City shared the building with the federal courts. Lewis' courtroom was on the second floor. The United States Supreme Court sat on the first floor from 1790 until 1800 while Philadelphia was the nation's capital.[85]

The tenure of Judge Lewis turned out to be even shorter than that of Hopkinson. He resigned in January 1792,[86] after only a few months on the bench, to return to his lucrative law practice.

After leaving the bench, he was involved as counsel in many important cases in both the state and federal courts, including the highly publicized John Fries trials of which more will be said later. During the 1790's, he was one of a small group of lawyers, mainly from Philadelphia, who regularly argued before the United States Supreme Court.[87] Indeed, he was one of the most distinguished and respected lawyers of his time.

For the last two years of his life, he lived with his second wife at his longtime country home on the banks of the Schuylkill, known to us today as Strawberry Mansion. He died on August 16, 1819, at the age of sixty-eight and is buried in the yard of St. Peter's Church in Philadelphia.[88]

The first two judges of the District of Pennsylvania, Francis Hopkinson and William Lewis, were distinguished citizens of Philadelphia and strong supporters of the Constitution. President Washington was to make a third appointment who fit the same description.

## Notes

1. The Convention opened its first official session on May 25, 1787, after it finally had a quorum. Rhode Island chose not to participate. Van Doren, Carl, *The Great Rehearsal*, pp. 9-14, 53 (Vintage Press, 1948). *See also*, Berkin, Carol, *A Brilliant Solution: Inventing the American Constitution*, pp. 5-7, 32, and 49 (Harcourt, 2002).
2. Goebel, Julius, Jr., *The History of the Supreme Court of the United States*, Vol. I, pp. 204-50 (The Macmillan Co., 1971).
3. Van Doren, Carl, *The Great Rehearsal*, pp. 268-73 (Vintage Press, 1948).
4. Berkin, Carol, *A Brilliant Solution: Inventing the American Constitution*, p. 54 (Harcourt, 2002).
5. Van Doren, Carl, *The Great Rehearsal*, p. 64 (Vintage Press, 1948).
6. Bowen, Catherine Drinker, *The Miracle at Philadelphia*, pp. 62, 65-66 (Little, Brown & Co., 1966); Van Doren, Carl, *The Great Rehearsal*, pp. 64-65 (Vintage Press, 1948). The Federalist No. 78 (Alexander Hamilton).
7. The Federalist No. 79 (Alexander Hamilton).
8. Koch, Adrienne, *Notes of Debates in the Federal Convention of 1787 Reported by James Madison*, pp. 67-68; Bowen, Catherine Drinker, *Miracle at Philadelphia*, p. 66 (Little, Brown & Co., 1966).
9. Van Doren, Carl, *The Great Rehearsal*, p. 135 (Vintage Press, 1948).
10. Art. II, § 2, ¶ 2. This paragraph of the Constitution continues: "... but the Congress may by Law vest the Appointment of such inferior Officers, as they think proper, in the President alone, in the Courts of Law, or in the Heads of Departments."
11. The provision giving the federal courts jurisdiction over controversies "between a State or Citizens thereof; -- and foreign States, Citizens, or Subjects" was changed by the Eleventh Amendment, ratified on February 7, 1795: "The Judicial power of the United States shall not be construed to extend to any suit in law or equity, commenced or prosecuted against one of the United States by Citizens of another State, or by Citizens or Subjects of any Foreign State."
12. U.S. Const. art. VII, § 1 provides: "The Ratification of the Conventions of nine States, shall be sufficient for the Establishment of this Constitution between the States so ratifying the Same."
13. Judiciary Act of 1789, ch. 20, 1 Stat. 73.
14. North Carolina and Rhode Island did not ratify the Constitution until November 1789 and May 1790, respectively.
15. Konkle, Burton Alva, *Joseph Hopkinson: 1770-1842*, p. 206 (Univ. of Pennsylvania Press, 1931). The Circuit Court for the District of Pennsylvania was also required to sit at Philadelphia and York Town. In 1796, Congress eliminated the requirement that the Circuit Court sit at "Yorktown." Act of May 12, 1796, ch. 24, 1 Stat. 463; interview with Michael E. Kunz, the Court Clerk, by the author.
16. *Journal of the Executive Proceedings of the Senate of the United States of America*, Vol. I, pp. 29-3 (1789-1805).
17. Wood, Gordon S., *Empire of Liberty*, pp. 411-12 (The Oxford University Press, 2009).
18. John Rutledge of South Carolina and John Blair of Virginia, two other Supreme Court nominees, as well as David Brearley, the New Jersey District Court nominee, and Gunning Bedford, Jr., the Delaware District Court nominee, had all been signers of the Constitution. William Paterson of New Jersey, a subsequent Supreme Court appointee of President Washington, had signed the Constitution while Samuel Chase of Maryland, likewise a later Washington Supreme Court appointee, had signed the Declaration of Independence.
19. Hastings, George E., *The Life and Works of Francis Hopkinson*, pp. 324-25, 459 (University of Chicago, 1926).
20. *Journal of the Executive Proceedings of the Senate of the United States of America*, Vol. I, p. 31 (1789-1805); *see* Copy of Commission of Francis Hopkinson, signed by President Washington, dated Sept. 26, 1789, National Archives, Mid-Atlantic Branch.
21. Letter from George Washington to Francis Hopkinson, dated Sept. 30, 1789; *The Pennsylvania*

*Magazine of History and Biography*, Vol. II, p. 323 (1878).

22. Hastings, George E., *The Life and Works of Francis Hopkinson*, pp. 28-30, 42-44 (University of Chicago, 1926).
23. *Id.* at 55-56, 68. *See also*, Inserted article by Mearble, Annie Russell, "Francis Hopkinson: Man of Affairs and Letters," pp. 289-302, found in Simpson, Henry, *The Lives of Eminent Philadelphians Now Deceased*, Extended by Fox, J.M., Vol. II (William Brotherhead, 1859).
24. Hastings, George E., *The Life and Works of Francis Hopkinson*, pp. 17-19, 119-49; Konkle, Burton Alva, *Joseph Hopkinson: 1770-1842*, p. 5 (University of Pennsylvania Press, 1931). Inserted article by Mearble, Annie Russell, "Francis Hopkinson: Man of Affairs and Letters," pp. 289-302, found in Simpson, Henry, *The Lives of Eminent Philadelphians Now Deceased*, Extended by Fox, J.M., Vol. II (William Brotherhead, 1859).
25. Hastings, George E., *The Life and Works of Francis Hopkinson*, pp. 158-64 (University of Chicago, 1926).
26. *Id.* at 168-71.
27. *Id.* at 212-14.
28. Van Doren, Carl, *Benjamin Franklin*, pp. 551-52 (The Viking Press, 1965).
29. Hastings, George E., *The Life and Works of Francis Hopkinson*, pp. 356-66, 448 (University of Chicago, 1926).
30. *Id.* at 214-19.
31. *Id.* at 256-57.
32. *Id.* at 227-33. *See also*, Inserted article by Mearble, Annie Russell, "Francis Hopkinson: Man of Affairs and Letters," pp. 289-302, found in Simpson, Henry, *The Lives of Eminent Philadelphians Now Deceased*, Extended by Fox, J.M., Vol. II (William Brotherhead, 1859).
33. Hastings, George E., *The Life and Works of Francis Hopkinson*, pp. 304, 320-22, 459 (University of Chicago, 1926).
34. A letter from "One of the People" addressed "To the Freemen of Pennsylvania," *American Museum* (Oct., 1787); Hastings, George E., *The Life and Works of Francis Hopkinson*, pp. 397-410, 480 (University of Chicago, 1926).
35. Hastings, George E., *The Life and Works of Francis Hopkinson*, p. 459 (University of Chicago, 1926). *See also*, Presser, Stephen B., *Studies in the History of the United States Courts of the Third Circuit*, (Government Printing Office, 1982), Flyleaf; Weigley, Russell F., ed., *Philadelphia: A 300-Year History*, p. 137 (W.W. Norton and Company, 1982); Mahan, Katherine Hines, "Hopkins and Reinagle: Patriot-Musicians of Washington's Time," *Music Educators Journal*, 62 pp. 40-50 (April 1976); Anderson, Gillian B., "'The Temple of Minerva' and Francis Hopkinson: A Reappraisal of America's First Poet-Composer," *Proceedings of the American Philosophical Society* 120, pp. 166-77 (June 15, 1976).
36. See generally, Hastings, George E., *The Life and Works of Francis Hopkinson*, (University of Chicago, 1926).
37. *Id.* at 69-81, 461-64, 483; Gough, Deborah Mathias, *Christ Church in Philadelphia*, pp. 93, 98 (University of Pennsylvania Press, 1995).
38. Hastings, George E., *The Life and Works of Francis Hopkinson*, pp. 290-95 (University of Chicago, 1926).
39. *The Miscellaneous Essays and Occasional Writings of Francis Hopkinson, Esq.*, Vol. II, pp. 248-49 (T. Dobson, Phila. 1792).
40. Goebel, Julius, Jr., *The History of the Supreme Court of the United States*, Vol. I, pp. 322-23 (The Macmillan Co., 1971).
41. Hastings, George E., *The Life and Works of Francis Hopkinson*, p. 448 (University of Chicago, 1926).
42. *Id.* at 360.
43. *Id.* at 176, 464-66.
44. *Id.* at 263-66, 705-66; Gough, Deborah Mathias, *Christ Church in Philadelphia*, pp. 93-98, 152, 160-61 (University of Pennsylvania Press, 1995).

45. Gough, Deborah Mathias, *Christ Church in Philadelphia*, pp. 70, 93-98, 138-42, 152, 156, 161 (University of Pennsylvania Press, 1995); Inserted article by Mearble, Annie Russell, "Francis Hopkinson: Man of Affairs and Letters," pp. 289-302, found in Simpson, Henry, *The Lives of Eminent Philadelphians Now Deceased*, Extended by Fox, J.M., Vol. II (William Brotherhead, 1859).
46. Robreno, Eduardo C., "Learning to Do Justice: An Essay on the Development of the Lower Federal Courts in the Early Years of the Republic," *Rutgers Law Journal*, p. 557 (Spring 1998).
47. Act of Apr. 10, 1790, ch. 8, 1 Stat. 111, §§ 4-6; Act of Feb. 21, 1793, ch. 11, 1 Stat. 323, §§ 5, 6, 10; Act of May 31, 1790, ch. 25, 1 Stat. 124; Act of Apr. 4, 1800, ch. 19, 2 Stat. 21.
48. Judiciary Act of 1789, ch. 20, 1 Stat. 75, § 9.
49. Wheeler, Russell R. and Harrison, Cynthia, *Creating the Federal Judicial System*, pp. 4-7 (Federal Judicial Center, 1994); Surrency, Erwin C., *History of the Federal Courts*, pp. 19-23, 55 (Oceana Publications, 2002).
50. Judiciary Act of 1789, ch. 20, 1 Stat. 78-79.
51. Act of Mar. 2, 1793, ch. 22, 1 Stat. 333.
52. The Judiciary Act of 1875, ch. 137, 18 Stat. 470, § 1.
53. Judiciary Act of 1789, ch. 20, 1 Stat. 75, § 12. The Seventh Amendment to the Constitution provides:

    In Suits at common law, where the value in controversy shall exceed twenty dollars, the right of trial by jury shall be preserved, and no fact tried to jury, shall be otherwise re-examined in any Court of the United States, than according to the rules of the common law.
54. *Id.* at § 14.
55. *Id.* at § 17.
56. *The Pennsylvania Packet*, p. 2 (Nov. 21, 1789); *Journal of the Executive Proceedings of the Senate of the United States of America*, Vol. I, pp. 29, 31 (1789-1805).
57. Wood, Gordon S., *Empire of Liberty*, pp. 412-13 (Oxford University Press, 2009).
58. *The Daily Advertiser*, p. 2 (Nov. 27, 1789).
59. *Id.*
60. Judiciary Act of 1789, ch. 20, 1 Stat. 75; Copy of Appointment document of Samuel Caldwell as Clerk, signed by Judge Hopkinson, dated Oct. 6, 1789.
61. *See* Records of the United States District Court for the Eastern District of Pennsylvania.
62. *Connor v. The Sloop Polly*, (D. Pa. Dec. 13, 1789).
63. *Rice v. The Polly & Kitty*, 20 F. Cas. 666, 667 (D. Pa. 1789) (No. 11,754).
64. *See* Records of the United States District Court for the Eastern District of Pennsylvania.
65. *Id.*
66. Hastings, George E., *The Life and Works of Francis Hopkinson*, pp. 447-49 (University of Chicago, 1926).
67. *Id.* at 473.
68. Records of Christ Church, Philadelphia.
69. *See* Document in Records of the United States District Court for the Eastern District of Pennsylvania; Rueter, Thomas J., "William Lewis: First United States Attorney," *The Shingle*, Vol. 52, pp. 36 ff. (Philadelphia Bar Association, Spring 1989).
70. Bell, Robert R., *The Philadelphia Lawyer: A History, 1735-1945*, pp. 83-86 (Selinsgrove: Susquehanna University Press, 1992); Primrose, William, "Biography of William Lewis," *The Pennsylvania Magazine of History and Biography*, Vol. 20, pp. 30-32 (April, 1896); Rueter, Thomas J., "William Lewis: First United States Attorney," *The Shingle*, Vol. 52, pp. 36, 38 (Philadelphia Bar Association, Spring 1989); Information provided by Mrs. George C. McFarland.
71. *Id.*
72. Bell, Robert R., *The Philadelphia Lawyer: A History, 1735-1945*, p. 86 (Selinsgrove: Susquehanna University Press, 1992); Rueter, Thomas J., "William Lewis: First United States Attorney," *The Shingle*, Vol. 52, p. 43 (Philadelphia Bar Association, Spring 1989).

73. Information provided by Mrs. George C. McFarland; Rueter, Thomas J., "William Lewis: First United States Attorney," *The Shingle*, Vol. 52, p. 36-39 (Philadelphia Bar Association, Spring 1989).
74. Information provided by Mrs. George C. McFarland; Rueter, Thomas J., "William Lewis: First United States Attorney," *The Shingle*, Vol. 52, p. 38 (Philadelphia Bar Association, Spring 1989).
75. Rueter, Thomas J., "William Lewis: First United States Attorney," *The Shingle*, Vol. 52, pp. 36-39, 42 (Philadelphia Bar Association, Spring 1989); Ludlum, Mabel Steward, "The Story of Strawberry Mansion," Bulletin of the Pennsylvania Museum, Vol. 26, No. 142, Part 2: Strawberry (May 1931), p. 5; Bell, Robert R., *The Philadelphia Lawyer: A History, 1735-1945*, pp. 83-86 (Selinsgrove: Susquehanna University Press, 1992); Information provided by Mrs. George C. McFarland.
76. Rueter, Thomas J., "William Lewis: First United States Attorney," *The Shingle*, Vol. 52, pp. 36-39, 42 (Philadelphia Bar Association, Spring 1989); Primrose, William, "Biography of William Lewis," *The Pennsylvania Magazine of History and Biography*, Vol. 20, pp. 30-40 (April 1896); *The Pennsylvania Manual*, Vol. 104, pp. 8-9 (Pa. Dept. of General Services, 1979); Information provided by Mrs. George C. McFarland.
77. Bell, Robert R., *The Philadelphia Lawyer: A History, 1735-1945*, pp. 83-86 (Selinsgrove: Susquehanna University Press, 1992); Information provided by Mrs. George C. McFarland.
78. *Journal of the Executive Proceedings of the Senate of the United States of America*, Vol. I, pp. 29, 31 (1789-1805).
79. Rueter, Thomas J., "William Lewis: First United States Attorney," *The Shingle*, Vol. 52, p. 40 (Philadelphia Bar Association, Spring 1989).
80. Bell, Robert R., *The Philadelphia Lawyer: A History, 1735-1945*, pp. 83-86 (Selinsgrove: Susquehanna University Press, 1992); Rueter, Thomas J., "William Lewis: First U.S. Attorney," *The Shingle*, Vol. 52, p. 43 (Philadelphia Bar Association, Spring 1989); Information provided by Mrs. George C. McFarland.
81. Sellers, Charles Coleman, "Rembrandt Peale, 'Investigator'", *Pennsylvania Magazine of History and Biography*, 79 (1955), pp. 339-40.
82. *The Philadelphia Lawyer*, Vol. 64, pp. 58-60 (The Philadelphia Bar Association, Winter 2002).
83. Information provided by Mrs. George C. McFarland.
84. Presser, Stephen B., *Studies in the History of the United States Courts of the Third Circuit*, p. 242 (Government Printing Office, 1982); Rueter, Thomas J., "William Lewis: First United States Attorney," *The Shingle*, Vol. 52, pp. 38-39 (Philadelphia Bar Association, Spring 1989).
85. Scharf, J. Thomas & Westcott, Thompson, *History of Philadelphia, 1609-1884*, p. 1771; Moss, Roger W. (Photograph by Tom Crane), *Historic Landmarks of Philadelphia*, pp. 38-41 (University of Pennsylvania Press, 2008).
86. *Journal of the Executive Proceedings of the Senate of the United States of America*, Vol. I, p. 97 (1789-1805).
87. Goebel, Julius, Jr., *The History of the Supreme Court of the United States*, Vol. I, p. 666 (The Macmillan Co., 1971).
88. Primrose, William, "Biography of William Lewis," *The Pennsylvania Magazine of History and Biography*, Vol. 20, p. 40 (April 1896); Rueter, Thomas J., "William Lewis: First United States Attorney," *The Shingle*, Vol. 52, p. 43 (Philadelphia Bar Association, Spring 1989).

# II
# Two Federalist Judges: 1792-1842

At the time of the resignation of Judge Lewis in January 1792, the political demarcation lines between the Federalists and the Republicans were becoming more pronounced. The Federalists, with Alexander Hamilton as one of their leaders, favored an energetic federal government including strong federal courts and an expansive interpretation of the powers granted to the federal government by the Constitution. They were also partisans of the commercial, banking, and manufacturing interests. In contrast, those who called themselves Republicans under the aegis of Thomas Jefferson and others supported state rights and emphasized the importance of the yeoman farmer, the artisan and mechanic, and individualism in American society. The Republicans tended to be more egalitarian than the Federalists at least with respect to the white male portion of the population.

The differing views of the two parties were not limited to domestic issues. Revolution was convulsing France at the time. The Federalists became alarmed particularly as it reached its radical phase while the Republicans continued to express support for those who had overthrown the old order. When Great Britain and France went to war in the 1790's, the Federalists sided with the British and the Republicans with the French. These seemingly faraway events in Europe would ultimately have ramifications for the federal courts.

President Washington, although denouncing party factions, was in the Federalist camp and promptly named another Federalist, Richard Peters, as his third appointee to the District Court of Pennsylvania to succeed Lewis. The Senate, again moving quickly, gave its advice and consent on January 13, 1792, a day after he was nominated.[1]

Upon confirmation, Peters still had some business to finish as a state senator and requested that Jefferson, the Secretary of State, withhold his Commission until that business was completed. Peters resigned his legislative office on February 1, 1792, and then took the oath of office.[2] In contrast to the short tenures of Judges Hopkinson and Lewis, Peters went on to serve as the District's sole federal judge for the next thirty-six years.

Peters was born on June 22, 1744, in Blockley Township, Philadelphia County at the family farm known as Belmont, in what is now part of the Fairmount Park in West Philadelphia. His father, William Peters, was a large landowner and successful lawyer who at one point held office as a colonial judge.[3] An uncle, The Reverend Richard Peters, served as the rector of Christ Church before the Revolution.[4] As had Hopkinson, Peters earned a degree from the College of Philadelphia (now the University of Pennsylvania) and subsequently read law.[5]

Although his family had maintained a close relationship with the Penns, the colonial proprietors of Pennsylvania, Peters supported the American cause during the Revolution. He resigned his post as Registrar of the Admiralty Court, which he had held since 1771 and became a captain in the Pennsylvania militia. On June 13, 1776, Congress appointed him Secretary of the Board of War. From this position, Peters exposed the peculations of Benedict Arnold and worked fervently and successfully at raising money and provisions for the Continental Army during the Revolution at a time when the situation was dire. He resigned in 1781 when a Department of War was created and then served a year in Congress. Thereafter, Peters was elected to the Pennsylvania Assembly and later to the state Senate. In each instance his fellow legislators chose him as that body's Speaker. Before his appointment as a District Judge, he had been offered but declined the position of Comptroller of the Treasury in the new federal government.[6]

Peters was a noted wit and conversationalist who made a delightful dinner companion. He was a classical scholar with a reading knowledge of Dutch, Spanish, French, and Italian. His proficiency in German helped his legal career among Pennsylvania's large German population.[7]

While most of his adult life was dominated by politics and his judicial career, his interests cut across a wide spectrum. He was a devout and influential Episcopalian, who like Francis Hopkinson was instrumental in the establishment of the Protestant Episcopal Church in the United States. After the Revolution, he sailed to England and met with the Archbishop of Canterbury to resolve certain ecclesiastical issues with the Church of England.[8]

He, like William Lewis, held membership in the Pennsylvania Abolition Society. Devoted to innovation in farming, he served as the first president of the Philadelphia Society for the Promotion of Agriculture and wrote a number of influential articles on agricultural subjects. His knowledge and practical experience were such that George Washington, retired at Mt. Vernon, sought his advice on what type of grain to plant to avoid destruction of his crops by the Hessian fly. Among a wide variety of civic improvement projects with which he was connected, one of the most important was the construction of the bridge over the Schuylkill at High (now Market) Street which made travel easier to and from the western part of Philadelphia County where he lived.[9]

At the time Peters was appointed to the bench in 1792, the District Court was still sitting in Philadelphia's City Hall at Fifth and Chestnut Streets. The Court remained there until 1824, except for a temporary absence during the summer and fall of 1799, when it sought refuge in the Montgomery County Courthouse in Norristown because of the yellow fever epidemic in Philadelphia. In 1824, the Court moved a few yards west from City Hall to Congress Hall, originally constructed as the Philadelphia County Courthouse, at Sixth and Chestnut Streets.

After a two year stay, the Court relocated again.[10] A ten-year lease, effective January 1, 1826, was signed for the use of the second floor of the Franklin Institute on Seventh Street, just south of Market Street. However, the Court occupied that venue only until April 1, 1830, when the United States Marshal, who had responsibility for leasing court space and paying the rent, negotiated a release of the Government's obligations to the Franklin Institute. The building still stands and now houses the Philadelphia History Museum at the Atwater Kent. Thereafter, the Court returned to Independence Hall where it sat on the second floor until 1854.[11]

When Peters was sitting as a District Judge on the Circuit Court, he was joined by one or more Supreme Court Justices as provided in the Judiciary Act. In his early years on the bench, Justices John Blair, Samuel Chase, James Iredell, William Paterson, and James Wilson presided with him at one time or another.

On December 19, 1798, President Adams appointed Bushrod Washington, the nephew of George Washington, to the Supreme Court to fill the seat left vacant by the death of Justice Wilson. The younger Washington, a Virginian, had studied law under Wilson in Philadelphia.[12] Within a few years of his appointment, he was the justice who regularly joined Peters on the Circuit Court. Washington's time on the Supreme Court (1798-1829) largely coincided with that of Peters on the District Court (1792-1828). The two men developed a close friendship. Both were Federalists, and both held Chief Justice John Marshall in high regard. Washington died in Philadelphia on November 26, 1829, while present for a court session. On the third floor of the present United States courthouse outside the judges' conference room is a marble relief of the Justice with an accompanying tablet which reads:

THIS TABLET RECORDS
the affection and respect,
of the members of the Philadelphia Bar, for
BUSHROD WASHINGTON
an associate Justice of the Supreme Court
of the United States:
alike distinguished
for simplicity of manners,
and purity of heart:
fearless, dignified, and enlightened as a Judge;
no influence or interest,
could touch his integrity, or
bias his judgment:
a zealous patriot, and a pious christian.

He died at Philadelphia,
on the 26th of November A.D. 1829;
leaving to his professional brethren,
a spotless fame;
and to his country, the learning, labour, and wisdom,
of a long judicial life.[13]

The main work of the District Court in the days of Judge Peters was presiding over and deciding admiralty and maritime cases, and it is in this setting that he earned an esteemed reputation. These lawsuits ranged widely in subject matter. They concerned the seizure of ships during wartime, the distribution of prize money from captured vessels, insurance coverage for lost or damaged cargo, and wages and medical care due seamen.[14] Criminal cases involving murder and assault on the high seas also came before the Court.[15] The highly respected Supreme Court Justice Joseph Story lauded Peters for his "rich contribution to the maritime jurisprudence of our country."[16]

It was also a time when there existed tens of thousands of acres of virgin land west of the developed areas of the eastern seaboard. A number of civil suits of note before Peters concerned land disputes and land speculators.[17]

Peters from the outset was sensitive to the separation of powers among the executive, legislative, and judicial branches of government. In 1792, Congress approved the Pension Act to benefit certain Revolutionary War veterans. The Act included a provision for the Circuit Courts to evaluate pension applications. The conclusions of the judges and the proofs upon which they relied were to be forwarded to the Secretary of War for his review and approval, with authority given the Secretary to deny a pension where he "shall have cause to suspect imposition or mistake."[18]

William Hayburn petitioned the Circuit Court for the District of Pennsylvania to be placed on the pension list. Justices James Wilson and John Blair along with Judge Peters, then sitting on the Circuit Court, decided "after due Deliberation" that they would "not proceed upon" the petition.[19] Instead of issuing an opinion setting forth the reasons why they refused to resolve the case on the merits, they addressed an explanatory letter to President Washington. They first stated that it was a "painful occasion" not to have been able to proceed with Hayburn's petition. Nonetheless, it was their conclusion that a part of the Pension Act was unconstitutional in that any judicial decision on his pension request was subject to revision "by an officer in the executive department." Consequently, the statutory scheme was "radically inconsistent with the independence of that judicial power which is vested in the courts; and consequently with that important principle which is so strictly observed by the constitution of the United States." The letter closed apologetically:

> These, Sir, are the reasons of our conduct. Be assured that, though it became necessary, it was far from being pleasant. To be obliged to act contrary either to the obvious directions of congress, or to a constitutional principle, in our judgment equally obvious, excited feelings in us, we hope never to experience again.[20]

The Circuit Courts in New York and North Carolina each took a similar stance. Attorney General Edmund Randolph thereupon filed a petition for mandamus on behalf of Hayburn in the Supreme Court.[21] While the matter was pending, Congress enacted a new procedure for processing pension applications without judicial involvement. As a result, the Supreme Court never ruled on the Attorney General's motion.[22] The decision of the Circuit Court for the District of Pennsylvania in *Hayburn's Case* in which Judge Peters participated was handed down some eleven years before the famous case of *Marbury v. Madison* in which the Supreme Court firmly established the right of the courts to invalidate an Act of Congress as repugnant to the Constitution.[23]

Peters had been the District Judge only a relatively short time when the Whiskey Rebellion erupted in Western Pennsylvania in 1794. It was precipitated by an excise tax on whiskey, to be paid by the distillers, which Congress had enacted to help pay for the massive fiscal program of Secretary of the Treasury Alexander Hamilton to assume the debt of the states incurred during the Revolution. Many of those living in that rugged area of Pennsylvania refused to pay the levy. There was even talk of establishing a separate country beyond the Allegheny Mountains and of marching on Philadelphia, the nation's capital.[24]

President Washington decided to dispatch some 13,000 militiamen to quell the revolt. He joined the troops as Commander-in-Chief in Carlisle, Cumberland County and accompanied them as far as Bedford County before returning to Philadelphia. As the Army marched westward, it met no opposition, and shots were never fired. The rebellion simply dissolved.[25]

What began as a political and military issue was transformed, as so often happens, into a judicial matter. Judge Peters and United States Attorney William Rawle, one of the initial twenty-six attorneys to have been admitted to practice before the Circuit Court in 1790, traveled with the soldiers into Western Pennsylvania. Arrests were made, and Peters sent some back to Philadelphia for trial. Indictments for treason were handed down, such as the one against Frederick Reamer, which charged him as "an evil, depraved person ... of a turbulent and seditious disposition."[26] Supreme Court Justice William Paterson of New Jersey and Judge Peters presided over the Circuit Court trials in Philadelphia. Of those indicted, two were convicted of treason and sentenced to death, but both were pardoned by President Washington.[27]

In early 1798, Justice Samuel Chase and Judge Peters decided a case involving the important but unsettled legal question as to whether federal common law crimes exist, that is, whether a court may deem to be a crime conduct which Congress had not made criminal. Robert Worrall was indicted for attempting to bribe a Government official in Philadelphia in connection with the construction contract for a lighthouse in Cape Hatteras, North Carolina. There was no federal statute at the time making such behavior a crime. Worrall was convicted by a jury. Justice Chase was of the view that the indictment should be dismissed because the Constitution only allowed conduct to be considered a federal crime pursuant to a law passed by Congress. Judge Peters disagreed. He reasoned:

> the existence of the Federal government would be precarious, it could no longer be called an independent government, if, for the punishment of offences of this nature, tending to obstruct and pervert the administration of its affairs, an appeal must be made to the State tribunals, or the offenders must escape with absolute impunity.

Chase ultimately relented, and Worrall was sentenced to jail and fined.[28]

The position of Peters that the Constitution countenanced federal common law crimes was widely held by federalist judges of that period and was consistent with the notion of an energetic federal government. Thomas Jefferson and his Republican adherents vehemently disagreed. They considered the Federalist position to be nothing less than a dangerous and illegal enhancement of federal judicial power.[29] It was not until 1812 that the Supreme Court finally settled the issue by deciding that Chase's original position had been correct. The Court concluded that neither the enumerated nor the implied powers granted under the Constitution authorize federal common law crimes.[30]

In 1798, a few years after the Whiskey Rebellion, Judge Peters was confronted with what is known as the Fries Rebellion. At that time, France and Great Britain were locked in war, with both nations seizing neutral American ships. In response, Congress enacted a series of taxes on real estate to raise revenue to finance an enlarged Army and Navy. The tax was calculated on the basis of the number of windows in a person's home. German-speaking residents of Bucks and Northampton counties, led by a John Fries, "revolted" against compliance with the tax. Fries was a Federalist who had served as an Army officer during the Revolution and during the Whiskey Rebellion. In civilian life he was an auctioneer. Poor communication about the tax in these areas as well as in Montgomery County played a role in the Fries Rebellion or, as it is sometimes known, the "Hot Water War." When revenue collectors arrived in the area, they were often met with hot water dumped on them from upper windows. The fleeing tax assessors were thus prevented from calculating the taxes owed.[31]

Judge Peters directed United States Marshal William Nichols to arrest those responsible. After making several arrests, Nichols was met by John Fries and other armed locals at the Sun Tavern in Bethlehem. Fries demanded the prisoners be tried in local courts rather than in the federal court in Philadelphia. Nichols refused the demand but being surrounded eventually turned the prisoners over to Fries and his men. Fortunately, no shots were fired during the standoff.[32]

President Adams thereafter ordered troops to seize those in revolt. That Fries had served his country in the army and was a Federalist mattered little. All that Federalists saw was yet another insurrection in Pennsylvania. Ultimately, Fries along with sixty others who had been with him during the standoff with Nichols were arrested and taken to Philadelphia where Fries was indicted for treason.[33]

Fries had able representation at his trial. His lawyers were William Lewis, the former District Judge, and Alexander James Dallas. Though the two counsels could not have been more different politically, and indeed had almost fought a duel, they were united in defending Fries.[34]

The first trial began in April 1799 in Philadelphia before Judge Peters and Supreme Court Justice James Iredell of North Carolina. Fries was convicted of treason by the jury. Nonetheless, before a death sentence could be imposed, it was brought to the Court's attention that some of the jurors had talked during a recess in the trial about how "Fries and the other insurgents" should be hanged. Lewis, on behalf of his client, moved for a new trial based on juror bias. The Court agreed and granted the motion.[35]

The second trial took place in 1800 before Justice Samuel Chase of Maryland and Judge Peters. In a dramatic move, Lewis and Dallas resigned from the case in the midst of the proceedings because of the rulings and intemperance of Chase whom Peters had unsuccessfully attempted to moderate.[36] While Chase and Peters offered to appoint new counsel, Fries declined the offer. He proceeded to represent himself. He was convicted by the jury of treason for the second time and sentenced to be hanged. Contrary to the unanimous recommendation of his cabinet and over the strong opposition of adherents of former Secretary of the Treasury Alexander Hamilton, President Adams pardoned Fries and the other individual who had been convicted.[37] Capitalizing on his notoriety, Fries thereafter opened a tin-ware shop in Philadelphia and was said to have attained "a respectable fortune, and a respectable character."[38]

The execution of Louis XVI, the onslaught of the Reign of Terror and the radical phase of the French Revolution, and the war between Great Britain and France in the 1790's had their deep-felt effects on domestic politics in the United States. The Federalists coalesced in support of the British, while the Republicans, led by Thomas Jefferson, advocated a pro-French policy. What has sometimes been called this country's quasi-war with France arose as part of this larger European conflict.

These events were the backdrop for the Alien and Sedition Acts passed by Congress sitting in Congress Hall in Philadelphia and signed by President Adams in July 1798. The Federalists sought to bolster the Adams administration against the increasingly virulent verbal attacks by the Jeffersonian Republicans and the Republican press on its record, including its handling of relations with France.

The key provision of the Sedition Act read:

> SEC. 2. ... That if any person shall write, print, utter or publish ... any false, scandalous, and malicious writing or writings against the government of the United States, or either house of the Congress of the United States, or the President of the United States, with intent to defame [them], or to bring them ... into contempt or disrepute; or to excite against them ... the hatred of the good people of the United States, or to stir up sedition within the United States ... then such person ... shall be punished by a fine not exceeding two thousand dollars, and by imprisonment not exceeding two years.[39]

Truth was a defense in any prosecution.[40] While the Act protected the President and Congress, it did not outlaw "false, scandalous and malicious writings" against the Vice-President, the office then held by Adams' political rival, Thomas Jefferson.

The Federalist administration of President Adams did not wait for the enactment of the Sedition Act to take legal action against its critics. It indicted Benjamin Franklin Bache, Benjamin Franklin's grandson, in June 1798, for what it deemed the federal common law crime of sedition. Bache, a vociferous critic of the Federalists, was the publisher of the widely read Philadelphia newspaper known as the *Aurora*.[41] For years, he had excoriated both George Washington and John Adams, accusing the latter on one occasion of being "blind, bald, crippled, toothless [and] querulous."[42] On June 26, 1789, United States Marshal Nichols arrested him on a warrant signed by Judge Peters. The indictment charged Bache with "libelling the President & the Executive Government in a manner tending to excite sedition and opposition to the laws, by sundry publications and re-publications." Bache was brought before Judge Peters who released him on bail pending trial.[43] His counsel, Alexander Dallas, had made it known that he would challenge any trial based on the existence of a federal common law crime, even though Peters had ruled in the *Worrall* case that such crimes exist.[44] Bache's trial in the Circuit Court, scheduled for October 1798, with all its potential legal and political ramifications, never took place much to the chagrin of the Federalists. Bache had died of yellow fever in September.[45]

Once the Sedition Act became law, the Government wasted no time in using it to bring indictments against its adversaries in the District of Pennsylvania and elsewhere. In total, fifteen indictments were handed down nationwide and ten cases went to trial between the passage of the Act in July 1798, and its expiration on the last day of the Adams administration on March 3, 1801. All ten resulted in convictions, fines, and jail terms.[46]

The Government's focus on the alleged libels emanating from the *Aurora* did not end with the death of Bache. William Duane, who married Bache's widow Margaret, continued the newspaper's publication with its virulent attacks on the Federalists. After a jury acquittal in an earlier common law sedition case against him where Joseph Hopkinson, the son of Francis Hopkinson, had been appointed the special prosecutor, the Government indicted Duane in July 1799 under the Sedition Act. The indictment was based on an article in the *Aurora* that the British government had exercised undue influence over the State Department.

Duane was brought before Judge Peters who released Duane on bond. The trial was scheduled for October before Peters and Justice Bushrod Washington in the Montgomery County Courthouse where the Circuit Court was sitting temporarily due to the yellow fever outbreak in Philadelphia. The trial, however, was delayed while awaiting the arrival of Justice Washington in Norristown for his circuit duties. Belatedly recognizing the difficulties with the case and recently aware that then Vice-President John Adams had written a letter in 1792 making the same accusation of British influence at the State Department, the Government withdrew the indictment. No trial ever took place.[47]

Duane's respite was temporary. He was indicted again for sedition on October 17, 1800, toward the end of the Adams Administration and appeared in Court that day before Justice Paterson and Judge Peters. The trial was postponed in order to provide Duane's counsel time to obtain evidence for his defense. With the expiration of the Sedition Act and the inauguration of Thomas Jefferson as President in March 1801, the protracted effort to prosecute Duane ultimately came to an end.[48]

Not so fortunate was Thomas Cooper, an attorney and the editor of the *Gazette* in Northumberland County, Pennsylvania. He was charged under the Sedition Act "with having published a false, scandalous and malicious attack on the character of the President of the United States [John Adams], with the intent to excite the hatred and contempt of the people of this country against the man of their choice." He had castigated the Adams administration for the expense of a permanent navy, the existence of a standing army, and the fact the credit of the country was so weak as to require it to borrow money at 8% in time of peace.[49]

Justice Samuel Chase and Judge Peters presided over the trial, which began in April 1800. United States Attorney William Rawle was the prosecutor while Cooper represented himself. Chase dominated the courtroom. He demonstrated extreme bias in favor of the Government and his rulings at every turn prevented Cooper from being able to present his defense. In his charge to the jury, Chase declared, "if a man attempts to destroy the confidence of the people in their officers," he undermines the "foundations of the government." He further instructed the jury that Cooper was doing nothing less than attempting to "arouse the people against the President so as to influence their minds against him on the next election."[50] The jury found Cooper guilty. Chase sentenced him to six months in prison and imposed a $400 fine.[51]

Cooper's conviction for seditious libel did not ruin his reputation or his career. In 1804, he was appointed as a Pennsylvania state judge. He later taught chemistry at Carlisle College (now Dickinson College) and the University of Pennsylvania and became President of South Carolina College.[52] In 1850, with the benefit of hindsight and some fifty years after his trial, Congress voted to refund his $400 fine with interest to his heirs.[53] Although it may seem surprising today, no challenge was ever made in any court to the constitutionality of the Sedition Act on free speech grounds.

Chase's total lack of impartiality and his intemperance during the Cooper and the second Fries trials were to play a role a few years later in his impeachment by the House of Representatives controlled by the Jeffersonian Republicans and in his subsequent trial in the Senate. In connection with its efforts to impeach Chase, a House Committee also investigated Peters, who had presided with Chase in both cases. Nonetheless, the Committee soon concluded that "no cause of accusation" existed against him.[54]

In 1801, not long after the second Fries trial and in the final days of his Federalist Administration, President John Adams signed a bill establishing six Circuit Courts with separate judgeships and expanding the jurisdiction of those courts to all types of cases authorized under Article III of the Constitution. The Act was quickly repealed once President Jefferson took office, and a new law was enacted in 1802. Although Congress had abolished the "mid-night" judgeships created by the Federalists, the Act of 1802 reauthorized the six circuits with Pennsylvania and New Jersey now placed in the new Third Circuit. It also allowed a District Judge to preside alone in a Circuit Court if a Supreme Court justice was not available.[55]

The supremacy of federal law was not always a universally accepted principle in Pennsylvania or elsewhere[56] in the early nineteenth century even though Article VI, ¶ 2 of the Constitution declares: "This Constitution and the Laws of the United States which shall be made in Pursuance thereof ... shall be the supreme Law of the Land; and the Judges in every State shall be bound thereby, any Thing in the Constitution or Laws of any State to the Contrary notwithstanding." A clash between federal power and state power came to a head in a case before Judge Peters. Gideon Olmstead and others had been captured by the British in 1778 and taken to Jamaica during the Revolution. Thereafter they were impressed to serve on the British sloop *Active*, which was taking supplies to the troops of King George III in New York. During the voyage to New York in September 1778, Olmstead and his associates seized control of the vessel and were sailing toward Egg Harbor, New Jersey, when an armed brig of the Commonwealth of Pennsylvania took possession of it and brought it to the Port of Philadelphia.[57]

The Olmstead group as well as the Commonwealth and another party each claimed the vessel and its cargo as a prize in the state admiralty court. After a trial, the court ruled primarily in favor of Pennsylvania and awarded only a quarter of the prize to Olmstead and his associates. On appeal, a court of commissioners of appeals of the United States of America under the Articles of Confederation overturned the state court verdict. It held that the vessel and cargo were the exclusive prize of the Olmstead group.[58]

As the result of a series of circumstances, the portion of the prize money awarded originally by the state admiralty court to Pennsylvania and another claimant was not paid to Olmstead and his associates. Instead, the Pennsylvania state treasurer, David Rittenhouse, had in his possession certain certificates representing this prize money. In 1803, Judge Peters, in the exercise of the District Court's admiralty and maritime jurisdiction, entered a decree requiring the Rittenhouse Estate, which held the certificates after the death of Rittenhouse, to deliver them to the Olmstead group. Throwing down the gauntlet, Pennsylvania passed a law requiring the certificate holders to turn them over to the Commonwealth. Ominously, the law also authorized the Governor "to protect the just rights of the state ... by any further means and measures that he may deem necessary for the purpose." The Rittenhouse Estate, not surprisingly, when faced with these competing demands, refused both.[59]

Olmstead requested Judge Peters to enforce the Court's order, but should Peters do so it was anticipated that Governor Simon Snyder would command the state militia to prevent the order from being carried out. Considering the seriousness of the situation, Peters declined to take any further steps until he had a ruling from the Supreme Court. A mandamus proceeding, that is, a proceeding to compel Judge Peters to act, followed. In *United States v. Peters*,[60] the high Court granted the writ of mandamus directed to Judge Peters. Chief Justice Marshall made it clear that the "highest judicial authority of the nation" had held that the Confederation court of appeals had full authority to reverse the decisions of the state admiralty courts in prize cases. While regretting to have to rule in this matter, he stated that "it is a solemn duty," and directed Judge Peters to enforce his order.[61]

Pennsylvania, however, was not mollified by the Supreme Court's decision and appeared in no mood to comply. President James Madison finally persuaded the Governor to withdraw his threat of calling out the militia to prevent enforcement of Judge Peters' order, and Olmstead and his associates finally obtained the certificates more than thirty years after the prize money had been awarded to them.[62]

As the years passed while Peters was serving as a federal judge, the population of both Philadelphia and Pennsylvania was rapidly expanding. According to the 1790 census, the City and County of Philadelphia had 82,852 residents while Pennsylvania's population stood at 434,373. By 1820, both had grown significantly. That year's census figures showed slightly more than 137,000 people living in Philadelphia and 1,049,393 in the Commonwealth.[63]

Recognizing this growth, Congress in 1818 divided the District of Pennsylvania into the Eastern District of Pennsylvania with court to be held at Philadelphia before Judge Peters, and the Western District with a new federal judge to be appointed to sit in Pittsburgh.[64] Congressman (later Judge) Joseph Hopkinson, at the behest of Judge Peters, had unsuccessfully opposed this division. In Peters' view there was not enough judicial business in the western reaches of Pennsylvania for the creation of a new court.[65] The smaller District over which Peters now presided consisted of twenty-six counties in the eastern half of the state.

Judge Peters died in late August 1828, at his home, known today as Belmont Mansion. He was eighty-four years old and was buried in St. Peter's Churchyard in Philadelphia.[66] Born thirty-two years before the Declaration of Independence, he had engaged in distinguished public service during and after the Revolution. President Washington named him to the District Court where he presided for thirty-six years in times of war and peace, tumult and tranquility, during the terms of six presidents.

For the first few years during which Peters sat on the bench, Philadelphia was not only the nation's capital but also the capital of Pennsylvania. Even after the seat of the federal government moved to Washington and the state capital moved first to Lancaster and then to Harrisburg, the City and County of Philadelphia remained vibrant with a bustling port, extensive commerce, and the Second Bank of the United States. But that was not all Philadelphia was. It continued to have an abundant intellectual and cultural life, in which Francis Hopkinson, William Lewis, and Richard Peters had all actively participated. The famous portrait painter Gilbert Stuart quite aptly described Philadelphia of this era as the "Athens of America."[67]

At the time of Peters' death, John Quincy Adams was in his last months as President of the United States. Adams chose as Peters' successor, Adams' long time friend Joseph Hopkinson,[68] a prominent Philadelphia lawyer and the son of Pennsylvania's first District Judge, Francis Hopkinson and the grandson of Thomas Hopkinson, a colonial admiralty judge. Hopkinson brought "a tone of dignity, learning, and urbanity" to the Philadelphia legal community.[69] He, like his father, was a Federalist in his political leanings. Such noteworthy figures as Chief Justice John Marshall as well as Justices Joseph Story and Bushrod Washington authored laudatory letters to the President recommending the appointment of Hopkinson to the District Court.[70] In his letter, Chief Justice Marshall wrote:

> ... If I take the liberty to bring to your notice a person who stands high in his profession, as one well qualified to be his [Peters'] successor, I must hope to find an apology in my conviction of the importance you attach to the judicial department, and of your desire to fill all vacancies which may occur in it with gentlemen in all respects entitled to the public confidence.
>
> I have been long and intimately acquainted with Mr. Joseph Hopkinson, and think highly of his legal attainments, as well as his fitness in all other respects for the office. I have heard him argue several important causes in the Supreme Court of the United States, in which he always displayed accurate knowledge of his subject, and very considerable power of mind. I forbear to speak of him otherwise than professionally, because I believe he is personally known to you.[71]

President Adams gave Hopkinson a recess appointment to the Court in October 1828. His nomination, however, was not considered by the Senate until February 23, 1829, less than two weeks before Adams was to leave office and Andrew Jackson, Adams' political adversary, was to succeed him. Not surprisingly, with a change of administration just over the horizon, a motion was made in the Senate to postpone consideration of the Hopkinson nomination to March 4, Inauguration Day, when his recess appointment would expire. Upon defeat of the motion, he was confirmed by a divided vote of 28 to 15, with one of the two Pennsylvania Senators voting against him.[72] Several days later, President Adams sent Hopkinson a letter enclosing his commission. The President likened Hopkinson's appointment to the historic appointment of Chief Justice Marshall by his father President John Adams in the final days of that administration in 1801:

> One of the last acts of my father's administration was the transmission of a commission to John Marshall as Chief Justice of the United States. One of the last acts of my administration is the transmission of the enclosed commission to you. If neither of us had ever done anything else to deserve the approbation of our country and of posterity, I would proudly claim it of both for these acts; as due to my father and to--your friend, J. Q. Adams.[73]

Born in Philadelphia on November 12, 1770, Hopkinson received his bachelor's degree at what was then known as The University of the State of Pennsylvania (now the University of Pennsylvania). Thereafter, he read law under James Wilson and

William Rawle and attended Wilson's celebrated law lectures at the University of Pennsylvania in 1791. He engaged in private practice in Philadelphia and also in Easton, in Northampton County. After completing two terms in the United States House of Representatives (1815-1819),[74] he moved to Bordentown, New Jersey, for a time in semi-retirement. He returned to Philadelphia in 1823 where he resumed his active law practice.[75]

As a young lawyer, he successfully represented Benjamin Rush, a signer of the Declaration of Independence and a noted Philadelphia physician, in a libel action in the Pennsylvania courts against William Corbett, the publisher of the *Porcupine Gazette*. The jury found that Corbett had defamed Rush when Corbett disparaged Rush's practice of bleeding patients during the several yellow fever epidemics in Philadelphia in the 1790's.[76]

Later in his legal career, Hopkinson participated as part of Justice Samuel Chase's defense team during his impeachment and his later trial in the Senate in 1804. Several of the Articles of Impeachment related to his actions at the Fries trial.[77] Chase, a staunch Federalist, was acquitted.[78]

Hopkinson appeared as counsel in a number of cases before the United States Supreme Court.[79] Among others, he was co-counsel with Daniel Webster in arguing and winning in 1819 a case upholding the original charter of Dartmouth College.[80] He also represented the State of Maryland, the losing party, in *McCulloch v. Maryland* in which the Supreme Court declared unconstitutional the state's tax on notes issued by the Bank of the United States. It was in the Court's opinion in that case that Chief Justice Marshall penned the well-known words "the power to tax involves the power to destroy."[81]

Hopkinson, in addition to his legal pursuits, was very active in the American Philosophical Society and the Pennsylvania Academy of Fine Arts. He also served as a trustee of the University of Pennsylvania.[82] Again, like his father, he was accomplished as a writer of both prose and poetry. His most famous composition, written in 1798, was the popular "Hail Columbia," sung to the tune known as "The President's March." It was an encomium to George Washington and was designed as a patriotic response to counter those in America who made a point of singing the "Marseillaise" to demonstrate sympathy with the revolutionary events occurring in France.[83]

The types of cases heard by Judge Hopkinson did not differ markedly from those that came before Judge Peters, although, of course, the Sedition Act had long ago expired. Hopkinson sat on numerous admiralty and maritime suits, including those in which seamen sued for wages and those involving alleged maltreatment of seamen by ship captains. Based on notions of fairness and equity, he crafted the law in favor of the seamen to prevent abuses by their powerful officers.[84] Other cases concerned the jurisdiction of United States courts over conduct on the high seas and claims for damages resulting from ship collisions. Bankruptcy matters also came before him.[85] On one occasion, he presided over a lawsuit involving the issue of diplomatic immunity for a minister of the King of Denmark who was arrested and imprisoned for failure to pay a debt.[86] Philadelphia was home to the Second Bank of the United States, headed by Nicholas Biddle. Cases involving bank notes and counterfeiting appeared on his docket.[87]

Judge Hopkinson, as had Judge Peters, recognized the importance of the separation of powers. He was careful not to encroach on the legislative sphere. In one decision, he stated:

> This is a case in which a court must be guarded to keep within the judicial pale; and not take a step into the legislative domain, under impulses given by the circumstances of the case. We must look closely and exclusively to what legislation has done on the subject, and be careful to do no more. .... But the courts have never assumed the office of supplying legislative defects; and a judge should especially look to the limitations of his powers, when he approaches a case of evil aspect and bad fame.[88]

When sitting as a Circuit Judge, Hopkinson was often joined by Justice Henry Baldwin, a Pennsylvanian from Pittsburgh, appointed in 1830 by President Andrew Jackson to succeed Justice Washington. Hopkinson and Baldwin had served together in Congress but did not have the same close relationship as Hopkinson had had with his fellow Federalist and longtime friend Bushrod Washington.[89]

One case of note before Justice Baldwin and Judge Hopkinson involved a robbery.[90] The stagecoach, during this era before the advent of the railroad, was a common means of transportation, not only for passengers but for the United States mail. Travel then, as is true now, was not always without incident. At 2:30 a.m. of December 6, 1829, a stagecoach left Philadelphia for Reading with a driver and one passenger beside him on the outside seat, nine passengers inside the coach, and bags of mail. Suddenly, along the route three highwaymen stepped out, pointed pistols at the driver, and ordered him to stop. The men extinguished the lamps on the coach by striking them with their firearms. In the darkness, after compelling the driver and the passenger beside him to climb down from their outside seat, they demanded that the other passengers exit the coach one by one and then robbed each of them. Next they proceeded to steal the contents of the mailbags, tie up the driver, and hitch the horses to a fence.

During the course of the robbery, a conversation ensued between the driver and one of the robbers. The driver reported he was asked "whether I didn't think it was a rough introduction." The driver replied, "I thought it was." When the robber further inquired whether the driver made his living by driving a stagecoach, he answered, "I did and it was a rather hard life too, the way I was used." The robber responded, "This is the way we make our living, and it's hard with us sometimes."[91]

Two of the malefactors were indicted for robbery of the United States mail with the use of a dangerous weapon and for placing the life of the carrier in jeopardy "against the peace and dignity of the United States of America." The United States Attorney was George Mifflin Dallas, later to be Vice-President of the United States under President Polk. The defendants also had distinguished lawyers, John Kane, who subsequently became a federal District Judge, and Joseph Ingersoll, later a Congressman and United States Minister to Great Britain.

The defendants were convicted by a jury and all post-trial motions were denied. The Court rejected the defendants' argument, among others, that the indictment had been deficient in failing to identify the county in which the offense occurred as was customary in England. The Court explained that it was sufficient, in accordance with the venue provision of the Sixth Amendment, that the trial took place in the state and the district, in this case the Eastern District of Pennsylvania, where the crime was committed.[92]

One of the most significant cases decided by Judge Hopkinson was *Wheaton v. Peters*,[93] a landmark decision in the field of copyright law. The plaintiffs were assignees of Henry Wheaton who had served by appointment of the Supreme Court as its third reporter of decisions from 1816 until 1827. Initially, Wheaton had received no compensation from the Government but made his money selling copies of the Supreme Court decisions, with notes and summaries, in volumes known as Wheaton's Reports. Because this was not sufficient to make a living, the Court later paid him a salary.

The complaint alleged that Wheaton had both a common law and a federal statutory copyright in the Wheaton Reports. Plaintiffs maintained that defendants, including Richard Peters, Jr., Wheaton's successor as the Supreme Court Reporter and son of Judge Peters, were selling volumes entitled "Condensed Reports of Cases of the Supreme Court of the United States" which contained the virtually identical reports of cases included in the first volume of Wheaton Reports. Plaintiffs sought an injunction to restrain defendants from continuing to sell their works.

Hopkinson ruled that there was no common law copyright in the United States and that Wheaton's assignees had not demonstrated an equitable right to relief under the copyright statute passed by Congress. In 1834, the Supreme Court reviewed Hopkinson's decision on appeal. The Court agreed with him that no federal common law copyright existed, although it remanded on the issue of whether Wheaton had met all the requirements for a copyright under the Copyright Act. The Supreme Court then declared: "It may be proper to remark that the court are unanimously of opinion that no reporter has or can have any copyright in the written opinions delivered by this court; and that judges thereof cannot confer on any reporter any such right."[94] Thus, even if plaintiffs won on the statutory copyright claim, they could only prevail with respect to any summaries and indices and could not prevent others from publishing the opinions themselves.

Hopkinson continued his interest and involvement in public affairs after he was appointed to the bench and apparently had the time to do so. In contrast to what would be permitted of a federal judge today, he was elected as a delegate from the City of Philadelphia to the Pennsylvania Constitutional Convention held intermittently from May 1837 into February 1838. One of the crucial issues it faced was whether state judges should continue to have the benefit of life tenure as provided in the Constitution of 1790, a document which William Lewis had had a hand in drafting. Hopkinson chaired the Convention's Committee on the Judiciary. Despite a valiant effort on his part to retain life tenure for state judges, he was unable to hold back the populist Jacksonian tide. The delegates voted to change the state constitution to provide for appointment of the judges of the Pennsylvania Supreme Court for fifteen-year terms and the judges of other courts for either ten or five-year terms.[95]

Hopkinson's last reported decision, a maritime matter, was handed down in December 1841. A captain of a sloop sued for payment of additional wages for painting and scraping the vessel at the owner's request. Based on the evidence and finding that these services did not customarily fall within the regular duties of a ship captain, Hopkinson entered a decree in his favor. Reflecting the less restrictive attitude in those days toward conflicts of interest, the record notes without fanfare that the judge's son Oliver Hopkinson represented the captain.[96]

Joseph Hopkinson died in January 1842, after presiding as the Judge in the Eastern District of Pennsylvania for over thirteen years. He was buried in the Hopkinson Cemetery in Bordentown.[97] Like his three judicial predecessors, he was a leader not only in the legal community but also in the civic, cultural, intellectual and political life of Philadelphia and beyond. His death marked the end of the era of judges in this District who had grown up in eighteenth century America.

By 1840, the population of the City and County of Philadelphia had climbed to over 258,000. Even though no longer the nation's largest city or the home of the Second Bank of the United States whose charter had expired, Philadelphia continued to be a major center of banking, shipping, and commerce. One of its most prominent citizens during the time when Peters and Hopkinson were judges was the merchant and banker Stephen Girard, who at his death in 1831 was said to have been the wealthiest person in America.[98] Little could anyone then imagine that his will would be the focus of major litigation in the Eastern District of Pennsylvania over 130 years later.

The issues facing the country and the federal courts would change dramatically in the years following the death of Judge Hopkinson. By the end of the decade, slavery would come to dominate the political discourse and then surface as an intractable judicial matter as well.

## Notes

1. *Journal of the Executive Proceedings of the Senate of the United States of America*, Vol. I, p. 97 (1789-1805).
2. Cullen, Charles T., ed., *The Papers of Thomas Jefferson*, Vol. 23, p. 82 (Princeton University Press, 1990).
3. Address by Judge J. William Ditter, Jr., at the Annual Meeting of the Historical Society of the United States District Court for the Eastern District of Pennsylvania, p. 2 (Apr. 11, 1986).
4. Gough, Deborah Mathias, *Christ Church, Philadelphia*, pp. 89-90, 95-106 (Philadelphia: University of Pennsylvania Press, 1995); Baltzell, E. Digby, *Puritan Boston and Quaker Philadelphia*, p. 225 (The Free Press, 1979).
5. Richard Peters Clipping File, Archives of the University of Pennsylvania; Weigley, Russell F., ed., *Philadelphia: A 300-Year History*, pp. 231-32 (W.W. Norton and Company, 1982); Salade, Robert F., *Judge Richard Peters of Belmont Mansion*, pp. 4-5 (Benjamin F. Emery Co., 1925).
6. Presser, Stephen B., *Studies in the History of the United States Courts of the Third Circuit*, p. 21 (Government Printing Office, 1982); Address by Samuel Breck to the Blockley and Merion Agricultural Society on the death of their late President, The Hon. Richard Peters, pp. 7-15, Sept. 20, 1828 (Phila.: Lydia R. Bailey, 1828).
7. Address by Samuel Breck to the Blockley and Merion Agricultural Society on the death of their late President, The Hon. Richard Peters, pp. 4-5, 26-27, Sept. 20, 1828 (Phila.: Lydia R. Bailey, 1828); Address by Judge J. William Ditter, Jr. at the Annual Meeting of the Historical Society of the United States District Court for the Eastern District of Pennsylvania, (Apr. 11, 1986).
8. Malone, Dumas, ed., *Dictionary of American Biography*, Vol. VII, pp. 509-10 (Charles Scribner's Sons, 1934); Address by Samuel Breck to the Blockley and Merion Agricultural Society on the death of their late President, The Hon. Richard Peters, pp. 20-25, Sept. 20, 1828 (Phila.: Lydia R. Bailey, 1828).
9. Malone, Dumas, ed., *Dictionary of American Biography*, Vol. VII, pp. 509-10 (Charles Scribner's Sons, 1934); Presser, Stephen B., Studies in the History of the United States Courts of the Third Circuit, pp. 23, 60 n.34, 242 (Government Printing Office, 1982); Gough, Deborah Mathias, *Christ Church, Philadelphia*, p. 197 (University of Pennsylvania Press, 1995); Weigley, Russell F., ed., *Philadelphia: A 300-Year History*, pp. 231-32 (W.W. Norton and Company, 1982); Address by Samuel Breck to the Blockley and Merion Agricultural Society on the death of their late President, The Hon. Richard Peters, Sept. 20, 1828 (Phila.: Lydia R. Bailey, 1828); Letter from George Washington to Richard Peters, dated June 26, 1797 (Historical Society of Pennsylvania); *see* Selections from Correspondence of Judge Richard Peters of Belmont, *Pennsylvania Magazine of History and Biography*, Vol. 44, pp. 325-26 (October 1941).
10. *Philadelphia in 1824*, p. 133.
11. Kimball, D., Chronology of Room Use in State House (1992) (Independence National Historical Park); Moss, Roger W. (Photographs by Tom Crane), *Historic Landmarks of Philadelphia*, pp. 116-18 (University of Pennsylvania Press, 2008).

12. Konkle, Burton Alva, *Joseph Hopkinson: 1770-1842*, p. 252 (University of Pennsylvania Press, 1931).
13. The relief and tablet were first erected in October 1830 in Independence Hall where the federal court was then sitting. Judge Joseph Hopkinson, Judge Peters' successor, delivered the Memorial Address. *See* Konkle, Burton Alva, *Joseph Hopkinson: 1770-1842*, pp. 269-70 (University of Pennsylvania Press, 1931).
14. *McFaden v. The Exchange*, 16 F. Cas. 85 (C.C.D. Pa. 1811) (No. 8786), *rev'd The Schooner Exchange v. McFaddon*, 11 U.S. (7 Cranch) 116 (1812); *Winthrop v. Union Ins. Co.*, 30 F. Cas. 376 (C.C.D. Pa. 1807) (No. 17,901); *Walton v. The Neptune*, 29 F. Cas. 142 (D. Pa. 1800) (No. 17,135); *Scott v. The Greenwich*, 21 F. Cas. 830 (D. Pa. 1802) (No. 12,531); *Findlay v. The William*, 9 F. Cas. 57 (D. Pa. 1793) (No. 4790). *See also*, Robreno, Eduardo C., "Learning to Do Justice: An Essay on the Development of the Lower Federal Courts in the Early Years of the Republic;" *Rutgers Law Journal*, pp. 555, 564-71 (Spring 1998).
15. *United States v. Smith*, 27 F. Cas. 1247 (C.C.E.D. Pa. 1819) (No. 16,345); *United States v. McGill*, 4 U.S. (4 Dall.) 426 (1806); *United States v. Worrall*, 2 U.S. (2 Dall.) 384, 28 F. Cas. 774 (C.C.D. Pa. 1798) (No. 16,766).
16. Presser, Stephen B., *Studies in the History of the United States Courts of the Third Circuit*, p. 61, n.38 (Government Printing Office, 1982).
17. *See*, e.g., *Huidekoper's Lessee v. Douglass*, 7 U.S. (3 Cranch) 1 (1805).
18. 1 Stat. 243 (1792); Presser, Stephen B., *Studies in the History of the United States Courts of the Third Circuit*, p. 24 (Government Printing Office, 1982).
19. *The Documentary History of the Supreme Court of the United States, 1789-1800*, Vol. 6, pp. 46, 48 (Columbia University Press, 1998).
20. *Hayburn's Case*, 2 U.S. (2 Dall.) 409 (1792).
21. *Id.*
22. *Id.* In 1794, in an unrelated case, the Supreme Court vindicated the principle of separate powers enunciated by Peters and his colleagues. *See United States v. Todd*, an unreported case summarized by the Supreme Court in *United States v. Ferreira*, 54 U.S. (13 How.) 40, 52-53 (1851).
23. 5 U.S. (1 Cranch) 137 (1803).
24. Chernow, Ron, Washington, *A Life*, pp. 718-28 (The Penguin Press, 2010); Flexner, James Thomas, *Washington, The Indispensable Man*, pp. 314-20 (Little, Brown & Co., 1974).
25. *Id.*
26. *United States v. Reamer*, Records of the U.S. Circuit Court for the Eastern District of Pennsylvania, Criminal Case Files 1791-1883, Record Group 21, Box 1, Nat'l Archives, Phila.
27. Hall, Kermit L., *The Magic Mirror: Law in American History* (New York: Oxford University Press, 1989), 76; Brookhiser, Richard, *Founding Father*, p. 88 (The Free Press, 1996).
28. *United States v. Worrall*, 2 U.S. (2 Dall.) 384, 28 F. Cas. 774, 779-80 (C.C.D. Pa. 1798) (No. 16,776).
29. Wood, Gordon S., *Empire of Liberty*, 416-18, 439-39 (Oxford University Press, 2009).
30. *United States v. Hudson*, 11 U.S. (7 Cranch) 32 (1812).
31. Elsmere, Jane Shaffer, "The Trials of John Fries," *Pennsylvania Magazine of History and Biography*, Vol. 93, p. 432 (October 1979).
32. Newman, Paul Douglas, "Fries's Rebellion and American Political Culture, 1798-1800," *Pennsylvania Magazine of History and Biography*, 119 (January/April 1995), 56-59; Robreno, Eduardo C., *Learning to do Justice: An Essay on the Development of the Lower Federal Courts* in the *Early Years of the Republic*, 29 Rutgers L.J. 575 (1998); Rosenfeld, Richard N., *American Aurora: A Democratic-Republican Returns. The Suppressed History of Our Nation's Beginnings and the Heroic Newspaper that Tried to Report It*, pp. 605, 609, 614, 625, 639 (St. Martin's Press, 1997); Larson, Edward J., *A Magnificent Catastrophe: The Tumultuous Election of 1800, America's First Presidential Campaign* (New York: Free Press, 2007), pp. 128-129; Elkins, Stanley and McKitrick, Eric, *The Age of Federalism, pp. 697-98* (New York: Oxford University Press, 1995).
33. Elkins, Stanley and McKitrick, Eric, *The Age of Federalism*, pp. 697-98 (New York: Oxford University Press, 1995).

34. Elsmere, Jane Shaffer, "The Trials of John Fries," *Pennsylvania Magazine of History and Biography*, Vol. 93, p. 437 (October 1979); Ludlum, Mabel Steward, "The Story of Strawberry Mansion," *Bulletin of the Pennsylvania Museum*, Vol. 26, No. 142, Part 2: Strawberry (May 1931), p. 5; Mrs. George C. McFarland, interview, May 28 2008; Bell, Robert R., *The Philadelphia Lawyer: A History, 1735-1945*, p. 86 (Selinsgrove: Susquehanna University Press, 1992).
35. *United States v. Fries*, 9 F. Cas. 826, 922-23 (C.C.D. Pa. 1799) (No. 5126).
36. Elsmere, Jane Shaffer, "The Trials of John Fries," *Pennsylvania Magazine of History and Biography*, Vol. 93, p. 441 (October 1979).
37. Smith, Page, *John Adams*, Vol. II, pp. 1033-34 (Doubleday & Co., Inc., 1962).
38. *Case of Fries*, 9 F. Cas. 924, 949 (C.C.D. Pa. 1800) No. 5127 (appended note).
39. Sedition Act, ch. 74, 1 Stat. 596-97 (1798).
40. *Id.*
41. Smith, James Morton, "The Aurora and the Alien and Sedition Laws," *Part I: The Editorship of Benjamin Franklin Bache; Pennsylvania Magazine of History and Biography*, Vol. 77, pp. 3-4 (January 1953).
42. Stone, Geoffrey R., *Perilous Times*, p. 35 (W.W. Norton & Co., 2004).
43. Smith, James Morton, "The Aurora and the Alien and Sedition Laws," *Part I: The Editorship of Benjamin Franklin Bache; Pennsylvania Magazine of History and Biography*, Vol. 77, pp. 18-20 (January 1953); Rosenfeld, Richard N., *American Aurora*, pp. 169, 174-76 (St. Martin's Press, 1997).
44. *Id.* at 19-20; *United States v. Worrall*, 2 U.S. (2 Dall.) 384, 28 F. Cas. 774, 779-80 (C.C.D. Pa. 1798) (No. 16,766); Robreno, Eduardo C., *Learning to Do Justice: An Essay in the Development of the Lower Federal Courts in the Early Years of the Republic*, 29 Rutgers L.J. 555, 573-74 (1998); Rosenfeld, Richard N., *American Aurora*, p. 175 (St. Martin's Press, 1997).
45. Smith, James Morton, "The Aurora and the Alien and Sedition Laws," *Part I: The Editorship of Benjamin Franklin Bache; Pennsylvania Magazine of History and Biography*, Vol. 77, pp. 20, 22 (January 1953).
46. Stone, Geoffrey R., *Perilous Times*, p. 63 (W.W. Norton & Co., 2004).
47. *Id.* at 65; Elsmere, Jane Shaffer, "The Aurora and the Alien and Sedition Laws, *Part II: The Editorship of William Duane," Pennsylvania Magazine of History and Biography*, Vol. 77, pp. 123-55 (April 1953); Rosenfeld, Richard N., *American Aurora*, pp. 221, 223, 701, 703, 707-10 (St. Martin's Press, 1997).
48. Elsmere, Jane Shaffer, "The Aurora and the Alien and Sedition Laws, *Part II: The Editorship of William Duane," Pennsylvania Magazine of History and Biography*, Vol. 77, pp. 123-55 (April 1953); Rosenfeld, Richard N., *American Aurora*, pp. 869-70 (St. Martin's Press, 1997).
49. Stone, Geoffrey R., *Perilous Times*, p. 55 (W.W. Norton & Co., 2004); Volokh, Eugene, "Thomas Cooper, Early American Public Intellectual," *New York University Journal of Law & Liberty*, Vol. 4, pp. 378-79 (2009).
50. Stone, Geoffrey R., *Perilous Times*, pp. 58-59 (W.W. Norton & Co., 2004); *United States v. Cooper*, 25 F. Cas. 631 (C.C.D. Pa. 1800) (No. 14,865).
51. *Id.* at 644.
52. Volokh, Eugene, "Thomas Cooper, Early American Public Intellectual," *New York University Journal of Law & Liberty*, Vol. 4, pp. 378-79 (2009).
53. Act of July 29, 1850, ch. XXXIV, 9 Stat. 799.
54. Presser, Stephen B., *Studies in the History of the United States Courts of the Third Circuit*, pp. 51-52 (Government Printing Office, 1982); Address by Samuel Breck to the Blockley and Merion Agricultural Society on the death of their late President, The Hon. Richard Peters, p. 18, Sept. 20, 1828 (Philadelphia: Lydia R. Bailey, 1828).
55. Act of Apr. 29, 1802, ch. 31, 2 Stat. 156.
56. *See also Martin v. Hunter's Lessee*, 14 U.S. (1 Wheat.) 304 (1816).
57. Higginbotham, Sanford W., *The Keystone in the Democratic Arch: Pennsylvania Politics, 1800-1816*, pp. 183-98 (Pennsylvania Historical and Museum Commission, 1952); Smith, Jean Edward, *John*

*Marshall: Definer of a Nation*, pp. 385-86 (Henry Holt & Co., 1996); Newmyer, R. Kent, *John Marshal and the Heroic Age of the Supreme Court*, p. 325 (Louisiana State University Press, 2001); Surrency, Erwin C., *History of the Federal Courts*, pp. 15-16 (Oceana Publications, 2002).

58. *Id.*
59. *United States v. Peters*, 9 U.S. (5 Cranch) 115 (1809).
60. *Id.*
61. *Id.* at 140. Chief Justice Marshall also determined that the certificates had been in the possession of David Rittenhouse as an individual and not in the possession of the Commonwealth of Pennsylvania so that the Eleventh Amendment of the Constitution that prohibited federal courts from using process against a state was not applicable.
62. "Maritime and Admiralty Historical Symposium," Historical Society of United States District Court for the Eastern District of Pennsylvania, p. 7 (Apr. 6, 1989).
63. Philadelphia County had a population of 54,330 in 1790 and by 1820, it had grown to 73,295.
64. Act of April 20, 1818, ch. 108, 3 Stat. 462 (1818). The Eastern District now consisted of the counties of: Adams, Berks, Bradford, Bucks, Chester, Columbia, Cumberland, Dauphin, Delaware, Franklin, Lancaster, Lebanon, Lehigh, Luzerne, Lycoming, Montgomery, Northampton, Northumberland, Philadelphia, Pike, Schuylkill, Susquehanna, Tioga, Union, Wayne, and York. In later years, some of these counties were divided and additional counties created.
65. Konkle, Burton Alva, *Joseph Hopkinson: 1770-1842*, p. 206 (University of Pennsylvania Press, 1931).
66. Address by Samuel Breck to the Blockley and Merion Agricultural Society on the death of their late President, The Hon. Richard Peters, p. 4, Sept. 20, 1828 (Phila.: Lydia R. Bailey, 1828).
67. Weigley, Russell F., ed., *Philadelphia, A 300 Year History*, p. 257 (W.W. Norton & Co., 1982).
68. Konkle, Burton Alva, *Joseph Hopkinson: 1770-1842*, p. 259 (University of Pennsylvania Press, 1931).
69. Weigley, Russell F., ed., *Philadelphia, A 300 Year History*, pp. 244-45 (W.W. Norton & Co., 1982).
70. Konkle, Burton Alva, *Joseph Hopkinson: 1770-1842*, pp. 256-67 (University of Pennsylvania Press, 1931).
71. *Id.* at p. 258.
72. *Journal of the Executive Proceedings of the Senate of the United States of America*, Vol. III, p. 650 (1715-1829).
73. Konkle, Burton Alva, *Joseph Hopkinson: 1770-1842*, p. 265 (Univ. of Pennsylvania Press, 1931).
74. *Id.* at pp. 175-214.
75. *Id.* at pp. 227-43.
76. *Id.* at pp. 58-68. While Hopkinson was lead counsel, several more experienced lawyers assisted him, including William Lewis.
77. *Id.* at p. 98.
78. *Id.* at p. 111.
79. *Id.* at 155-60, 215-26.
80. The Supreme Court, in an opinion of Chief Justice Marshall, held that the Charter of Dartmouth College was a contract protected from impairment of its obligations under Article I, § 10 of the Constitution. The Court declared void an Act of the New Hampshire legislature amending the Charter. *Trustees of Dartmouth College v. Woodward*, 17 U.S. (4 Wheat.) 518 (1819).
81. 17 U.S. (4 Wheat.) 316, 431 (1819).
82. Konkle, Burton Alva, *Joseph Hopkinson: 1770-1842*, pp. 148, 243, 247, 349 (University of Pennsylvania Press, 1931).
83. *Id.* at pp. 69-84; Presser, Stephen B., *Studies in the History of the United States Courts of the Third Circuit*, p. 243 (Government Printing Office, 1982).
84. Robreno, Eduardo C., Learning to Do Justice: An Essay on the Development of the Lower Federal Courts in the Early Days of the Republic, 29 *Rutgers L.J.* 555, 570-71 (1998).

85. *See* Konkle, Burton Alva, *Joseph Hopkinson: 1770-1842,* pp. 284-308 (University of Pennsylvania Press, 1931). Hopkinson, years before, had argued a major bankruptcy case in the Supreme Court, *Sturges v. Crowninshield,* 17 U.S. (4 Wheat.) 122 (1819). *Id.* at 216-17.
86. *United States v. Benner,* 24 F. Cas. 1084 (C.C.E.D. Pa. 1830) (No. 14,568).
87. Mihm, Stephen, *A Nation of Counterfeiters: Capitalists, Con Men, and the Making of the United States,* pp. 130, 146-48 (Harvard University Press, 2007).
88. *United States v. Twenty-Eight Packages of Pins,* 28 F. Cas. 244, 249 (E.D. Pa. 1833) (No. 16,561); Konkle, Burton Alva, *Joseph Hopkinson: 1770-1842,* pp. 297-98 (University of Pennsylvania Press, 1931).
89. Konkle, Burton Alva, *Joseph Hopkinson: 1770-1842,* pp. 284-87 (University of Pennsylvania Press, 1931).
90. *United States v. Wilson,* 28 F. Cas. 699 (C.C.E.D. Pa. 1830) (No. 16,730).
91. *Id.* at 702-04.
92. *Id.* at 716. The Sixth Amendment provides in relevant part: "In all criminal prosecutions, the accused shall enjoy the right to a speedy and public trial, by an impartial jury of the State and district wherein the crime shall have been committed ...." U.S. Const. amend. VI.
93. 29 F. Cas. 862 (C.C.E.D. Pa. 1832) (No. 17,486), *rev'd* 33 U.S. (8 Pet.) 591 (1834).
94. *Wheaton,* 33 U.S. (8 Peters) at 668; Abrams, Howard B., "The Historic Foundation of American Copyright Law: Exploding the Myth of Common Law Copyright," *Wayne Law Review,* Vol. 29, pp. 1178-87 (Spring 1983).
95. *Proceedings and Debates of the Convention of the Commonwealth of Pennsylvania to Propose Amendments to the Constitution Commenced and Held at Harrisburg on the Second Day of May 1837,* Vol. I, p. 11 (Parker, Barrett & Parks, 1837); *id.* Vols. I-XIV; Act of March 29, 1836, Pa. Session Laws, No. 70; Konkle, Burton Alva, *Joseph Hopkinson: 1770-1842,* pp. 309-23 (University of Pennsylvania Press, 1931); Pa. Constitution of 1838, Art. II & V.
96. *String v. Hill,* 23 F. Cas. 235 (E.D. Pa. 1841) (No. 13,535). Konkle, Burton Alva, *Joseph Hopkinson: 1770-1842,* p. 307 (University of Pennsylvania Press, 1931).
97. Konkle, Burton Alva, *Joseph Hopkinson: 1770-1842,* pp. 348-49 (University of Pennsylvania Press, 1931).
98. Weigley, Russell F., ed. *Philadelphia, A 300-Year History,* p. 215 (W.W. Norton & Co., 1982).

# III
# Slavery, Civil War, and Reunion: 1842-1879

At the time of Judge Hopkinson's death in January 1842, John Tyler was President of the United States. Less than a year before, on April 4, 1841, he had succeeded William Henry Harrison upon the latter's death after only one month in office. Harrison, the victorious general at the Battle of Tippecanoe against the Shawnee Indians, and Tyler, a former Senator from Virginia, had run successfully together on the Whig ticket with the slogan "Tippecanoe and Tyler too." Once in the White House, Tyler rejected some of the key Whig principles such as the party's endorsement of a national bank, and as a result he earned the enmity of many Whigs who controlled Congress.[1]

Tyler's appointment of a successor to Joseph Hopkinson did not go smoothly, at least at first. Initially, Tyler selected Horace Binney, a prominent Philadelphia lawyer, who was a Whig and former anti-Jacksonian congressman (1833-1835). His name had been mentioned years before as a possible Supreme Court nominee. In what seems like a rather unorthodox move, the President nominated Binney, and the Senate confirmed him for the District Court without having obtained his consent. When Secretary of State Daniel Webster forwarded to Binney his commission signed by the President, he declined the appointment. He was then sixty-two years old and had been retired from the practice of law.[2]

The President then turned to Thomas Bradford, another accomplished Philadelphia lawyer and a prominent Presbyterian layman, whose uncle William Bradford had been the Attorney General under President Washington and whose ancestors had been successful printers during the Revolutionary War era. Unfortunately for Bradford, he had spoken out publicly against the rechartering of the Bank of the United States which was supported by the influential Senator Henry Clay, among others. Consequently, the Whig-controlled Senate rejected him for a federal judgeship.[3]

On the third try, Tyler nominated Archibald Randall. This time the President met with success. The Senate confirmed Randall in March 1842, five days after his nomination. Born in Philadelphia in 1797, he had practiced law since 1818, had been active in Democratic politics, and had served for a time as Clerk of Philadelphia's Select Council. In 1834, he was named a judge of the Court of Common Pleas of Philadelphia County, a position he held until his appointment as a District Judge.[4] Randall was involved in philanthropic causes, including the Philadelphia Society for Alleviating the Miseries of Public Prisons. At one point, he had responsibilities as a

Director of the Philadelphia Schools.[5] He was also the first Roman Catholic to sit on the bench of the Eastern District of Pennsylvania. It appears that Tyler, in thinking about the next presidential election, was attempting to solidify his support among the Irish community of Philadelphia.[6]

Within a month or so after Randall took office, Justice Baldwin and he presided over the trial of Alexander William Holmes for manslaughter on high seas. It was a case fraught with difficult legal and moral issues.[7] In March 1841, the ship *William Brown* left Liverpool bound for Philadelphia with seventeen crew members, sixty-five Scottish and Irish immigrants, and heavy cargo. During the voyage the ship hit an iceberg off the coast of Newfoundland and began to sink. Two smaller boats were lowered into the water. Some passengers and crew were able to scramble aboard while those not so fortunate went to their deaths on the *William Brown*. Thereafter, one of the smaller boats in the charge of Holmes, a crew member, began to leak as it was buffeted by a severe rainstorm and high waves. Finally, after twenty-four hours, the crew, including Holmes, threw overboard fourteen male passengers in order to save the boat from sinking and to prevent those remaining from perishing. Two women were also lost although it was not clear if they were tossed out of the boat. The next day, after the inclement weather had subsided, the survivors were rescued by a passing ship.

At his homicide trial in Philadelphia, Holmes was described as an able, brave, and compassionate seaman.[8] In a detailed charge to the jury, Justice Baldwin with the concurrence of Judge Randall explained the obligation of a sailor to a passenger. He instructed the jury that a sailor had no right to invoke the law of necessity as a defense unless all ordinary means of self-preservation were exhausted. He outlined the duties of a sailor to undergo whatever hazard is necessary to preserve the boat and passengers. When danger is extreme with destruction imminent and when time exists, the Court declared that the proper method for determining who should be thrown overboard is by casting lots, "the fairest mode, and in some sort, as on appeal to God, for selection of the victim." The Court also recognized that homicide is "sometimes justifiable." Finally, the Court concluded in its charge that the case "involved questions of the gravest consideration and ... the facts, in some sort were without precedent." The jury struggled with its decision and at one point advised the Court it was unable to agree. "With some difficulty" it ultimately returned a verdict of guilty of manslaughter but recommended mercy. Holmes was sentenced to six months in prison in solitary confinement at hard labor at the Eastern Penitentiary of Pennsylvania and fined $20. While President Tyler refused to grant a pardon, the record states that the "penalty was subsequently remitted."[9]

In late 1842, not long after the *Holmes* case was decided, Francis P. Kenrick, the Roman Catholic Bishop of Philadelphia, wrote a letter to the Board of Controllers of the public schools requesting that Catholic children be permitted to use their own Bible rather than the Protestant King James version and be excused from what in effect was Protestant religious instruction in the public schools. After months of correspondence between the Bishop and school officials, Protestant-Catholic friction escalated. In May 1844, an anti-Catholic riot broke out in the Kensington District of Philadelphia after outsiders allegedly disrupted a meeting being held by a group of Protestants. A second more serious riot erupted in the Southwark District of Philadelphia in July. In this instance, the militia had to be called out to quell the violence.[10]

After the May riot, a state grand jury was impaneled. It issued a report that was critical of "efforts of a certain portion of the community to exclude the Bible from our public schools." It concluded that the riot had been caused after a "band of lawless irresponsible men, some of whom had resided in our country only for a short period," had disturbed and fired upon those of the District of Kensington who sought "the peaceful exercise of the sacred rights and privileges guaranteed to every citizen by the Constitution and laws of our State and Country."[11] This was a thinly veiled attack on the Irish Catholic community.

Judge Randall chaired a meeting of Catholic citizens at St. Mary's Cathedral on Fourth Street in June 1844 to prepare a public response to the grand jury report. The "Address," which he signed and which was printed in the newspaper, criticized the grand jury for failing to call all witnesses and fully examine the circumstances as to what had occurred. Randall denied that the Catholic community ever sought to exclude the Bible from the public schools. He then wrote eloquently about religious freedom, the rights of minorities, and the Constitution:

> [T]hey [the Catholic community] limited their request to the liberty of using their own version [of the Bible], and did not in any way interfere with the use of the Protestant version by such as chose to adopt it. In this age and country, and especially in the city to which William Penn gave the name and impress of brotherly love, we presume it is unnecessary to put forward any plea in support of our constitutional and legal right to have our religious predilections respected. Freedom of conscience is a fundamental article of the social compact which we are bound to maintain, and we cannot consent to see it violated, in ourselves, or our fellow citizens. We appeal to all whether we do not scrupulously respect it in all the various relations of life.
>
> ...
>
> We have heard it affirmed that because Catholics are a minority, they must submit to the regulations which the majority may please

> to adopt. We are willing that the principle should be applied to all things wherein public interest and order are concerned, saving always those principles and rights which the Constitution holds to be inviolable. We are the minority; and for us, therefore, does the Constitution exist. The majority need not its protection, for they have the power to take care of their own interests. Unless for the shield which the Constitution gives to those who are the smaller, and, therefore, the weaker party, this government would be a Despotism, for the governing power would be uncontrolled. To-day one class may be lashed by the tyrant of numbers, and to-morrow another may feel the scourge. No man, no sect, no party, would ever be safe. Peace and order would be destroyed, and soon the wreck of the Republic would add another to the many melancholy instances of the danger which always attends the conferring of unbounded power.[12]

In Randall's day, the federal court was not the place to obtain redress against a school board in matters of Bible reading or religion. The First Amendment, which was ratified as part of the Constitution in 1791, provided that "Congress shall make no law respecting an establishment of religion or prohibiting the free exercise thereof ..." It was not until the third decade of the Twentieth Century that the Supreme Court held that these provisions of the First Amendment also applied to the actions of the states and their municipalities and school boards as a result of the post-Civil War Fourteenth Amendment.[13] Thereafter, the Eastern District was destined to decide a number of significant cases on the issues of religious liberty and the separation of church and state. But all of this lay well into the future.

On the bench, Judge Randall presided primarily over admiralty and maritime matters as well as criminal offenses committed at sea such as *Holmes*. He also adjudicated cases alleging violations of the postal laws. On one occasion he heard a lawsuit in which the Government sought penalties of $2,000 from a person for carrying mail for a fee on railroads and steamboats between Philadelphia and New York in competition with the Post Office.[14] The jury found in favor of the United States. Judge Randall rejected the contention that the statute providing the Government with exclusive authority to establish and regulate post roads was unconstitutional. He cited Article I, § 8 of the Constitution which gives Congress the power "to establish Post Offices and Post Roads" and "to make all Laws which shall be necessary and proper for carrying into Execution the foregoing Powers." Relying on Supreme Court precedent, he concluded that "the presumption is always in favor of the validity of the law, if the contrary is not clearly demonstrated."[15]

When Judge Randall died in June 1846, only four years after he began his federal judicial service, a "Tribute of Respect" appeared in a local newspaper. It referred to him as "the Judge in Admiralty" and reported that the flags of all vessels in the port of Philadelphia had been flown at half mast in his memory.[16]

President James K. Polk, a Democrat, had taken office in March 1845, after having defeated Henry Clay, the Whig candidate. He chose John Kintzing Kane for the seat previously held by Judge Randall. Kane was born in Albany, New York, in 1795, the son of Elisha Kane, a successful merchant, and Alida Van Rensselaer, a member of one of New York's old Dutch patroon families. After her death when their son was four years old, Elisha moved to Philadelphia where he remarried. John Kane later took as his middle name the maiden name of his step-mother.

Following Kane's graduation from Yale College, he read law under Joseph Hopkinson before the latter became a federal District Judge. He was admitted to the Bar in 1817 and two years later married Jane Leiper whose father was prominent in Philadelphia business and political circles. Thereafter, Kane was elected to the Pennsylvania House of Representatives for a term, served as the City Solicitor of Philadelphia, and was chosen by President Andrew Jackson in the 1830's as one of the United States Commissioners to settle claims against France for attacks on American shipping during the Napoleonic era. At this time, his cousin Elias Kane was a United States Senator from Illinois. While originally a Federalist, John Kane had become an active member of the Democratic party and partisan of Jackson after John Quincy Adams and Henry Clay allegedly made a "corrupt bargain" to deprive Jackson of the Presidency when the election of 1824 was thrown into the House of Representatives.[17]

During the 1844 presidential campaign, Kane was a strong supporter of and advisor to Polk.[18] In 1845, Governor Francis Shunk appointed him the Attorney General of Pennsylvania.[19] While holding this office, he prosecuted those who were arrested during the anti-Catholic riots in the Kensington District of Philadelphia during the mid-1840's.[20]

In addition to his political activity and public service, Kane, like his predecessors, had a wide range of interests. He served for many years as an officer of the American Philosophical Society and as its president for the last year of his life. He also sat on the boards of a canal company and a bank, held various offices in the Presbyterian Church, and was a vice-president of the Pennsylvania Institution for the Instruction of the Blind.[21] During the time he was a judge, he and his family lived in center city Philadelphia in the winter and in the summer at a home he had built in the outskirts of Philadelphia County called Fern Rock.[22]

In the first part of the nineteenth century, nepotism was an accepted Government employment practice. At Kane's installation as a federal judge in June 1846, his commission was read by the Court Clerk, who was Francis Hopkinson, Esquire, the grandson and namesake of the first District Judge.[23] He had been appointed to this position by his father, Judge Joseph Hopkinson. Not long thereafter, Kane took the same course and replaced Hopkinson as the Clerk with his own son, Thomas L. Kane. Consideration of family relationships was nothing new in the appointment of court clerks. In 1798, Judge Peters had hired David Caldwell as the clerk to succeed his father Samuel Caldwell after the latter's death.[24]

The rules of conduct for judges were different then than they are now. The strict separation of judges from politics was not required in the mid-nineteenth century. At the urging of Vice-President George Mifflin Dallas, a fellow Pennsylvanian, Kane organized a rally in Philadelphia in 1847 on behalf of the Polk Administration to support the war with Mexico.[25]

One of the first cases Judge Kane encountered on his docket was an unfinished criminal matter.[26] A jury had found a seaman named Harding guilty of murder of the second mate on the barque *Cactus* at a trial before Justice Baldwin and Judge Randall, while two other seaman, Grimes and Williams, had been found guilty of manslaughter. The defendants had filed post-trial motions in which, among other arguments, they maintained that the evidence was insufficient for conviction. Before the Court could rule on the motions, Justice Baldwin had died. Judge Randall was about to decide the issue when he suddenly became ill and also died. Complicating matters further was the fact that there was no verbatim trial transcript. All that existed, according to Judge Kane, were notes of the prosecutor and "the columns of an irresponsible newspaper, that gives sometimes the language of the witness, sometimes its import, and sometimes the reporter's opinion of its value,–these, and nothing more, are to form the basis of our judicial action."[27]

Justice Robert C. Grier, who had replaced the deceased Justice Baldwin as the Circuit Justice, deferred to Judge Kane with respect to the post-trial motions. In his opinion, Judge Kane explained that "To my mind, the principle of the law is clear. The defendant, before sentence can be pronounced on him, has a right to the judicial determination of his guilt by the Court, as well as by the jury. If the verdict does not satisfy the conscience of the judge, the prisoner is entitled to a new trial."[28]

While there was some indication about how Judge Randall had intended to rule if he had lived, Judge Kane rejected the notion of relying on what he had learned in this regard. He reasoned that "a judge's opinions became operative only when they are solemnized by their assertion from the bench."[29] After reviewing the American and English precedents, Judge Kane, with the concurrence of Justice Grier, exercised the Court's discretion to grant a new trial for all three defendants. At the retrial, Harding and Grimes were convicted of manslaughter and Williams was acquitted.[30]

There are times in the life of a judge when he or she is called upon to enforce a statute or adhere to a Supreme Court decision which is unpopular with a significant segment of the community. Judge Peters presided over prosecutions under the Sedition Act of 1798, a statute with which he was in sympathy. Some 50 years later, Judge Kane faced an even more controversial and challenging set of circumstances.

As sectional antagonism increased over slavery in the later 1840's, Congress ultimately enacted a series of statutes, signed by President Millard Fillmore, known as the Compromise of 1850. Among this legislation was the Fugitive Slave Act, which was designed to placate Southern slave owners who wanted more effective assistance from the federal government to recover their slaves who fled to the North and freedom.[31]

Judge Kane sat in a particularly difficult milieu in Pennsylvania with its history of hostility to slavery. There was a strong Quaker presence which had long opposed human bondage.[32] As previously noted, in 1780, taking the lead among the states, Pennsylvania had enacted a law, drafted by William Lewis, that provided for the gradual abolition of slavery in the Commonwealth. In 1826, the General Assembly approved an Act making it a crime, punishable by a mandatory minimum term of imprisonment of seven years and a maximum term of twenty-one years as well as confinement at hard labor, for taking or carrying away by force and violence any Negro or mulatto to a place outside the Commonwealth with the intent to sell, detain or keep such person as a slave. In 1847, after the United States Supreme Court had declared the 1826 law unconstitutional,[33] the General Assembly enacted the Liberty Law which, among other provisions, made a slave free once he or she stepped onto Pennsylvania soil.[34] Yet, many leading citizens of Philadelphia had married into Southern families and had commercial ties with and sympathy for the South. The textile industry in Philadelphia depended on Southern cotton. While the Underground Railroad existed in Philadelphia, bias against free people of color was commonplace among the general population.[35]

The Fugitive Slave Act provided for the appointment of commissioners to aid in the arrest, capture and return of runaway slaves. It authorized owners to obtain arrest warrants for their slaves and to seize and arrest them without a warrant if it could be done without breach of the peace. The slaves were then to be taken before a judge or commissioner whose duty it was to hear and determine the case of a claimant in a summary manner and upon satisfactory proof "by deposition or affidavit." Once the Court issued a certificate of ownership, a claimant was allowed to use "such reasonable force and restraint as may be necessary" to return the slaves to the state or territory from which they had fled. Significantly, the fugitive slaves were not allowed to tell their side of the story at any trial or hearing. The statute specifically prohibited their testimony from being admitted into evidence.[36]

With respect to compensation, the commissioners and Deputy United States Marshals were to be paid more if the fugitive was returned to slavery after a hearing than if the claimant-slave owner was unsuccessful. Finally, the Act made it a crime for anyone to prevent the arrest of a fugitive, to harbor or conceal a fugitive, or to refuse to aid the government when called on by a Deputy United States Marshal in procuring an arrest of a fugitive.[37]

The fugitive slave cases defined the remaining years of Judge Kane's tenure on the bench. One of the most highly publicized cases arose out of an incident that occurred in Christiana, Lancaster County, Pennsylvania in September 1851.[38] A slave owner from Maryland named Gorsuch had obtained from a United States Commissioner a warrant to arrest certain of his slaves who had fled across the border to Christiana. Gorsuch arrived with a number of others, including a Deputy United States Marshal, at the house where they were being harbored. The slaves refused to come out despite a "promise" they would be treated fairly. While in the vicinity, the defendant Castner Hanway, a Caucasian, explicitly rejected the request from the Deputy Marshal to assist in the apprehension of Gorsuch's slaves. He asserted that the slaves had a right to defend themselves and that he was opposed to the Act of Congress under which they were being seized. Ultimately, the slaves, together with some of a group of about 150 Blacks who had gathered, fired weapons at those who attempted to seize them. A gun battle erupted and Gorsuch was killed. Numerous indictments followed both in the federal and state courts.

Reflecting the temper of the times and the passions that the Christiana Riot, as it came to be known, had generated, Hanway was indicted for treason and tried before Justice Grier, Judge Kane, and a jury.[39] Thaddeus Stevens, the Whig and later Radical Republican Congressman from Pennsylvania, headed the defense team. The prosecutors included not only John W. Ashmead, the United States Attorney for the Eastern District of Pennsylvania, but also James Cooper, one of Pennsylvania's senators. Because of the insistence of Maryland's Governor, the Maryland Attorney General, Robert J. Brent, also actively participated in representing the federal Government.[40] Attending the trial in the crowded courtroom was Lucretia Mott, the Quaker abolitionist and a leader of the nineteenth-century women's rights movement.[41]

> The indictment charged that:
>
> Hanway, wickedly intending and devising the peace and tranquillity of the United States to disturb, and prevent the execution of the laws thereof, to wit, "An act, &c.," and another act, supplementary to the same, passed on the 18th September 1850, did on the 11th of September 1851, wickedly and traitorously intend to levy war against the United States.[42]

In the charge to the jury, Justice Grier, with the concurrence of Judge Kane, expressed the Court's view of the facts "without desiring to invade the prerogatives of the jury in judging the facts of this case." The Court conceded that Hanway's conduct did not constitute treason by levying war against the United States. On the other hand, it was quick to advise the jury that it disapproved of resistance to the Fugitive Slave Act:

> The act of 1850, passed to secure them [the people of Maryland] in the enjoyment of their acknowledged rights, had been received with a shout of disapprobation, in certain parts of the country. Meetings had been held in many places in the North, denouncing the law, and advising a traitorous resistance to its execution; conventions of infuriated fanatics had incited to acts of rebellion, and even the pulpit had been defiled with furious denunciations of the law, and exhortations to a rebellious resistance to it. The government was perfectly justified in supposing that this transaction was but the first overt act of a treasonable conspiracy extending over many of the Northern states to resist by force of arms the execution of this article of the constitution and the laws framed in pursuance of it. In making these arrests, and having this investigation, the officers of government have done no more than their strict duty. The activity, zeal, and ability which have been exhibited by the learned attorney of the United States in endeavoring to bring to condign punishment the perpetrators of this gross offence, are deserving of all praise.[43]

The jury accepted the Court's view of the evidence and found the defendant not guilty of treason. The abolitionists were elated and the partisans of slavery were outraged.[44]

In another high profile case,[45] John Wheeler, a North Carolinian and the United States Minister to Nicaragua, was passing through Philadelphia to New York in 1855 with his slave Jane Johnson and her two children. While they were on a steamship awaiting departure from Philadelphia, one Passmore Williamson, a Quaker and an abolitionist, boarded the vessel. He inquired of Johnson whether she desired to be free and received an affirmative answer. He then separated her and her children from Wheeler, took them ashore, and released them. A habeas corpus proceeding followed in which Judge Kane ordered Williamson, a friend of Kane's son Thomas, to produce the bodies of the slaves. When he failed to do so, Judge Kane jailed him for contempt at Moyamensing Prison.[46] After much legal wrangling, Williamson was freed but only after 100 days of confinement.[47] This decision to imprison Williamson caused much public uproar and even calls for Kane's impeachment.[48]

In one of his opinions in this case, he expounded at length his views, undoubtedly commonly held at the time, about slavery. He began with the proposition that the United States Constitution recognized slaves as property. According to Judge Kane, it secured the rights to slave property to the same extent as it protected other property.

He then acknowledged, "We revolt in Pennsylvania, and honestly no doubt, at this association of men with things as the subjects of property ..." Yet, he noted that even in Pennsylvania Blacks were denied political rights. Quoting from the late Justice Baldwin,[49] he wrote that the right of the master to the services of a slave was no different than the right of a parent to the services of his minor children. If it was unjust and oppressive to have property in human beings for life, "the sin is on the makers of laws which tolerate slavery" and not on those who honestly acquire slaves. To blame the latter is "the rankest injustice towards our fellow men."[50] Judge Kane's ambivalence about slavery was evident, but in the end he adhered to the principle that the law must be obeyed, however distasteful:

> The only permanent danger is in the indulgence of the humane and benevolent feelings of our nature, at what we feel to be acts of oppression towards human beings, endowed with the same qualities and attributes as ourselves, and brought into being by the same power which created us all; without reflecting, that in suffering these feelings to come into action against rights secured by the laws, we forget the first duty of citizens of a government of laws, obedience to its ordinances.[51]

In November 1855, after his release, Williamson lost no time in suing Judge Kane in the Court of Common Pleas of Delaware County for damages for false imprisonment. The case was still pending when Kane died several years later and only then was it dismissed. The federal government had rebuffed all of Kane's efforts to obtain reimbursement from it for the expenses of his defense.[52]

The records of the Eastern District reflect that Judge Kane presided over numerous other fugitive slave cases during his years on the bench. Sometimes the fugitives were returned to the South and other times they were not. In some instances the identification of the slave was a thorny issue as in the case of one Henry Garnet.[53] In all instances, moral issues were clearly present. He wrote to one of his sons that in Pennsylvania the Fugitive Slave Act "has been carried out firmly and honestly."[54]

During the time Kane sat as a federal judge, his son Robert Patterson Kane was a practicing attorney. The court records identify him as representing parties in lawsuits over which his father presided. He was defense counsel for some of the Blacks in state trials arising out of the Christiana Riot and also represented the fugitive slave Henry Garnet in another case.[55] No one seemed to have raised any concern about the close familial relationship between the Judge and the lawyer for a litigant before him.

Judge Kane had appointed another son Thomas Kane not only as the court clerk but also as a commissioner under the Fugitive Slave Act. Thomas soon resigned the latter position as an act of conscience. He, like his brother Robert, was a vocal opponent of slavery and on the eve of the *Hanway* trial delivered "six superior turkeys" and a pound cake to the prison for Hanway and other prisoners to enjoy. He even went so far as to aid runaway slaves by using the family home at Fern Rock as a way station. Incensed by his son's indignant letter of resignation as a United States Commissioner, the judge ruled him in contempt and sentenced him to prison, but Supreme Court Justice Grier quickly overturned the order. The record is unclear whether Thomas Kane ever served any time behind bars.[56]

In addition to issues concerning fugitive slaves, Judge Kane presided over a trial of a sea captain named Darnaud who was indicted for engaging in the slave trade on the high seas, a capital offense.[57] In his charge to the jury, Kane explained that unlike piracy which was against the law of nations and punishable by all countries regardless of the citizenship of the pirates, trading in slaves on the high seas was legal under the laws of many countries, although not under the laws of the United States. Consequently, the defendant could be convicted only if the vessel involved was owned in whole or in part by an American citizen or the sea captain himself was an American citizen and had the intent to engage in the slave trade.

The indictment charged that Darnaud had captained the *Grey Eagle* which had picked up Blacks on the coast of Africa and had confined them with the intent to sell them as slaves. Because the evidence was equivocal on the ownership of the vessel and there was strong evidence that Darnaud was a French rather than an American citizen, Judge Kane cautioned the jury particularly in light of the "awful and solemn consequences to the defendant" that it may only find the defendant guilty if it did so beyond a reasonable doubt. The jury returned a verdict of not guilty.

Until 1854, the County of Philadelphia consisted of more than two dozen townships, boroughs, and districts in addition to the City of Philadelphia whose boundaries at that time encompassed only the area between Vine and South Streets from the Delaware River on the East to the Schuylkill on the West. In 1854, the Pennsylvania General Assembly consolidated the City and County, making the two jurisdictions co-terminus.[58]

With this consolidation, the District Court moved out of Independence Hall where it had sat since 1830. In June 1854, the Government leased for the Court the ground and second floors of the Hall of the American Philosophical Society situated immediately south of Philadelphia's City Hall on the west side of Fifth Street. The space had previously housed the offices of the City's Mayor, among others.[59] Undoubtedly, Judge Kane was instrumental in bringing about this contractual arrangement since at the time he was also the vice-president of the Society. In 1856, the government offered to purchase the Hall and its lot for the Court for $78,000, but because of a deed restriction, the United States Attorney General refused to approve the acquisition. This space continued to be leased for the Court until 1863.[60]

Judge Kane died in Philadelphia in February 1858 some three years before the beginning of the Civil War. His judicial career was the subject of much controversy.[61] His decision to jail Williamson for contempt had inflamed a large segment of the community in the North. According to a local newspaper, "The manner in which he discharged his judicial duties has caused much excited discussion, and Judge Kane has been denounced as tyrannical and arbitrary. But of his legal acquirements, there could not be two opinions. He was both a ripe scholar and an able lawyer. In the social relations he was perfectly exemplary .... His manners were those of a finished gentleman."[62] Another newspaper commented, "His judicial career was chiefly distinguished by a decision which excited, at the time it was given, the keenest controversy, and the principles involved in which, applied on a larger scale, are now agitating the whole country to its very foundation."[63]

Judge Kane did not live long enough to know about the later achievements of his sons Thomas and Robert. For a time, Robert served as Acting United States Attorney for the Eastern District and became a Colonel in the Union Army during the Civil War. Thomas was also commissioned a Union officer. He was wounded twice, taken prisoner, exchanged, cited for gallantry at Gettysburg, and finally breveted a Major General. Francis Fisher Kane, the judge's grandson and Robert's son, would be appointed by President Woodrow Wilson in 1913 as the United States Attorney for the Eastern District of Pennsylvania.[64]

Judge Kane was succeeded by John Cadwalader, who was selected for the Court in April 1858, by President James Buchanan. Cadwalader, who was born in 1805, came from a distinguished Philadelphia family and was known to the President. His grandfather, also named John Cadwalader, had served as an officer under George Washington during the Revolutionary War. His brother, George, was a lawyer and a General in the Pennsylvania militia.[65] After his graduation from the University of Pennsylvania in 1821, the future judge studied law under Horace Binney, who, as noted previously, refused an appointment by President Tyler to the District Court. Cadwalader's first wife was Binney's daughter. Following admission to the bar, he soon developed a lucrative practice. At one point he was a solicitor to the Bank of the United States. He was elected as a Democrat to the House of Representatives from Philadelphia and served one term (1855-1857). Choosing not to seek reelection, he returned to private practice, and a year later President Buchanan nominated him to the Eastern District.[66] He was confirmed shortly thereafter.

In the years immediately prior to and following the death of Judge Kane, sectional rhetoric and strife continued to escalate at a quicker and quicker pace. In March 1857, the Supreme Court handed down its infamous *Dred Scott* decision, in which Chief Justice Roger Brooke Taney declared that a Black person could not be a citizen of the United States or any state under the Constitution.[67] In 1859, John Brown and his small band of militant abolitionists raided the federal armory at Harper's Ferry, Virginia. They were quickly captured and then hanged.[68] The election of Abraham Lincoln as the President of the United States in November 1860 precipitated the rupture between the North and South, and before that year had come to a close, South Carolina had seceded from the Union.[69]

Against this ever more inflamed background, Judge Cadwalader, like his predecessor Judge Kane, encountered fugitive slave cases on his docket. In 1860, he had before him the criminal trial of Jeremiah Buck who had attempted to free a fugitive slave in the custody of Deputy United States Marshals.[70]

At a prior hearing at the American Philosophical Society Hall where the Court was sitting at that time, Judge Cadwalader had issued a certificate under the Fugitive Slave Act which allowed a claimant to remove a fugitive slave from Pennsylvania. Once the judge had handed down his ruling in the packed courtroom where the Marshal had excluded virtually every Black person allegedly for security reasons, the fugitive was led out of the Fifth Street doorway of the building.[71] He was placed in a carriage with several deputy marshals inside and a deputy marshal on the outside seat beside the driver. As the carriage moved north toward Chestnut Street, efforts were made by some of the gathered crowd to impede its movement. The horses pulling the carriage increased their speed and were able to proceed several blocks westward on Chestnut Street when Buck, "violently excited and exerting great strength" along with others, seized and held the heads of the horses and forced them onto the sidewalk against an iron awning post. At that point, a little beyond Seventh Street and about sixty yards from the courthouse, Buck was arrested by a Philadelphia police officer.[72]

Judge Cadwalader, after reviewing the relevant law for the jury, suggested that it should find Buck guilty of attempting to rescue a fugitive slave from official custody. Following the judge's suggestion, the jury did precisely that.[73]

Shortly thereafter, in early 1861, Abraham Lincoln, the President-elect, made his way by train from Illinois to Washington for his inauguration as the secessionist crisis beckoned. Taking a circuitous route through the Northern states, he stopped in a number of cities, including Philadelphia where he was warmly greeted.[74] To great applause, he delivered a few remarks inside of Independence Hall before the members of the Select and Common Councils of the City on Washington's birthday, February 22. He then proceeded outside to raise an American flag. His remarks to the council members began:

> I am filled with deep emotion at finding myself standing here in the place where were collected together the wisdom, the patriotism, the devotion to principle from which sprang the institutions under which we live.[75]

Those institutions, which included the federal courts, would be challenged mightily after Lincoln took the oath of office on March 4.

In the early morning hours of April 12, 1861, Confederate batteries, under the command of General Pierre G.T. Beauregard, opened fire on Fort Sumter in Charleston Harbor. Major Robert Anderson and his small Union garrison surrendered thirty-three hours later.[76] President Lincoln immediately called for the states to supply 75,000 militiamen to suppress the rebellion.[77] He also proclaimed a blockade of southern ports, and as a result ships attempting to enter or leave those ports were seized. Actions were then instituted in the various federal courts sitting in admiralty to determine whether these ships and their contents should be condemned as prizes of the United States. The legality of the blockade, which was a major wartime strategy of the Lincoln Administration, would soon be tested.[78]

In May 1861, within weeks after the blockade was proclaimed, a government frigate captured a vessel, *The Parkhill*, off the coast of Charleston, South Carolina, on a voyage from Liverpool. The vessel was brought to Philadelphia for a determination by Judge Cadwalader whether it should be condemned on behalf of the United States.[79] The libel filed by the Government contended that the ship attempted to avoid the blockade and was "the property of insurgents, traitors, and public enemies." The owners, residents of South Carolina, sought the return of their property.

Judge Cadwalader, in his opinion, recited the recent history of the insurgency. He recounted that in December 1860, South Carolina at a convention had "proclaimed her independence of the constitutional government of the United States. This revolutionary attempt has been followed by similar acts of such conventions in 10 other states" and "[a] revolutionary constitutional confederation has been organized in them." He observed that the laws of the United States were not presently enforceable anywhere in nine of the eleven Confederate states including South Carolina and were enforceable only in limited places in the other two,[80] that is, in the Western District of Virginia and the Eastern District of Tennessee. His opinion proceeded to detail the English and American precedents on the seizure of vessels as prizes during times of war between nations as well as during civil wars and other hostilities.

Upon completion of his erudite review of the law, Judge Cadwalader held that the Government properly seized the vessel as a prize because of the existence of hostilities with South Carolina. Since *The Parkhill's* destination was Charleston, it did not matter whether the owners were loyal to the United States. He rejected the argument that the seizure was illegal because the Congress has "not legislated upon the existing war" and "the president alone had directed and regulated the prosecution of hostilities." When the courts cannot function and the Marshal cannot execute process, he wrote, "a state of war exists" and the President has a duty "to take care that the laws be faithfully executed."[81] The Government retained *The Parkhill* and its contents as a prize, and the claim of the owners was rejected.

In the summer of 1862, Justice Robert Grier, sitting as the Circuit Justice in Philadelphia, sustained a decision of Judge Cadwalader which upheld the Government's right to seize and retain as prizes ships and cargo belonging to citizens of states in rebellion even though the owners were not attempting to aid the rebellion. The *Philadelphia Public Ledger* reported that "Judge Grier's opinion is the more important from the fact that it is the first given by a member of the Supreme Court."[82]

Thereafter, the constitutionality of the blockade reached the Supreme Court in four consolidated cases involving vessels condemned in the District Courts in Boston, New York, and Key West. It was Justice Grier who wrote the 5 to 4 decision in March 1863 which held that President Lincoln's blockade of the Confederate ports during the insurrection was constitutional and that even if some defect existed as to what he had done, the blockade had been ratified by Congress.[83] Some have considered the Supreme Court's decision in the *Prize Cases* to be the most crucial that it rendered during the Civil War.[84]

In the same year that Judge Cadwalader decided *The Parkhill* seizure, he ruled on another case involving a military incident that had occurred in the South. Charles Greiner, a Philadelphian, was engaged in agricultural pursuits in Georgia. In January 1861, several months before the surrender of Fort Sumter, he was a member of an artillery company in that state which seized Fort Pulaski from the United States without resistance, garrisoned it for a time, and then turned it over to the state authorities. Within a few months thereafter, Greiner returned to Philadelphia to visit with his wife and child. While here, he was charged with treason by levying war against the United States.[85]

Under the Constitution, an accused is entitled to a speedy trial by a jury in the state and district where the crime was committed.[86] Because the federal court was not open in Georgia, Greiner could not be sent there for trial. Nor did anyone know in mid-1861 when it would again be functioning. The question before the Eastern District was whether Greiner should be held in custody until that future day arrived or instead be admitted to bail in the meantime. After consulting with Justice Grier, Judge Cadwalader allowed Greiner to remain free, although on bail of $10,000. Under the circumstances presented, where pretrial imprisonment could be lengthy, he expressed great concern that an order of commitment "would be a dangerous precedent."[87]

The imprisonment of civilians during the Civil War was not always the result of judicial process. In late April 1861, shortly after taking office, President Lincoln, relying on his constitutional power as Commander in Chief of the Army and Navy,[88] authorized General Winfield Scott or a subordinate officer to suspend the privilege of the writ of habeas corpus if necessary for the public safety "at any point on or in the vicinity of the military line which is now used between the City of Philadelphia and the City of Washington via Ferryville, Annapolis City and Annapolis Junction."[89]

The ancient writ of habeas corpus allows the courts to decide whether a person was being legally detained. The Constitution, recognizing its significance, provides that "The Privilege of the Writ of Habeas Corpus shall not be suspended, unless when in Cases of Rebellion or Invasion the public Safety may require it."[90]

In August 1861, without specifically mentioning habeas corpus, Congress ratified all acts and orders of the President relating to the military since his inauguration.[91] Lincoln thereafter suspended habeas corpus from time to time in various parts of the country. In early August 1862, Secretary of War Edwin M. Stanton, acting for the President, suspended the writ nationwide. In September 1862, the President himself issued a nationwide suspension order. It declared that "all persons guilty of any disloyal practice shall be subject to martial law."[92]

With the writ's suspension, civilians were sometimes arrested and imprisoned without the involvement of the courts for speech that was viewed to be inimical to the war effort. Probably the most highly publicized incident arose out of the seizure of former Congressman Clement Vallandigham of Ohio.[93] Another such incident occurred in Philadelphia in which Charles Ingersoll, a successful lawyer and leading citizen, was the target. He was the grandson of Jared Ingersoll, a signer of the Constitution and a former United States Attorney, and the son of Charles Jared Ingersoll, a renowned lawyer and a longtime member of Congress.[94]

Charles Ingersoll, who was married to the daughter of a former Tennessee Senator, defended slavery and was an arch foe of the abolitionists. He blamed the intransigence of the North and the Lincoln Administration for the South's secession and the Civil War. In August 1862, he spoke at a large rally in Philadelphia where he denounced the Lincoln Administration and its conduct of the war. He urged a vote for the Democratic ticket in the fall election and accused the Lincoln Administration of corruption and profiteering. Two days later, the local Provost Marshal arrested him. Upon being released on bail, he was taken into custody by the United States Marshal who held him pursuant to a standing order of the War Department which had authorized the arrest of anyone who, among other misdeeds, "give[s] aid and comfort to the enemy."[95]

Ingersoll petitioned Judge Cadwalader for a writ of habeas corpus, and Cadwalader thereupon ordered him to be brought before the Court for a determination as to whether he was being held lawfully. Counsel for the Marshal argued that he did not have to produce Ingersoll because the privilege of the writ of habeas corpus had been suspended. Cadwalader postponed the hearing for a day but warned the Marshal not to remove Ingersoll outside of the jurisdiction. The Marshal, in the meantime, had been commanded to take Ingersoll to Washington for confinement in the Old

Capitol Prison. Before any removal of Ingersoll had taken place and before any critical confrontation between the executive and judicial branches of government erupted, Secretary of War Stanton learned of the arrest and defused the situation by directing Ingersoll to be released. Consequently, Judge Cadwalader never had to resolve this potentially explosive issue.[96]

In addition to the important constitutional question involved, this case illustrates the often close web of personal relationships that existed among the leading families in Philadelphia in this era. Judge Cadwalader, Ingersoll, Ingersoll's father, and one of Ingersoll's attorneys Peter McCall were all fellow parishioners at Philadelphia's Christ Church.[97]

The Ingersoll case also had a familial twist for Judge Cadwalader. A year or so before the arrest of Ingersoll, the Judge's brother George Cadwalader, a Philadelphia lawyer and a Brevet Major General, had played a leading role in a similar habeas corpus matter. In May 1861, shortly after Lincoln had authorized the suspension of habeas corpus in the area between Philadelphia and Washington, John Merryman was arrested at his home north of Baltimore for "acts of treason" as a Lieutenant in the rebel forces. He was taken to Fort McHenry which happened to be under the command of Brevet Major General Cadwalader.

Attorneys for Merryman sought and obtained a writ of habeas corpus from the aged Chief Justice Taney, an appointee of President Andrew Jackson. The writ was served on General Cadwalader who was ordered to produce Merryman in court. Cadwalader, through a representative, respectfully requested a postponement until he received further instructions from the President. Refusing to defer, Taney again ordered Merryman to be produced. Cadwalader refused to do so.[98]

In a Baltimore courtroom in which both Cadwalader and Merryman were absent, Taney, describing himself as "Chief Justice of the Supreme Court of the United States at chambers," quickly proceeded to hand down his decision. He declared that only Congress could suspend habeas corpus and that the President had violated the Constitution in doing so without Congressional approval. Taney directed that Merryman be freed.[99] Lincoln and Cadwalader declined to comply.[100]

Nonetheless, like Ingersoll, Merryman was released at the direction of the Secretary of War, but in his case after a few weeks of confinement. Although Merryman was then indicted for levying war against the United States, he was granted bail and the charges were ultimately dismissed.[101]

The intervention of the Secretary of War in the Merryman case and later in the Ingersoll case averted a serious clash between the President and the federal courts over habeas corpus. In particular, it enabled Judge Cadwalader to avoid the need to decide whether to follow Chief Justice Taney's ruling in *Merryman* in which the judge's brother was a principal player. On a personal level, a potentially difficult issue between Judge Cadwalader and his brother was obviated.

Habeas corpus as a significant constitutional issue faded from view in the Eastern District as of March 1863, when Congress ratified the President's suspension of the writ of habeas corpus and empowered him to suspend the writ anywhere in the nation "during the present rebellion ... whenever, in his judgment, the public safety may require it."[102] On the same day in March 1863, Congress also enacted a national draft.[103] Cases involving conscription, enlistment, and desertion thereafter appeared on Judge Cadwalader's docket.

He discharged one soldier, James Burke, on petition of his mother, because the soldier had enlisted at the age of seventeen without her consent.[104] Frederick Stingle, a married man over thirty-five years old who had been drafted in violation of law, was also released from military service.[105] In another case, Cornelius McCall had allegedly been drafted and had failed to appear at the Montgomery County Courthouse for induction at the appointed time. He was charged with desertion. Judge Cadwalader freed him after finding that the military enrollment list had misstated his first name.[106]

In *Antrim's Case*,[107] W.H.H. Antrim claimed he was entitled to a draft exemption as the only son of a widow dependent for support on his labor. He lost before a three- person local commission, known as the Board of Enrollment. After he reported for duty and received his uniform, he filed a habeas corpus petition before Judge Cadwalader in which he sought to be discharged. The Board which had decided against Antrim consisted of three members: its president who was the Provost Marshal of the district with the rank of a Captain of Cavalry; the local surgeon whose duty it was to examine those drafted to determine whether they were fit to serve; and a citizen-at-large. The crucial question was whether the Court had jurisdiction in a habeas corpus proceeding to decide whether the decision of a local Board of Enrollment denying a draft exemption could be reviewed by a court when the draft law provided that the Board's decision was final. Judge Cadwalader held that he did have jurisdiction. Interpreting the law to give the Board's decision finality without judicial review, said Judge Cadwalader, would render it unconstitutional as vesting judicial powers in a body whose decision-makers were not judges appointed by the President and confirmed by the Senate. Finally, he rejected the argument that the writ of habeas corpus had been suspended with respect to draft cases such as this.

Not all cases before Judge Cadwalader during the Civil War involved war-related issues. In 1861, for example, he decided a lawsuit brought by the well-known actress Laura Keene who claimed certain rights in the British comedy *Our American Cousin*. Unbeknown to him or anyone else at the time, both the actress and the play were later to make a cameo appearance on the stage of American history. On the evening of April 14, 1865, President and Mrs. Lincoln were attending a performance of *Our American Cousin* featuring Keene at Ford's Theater when John Wilkes Booth fired his fatal shot.[108]

According to Judge Cadwalader's findings in the lawsuit before him, the play was written in England in 1852 by a man named Tom Taylor. In 1858, after a rewriting of the manuscript, Taylor transferred all rights to it to Keene, who at the time was a lessee and proprietor of a theater in New York. It was first performed there in October 1858, where it met with great success. Although Keene was willing to grant the defendants William Wheatley and John Sleeper Clarke[109] the right to perform the play in Philadelphia for a fee, they decided to go forward without any agreement with her. They asserted in their defense that they had legally obtained a copy of the play from the former wife of an English actor. Defendants repeatedly performed the play thereafter in Philadelphia with profitable results.

Judge Cadwalader first decided that Keene had no federal statutory copyright in the manuscript. Nonetheless, he exercised his "general equitable jurisdiction" as the citizenship of the parties was diverse. He ruled that Keene had literary proprietorship in *Our American Cousin* and was entitled to a decree against defendants. After the matter of damages was referred to a master, she was ultimately awarded $500.[110]

During this period and up until July 1, 1863, the American Philosophical Society Hall continued to be leased for the use of the Eastern District, although the Court had vacated the premises before that time.[111] The minutes of the Society reflect that in June the Court sought permission to remove its papers from the Hall's "N.E. attic."[112]

In February 1863, in the midst of the Civil War, a new post office and courthouse costing $60,000 was dedicated. It was located on the south side of Chestnut Street east of Fifth Street, less than a block from the American Philosophical Society Hall and next to what had been the Second Bank of the United States. A wing extended south to Library Street. The new structure contained marble floors and steam heat and was the first building constructed in Philadelphia specifically to house a federal court. Many dignitaries including Postmaster General Montgomery Blair, Secretary of Interior John Usher, and Governor Andrew Curtin, were present for the festivities which featured a band, a dinner, and the unfurling with great fanfare of an American flag from a rooftop staff. The second floor of the wing that bordered on Library Street provided accommodations for the Court, which moved into that space in May 1863.[113] A contemporary newspaper article commented, "The whole arrangement tends to the comfort and will meet the wants of the Post Office as well as the United States Courts, in an admirable manner, there being convenience within the structure for both departments."[114] It was here that Judge Cadwalader sat for his remaining years on the bench.

In the fall of 1868, he was called upon to decide who was the rightful United States Attorney for the Eastern District of Pennsylvania.[115] In doing so, he was confronted with the then highly publicized Tenure of Office Act, which the Radical Republican Congress had passed over the veto of President Andrew Johnson in 1867.

It was designed to curb the power of the President by limiting his right to dismiss certain high level government officials, including cabinet members, without the advice and consent of the Senate.[116] When Johnson "suspended" Secretary of War Edwin M. Stanton without the Senate's approval in the summer of 1867, Johnson's conduct in allegedly violating the Tenure of Office Act was made one of the subjects of the Articles of Impeachment voted against him by the House of Representatives. Johnson's trial in the Senate, which resulted in his acquittal by one vote, had ended in May 1868.[117]

In April 1868, while the Senate was in session, President Johnson had nominated John P. O'Neill as the new United States Attorney. The Senate adjourned in July without acting on the nomination. In August, Johnson gave O'Neill a recess appointment to the position with his commission to expire at the end of the next session of the Senate.

Charles Gilpin, who had previously been appointed the United States Attorney by President Lincoln, contested O'Neill's right to the office. Gilpin's four-year term had come to an end on March 15, 1868, but he had continued to serve. Gilpin contended that his term as the United States Attorney was extended under the Tenure of Office Act since the Senate had not concurred in his being replaced. Judge Cadwalader rejected the argument on the ground that the Act specifically exempted from its grasp those offices for which the law provided a specific term.[118]

This, however, did not mean vindication for O'Neill. Cadwalader ruled that he too was not entitled to the office because the Constitution allows the President to make recess appointments only when the vacancy occurs while the Senate was not in session.[119] At the time Gilpin completed his four-year term on March 15, 1868, the Senate was sitting. Nonetheless, Cadwalader recognized O'Neill's right to act, not as the United States Attorney as such, but rather under the instructions and authorization of the Attorney General.[120]

The Civil War, among many other consequences, had severely disrupted everyday commercial activities between the North and the South. Once the conflict ended in the spring of 1865, federal courts were often called upon to untangle what it had wrought. In 1847, a man named Henry Bird, a resident of Virginia, had purchased an insurance policy on his life from the Penn Mutual Life Insurance Company in Philadelphia. He had dutifully paid the annual premiums until 1861 when hostilities prevented him from continuing to do so. Penn Mutual declared the policy lapsed, and in correspondence with the policyholder after the war refused to change its position. Bird brought suit in the Eastern District for an order to allow him to pay the unpaid premiums, to have the policy declared in force, and to obtain an accounting of any dividends due. Based upon equitable considerations due to impossibility, Judge Cadwalader found in his favor and ordered reinstatement of the policy on payment of the premiums and an accounting with respect to dividends.[121]

In the years after the Civil War, the calendar of Judge Cadwalader contained a wide variety of other cases reflecting the fact that Philadelphia was a major railroad and banking center as well as an important port. In 1876, the nation's centennial year, it was estimated to have a population of 817,000 and was the second largest city in the United States behind New York.[122]

The railroads were no strangers to the courtroom.[123] Taxation of banks and the right to engage in banking also came before the Court.[124] Disputes continued to arise in admiralty. Among them were cases involving the licensing of a vessel, the delay in the delivery of a cargo of goat skins originating in Trieste, and the delivery of a wet potato shipment after a long tumultuous voyage.[125]

Harkening back to the days of the Whiskey Rebellion and Judge Peters, the Government instituted a proceeding before Judge Cadwalader to seize equipment used for the production of distilled spirits. It did so because of the failure of the distiller to pay certain taxes due on his whiskey.[126] This time, however, the flames of rebellion were not ignited.

One of the most far-reaching results of the Union victory in the Civil War was the ratification of the Thirteenth, Fourteenth, and Fifteenth Amendments to the Constitution. These amendments abolished slavery, declared former slaves to be citizens, prohibited a state from depriving a citizen of life, liberty, or property without due process or of the equal protection of the laws and from denying the right to vote on account of race, color or previous condition of servitude. The Fugitive Slave Act, which Judges Kane and Cadwalader had expended so much time and energy to enforce, was now a dead letter. Congress undertook the Reconstruction of the South and expanded the reach of the federal government in the process. From now on, it would be the United States is, not the United States are.

During Reconstruction, Congress granted the federal trial courts for the first time general jurisdiction over cases arising under federal law.[127] No longer would such suits be relegated to the state courts. As Felix Frankfurter and James Landis wrote many years ago, the Judiciary Act of 1875 now made the federal courts "the primary and powerful reliances for vindicating every right given by the Constitution, the laws, and treaties of the United States."[128]

Judge Cadwalader died in Philadelphia in January 1879, less than four years later and after almost twenty-one years on the bench. He had lived through and had weathered the most momentous events in American history since the creation of the federal courts. A newspaper article at the time of his death recorded, "He was loved and respected by all with whom he came in contact, and he dies leaving an illustrious name."[129] A marble tablet, containing a bronze frieze of his profile, was commissioned and remains to this day on the third floor of the present courthouse. It reads:

JOHN CADWALADER

JUDGE OF THE DISTRICT COURT

OF THE UNITED STATES

FOR THE EASTERN DISTRICT

OF PENNSYLVANIA

FROM APRIL 26TH 1858

UNTIL HIS DEATH JANUARY 26TH 1879

---

PACE AC BELLO

INTER CIVES ET INTER GENTES

SALVA JUSTITIA PATRIA SALVA

JUS DIXIT[130]

## Notes

1. Peterson, Merrill D., *The Great Triumvirate*, pp. 301-13 Oxford University Press, 1987).
2. Bell, Robert R., *The Philadelphia Lawyer: A History, 1735-1945*, p. 148 (Selinsgrove: Susquehanna University Press, 1992); Binney, Charles C., *The Life of Horace Binney*, p. 213 (J.B. Lippincott Co., 1903); *Journal of Executive Proceedings of the Senate* (Jan. 18, 1842; Jan. 25, 1842); *Biographical Directory of the United States Congress 1774-2005*, p. 657 (Government Printing Office, 2005). While Binney was retired at that time, he later resumed his practice. Bell, Robert R., *The Philadelphia Lawyer: A History, 1735-1945*, pp. 145-56 (Selinsgrove: Susquehanna University Press, 1992).
3. Dwight, Henry E., *The Life and Writings of Hon. Vincent L. Bradford*, pp. 4-7 (1885); *Journal of Executive Proceedings of the Senate* (Feb. 8, 1842; Feb. 21, 1842).
4. Biography supplied by the Federal Judicial Center; Scharf, J. Thomas and Westcott, Thompson, *History of Philadelphia, 1609-1884, Volume II*, p. 1544 (L.J. Everts and Co., 1884).
5. Presser, Stephen B., *Studies in the History of the United States Courts of the Third Circuit*, p. 243 (Government Printing Office, 1982).
6. Goldman, Sheldon, "The Politics of Appointing Catholics to the Federal Courts," *Univ. of St. Thomas Law Journal*, Vol. 4, p. 204 (2006-07).
7. *United States v. Holmes*, 26 F. Cas. 360 (C.C.E.D. Pa., 1842) (No. 15,383); *The North American and Daily Advertizer*, p. 1 (April 25, 1842).
8. *United States v. Holmes*, 26 F. Cas. 360 (C.C.E.D. Pa., 1842) (No. 15,383).
9. *Id.* at 366-69. *See also*, Brown, David Paul, *The Forum; or Forty Years Full Practice at the Philadelphia Bar*, p. 1856 (R.H. Small, Law Bookseller, 1856).
10. Weigley, Russell F., ed., *Philadelphia, A 300-Year History*, pp. 356-58 (W.W. Norton & Co., 1982).
11. *The North American and Daily Advertizer*, pp. 1-2 (June 22, 1844); "Address of the Catholic Lay Citizens of the City and County of Philadelphia, to their fellow-Citizens, in reply to the Presentment of the Grand Jury of the Court of Quarter Sessions of May Term 1844, in Regard to the Causes of the Late Riots in Philadelphia," *The Philadelphia Riots of 1844: Reporting Ethnic Violence* (The Historical Society of Pennsylvania).

12. *Id.*
13. *See Meyer v. Nebraska*, 262 U.S. 390 (1923). The Supreme Court held that these provisions were incorporated into the Fourteenth Amendment which was ratified after the Civil War and which apply to the states. That Amendment reads in relevant part, "... nor shall any State deprive any person of life, liberty, or property without due process of law ...."
14. *United States v. Hall*, 26 F. Cas. 75 (C.C.E.D. Pa., 1844) (No. 15,281).
15. *Id.* at 77.
16. *The North American*, Vol. VIII, p. 1 (June 10, 1846).
17. Grow, Matthew J., *Liberty to the Downtrodden*, pp. 1-5 (Yale University Press, 2009); Peterson, Merrill D., The Great Triumvirate, pp. 116-31 Oxford University Press, 1987); Burt, Nathaniel, *The Perennial Philadelphians: The Anatomy of an American Aristocracy*, p. 461 (Little, Brown and Co., 1963); Legal Papers Misc. File, John Kintzing Kane Papers, American Philosophical Society, Philadelphia, Pennsylvania).
18. Dusinberre, William, *Slavemaster President: The Double Career of James Polk* (Oxford University Press, 2003); Borneman, Walter R., *Polk: The Man Who Transformed the Presidency and America*, p. 142 (Random House, 2008); Hall, Kermit L., *The Magic Mirror: Law in American History*, pp. 140-41 (Oxford University Press, 1989); Borneman, Walter R., *Polk: The Man Who Transformed the Presidency and America*, p. 116 (Random House, 2008). For examples of the Kane/Polk correspondence *see* Sept. 16, 1844, Oct. 31, 1844, Nov. 4, 1844; Jan. 29, 1845, Feb. 4, 1845, Feb. 14, 1845, April 14, 1845, April 28, 1845, Oct. 9, 1845, Jan. 30, 1847, June 15, 1847, Feb. 13, 1848, and May 5, 1848.James Knox Polk Papers, Microfilm Reel 56, Library of Congress, Washington, D.C.
19. Grow, Matthew J., *Liberty to the Downtrodden*, pp. 35-36 (Yale University Press, 2009).
20. Brandt, Nat and Brandt, Yanna Kroyt, *In the Shadow of the Civil War*, p. 65 (University of South Carolina Press, 2007).
21. Presser, Stephen B., *Studies in the History of the United States Courts of the Third Circuit*, p. 243 (Government Printing Office, 1982); Records of the American Philosophical Society.
22. Brandt, Nat and Brandt, Yanna Kroyt, *In the Shadow of the Civil War*, p. 65 (Univeresity of South Carolina Press, 2007).
23. "Local Affairs," *The North American*, p. 1, June 23, 1846.
24. Records of the United States District Court for the Eastern District of Pennsylvania.
25. James R. Snowden to John K. Kane, June 23, 1846, James R. Snowden File; James K. Polk to John K. Kane, June 11, 1846, James K. Polk File; J.R. Ingersoll to John K. Kane, Feb. 1, 1847, Feb. 26, Feb. 28, March 3, March 16, March 23, June 23, 1848, J.R. Ingersoll File, G.M. Dallas to John K. Kane, Feb. 14, 1847, G.M. Dallas File, John Kintzing Kane Papers, American Philosophical Society, Philadelphia, Pennsylvania.
26. *United States v. Harding*, 26 F. Cas. 131 (C.C.E.D. Pa., 1846) (No. 15,301).
27. *Id.* at 136.
28. *Id.*
29. *Id.*
30. *Id.* at 138-39.
31. Peterson, Merrill D., *The Great Triumvirate*, pp. 449-76, 480-83 (Oxford University Press, 1987).
32. Weigley, Russell F., ed., *Philadelphia, A 300-Year History*, pp. 45-46, 75, 355, 386-87 (W.W. Norton & Co., 1982).
33. The United States Supreme Court declared the 1826 statute unconstitutional in *Prigg v. Pennsylvania*, 41 U.S. (16 Pet.) 539 (1842). The Court ruled that it violated Article IV, § 2, ¶ 3 of the Constitution which provided: "No person held to Service or Labour in one State, under the Laws thereof, escaping into another, shall, in Consequence of any Law or Regulation therein, be discharged from such Service or Labour, but shall be delivered up on Claim of the Party to whom such Service or Labour may be due." The Court explained that this provision gave the federal government exclusive jurisdiction over the return of fugitive slaves and that Congress had passed a law in 1793 to enforce it.

34. Brandt, Nat and Brandt, Yanna Kroyt, *In the Shadow of the Civil War*, p. 39 (University of South Carolina Press, 2007).
35. Weigley, Russell F., ed., *Philadelphia, A 300 Year History*. pp. 383-94 (W.W. Norton & Co., 1982); Greenberg, Irwin, "Charles Ingersoll: The Aristocrat as Copperhead," *The Pennsylvania Magazine of History and Biography*, Vol. 93, pp. 197-98 (April 1969); Brandt, Nat and Brandt, Yanna Kroyt, *In the Shadow of the Civil War*, p. 43 (University of South Carolina Press, 2007).
36. Fugitive Slave Act of 1850, ch. 60, 9 Stat. 462.
37. *Id.*
38. *United States v. Hanway*, 26 F. Cas. 105 (C.C.E.D. Pa., 1851) (No. 15,299).
39. *Id.*; Slaughter, Thomas P., *Bloody Dawn: The Christiana Riot and Racial Violence in the Antebellum North*, pp. 112-14 (Oxford University Press, 1991).
40. Slaughter, Thomas P., *Bloody Dawn: The Christiana Riot and Racial Violence in the Antebellum North*, pp. 106-09, 116 (Oxford University Press, 1991); Trefousse, Hans L., *Thaddeus Stevens* (Stackpole Books, 2001).
41. Slaughter, Thomas P., *Bloody Dawn: The Christiana Riot and Racial Violence in the Antebellum North*, p. 120 (Oxford University Press, 1991); Brandt, Nat and Brandt, Yanna Kroyt, *In the Shadow of the Civil War*, p. 71 (University of South Carolina Press, 2007); Malone, Dumas, ed., *Dictionary of American Biography*, Vol. VII, p. 288 (Charles Scribner's Sons, 1934).
42. *Hanway*, 26 F. Cas. at 114.
43. *Id.* at 129.
44. Slaughter, Thomas P., *Bloody Dawn: The Christiana Riot and Racial Violence in the Antebellum North*, pp. 135-36 (Oxford University Press, 1991).
45. *United States ex rel. Wheeler v. Williamson*, 28 F. Cas. 682 (E.D. Pa. 1855), 28 F. Cas. 686 (E.D. Pa. 1855) (No. 16,725).
46. *Id.* at 686.
47. *United States ex rel. Wheeler v. Williamson*, 28 F. Cas. 686 (E.D. Pa. 1855) (No. 16,726).
48. *Id.*
49. *Id.* at 693, quoting *Johnson v. Tompkins*, 13 F. Cas. 840, 843 (C.C.E.D. Pa. 1833) (No. 7,416).
50. *United States ex rel. Wheeler*, 28 F. Cas. at 693.
51. *Id.* at 694.
52. Brandt, Nat and Brandt, Yanna Kroyt, *In the Shadow of the Civil War*, p. 144-51 (University of South Carolina Press, 2007).
53. Garnet Folder, Records of the United States District Court for the Eastern District of Pennsylvania - Circuit Court Fugitive Slave Cases 1850-1860.
54. Grow, Matthew J., *Liberty to the Downtrodden*, p. 117 (Yale University Press, 2009).
55. Grow, Matthew J., *Liberty to the Downtrodden*, p. 116 (Yale University Press, 2009); Brandt, Nat and Brandt, Yanna Kroyt, *In the Shadow of the Civil War*, p. 71 (University of South Carolina Press, 2007); Garnet Folder, Records of the United States District Court for the Eastern District of Pennsylvania - Circuit Court Fugitive Slave Cases 1850-1860.
56. Grow, Matthew J., *Liberty to the Downtrodden*, p. 115 (Yale University Press, 2009); Slaughter, Thomas P., *Bloody Dawn: The Christiana Riot and Racial Violence in the Antebellum North*, pp. 118-19 (Oxford University Press, 1991); Brandt, Nat and Brandt, Yanna Kroyt, *In the Shadow of the Civil War*, pp. 67-68 (University of South Carolina Press, 2007).
57. *United States v. Darnaud*, 25 F. Cas. 754 (C.C.E.D. Pa. 1855) (No. 14,918).
58. Weigley, Russell, F., ed., *Philadelphia, A 300-Year History*, pp. 359-62, 368-72 (W.W. Norton & Co., 1982).
59. Minutes of the American Philosophical Society (June 16, 1854).
60. Carter, Edward C., II, "*One Grand Pursuit,*" *A Brief History of the American Philosophical Society*, p. 42 (1993).
61. See Wainwright, Nicholas B., ed., *A Philadelphia Perspective: The Diary of Sidney George Fisher Covering the Years 1834-1871*, p. 390 (The Historical Society of Pennsylvania, 1967).

62. *Patriot* (Harrisburg, Pa.), p. 2 (Feb. 24, 1858).
63. *The North American,* (Phila., Pa.), p. 2 (Feb. 23, 1858).
64. Brandt, Nat and Brandt, Yanna Kroyt, *In the Shadow of the Civil War,* p. 151 (University of South Carolina Press, 2007). Elisha Kane, another son of Judge Kane, was a physician, naval officer and famed explorer of the North Pole, who died in 1857. He was accorded the rare honor to lie in state in Independence Hall. *Id.* at 67; *Philadelphia Inquirer,* p. 1 (Nov. 29, 1906); "Kane, Francis Fisher," *Who's Who in America,* Vol. 3, p. 461 (1950).
65. Weigley, Russell F., ed., *Philadelphia, A 300-Year History,* p. 331 (W.W. Norton Co., 1982); McGinty, Brian, *Lincoln & The Court,* p. 74 (Harvard University Press, 2008).
66. *The North American and United States Gazette,* p. 2 (Apr. 20, 1858); *The North American,* p. 1 (Jan. 21, 1879). *See also,* John Cadwalader Clipping File, Archives of the University of Pennsylvania; Gough, Deborah Mathias, *Christ Church, Philadelphia,* p. 229 (University of Pennsylvania Press, 1995).
67. *Dred Scott v. Sandford,* 60 U.S. (19 How.) 393 (1857); Fehrenbacher, Don E., *The Dred Scott Case* (Oxford University Press, 1978).
68. McPherson, James M., *Battle Cry of Freedom,* pp. 202-06 (Oxford University Press, 1988).
69. Goodwin, Doris Kearns, *Team of Rivals,* pp. 276-78, 293 (Simon & Schuster, 2005).
70. *United States v. Buck,* 24 F. Cas. 1289 (E.D. Pa. 1860) (No. 14,680).
71. The American Philosophical Society Hall, with its Fifth Street doorway, is still standing and occupied by the Society.
72. *United States v. Buck,* 24 F. Cas. 1289 (E.D. Pa. 1860) (No. 14,680).
73. *Id.*
74. Goodwin, Doris Kearns, *Team of Rivals,* pp. 305-12 (Simon & Schuster, 2005).
75. *The Philadelphia Inquirer,* p. 2 (Feb. 23, 1861).
76. McPherson, James M., *Battle Cry of Freedom,* pp. 264-65, 267, 273-74 (Oxford University Press, 1988).
77. Donald, David Herbert, *Lincoln,* p. 296 (Simon & Schuster, 1995).
78. McGinty, Brian, *Lincoln & The Court,* pp. 118-42 (Harvard University Press, 2008).
79. *In re The Parkhill,* 18 F. Cas. 1187 (E.D. Pa. 1861) (No. 10,755a).
80. *Id.*
81. *Id.* at 1197-98.
82. *The Philadelphia Public Ledger,* p. 1 (July 1, 1862); McGinty, Brian, *Lincoln & The Court,* pp. 132-33 (Harvard University Press, 2008).
83. *The Prize Cases,* 67 U.S. (1 Wall.) 635 (1863).
84. McGinty, Brian, *Lincoln & The Court,* p. 142 (Harvard University Press, 2008).
85. *United States v. Greiner,* 26 F. Cas. 36 (E.D. Pa. 1861) (No. 15,262).
86. The Sixth Amendment to the Constitution provides in part: "In all criminal prosecutions, the accused shall enjoy the right to a speedy and public trial, by an impartial jury of the State and district wherein the crime shall have been committed ...." U.S. Const. amend. VI.
87. *Greiner,* 26 F. Cas. at 41.
88. U.S. Const., art. II, § 2, ¶ 1.
89. McGinty, Brian, *Lincoln & The Court,* pp. 70-71 (Harvard University Press, 2008).
90. *Id.* at pp. 68-69, U.S. Const., art I, § 9, ¶ 2.
91. Act of August 6, 1861, ch. 63, § 3, 12 Stat. 326. McGinty, Brian, *Lincoln & The Court,* p. 84 (Harvard University Press, 2008); *Ex parte Merryman,* 17 F. Cas. 144 (C.C.D. Md. 1861) (No. 9487). While the Constitution does not state explicitly whether the President or Congress may suspend habeas corpus, the Suspension Clause, as it is known, is contained in Article I which describes the powers of Congress. U.S. Const., art. I, § 9, ¶ 2.
92. Stone, Geoffrey R., *Perilous Times,* pp. 123-24, including fn. 172 & 174 (W.W. Norton & Co., 2004).
93. McGinty, Brian, *Lincoln & The Court,* pp. 182-92, 274 (Harvard University Press, 2008).

94. Greenberg, Irwin, "Charles Ingersoll: The Aristocrat as Copperhead," *Pennsylvania Magazine of History and Biography*, Vol. 93, pp. 190-23 (April 1969).
95. *Id.*
96. *Id.*
97. Gough, Deborah Mathias, *Christ Church, Philadelphia*, p. 242 (University of Pennsylvania Press, 1995); Greenberg, Irwin, "Charles Ingersoll: The Aristocrat as Copperhead," *The Pennsylvania Magazine of History and Biography*, Vol. 93, p. 200 (April 1969). Charles Ingersoll was buried at Christ Church.
98. McGinty, Brian, *Lincoln & The Court*, pp. 72-75 (Harvard University Press, 2008); Stone, Geoffrey R., *Perilous Times*, pp. 85-87 (W.W. Norton & Co., 2004).
99. *Ex parte Merryman*, 17 F. Cas. 144 (C.C.D. Md. 1861) (No. 9487).
100. Stone, Geoffrey R., *Perilous Times*, p. 87 (W.W. Norton & Co., 2004).
101. McGinty, Brian, *Lincoln & The Court*, pp. 87-88 (Harvard University Press, 2008).
102. Act of March 3, 1863, ch. 81, 12 Stat. 755; Stone, Geoffrey R., *Perilous Times*, p. 124 (W.W. Norton & Co., 2004).
103. Act of March 3, 1863, ch. 75, 12 Stat. 731; McPherson, James M., *Battle Cry of Freedom*, pp. 600-01 (Oxford University Press, 1988).
104. *Ex Parte Burke*, 4 F. Cas. 731 (E.D. Pa. 1863) (No. 2156a); *see* Records of the United States District Court for the Eastern District of Pennsylvania.
105. *Stingle's Case*, 23 F. Cas. 107 (E.D. Pa. 1863) (No. 13,458).
106. *McCall's Case*, 15 F. Cas. 1225 (E.D. Pa. 1863) (No. 8669).
107. 1 F. Cas. 1062 (E.D. Pa. 1863) (No. 495).
108. Kauffman, Michael, *American Brutus*, p. 4 (Random House, 2004).
109. In April 1859, Clarke had married John Wilkes Booth's sister, Asia. Kauffman, Michael W., *American Brutus*, p. 103 (2004).
110. *Keene v. Wheatley*, 14 F. Cas. 180 (C.C.E.D. Pa. 1861) (No. 7644); Kauffman, Michael W., *American Brutus*, p. 103 (Random House, 2004).
111. Cash Account of the Treasurer, American Philosophical Society (July 11, 1863).
112. Rough Minutes of the American Philosophical Society (June 19, 1863).
113. Stets, R.J., *Philadelphia Postal History*, p. 30 (The Associated Stamp Clubs of Southeastern Penna. & Delaware, 1980).
114. *The Philadelphia Inquirer*, p. 4 (Feb. 23, 1863).
115. *Case of District Attorney of United States*, 7 F. Cas. 731 (E.D. Pa. 1868) (No. 3,924).
116. Act of Mar. 2, 1867, ch. 154, 14 Stat. 430.
117. Trefousse, Hans L., *Andrew Johnson*, pp. 276-328 (W.W. Norton & Co., 1989).
118. *Case of District Attorney of United States*, 7 F. Cas. 731, 733-34 (E.D. Pa. 1868) (No. 3,924).
119. Article II, § 2 ¶ 3 of the Constitution provides, "The President shall have Power to fill up all Vacancies that may happen during the Recess of the Senate, by granting Commissions which shall expire at the End of their next Session."
120. *Case of District Attorney of United States*, 7 F. Cas. 731, 744-45 (E.D. Pa. 1868) (No. 3,924).
121. *Bird v. Penn Mut. Life Ins. Co.*, 3 F. Cas. 430 (C.C.E.D. Pa. 1876) (No. 1430); *see also*, Docket in the records of the United States District Court for the Eastern District of Pennsylvania.
122. Weigley, Russell F., ed., *Philadelphia, A-300 Year History*, pp. 419-20, 430-33 (1982).
123. *Camblos v. Phila. & R.R. Co.*, 4 F. Cas. 1089 (C.C.E.D. Pa. 1873) (No. 2331); *DuPont v. Boshong*, 8 F. Cas. 109 (C.C.E.D. Pa. 1875) (No. 4184); *Kemble v. Wilmington & N.R. Co.*, 14 F. Cas. 280 (C.C.E.D. Pa. 1878) (No. 7684).
124. *Nat'l State Bank v. Pierce*, 17 F. Cas. 1238 (C.C.E.D. Pa. 1878) (No. 10,052).
125. *United States v. The Ohio*, 27 F. Cas. 219 (E.D. Pa. 1872) (No. 15,915); *Schmidt v. The Pennsylvania*, 21 F. Cas. 706 (E.D. Pa. 1878) (No. 12,464), *aff'd* 4 F. 548 (C.C.E.D. Pa. 1880); and *In re The Muriel*, 17 F. Cas. 1026 (E.D. Pa. 1877) (No. 9944).

126. *United States v. Whiskey*, 28 F. Cas. 536 (E.D. Pa. 1870) (No. 16,671).

127. The Judiciary Act of 1875, ch. 137, 18 Stat. 470, § 1.

128. Frankfurter, Felix and Landis, James, *The Business of the Supreme Court*, p. 65 (The Macmillan Company, 1928).

129. *The North American*, p. 1 (Jan. 21, 1879).

130. In time of war and peace
Among citizens and among nations
With Justice being secure and the homeland safe
He spoke the law.

Francis Hopkinson (1737 – 1791)
District Judge: 1789 – 1791

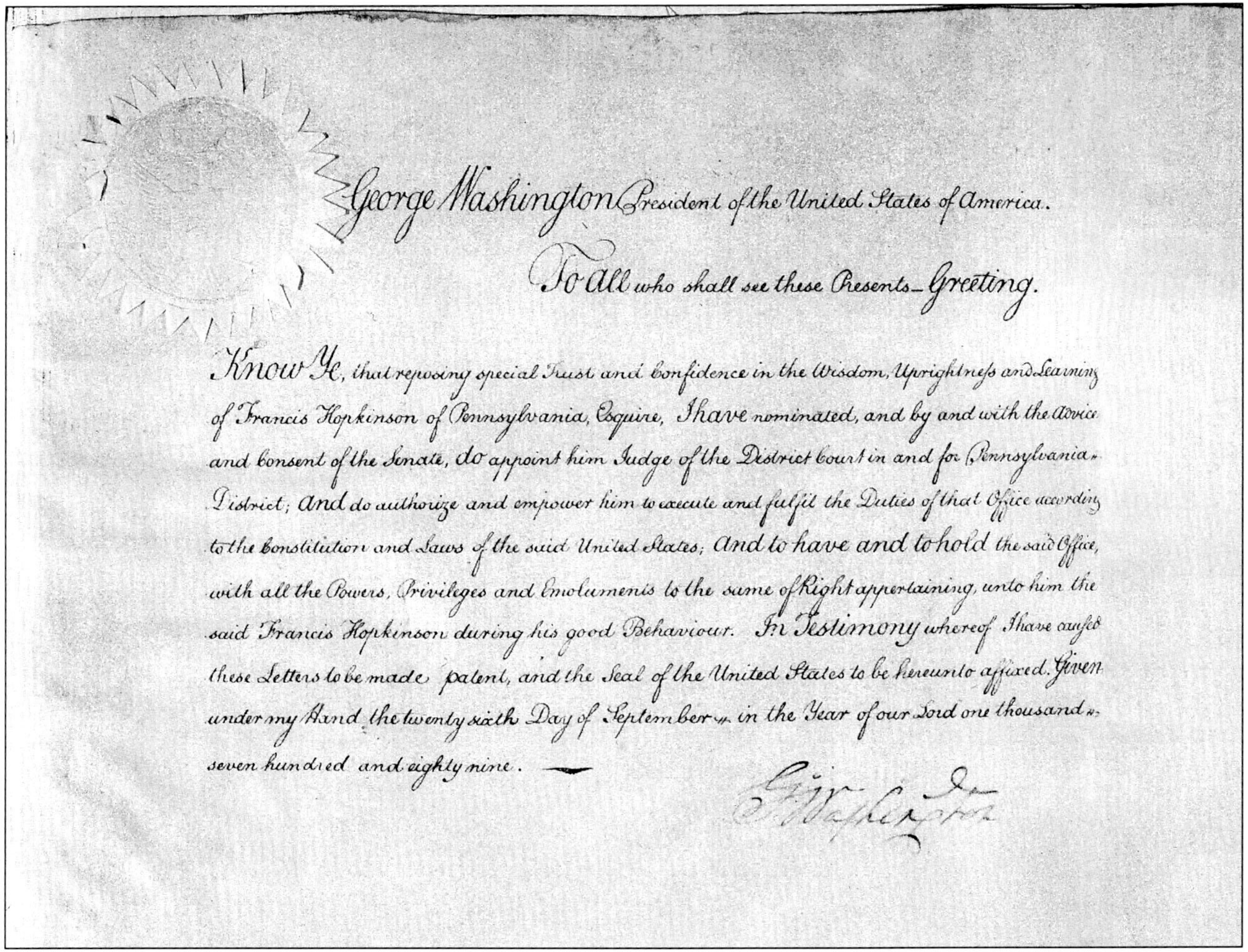

George Washington President of the United States of America.

To All who shall see these Presents—Greeting.

Know Ye, that reposing special Trust and Confidence in the Wisdom, Uprightness and Learning of Francis Hopkinson of Pennsylvania, Esquire, I have nominated, and by and with the Advice and Consent of the Senate, do appoint him Judge of the District Court in and for Pennsylvania District; And do authorize and empower him to execute and fulfil the Duties of that Office according to the Constitution and Laws of the said United States; And to have and to hold the said Office, with all the Powers, Privileges and Emoluments to the same of Right appertaining, unto him the said Francis Hopkinson during his good Behaviour. In Testimony whereof I have caused these Letters to be made patent, and the Seal of the United States to be hereunto affixed. Given under my Hand the twenty sixth Day of September in the Year of our Lord one thousand seven hundred and eighty nine.

G° Washington

Commission of
Judge Francis Hopkinson

Signed by President
George Washington

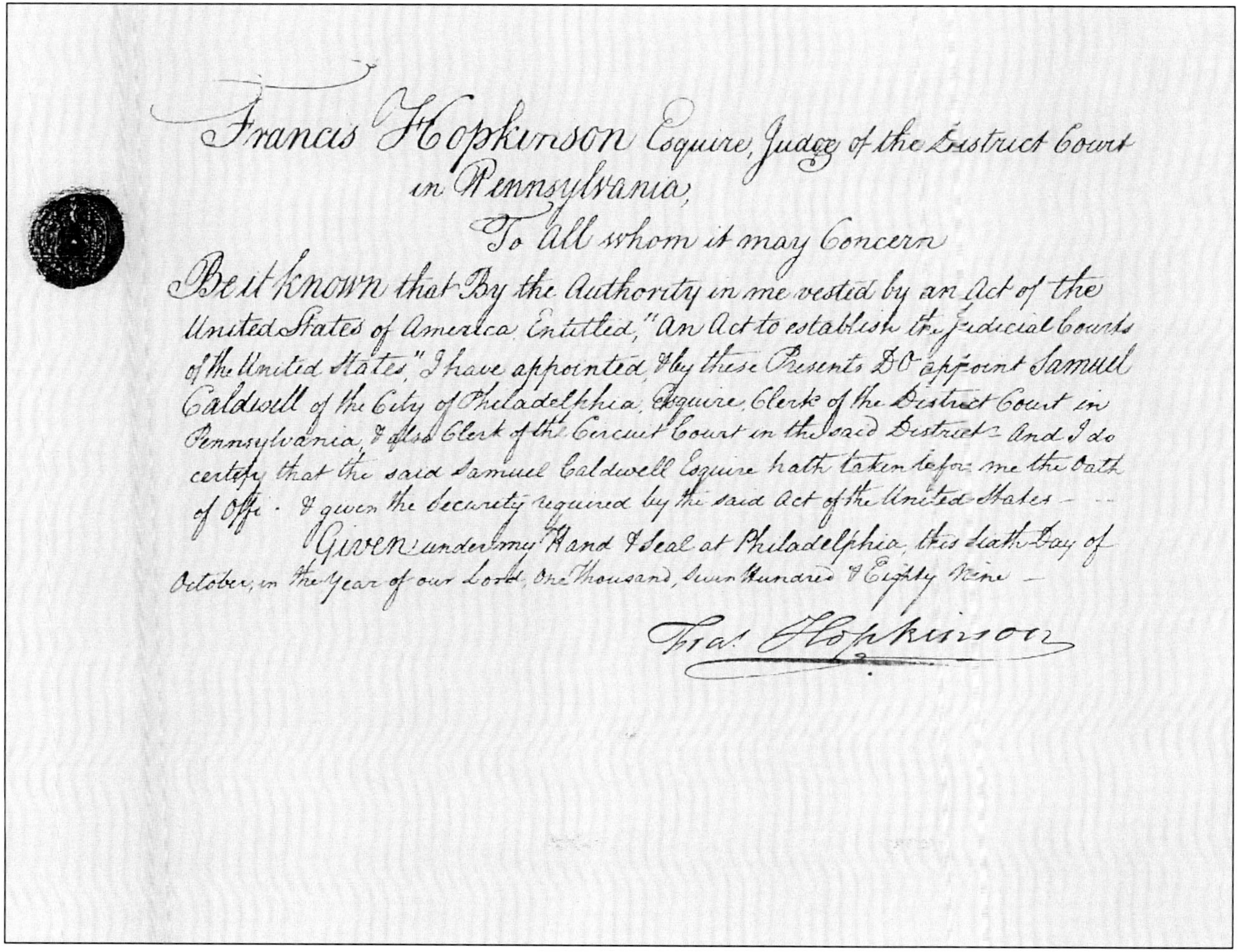

Francis Hopkinson Esquire, Judge of the District Court in Pennsylvania;

To All whom it may Concern

Be it known that By the Authority in me vested by an Act of the United States of America Entitled, "An Act to establish the Judicial Courts of the United States," I have appointed, & by these Presents DO appoint Samuel Caldwell of the City of Philadelphia, Esquire, Clerk of the District Court in Pennsylvania, & also Clerk of the Circuit Court in the said District – And I do certify that the said Samuel Caldwell Esquire hath taken before me the Oath of Office & given the Security required by the said Act of the United States – – –

Given under my Hand & Seal at Philadelphia, this Sixth Day of October, in the Year of our Lord, One Thousand, Seven Hundred & Eighty Nine –

Fras. Hopkinson

Commission of the First Court Clerk Samuel Caldwell

Signed by Judge Francis Hopkinson

William Lewis (1752 – 1819)
District Judge: 1791 – 1792

Richard Peters (1744 – 1828)
District Judge: 1792 – 1828

Joseph Hopkinson (1770 – 1842)
District Judge: 1828 – 1842

James Wilson (1742 – 1798)
Supreme Court Justice: 1789 – 1798

Alexander Hamilton (1755? – 1804)
Author of the Federalist Papers
Concerning the Judiciary

Bushrod Washington (1762 – 1829)
Supreme Court Justice: 1799 – 1829

Henry Baldwin (1780 – 1844)
Supreme Court Justice: 1830 – 1844

Archibald Randall (1797 – 1846)
District Judge: 1842 – 1846

John K. Kane (1795 – 1858)
District Judge: 1846 – 1858

John Cadwalader (1805 – 1879)
District Judge: 1858 – 1879

William Butler (1822 – 1909)
District Judge: 1879 – 1899

Back of the Pennsylvania State House as it appeared at the time of the Constitutional Convention in 1787 and the first sitting of the District Court for the District of Pennsylvania in 1789.

The original tower had been removed in 1781.

Old City Hall - Independence Hall - Congress Hall
Chestnut Street between Fifth and Sixth Streets, Philadelphia

The first session of the District Court was held in the Pennsylvania State House, now known as Independence Hall, in 1789. In 1791, the Court moved to what was then Philadelphia's City Hall and remained there until 1824. The Supreme Court also occupied this building from 1790 to 1800. From 1824 to 1826, the District Court sat at the Philadelphia County Courthouse, now known as Congress Hall. Independence Hall again became the Court's venue from 1830 to 1854. The present tower on Independence Hall was constructed in the late 1820's.

Old Mongomery County Courthouse
Penn and Swede Streets, Norristown

The Court vacated Philadelphia's Old City Hall and moved temporarily to Norristown in the summer and fall of 1799 due to the Yellow Fever Epidemic in Philadelphia. This courthouse was torn down many years ago.

The Franklin Institute
15 South Seventh Street, Philadelphia

The Court occupied space here from 1826 to 1830. It later became the home of the Atwater Kent Museum, now the Philadelphia History Museum at the Atwater Kent.

American Philosophical Society Hall
104 South Fifth Street, Philadelphia

The Court was situated at this location from 1854 until it moved to the Library Street Courthouse in 1863 during the Civil War.

United States Courthouse
Library Street between Fourth and Fifth Streets, Philadelphia

The Courthouse was a wing of the larger Post Office building which faced Chestnut Street, just west of the Second Bank of the United States. The Court sat here from 1863 to 1884. The edifice no longer stands.

United States Post Office
South side of Chestnut Street between Fourth and Fifth Streets
Philadelphia

This building was erected in 1863 with a smaller wing in the rear for a federal courthouse. This photograph shows in the background a bit of the courthouse with its peaked roof, just west of the Second Bank.

United States
Courthouse and
Post Office

Ninth & Market Streets
Philadelphia

This was the Court's home from 1884 until 1937 when it was razed to make way for a new courthouse on the same site.

"Law, Prosperity and Power"

This allegorical sculpture by Daniel Chester French stood on a cornice high above the Ninth Street entrance to the 1884 Courthouse and Post Office. The central figure holding the tablet symbolizes Law, the figure to the right with the cornucopia represents Prosperity, and the figure to the left with a sword depicts Power.

When the building was razed, the sculpture was moved to Fairmount Park. French later carved the statue of Abraham Lincoln at the Lincoln Memorial in Washington, D.C.

United States Custom House
Second & Chestnut Streets, Philadelphia

The Court had space here from 1937 to 1940 while the new courthouse was being constructed at Ninth and Market Streets.

United States Courthouse and Post Office
Ninth & Market Streets, Philadelphia

The Court sat at this site from 1940 to 1975. Magistrate Judges and Bankruptcy Judges still occupy part of this building.

United States Courthouse
601 Market Street
Philadelphia

The present courthouse in Philadelphia has been in use since 1975.

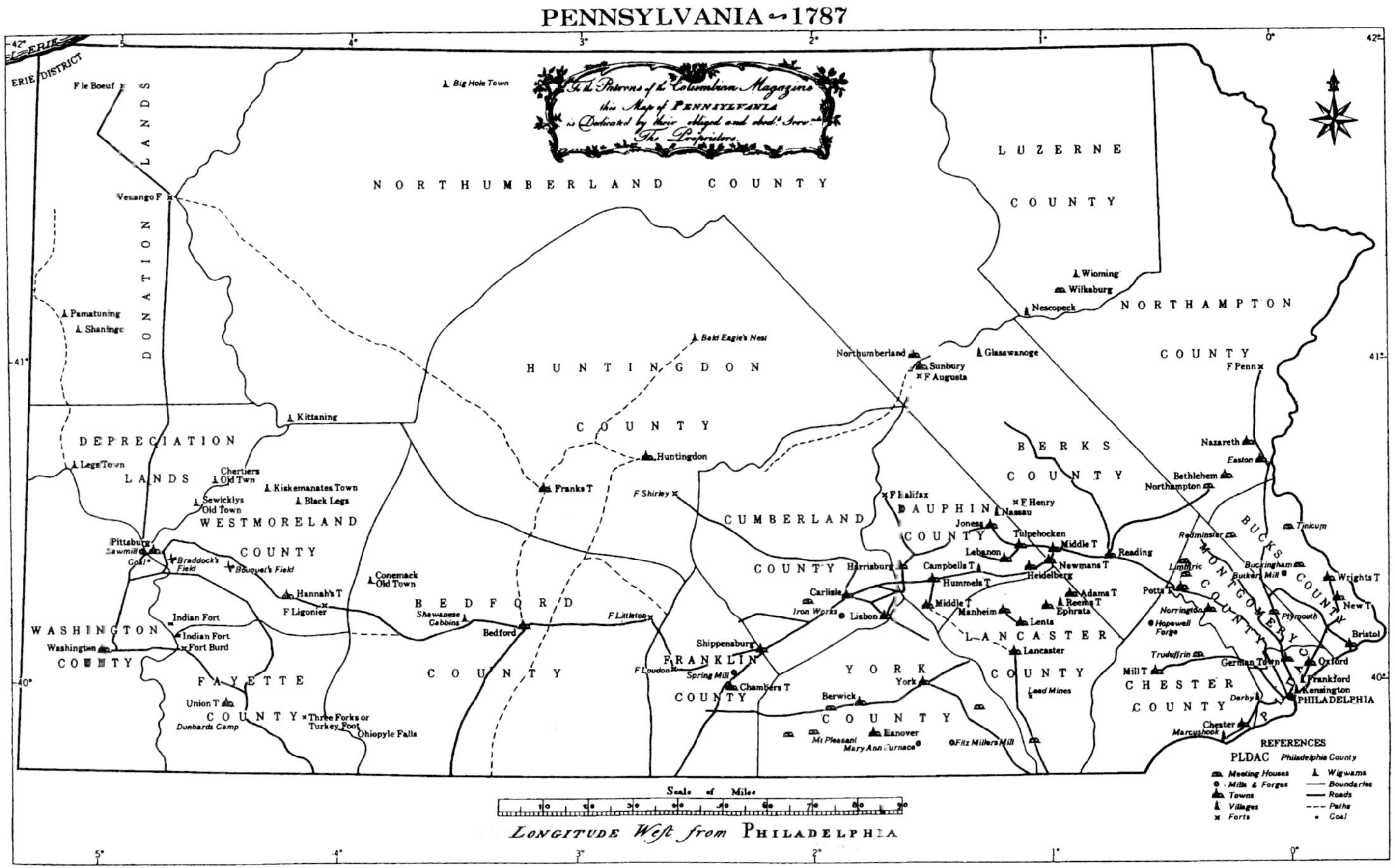


Pennsylvania – 1787

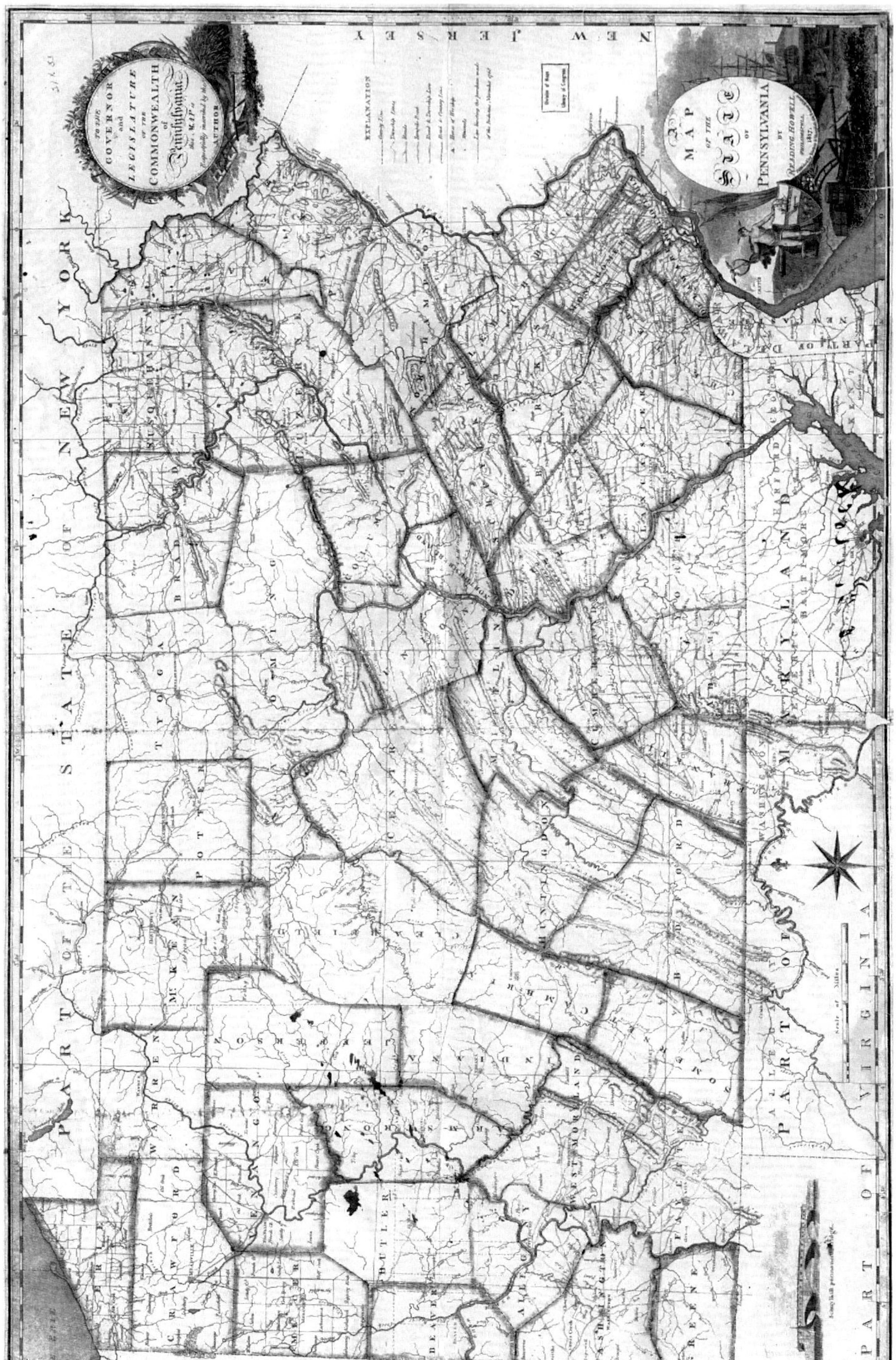


Pennsylvania – 1817

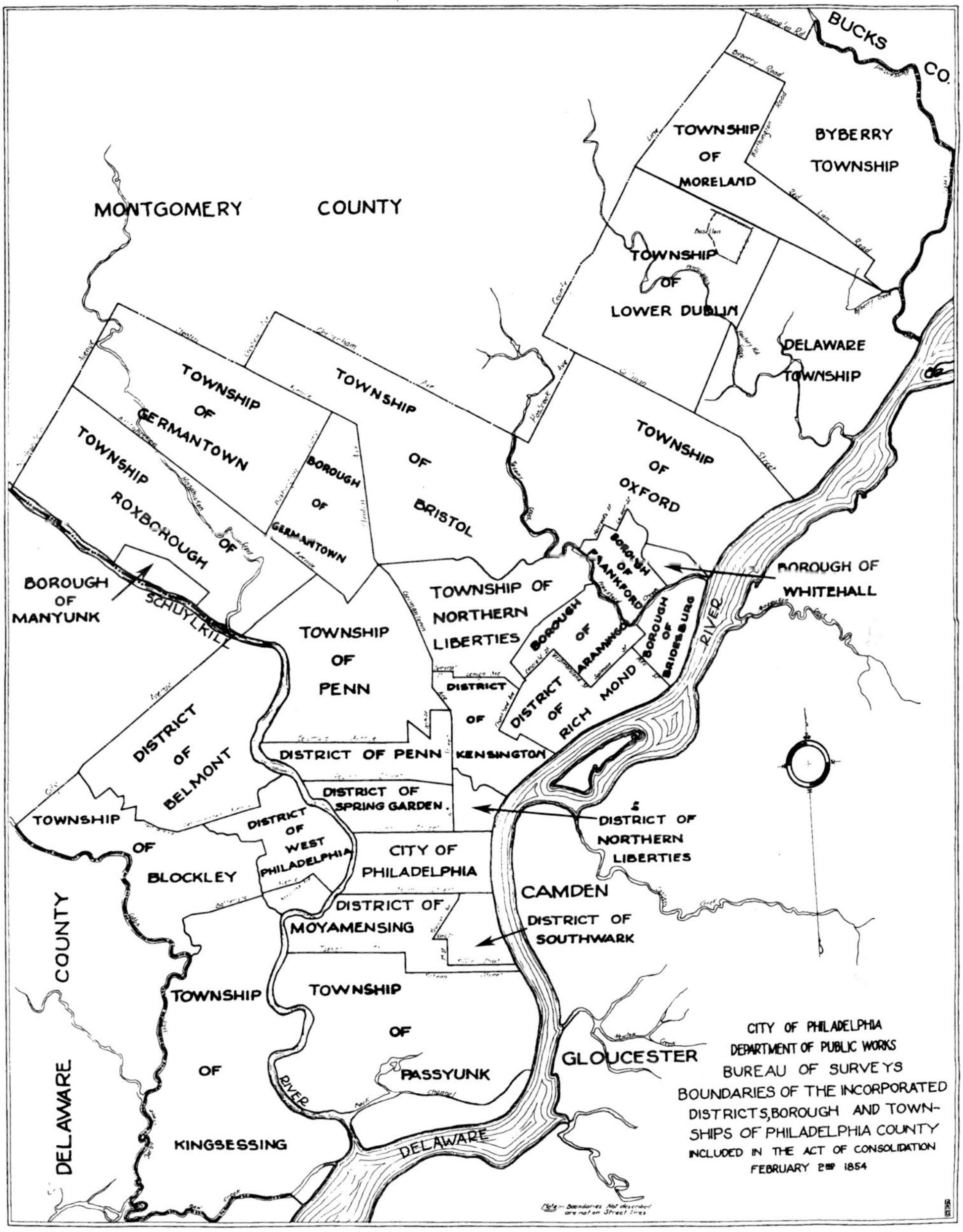


Philadelphia County prior to the 1854 City-County Consolidation

Pennsylvania – 2011

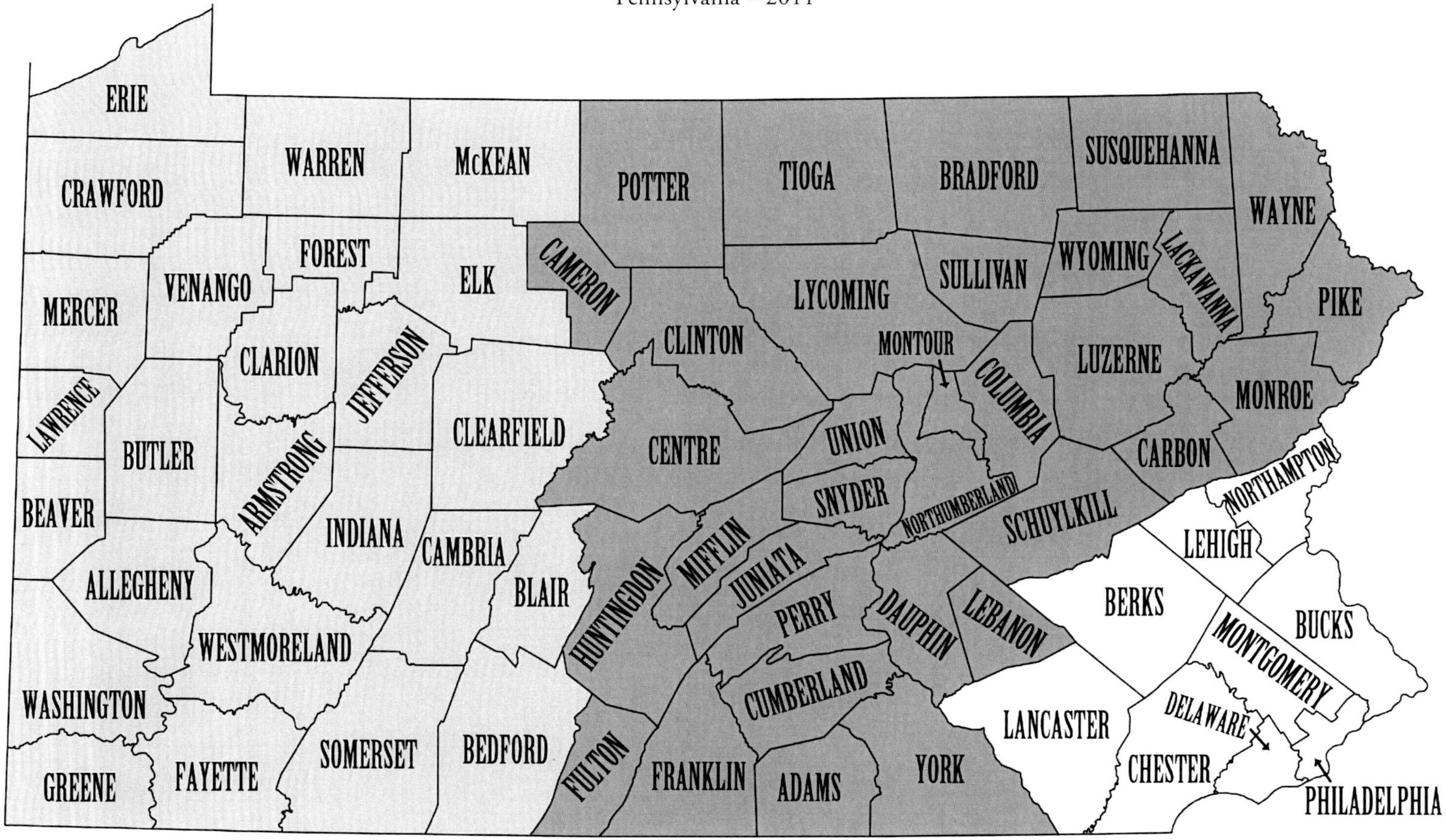


Western District

Middle District

Eastern District

# IV
# The Emergence of a Multi-Judge Court: 1879-1930

On March 4, 1877, less than two years before Judge Cadwalader's death, Rutherford B. Hayes, the Republican Governor of Ohio and a Brevet Major General during the Civil War, took the oath of office as President after a bitterly contested election. Although he received fewer popular votes than Samuel Tilden, he was awarded one more vote in the Electoral College than his Democratic opponent as part of the Compromise of 1877. The Compromise also brought to a close the Reconstruction of the South, including the end of the occupation of Southern states by federal troops.[1]

The post-Civil War era was a time of prosperity for Philadelphia. The Pennsylvania and Reading Railroads as well as the Baldwin Locomotive Works, all headquartered in the city, were in the midst of some of their halcyon days. By the end of the 1870's, the lines and operations of the Pennsylvania Railroad extended to Pittsburgh and west to Chicago and St. Louis, east into New Jersey, and south to Baltimore and Washington.[2] The Reading Railroad, while smaller, was a major freight line hauling millions of tons of anthracite coal annually from Northeastern Pennsylvania and delivering it to and shipping it from its docks at Port Richmond in Philadelphia.[3] Coal, iron and steel, and textiles were important products of the region. The Bethlehem Iron Company was a major industrial enterprise in the Lehigh Valley in the northern part of the Eastern District.[4]

In February 1879, as the ninetieth anniversary of the establishment of the federal courts was approaching, President Hayes chose William Butler to succeed Judge Cadwalader as the District's eighth judge and the first who was not a resident of Philadelphia County at the time of his appointment.

Butler was born in 1822 into an old Chester County family which had been in Pennsylvania since the seventeenth century. One of his ancestors on his mother's side had been a member of the Province's first Assembly established by William Penn.[5] His brother was the State Treasurer in the early 1880's.[6] After initially working as a printer's apprentice and newspaper publisher, Butler shifted careers and read law. Admitted to the Chester County Bar in 1845, he thereafter served as the County's District Attorney from 1856 through 1859. In 1861 he was elected to the Court of Common Pleas and was in his second term when named to the federal bench.[7] In 1873, he was the favorite son from the eastern part of the Commonwealth for a seat on the Pennsylvania Supreme Court but lost out for the nomination at the Republican state convention.[8]

*The Philadelphia Inquirer*[9] reported on his induction as a federal judge, which was attended by United States Supreme Court Justice William Strong. The article described Butler in glowing terms:

> Judge Butler is not only a learned, experienced jurist, but his whole social and judicial life has been so pure and elevated as to render his transfer to the presidency of our District Court a matter of common congratulation. There is nothing so desirable in government as a wise and pure judge, and nothing so much to be deplored as an unwise or impure one. Judge Butler's promotion to the bench of the United States District Court is an assurance that the law there will be well and justly administered.[10]

When Butler was sworn into office, the Court was continuing to sit in the Library Street Courthouse built during the Civil War. Within a few years, however, the Court would have yet another new home. In 1872, the University of Pennsylvania vacated its property a few blocks away on the west side of Ninth Street between Market and Chestnut Streets and moved to its more spacious campus in West Philadelphia. The Government, having purchased the property, constructed a large five-story granite courthouse and post office on the site with the main post office on the first floor and the Court on the second. It was designed in the French Second Empire style and was completed in 1884.[11] On the cornice high above the entrance on Ninth Street stood a large allegorical sculpture in marble entitled "Law, Prosperity, and Power" by Daniel Chester French. He later sculpted the widely acclaimed statue of Abraham Lincoln at the Lincoln Memorial in Washington, D.C.

The new edifice exhibited a far grander appearance than its more modest predecessor and evidenced the wider role that the federal courts were destined to play in American life. Nonetheless, the building would be dwarfed by Philadelphia's new City Hall which was being erected in the same architectural style at Broad and Market Streets. This elegant structure with its tower topped with Alexander Calder's statue of William Penn would occupy an entire block and contain not only a number of large courtrooms for the various state trial courts serving Philadelphia County but also a courtroom to accommodate the Supreme Court of Pennsylvania.

Butler's judicial responsibilities after the move into the new courthouse extended for a time beyond the boundaries of the Eastern District of Pennsylvania. In the 1880's, the New Jersey District Judge, John T. Nixon, was unable to fulfill his duties because of age and failing health. Third Circuit Judge William McKennan named Butler along with District Judge Leonard Wales of Delaware to travel into their neighboring district to assist with its workload.[12] Butler and Wales did so from 1886 to 1889.[13] This was to be the first of many future temporary assignments of Eastern District judges to other venues.

Due to the increased volume of litigation, Congress in 1891 created a separate Circuit Court of Appeals for each circuit. Appeals in the first instance from the federal trial courts would now be heard by these new tribunals. Each Circuit Court of Appeals was initially authorized two circuit judges to sit in panels of three with either a District Judge or a Supreme Court Justice. Since 1866, the Third Circuit has included Pennsylvania, New Jersey, and Delaware.[14] The old circuit trial courts created in 1789 languished until 1911 when Congress finally abolished them.[15] From that point on, the District Court was the place where federal trials would be held.

Congress was also active in other spheres. In 1890 it passed the Sherman Act which would significantly add to the judicial workload in the years ahead. This landmark legislation was enacted in order to rein in America's powerful monopolies and business trusts. It declared illegal "every contract, combination in the form of trust or otherwise, or conspiracy in restraint of trade or commerce among the several states, or with foreign nations." Congress enacted the law pursuant to its power under Article I, § 8 of the Constitution "To regulate Commerce ... among the several States, ...." The most well-known case over which Judge Butler presided while on the federal bench was *United States v. E.C. Knight Co.*, an antitrust action under the Sherman Act that ended up in the Supreme Court.[16]

The Government filed this equitable action in the Eastern District against five sugar refining companies. It sought the cancellation of certain contracts the defendant American Sugar Company had signed with the other four corporate defendants, all of which were based in Philadelphia. The Government contended that the contracts violated the Sherman Act in that they were the result of a conspiracy or combination to monopolize or restrain interstate commerce. The evidence established that the four Philadelphia companies produced 33% of the refined sugar in the United States in 1892 and that the American Sugar Company had purchased the stock of each of those companies, although apparently without any concert of action among the four. Nonetheless, as a result of these contracts, American Sugar now controlled virtually all of the refining and sale of sugar in the United States.

Judge Butler conceded that the conduct of American Sugar "tends" to the result of a commercial monopoly but found that no monopoly had been established. He concluded that for purposes of the Constitution and the Sherman Act, manufacturing was distinct from commerce and that nothing American Sugar had done in buying its competitors constituted interstate commerce. As he explained, "The contracts and acts of the defendants related exclusively to the acquisition of sugar refineries and the business of sugar refining, in Pennsylvania. They have no reference and bear no relation to commerce between the states or with foreign nations."[17] Judge Butler further noted that simply because a contract may "incidentally affect" interstate commerce was not enough to allow Congress to regulate it.[18]

The newly created Court of Appeals affirmed[19] as did the Supreme Court in an opinion by Chief Justice Melville Fuller. The high Court took the same narrow view of the Commerce Clause of the Constitution and the Sherman Act as had Judge Butler and the Court of Appeals. Correctly foreseeing the future decisions of the Supreme Court, Justice John Marshall Harlan dissented.[20] In the early Twentieth Century, the Supreme Court overturned *Knight* and adopted a more expansive understanding of what constitutes interstate commerce.[21]

The issue of interstate commerce appeared in another context before Judge Butler. This time it involved the telegraph which by the 1880's had become a widely used means of communication throughout the country. The City of Philadelphia had imposed on Western Union Telegraph Company what the City characterized as a license fee to defray the cost of inspecting Western Union's telegraph poles and wires. The fee amounted to $16,000 per year. When the company refused to pay, the City sued it in the Court of Common Pleas. Western Union removed the case to the federal court because of the parties' diversity of citizenship and argued that the amount being extracted was tantamount to an unconstitutional tax. While the City won before the jury, Judge Butler entered judgment for Western Union. He found that it was only necessary for the City to expend up to $3,500 for its supervisory activities to ensure public safety. The exorbitant fee charged by the City, Judge Butler held, was in reality a tax which affected telegraphic communications across state lines in violation of the Commerce Clause of the Constitution.[22]

The assassination of President James A. Garfield by Charles Guiteau, a disappointed office seeker, in 1881 provided the impetus for the passage of the Pendleton Civil Service Act of 1883, after years of failed efforts. Up to that time, patronage was the path to government employment. By the mid-1890's, some 86,000 federal jobs were covered by the merit system administered by the Civil Service Commission.[23]

Perhaps inevitably, with written applications and qualifying examinations, cheating would sometimes occur and with cheating would come criminal indictments in the District Court. Judge Butler presided over such a case. A person named Henry Bunting applied for a government clerkship, completed a sworn application, and was notified in due course to present himself for an examination. Instead of doing so, an impersonator, John Delany, appeared in his place and answered written questions about Bunting and signed Bunting's name. Delany was recognized, and he and Bunting were arrested. Both pleaded guilty after being indicted for defrauding the United States. Bunting was sentenced to three months in the Philadelphia County Prison and Delany to two months.[24]

Judge Butler, as had all his predecessors, continued to deal with admiralty cases, including those involving ship collisions, maritime insurance disputes, deductions from seamen's pay, and the disciplining of seamen.[25]

In 1899, after two decades on the bench, Butler retired and lived for another ten years. Except for Judge Lewis who had resigned in 1792, all his predecessors on the District Court had died in office. Butler took advantage of legislation approved by Congress in 1869 which for the first time allowed any federal judge who had attained the age of seventy and had at least ten years of service to retire and receive for the rest of his life the same salary he was receiving at the time of his retirement.[26]

After Judge Butler's departure, President William McKinley chose John Bayard McPherson for the Court. McPherson was born in Harrisburg in 1846. He was graduated from the College of New Jersey (now Princeton University) in 1866 and then read law. He served as District Attorney of Dauphin County from 1874 to 1877. Thereafter, he sat as a judge of the Court of Common Pleas of Dauphin and Lebanon Counties until his appointment to fill Judge Butler's vacancy. Following his move to Philadelphia to undertake his duties on the federal bench, the University of Pennsylvania Law School engaged him as a part-time lecturer on the subject of evidence. Both Penn and Princeton later awarded him an honorary LL.D. In 1912, President William Howard Taft tapped him for the Circuit Court of Appeals where he remained until his death in January 1919 after a long illness. McPherson was a Presbyterian and a member of a scholarly group known as the Shakespeare Society.[27]

In 1901, shortly after McPherson became a District Judge, Congress carved the Middle District of Pennsylvania out of portions of the Eastern and Western Districts.[28] By this time, the population of Philadelphia had grown to almost 1,300,000 and that of Pennsylvania to over 6,300,000. The Eastern District, which had heretofore encompassed the eastern half of the Commonwealth, was now reduced in area to include only ten counties of Southeastern Pennsylvania: Berks, Bucks, Chester, Delaware, Lancaster, Lehigh, Montgomery, Northampton, Philadelphia, and Schuylkill. While the geographic size of the Eastern District decreased, its complement of judges was soon to increase. In 1904, Congress added a second judgeship.[29]

Rival candidates vied to fill this new seat. Pennsylvania's two Republican Senators Matthew S. Quay and Boies Penrose supported United States Attorney James Buchanan Holland while several Court of Appeals judges, District Judge John McPherson, and some "influential men" identified with the University of Pennsylvania had endorsed another individual for the position.[30] Quay and Penrose were powerful figures who together controlled the Republican Party in Pennsylvania. Attesting to the leading roles they played on the political stage, a statue of Quay stands in the Rotunda of the State Capitol in Harrisburg, while a statue of Penrose is situated nearby on the capitol grounds. Not unexpectedly, President Theodore Roosevelt nominated Holland.[31] He was confirmed on April 19, 1904.

Holland was born in Montgomery County in 1857. Starting his working life as a laborer, he later became a school teacher and then a lawyer. Like all his judicial predecessors, he had been active in politics, in his case with the Republican Party, and had engaged in extensive public service. His resume included service as the Clerk of the Montgomery County Commissioners, the County Solicitor, and from 1893 to 1896 the County District Attorney. On one occasion when Senator Quay was in political "peril," it is said that Holland, the Republican party chairman in Montgomery County, "restored his supremacy."[32] He interrupted his political career to become a Naval officer during the Spanish-American War. As a result of the sponsorship of Quay and Penrose, he held the office of United States Attorney for the Eastern District from 1900 until his appointment as a federal judge.

Holland died in office on April 24, 1914, at the age of fifty-seven. After his death, a newspaper article described his judicial career in laudatory terms. According to a eulogist, one of his praiseworthy traits was his willingness to reverse himself if he thought he had committed error. The eulogist is reported to have said of Judge Holland, perhaps with a touch of hyperbole:

> His greatness of mind as a judge ... was shown in the calmness and frankness with which he would reverse his own decisions upon ground of reason shown with a freedom from vanity and acknowledgment of fallibility equal to George Washington's.[33]

Upon Judge McPherson's induction as a Court of Appeals judge in 1912, President Taft turned to Joseph Whitaker Thompson as McPherson's replacement on the District Court. Thompson had been an Assistant United States Attorney under Holland and had followed him as United States Attorney after Holland was appointed as a District Judge in 1904. Both men would again be colleagues for the short time before Holland's death.

The son of a Methodist minister, Thompson hailed from Stroudsburg, Monroe County, Pennsylvania where he was born in 1861. He received both his bachelor's and law degrees from the University of Pennsylvania. Following law school, he joined the law firm of his cousin Samuel Whitaker Pennypacker. The latter became Governor of Pennsylvania in 1903 with the help of Senator Quay, who also happened to be Pennypacker's cousin. Thompson was involved in Republican politics and served as a trustee of the University of Pennsylvania. He remained a District Judge until January 1931. At that time, the Senate confirmed him as a judge of the Court of Appeals on the nomination of President Herbert Hoover.[34]

Thompson was the first federal judge in the Eastern District to have been graduated from law school. All his predecessors were admitted to the Bar after reading and studying law under an experienced practitioner.

By the early 1900's, the Court was seeing more and more cases arising under recently enacted federal legislation. In addition to the Pendleton Act and the Sherman

Act, Congress had passed the Chinese Exclusion Act in 1882, as a result of the hundreds of thousands of Chinese laborers who had emigrated to the West Coast, primarily to help construct the railroads and to find employment as gold miners, farm laborers, and small businessmen. The Act was renewed in 1892 and again in 1902.[35] Xenophobia was not confined to the West. Judge McPherson had before him in 1909 an indictment of the master of a British steamship for landing or permitting the landing at the Port of Philadelphia of the vessel's Chinese Chief Cook. The judge ruled that under the statute the defendant could only be found guilty if he knowingly attempted or knowingly permitted the Chief Cook to land. Since the indictment was deficient in this regard, it was dismissed.[36]

Federal courts, in the Progressive Era of the early twentieth century, were also dealing for the first time with health and safety laws enacted by Congress. In a proceeding initiated by the Government, Judge McPherson condemned a shipment of decomposed black olives from Greece under the Food and Drug Act of 1906.[37]

McPherson also had on his docket an action by the Government to condemn certain bottles of gin for being mislabeled "London Dry Gin" when the gin had not been distilled in London but rather in the United States. The jury found in answer to special interrogatories that no mislabeling had occurred since London Dry Gin was a "distinct kind of gin," its place of production or manufacture was irrelevant, and the maker had no intent to deceive or mislead. In reversing that verdict, the Court of Appeals held that the intent of the maker was not pertinent and ordered a new trial.[38]

Another statute passed by Congress during the Progressive Era was the Mann Act which made it illegal to transport any person across state lines with the intent that such person engage in prostitution. Defendant Evan Gwynne was indicted for taking Anna Ward from Philadelphia to Baltimore for that illicit purpose. The case, which was heard by Judge Thompson shortly after he joined the bench, had a highly unusual twist. After the alleged offense occurred but before the trial, Gwynne and Ward were married. Gwynne's counsel objected at trial to the Government's calling his wife as a witness against him. Judge Thompson overruled the objection, and Gwynne was convicted.[39]

Gwynne then filed a motion for a new trial and upon further consideration, Thompson granted the motion. He noted that the admission of testimony in criminal cases in federal court is governed by state law as it existed when the Judiciary Act of 1789 was passed. It was well settled at the time that a wife was not a competent witness against a husband except in circumstances involving violence against the wife. Here, however, even assuming that the crime was one of violence, Ward was not Gwynne's wife at the time the crime was committed. Thompson held that the exception allowing a wife to testify applies only when injuries are inflicted or threatened during the marital relationship. Accordingly, he concluded he should not have compelled her to testify against her husband. While the government argued that such a ruling would allow a defendant to marry the woman who may be the only witness against him and thus avoid conviction, the judge responded that it was for Congress and not the Court to change the law in this regard.[40]

Antitrust actions continued to be filed in the Eastern District. In 1915, Judge Thompson presided over the vigorously contested case of *Bluefields Steamship Co. v. United Fruit Co.* involving an alleged monopoly and restraint of trade in the importation and distribution of bananas from Nicaragua into the United States. Plaintiff sought $5,000,000 in damages which would be trebled under the Sherman Act if it were to win the lawsuit. That was a huge sum of money in those days. The jury trial, which lasted from the beginning of November 1915 to the end of January 1916, was the longest of its kind in the Eastern District up to that time. A defense verdict resulted, and it was affirmed on appeal.[41]

As always, cases involving state law where the parties were of diverse citizenship made up a portion of the Court's calendar. Judge Holland tried a public accommodations case in 1910 that had nothing to do with race, gender, religion, national origin, age, sexual orientation, or disability. A champion light-weight prize fighter, Oscar "Battling Matthew" Nelson, who had won nearly 100 pugilistic contests, had checked into the Bellevue-Stratford Hotel in Philadelphia but was refused lodging when it was learned what he did for a living. Boxing at that time was a criminal offense in Pennsylvania and other states although the record is silent as to whether Nelson had engaged in any prize fights here. Although Pennsylvania law required an innkeeper to receive all travelers if a room was available, it also authorized the refusal to accommodate a person if the innkeeper had "good reason." Judge Holland charged the jury that the hotel was under no duty to accommodate Nelson if he was not a reputable person or not a law abiding citizen because of engaging in an unlawful business or occupation. The jury found that the hotel was within its rights not to lodge him.[42]

In February 1914, Congress created a temporary judgeship for the Eastern District with the proviso that the next vacancy on the Court would not be filled.[43] This brought the number of authorized judgeships in the District, at least for a time, to three. Several hopefuls for the position quickly emerged, some of whom had important political sponsors. Pennsylvania Democratic Congressman A. Mitchell Palmer, who would later serve as President Woodrow Wilson's Attorney General, pressed hard for the appointment of William A. Carr, a Philadelphia lawyer.[44] Carr was also supported by Common Pleas and Municipal Court judges as well as "over a thousand lawyers in the city."[45] A state court judge in Schuylkill County and one in Berks County also had political endorsements. Finally, there was Oliver Booth Dickinson, a leading lawyer in Chester, Delaware County, who had a group of friends urging his selection. One of the points made in favor of Carr was his residence in Philadelphia. It would be easier, so the argument went, to obtain emergency orders from Carr when the Court was out of session than it would be from a judge who lived in one of the outlying counties.[46]

The decision was in the hands of Attorney General James C. McReynolds who would make a recommendation to President Wilson. Despite the strong political support for Carr, McReynolds urged Dickinson's appointment, and the President thereupon nominated him for the new seat on March 31, 1914.[47]

Dickinson was born in 1857 in Dayton, Ohio. When he was five years old, his family moved to Marcus Hook where his father, a Baptist minister, had accepted a pastorate. Dickinson remained a resident of Delaware County for the rest of his life. He attended Lewisburg College (now Bucknell University) but left in his junior year because of the death of his father. Some years later, the college conferred on him an honorary Master's Degree. He read law under his brother, who was a lawyer, and was admitted to the Bar in 1878. He was a generous contributor to the Democratic Party and participated as a delegate at its 1892 national Convention which nominated Grover Cleveland for President. Twice he was a candidate for a Common Pleas judgeship on the Democratic ticket, and twice he was defeated in overwhelmingly Republican Delaware County. His interests extended beyond politics. He served as a trustee of Crozer Theological Seminary, the J. Louis Crozer Home and Hospital, the Y.W.C.A. of Chester, and the Pennsylvania Military College. There was great demand for him as a public speaker.[48] Dickinson was the first District Judge who had not held prior elected or appointed public office and was the last who never attended law school.

Dickinson was confirmed by the Senate on April 28, 1914, four days after Judge Holland died. Consequently, the Eastern District's complement of judges did not increase to three as anticipated but remained at two until another temporary judgeship was created in the 1920's. Known for his witticisms both on and off the bench, he served as a District Judge for twenty-five years. At the time of his death in September 1939 at the age of eighty-one, he was one of the oldest active judges in the federal system.[49]

Some jurists display their own distinctive habits or customs in the courtroom. Dickinson was one of them. He did not remain seated during Court proceedings but was known to pace back and forth on the bench.[50] When he was presiding over an admiralty case, he hung a silver oar, the traditional symbol of the authority of the admiralty court, in the front of the bench and would begin the day with the phrase, "May there be no moaning at the bar when I put out to sea."[51] Apparently, at some later time, a brass oar came to replace the silver oar in the Eastern District. Unhappily, both the silver and brass oars have disappeared, and with their disappearance a venerable tradition dating back at least to the reign of Elizabeth I has vanished from the Court.[52]

From the earliest days of the republic, federal courts have had jurisdiction over cases involving the mails, pursuant to the power given to Congress under the

Constitution "to establish Post Offices and post Roads."[53] Sometimes the cases involved theft of the mail, sometimes unauthorized competition with the delivery of the mail by the Post Office, and sometimes the use of the mails for fraudulent purposes. In a prosecution before Judge Dickinson in 1915, W.O. Smith, a physician specializing in the treatment of nervous diseases, was charged with the fraudulent use of the mails. The evidence established that he would promote his medical expertise to his victims through the mail and obtain statements of their symptoms. Once received, he would inform them that they had "serious ailments and in dire need of medical attention" even though they were in normal health. As the final step in the scheme, he induced those duped to forward him money purportedly for treatment. The jury found the defendant guilty, and Judge Dickinson sentenced him to pay a fine.[54]

Judge Thompson, like Judge Butler before him, was assigned to preside outside the Eastern District but in this instance for one specific case. In 1917, he was designated to sit in the District Court of Delaware to decide *DuPont v. DuPont*, a high profile, contentious, and complex corporate litigation pitting members of the DuPont family against one another for control of E.I. DuPont de Nemours & Co. The Delaware District Judge had recused himself because of familial relationships with both sides of the dispute.[55] Judge Thompson decided the case without a jury, and the Court of Appeals affirmed in all essential respects.[56]

During this period, events in Europe were entangling the United States. World War I had begun in August 1914, shortly after the assassination in Sarajevo of Archduke Franz Ferdinand, the heir to the Austro-Hungarian throne.[57] The United States remained neutral, although not unaffected, until Germany made its fateful decision in early 1917 to undertake unrestricted submarine warfare with attacks on all sea traffic, including American merchant ships, around Great Britain, France, Italy, and the Eastern Mediterranean.[58]

On April 6, at the urging of President Wilson, Congress declared war against Germany. Congress enacted the Selective Service Act shortly thereafter in May. The Espionage Act followed and became law on June 15, 1917. Philadelphia area industries became involved in the war effort. The Cramp Shipyard built torpedo boat destroyers, Midvale Steel manufactured guns for destroyers, and Baldwin Locomotive Works produced artillery shells and railroad gun-mounts. While there was a ground swell of patriotic fervor, the Socialist Party and others opposed conscription and the war effort.[59] The District Court would soon be drawn into this clash.

In the midst of the war, Charles T. Schenck, the General Secretary of the Socialist Party in Philadelphia, directed that a circular be printed and distributed through the mail to men who had been drafted. The circular compared conscription with slavery outlawed by the Thirteenth Amendment and declared "Do not submit to intimidation" although urging only peaceful measures such as petitioning to repeal the draft law. It called the draft the work of "cunning politicians and a mercenary capitalist press," promulgated "in the interest of Wall Street's chosen few." It denied the power of the Government to order citizens to "foreign shores to shoot up people of other lands."[60]

Schenck and others were indicted for conspiracy to violate the Espionage Act. Schenck was charged with causing and attempting to cause insubordination in the armed forces of the United States and obstruction of recruiting and enlistment when the United States was at war with the German Empire. He was also indicted for mailing prohibited material.[61] The United States Attorney at the time was Francis Fisher Kane, the grandson of the John Kane, who had been the Judge in the Eastern District of Pennsylvania from 1846 to 1858.

The jury convicted Schenck and codefendant Dr. Elizabeth Baer, but Judge Thompson directed the jury to acquit three others for insufficient evidence. Thereafter, the post-trial motions of the two remaining defendants claiming lack of evidence were denied.[62] However, at sentencing, he commented that Schenck and Baer were really minor players and imposed on them prison terms of only six months and ninety days, respectively. The defendants remained free pending appeal.[63]

Judge Thompson's opinion denying the post-trial motions makes no reference to free speech.[64] However, this issue was at the heart of the decision of the Supreme Court which agreed to hear the matter. Indeed, it was the first significant case in which the Supreme Court had construed the clause of the First Amendment prohibiting Congress from making any law "abridging the freedom of speech."[65] In unanimously upholding the convictions, the Court through Justice Oliver Wendell Holmes determined that Schenck intended his mailings to influence people to obstruct the draft. Holmes then wrote these oft-quoted words:

> We admit that in many places and in ordinary times the defendants in saying all that was said in the circular would have been within their constitutional rights. But the character of every act depends upon the circumstances in which it is done.... The most stringent protection of free speech would not protect a man in falsely shouting fire in a theatre and causing a panic.... The question in every case is whether the words used are used in such circumstances and are of such a nature as to create a clear and present danger that they will bring about the substantive evils that Congress has a right to prevent. It is a question of proximity and degree. When a nation is at war many things that might be said in time of peace are such a hindrance to its effort that their utterance will not be endured so long as men fight and that no Court could regard them as protected by any constitutional right.[66]

*Schenck* was not the only case of this kind in the Eastern District during World War I. In another prosecution, five individuals who were involved with the German language newspapers *Philadelphia Tageblatt* and the *Philadelphia Sonntagsblatt* were indicted and convicted before Judge Dickinson under the Espionage Act for conspiracy and for the substantive acts of promoting the success of the Imperial German Government, obstructing recruitment and enlistment in the United States military, and making false statements intended to promote the success of the nation's enemies as a result of articles and editorials appearing in their newspapers. All defendants appealed to the Supreme Court. Although emphasizing the constitutionality of the Espionage Act, the Court reversed the convictions of two of the defendants for lack of evidence. It sustained the convictions of the remaining three.[67]

Whenever the country is at war, there are always some who seek to evade any draft law or who desert their military posts. World War I was no exception. The most notorious cases in the annals of Philadelphia in that era involved Grover Cleveland Bergdoll, his brother, Erwin Rudolph Bergdoll, and their mother, Emma C. Bergdoll, the widow of a wealthy brewer Louis Bergdoll Jr. All three became well known to the District Court and to the public-at-large.

The family at one time resided in a large house on North 29th Street and then in a thirty-two room mansion at 52nd Street and Wynnefield Avenue known locally as "The Castle." In his youth Grover Bergdoll drove fast cars, had numerous minor brushes with the law, and flew his Wright Brothers biplane over Philadelphia and to Atlantic City.[68] In 1914, at the outbreak of World War I in Europe, he approached the German consul in Philadelphia and offered to serve as an aviator for Germany. He was turned down.[69]

In August 1917, Grover received a notice to report for a physical examination pursuant to the Selective Service Act but failed to appear on the appointed date. In July 1918, he was mailed a notice of induction into the Army which he ignored. Grover had fled. He traveled to the Midwest, Southwest and the South as well as to Maryland and always was able to stay a step ahead of federal agents. He even returned to his home in Philadelphia on occasion. With a flair for the dramatic, he taunted federal authorities by sending post cards to his local draft board and others from various places he had been and by writing a letter to the *Public Ledger*.[70] Agents searched the family home from time to time on tips that he was hiding there. Once his mother, with a pistol in hand, barred their entrance.[71] Finally, in early 1920, during a search of the house, Grover was arrested while hiding under pillows in a window seat.[72] He was court-martialed and sentenced to five years imprisonment at Governor's Island in New York.[73]

In the meantime his brother Erwin also failed to appear for his physical in 1917 and absconded. Like Grover, he did not report when later called for military duty. After being a fugitive for two years, sometimes with Grover, he surrendered to authorities in August 1920. He was promptly court-martialed and sentenced to a term of four years imprisonment at Fort Leavenworth, Kansas.[74] At Christmas 1933, President Franklin Roosevelt issued a general pardon of 1,500 persons convicted of evading service in World War I. Erwin Bergdoll, but not Grover, had his full rights of citizenship restored.[75]

The incredible story of Grover Bergdoll played out in the headlines for several more decades. In 1920, not long after his court-martial, his lawyers persuaded the War Department to furlough him from Governor's Island for three days to locate $105,000 in gold that he said he had buried in Maryland.[76] When on furlough he made an overnight visit under guard to his mother's home in Philadelphia before the scheduled journey to Maryland to unearth the treasure trove. During his stay, he escaped in a waiting car with the help of a friend and fled to Canada.[77] He promptly sailed to Liverpool and then made his way to Germany's Black Forest, where he had relatives.[78] Two unsuccessful attempts to kidnap and transport him to the United States took place. In the midst of one attempt, he shot and killed one of his assailants.[79] He married a German woman with whom he fathered a number of children.[80]

There is evidence he slipped back into the United States undetected in 1929. His wife and children arrived separately, and they all lived at 52nd and Wynnefield with Emma Bergdoll while Grover always remained out of sight. They departed for Germany in 1934.[81] Before doing so, Grover retrieved the pot of gold which had been hidden all along in the house and not in Maryland.[82] After only a short time in Germany, his family again returned to Philadelphia. He purportedly traveled back into this country secretly and remained hidden in his mother's home as his children attended school in Philadelphia.[83]

In the 1930's, his wife and mother sought and failed to obtain clemency for him from President Franklin Roosevelt.[84] He quietly sailed back to Germany in 1938. As World War II approached and after being a fugitive for nineteen years, he decided it was time to accept his fate and traveled back to the United States in 1939 after notifying the authorities.[85] He was immediately taken into custody and again court-martialed.[86] Three years were added to his previous five year sentence.[87] He was paroled from custody at Fort Leavenworth in 1944.

Grover, his wife, and family lived in the Philadelphia suburbs for a number of years and then moved to Virginia.[88] Death came to him in a psychiatric hospital in Richmond in 1966 at the age of seventy-two.[89]

After Grover's daring escape and flight in 1920, Emma Bergdoll, an American citizen who had been born in Germany, and several others, including her son Charles,[90] were tried before Judge Dickinson and a jury in the Eastern District on a number of charges including conspiracy to aid Grover and Erwin in deserting the United States

Army. She and her co-defendants were all convicted[91] at the trial closely followed by the news media. Grover had also been indicted but was not tried because he was a fugitive.

At the time, there was still significant anti-German sentiment. Nonetheless, at her sentencing in May 1921, Judge Dickinson showed sympathy for a mother in her predicament. He sentenced her to imprisonment for a year and a day and fined her a total of $7,000 on two indictments but ordered that if the fines were paid promptly, the prison sentence would be remitted. Judge Dickinson told her, "Perhaps the severest punishment you, as a mother, can feel, is that the disgrace into which you came has been brought upon you by your own sons." While acknowledging her guilt, he added, "No one would wish to see a mother sent to jail for merely helping her sons, guilty as they were."[92] She timely paid the fines, but under protest, and then appealed her sentence. The Court of Appeals held that her payment of the fines was voluntary and that as a result her appeal was moot.[93]

Emma Bergdoll's interaction with the Court continued well into the 1920's and 1930's. In 1926, Judge Dickinson found in her favor in a lawsuit she brought against the Alien Property Custodian to recover $500,000 which the Custodian has seized from her on the ground that the property belonged to her son, Grover Bergdoll. She was also vindicated in refusing to turn over to the Custodian an additional $439,000 which the Custodian claimed was the property of her son Grover. Judge Dickinson called her "a foolish mother" but then commented, "Many of us, however, have reason for gratitude for that folly of motherhood which sees the promise of good in sons to which other and wiser eyes are blind ..."[94]

Not all her lawsuits resulted in her favor. In the 1930's the Court denied her request to return to her "The Castle" at Fifty-second Street and Wynnefield Avenue, which, the Court found, had rightly been seized by the Government since she had deeded it to Grover, who had forfeited his ownership as a fugitive from justice. Nonetheless, she was not presently to be evicted.[95] She died in the Philadelphia suburbs in December 1944, shortly after Grover was paroled.[96]

As for Grover, back in August 1918, this Court had issued a bench warrant for his arrest as a result of his failure to appear for a physical examination for the military. As noted, he had been indicted along with his mother in 1920, but was never tried in the Eastern District because he was a fugitive at that time. Again in August 1938, a bench warrant was issued, but it was nol prossed, that is, dismissed in 1941.[97]

As the Court was dealing with the Bergdolls who were heirs to a brewery fortune, it was also grappling with issues of breweries in general. At the time of World War I, the temperance movement was gaining additional momentum nationally.[98] Congress passed legislation prohibiting the manufacture of alcoholic beverages to conserve grain for food for the armed forces. In 1917, the "drys" were victorious over the "wets" in persuading Congress to propose to the states the Eighteenth Amendment to the

Constitution establishing Prohibition. The requisite number of states had ratified the Amendment by January 1919. It read in relevant part:

> After one year from the ratification of this article the manufacture, sale, or transportation of intoxicating liquors within, the importation thereof into, or the exportation thereof from the United States and all territory subject to the jurisdiction thereof for beverage purposes is hereby prohibited.

To implement the amendment, Congress passed the Volstead Act over the veto of President Wilson. It created the mechanisms for the enforcement of Prohibition and set forth penalties for violations of its provisions.[99] The criminal caseload of the federal courts throughout the country increased significantly as a result of Prohibition related prosecutions.[100] Again, as with the Sedition Act of 1798 and the Fugitive Slave Act, the federal courts were thrust into the thicket of enforcing what in some circles was an unpopular law.

In the ensuing years, the District Court faced issues over the definition of beer and the legality of a search and seizure of beer and other property from a brewery. Other cases involved the indictment and conviction of individuals for maintaining a common nuisance by selling whisky to patrons or for operating an illicit still for the manufacture of intoxicating liquor. There was also a forty-seven-defendant indictment, including Federal Prohibition Director for Pennsylvania and a Federal Prohibition Inspector, for conspiracy to defraud the United States in the issuance of permits to purchase liquor in amounts and character to which the permitees were not entitled. Another action concerned the authority of Prohibition agents to conduct searches. Yet another dealt with the question whether a corporation sought to withdraw specially denatured alcohol from a warehouse for a licit or illicit purpose.[101]

In 1919, in addition to wrestling with prohibition, Congress enacted legislation allowing federal judges under certain conditions to take what has commonly come to be known as senior status. As previously noted, Congress in 1869 authorized a judge to retire on full salary once he had attained the age of seventy and had completed ten years of service. Under the new law, a judge could retire at his then salary after meeting these criteria, but he could be called upon to perform "such duties ... as such retired judge may be willing to undertake." When a judge took senior status, a vacancy was created for the appointment of a replacement.[102] Thus, a retired judge could continue to decide cases while a new judge would be added to help with the workload. In 1948, the law was amended to allow those retired judges on senior status to receive future salary increases provided to judges in active service.[103]

The sudden death of long-time Senator Boies Penrose on December 31, 1921 had a number of important political consequences, including an effect on future judicial appointments. Governor William Sproul, a Republican, chose patrician George Wharton Pepper, a distinguished Philadelphia lawyer, to fill the vacancy in the United States Senate, and State Senator Edwin H. Vare and his younger brother Congressman William S. Vare took over from Penrose as the bosses of the Philadelphia Republican organization.

Pepper was elected in the fall of 1922 to complete the little more than four years remaining in Penrose's term. The Vares eyed him with suspicion. Pepper refused to surrender his independence on appointments but was willing to consult with the organization on certain patronage matters. Nonetheless, he made it clear that federal judgeships were off limits. Edwin Vare had warned Pepper at a meeting, '... there's something I think you should know. It is that with our power over the organization we can send anybody we want to the United States Senate -- anybody.'[104] It was not an idle boast.

Pepper defied the Vares in recommending to President Warren Harding the nomination of his friend Charles Louis McKeehan, who had no political organization support, for the temporary judgeship that had been created for the Eastern District in September 1922. The President thereafter sent McKeehan's name to the Senate. He was confirmed in February 1923.[105]

Born in 1876 in Philadelphia, McKeehan was the son of a lawyer. He obtained his undergraduate degree from the University of Pennsylvania where he was President of his class and later his law degree from the same institution. As a law student, he spent time in the office of George Wharton Pepper, who in effect acted as his preceptor. He volunteered for military service at the outbreak of World War I, even though he was over forty years old. Although refused permission to serve in combat because of a recent appendectomy, he held non-combatant positions in the Army and achieved the rank of Lieutenant Colonel. During his legal career, he and Owen J. Roberts, later a Justice of the United States Supreme Court, were law partners. McKeehan also taught negotiable instruments and contracts at Penn Law School. From the time of its inception in 1902 until his appointment to the bench, he was the Secretary of the Board of Law Examiners, which had responsibility for examination and admission of lawyers to the Pennsylvania Bar. When not engaged in professional pursuits, he often sailed a small boat at Barnegat Light, New Jersey, where he had a summer home. Like Pepper, he was an active Episcopal churchman.[106]

McKeehan was also a member of the Executive Committee of the Association Against the Prohibition Amendment. Needless to say, this was a problem for someone who was going to be required to enforce the Volstead Act as a federal judge. Before his confirmation, Pepper and the Anti-Saloon League worked out an agreement that McKeehan would issue a statement that he would uphold the Prohibition Amendment and related laws. He did so and thereafter was approved by the Senate.[107] He died in

March 1925, at the age of forty-eight after only two years on the bench.[108] His funeral was attended by hundreds of leading citizens, including Senator Pepper, ex-Governor Edwin Stuart, and numerous judges and members of the bar.[109] With his death, his temporary seat was not to be filled, and the Court continued to function with his two older colleagues, Whitaker Thompson and Oliver Dickinson.

In 1926, William Vare put into action his late brother's warning to Pepper. Vare ran against and defeated Pepper and Governor Gifford Pinchot in the three-way Republican primary for the United States Senate by carrying only two of Pennsylvania's sixty-seven counties, Philadelphia and Dauphin. Vare went on to win the general election against his Democratic opponent.

In the last days of his term which was scheduled to end on March 4, 1927, Pepper succeeded in having Congress add a new permanent judgeship for the Eastern District of Pennsylvania. He sought to have William Huntington Kirkpatrick named to fill the seat before Vare, who had a different candidate in mind, was to take office.[110] At Pepper's request, President Calvin Coolidge nominated Kirkpatrick but did not do so until March 3, when the Act creating the new judgeship took effect.[111] It was the day before Pepper's term was to expire. Since the Judiciary Committee was not scheduled to meet on the eve of adjournment, Pepper persuaded the Chairman of the Committee, Senator George Norris, to poll the members, all of whom gave their approval of the nominee. Norris, in a closed Executive Session of the Senate, then asked the Vice-President for immediate consideration, which was granted. A unanimous affirmative vote was obtained, and Kirkpatrick was confirmed, literally at the eleventh hour.[112] Such a speedy confirmation process would be impossible today.

Kirkpatrick was born in 1885 and grew up in Easton in Northampton County. His father had served as a state court judge, the Attorney General of Pennsylvania in the late 1880's, and later as a Congressman. After being graduated from Lafayette College, Kirkpatrick attended the University of Pennsylvania Law School for a year where he impressed one of his professors, George Wharton Pepper. He served as a Judge Advocate in the Army during World War I with the rank of Lieutenant Colonel. He then returned to private practice in Easton. Following in his father's footsteps, he was elected to Congress on the Republican ticket for one term (1921-1923) representing Carbon, Monroe, and Northampton Counties. He was defeated for re-election in the Republican primary and resumed his law practice until sworn in as a federal judge. In the 1940's, Kirkpatrick was president of the Board of Trustees of his alma mater Lafayette College. Finding golf too slow a sport, he turned to hiking, a swifter form of recreation.[113]

Kirkpatrick's tenure on the Court lasted for over forty years and during that time he was invariably seen on the bench wearing his trademark green eyeshade and heard speaking in a casual "country boy style."[114] Unlike many judges, he enjoyed patent cases and frequently sat by designation on the Court of Customs and Patent Appeals in Washington. He died in 1970 in Cumberstone, Maryland, where he was living at the time.[115]

## Notes

1. McPherson, James M., Gen. ed., *To the Best of My Ability,* pp. 140-41 (Dorling Kindersley Publishing, Inc., 2000); Woodward, C. Vann, *Revision & Reaction* (Doubleday & Co., Inc., 1956).
2. Burgess, Geo. & Kennedy, Miles C., *Centennial History of the Pennsylvania Railroad Company*, pp. 195-06, 241-81 (1949).
3. Weigley, Russell F., ed., *Philadelphia, A 300-Year History*, pp. 323, 430 (W.W. Norton & Co., 1982).
4. *Id.* pp. 471-87.
5. *The Philadelphia Inquirer*, p. 3 (Nov. 3, 1909).
6. *Id.*; *The Pennsylvania Manual*, Vol. 91, p. 662 (1953-1954).
7. *The Philadelphia Inquirer*, p. 3 (Nov. 3, 1909). The Pennsylvania Constitution of 1838 had been amended in 1850 to provide for the election, rather than the appointment, of state judges.
8. Evans, Frank B., *Pennsylvania Politics, 1872-1877: A Study in Political Leadership*, pp. 48-49 (The Pennsylvania Historical and Museum Commission, 1966); Editorial Clipping, William Butler file, Box 598, RG 60 Department of Justice, Records Relating to the Appointment of Federal Judges, Marshals, and Attorneys 1853-1901; NARA II, College Park, Maryland.
9. *The Philadelphia Inquirer*, p. 4 (Feb. 27, 1879).
10. *Id.*
11. *See* Records of the General Services Administration.
12. In 1869, Congress authorized the appointment of one Circuit Judge for each circuit. The Circuit Judge had the same role as would a Supreme Court Justice sitting on the Circuit Court. The intention was to relieve the circuit riding burden on the justices. McKennan was appointed by President Ulysses S. Grant and was from the Western District of Pennsylvania. Surrency, Erwin C., *History of the Federal Courts*, Second ed., pp. 52-53 (Oceana Publications, Inc., 2002).
13. Lender, Mark Edward, *This Honorable Court: The United States District Court for the District of New Jersey*, 1789-2000, p. 127 (Rutgers University Press, 2006).
14. Wheeler, Russell and Harriman, Cynthia, *Creating the Federal Judicial System*, Second ed. (Federal Judicial Center 1994).
15. Presser, Stephen B., *Studies in the History of the United States Courts of the Third Circuit*, pp. 8-11 (Government Printing Office, 1982).
16. *United States v. E.C. Knight Co.*, 60 F. 306 (C.C.E.D. Pa.), *aff'd*, 60 F. 934 (3d Cir. 1894), *aff'd*, 156 U.S. 1 (1895).
17. *Id.* at 309.
18. *Id.* at 309-10.
19. 60 F. 394 (3d Cir. 1894).
20. 156 U.S. 1, 18-46 (1895).
21. *See Standard Oil Co. of New Jersey v. United States*, 221 U.S. 1 (1911); *Swift & Co. v. United States*, 196 U.S. 375 (1905).
22. *City of Philadelphia v. Western U. Tel. Co.*, 40 F. 615 (C.C.E.D. Pa. 1889).

23. Ackerman, Kenneth D., *Dark Horse: The Surprise Election and Political Murder of President James A. Garfield*, p. 446 (Carroll & Graf Publishers, 2003).
24. *United States v. Bunting*, 82 F. 883 (E.D. Pa. 1897); *see* E.D. Pa. Criminal Dockets, *United States v. John J. Delany*, Aug. Session, 1897, No. 7 and *United States v. Henry K. Bunting and John J. Delany*, Aug. Session, 1897, No. 8.
25. *In re The Illinois*, 84 F. 697 (E.D. Pa. 1898), *aff'd* 87 F. 574 (3d Cir. 1898); *Warner v. Great Western Ins. Co.*, (1884) (Record of U.S. Dist. Ct. for E.D. Pa., Law & Appellate Case Files, Record Group 21, Box 197, Nat'l Archives, Phila.); *United States v. Tobey*, 12 F. 347 (E.D. Pa. 1882); *In re The Yamoiden*, 49 F. 591 (E.D. Pa. 1892); and *In re The Viola*, 52 F. 172 (C.C.E.D. Pa. 1892), *aff'd*, 55 F. 829 (3d Cir. 1893).
26. Act of April 10, 1869, ch. 22, 16 Stat. 44, § 5.
27. *The Philadelphia Inquirer*, p. 13 (March 17, 1912); *The Philadelphia Inquirer*, p. 3 (Jan. 21, 1919).
28. Act of March 2, 1901, ch. 801, 31 Stat. 881.
29. Act of April 1, 1904, ch. 857, 33 Stat. 155.
30. *The Philadelphia Inquirer*, p. 16 (April 14, 1904).
31. *Id.*
32. *The Philadelphia Inquirer*, p. 6 (April 30, 1914).
33. *Id.*
34. *Id.*, p. 1 (Jan. 8, 1946).
35. Zimmermann, Warren, *First Great Triumph*, pp. 464-65 (Ferrar, Straus and Giroux, 2002).
36. *United States v. Rout*, 170 F. 201 (E.D. Pa. 1909).
37. *United States v. Nine Barrels of Olives*, 179 F. 983 (E.D. Pa. 1910).
38. *United States v. Thirty-Six Bottles of London Dry Gin*, 205 F. 111 (E.D. Pa. 1913), *rev'd*, 210 F. 271 (3d Cir. 1914). Judge McPherson presided over this matter in the District Court even though he was then a Judge on the Court of Appeals.
39. *United States v. Gwynne*, 209 F. 993 (E.D. Pa. 1914).
40. *Id.*
41. *Bluefields S.S. Co. v. United Fruit Co.*, 243 F. 1 (3d Cir. 1917), *appeal dismissed*, 248 U.S. 595 (1919). *See also*, *Bluefields Steamship Co. Ltd. v. United Fruit* (1911), Records of the United States District Court for the Eastern District of Pennsylvania. Depositions, #1428 Folder 1, Box 636 and #1428 Folder 2 and Folder 4, Box 637, George W. Pepper, to Clerk of the Eastern District, Nov. 15, 1912, #1428 Folder 1, Box 636, Alex Simpson and Francis Shunk Brown to Judge J. Whitaker Thompson, Jan. 24, 1916, #1428 Folder 3, Box 637, Records Group 21, National Archives Mid-Atlantic Division, Philadelphia, Pennsylvania; George Wharton Pepper, *Philadelphia Lawyer, An Autobiography*, pp. 354-56 (J.B. Lippincott Co., 1944); Chapman, Peter, *Bananas: How the United Fruit Company Shaped the World*, pp. 38, 65 (Canongate, 2007).
42. *Nelson v. Boldt*, 180 F. 779 (C.C.E.D. Pa. 1910).
43. Act of February 16, 1914, Pub. L. No. 63-56, 38 Stat. 283.
44. Palmer represented the 26th Congressional District which was composed of Carbon, Monroe, Northampton, and Pike Counties. Only Northampton County was in the Eastern District of Pennsylvania.
45. *The Philadelphia Inquirer*, p. 1 (March 26, 1914).
46. *Id.* at pp. 1, 9.
47. *Id.*, p. 16 (Mar. 3, 1914); p. 4 (Mar. 15, 1914); p. 1 (Mar. 26, 1914); Oral History of Judge Albert Maris, Conducted by Judge Francis Van Dusen (Feb. 19, 1984).
48. Bliss, Ward Raymond & Geary, Alexander Brooke, "Oliver Booth Dickinson," *Delaware County Reports*, Vol. 12, pp. 646-50; *The Philadelphia Inquirer*, p. 4B (Sept. 17, 1939); *The Evening Bulletin*, p. E3 (Sept. 16, 1939); "Hon. Oliver B. Dickinson," *The Shingle*, Vol. II, pp. 4-5 (Philadelphia Bar Ass'n, Jan., 1939).
49. *The Philadelphia Inquirer*, p. 4B (Sept. 17, 1939); *The Evening Bulletin*, p. E3 (Sept. 16, 1939).

50. Borneman, Harold B., "More About the Way Things Used to Be," *The Shingle*, p. 35 (Philadelphia Bar Ass'n, Nov. 1972).
51. *Id.*
52. Rose, Leonard, "The Silver Oar of the Admiralty," *The JAG Journal, United States Navy*, Vol. XXI, pp. 13-14 (July-August 1969); Sweeney, Joseph C., "The Silver Oar and Other Maces of the Admiralty: Admiralty Jurisdiction in America and the British Empire," *Journal of Maritime Law and Commerce*, p. 159 (April 2007).
53. U.S. Const., art. I, § 8, cl. 7.
54. *United States v. Smith*, 222 F. 165 (E.D. Pa. 1915); Criminal Docket, Sept. Session 1914, p. 123 (Records of United States District Court for the Eastern District of Pennsylvania).
55. Presser, Stephen B., *Studies in the History of the United States Courts of the Third Circuit*, pp. 145-57 (Government Printing Office, 1982).
56. 251 F. 937 (D. Del. 1918), *aff'd* with modification 256 F. 129 (3d Cir. 1919), *cert. denied*, 250 U.S. 642 (1919).
57. Howard, Michael, *The First World War*, pp. 16-31 (Oxford University Press, 2002).
58. Cooper, John Milton, Jr., *Woodrow Wilson*, pp. 362-89 (Alfred A. Knopf, 2009).
59. Lynskey, Bill, "Reinventing the First Amendment in Wartime Philadelphia," *Pennsylvania Magazine of History and Biography*, Vol. 131, pp. 33, et seq. (Jan. 2007).
60. *Schenck v. United States*, 249 U.S. 47, 51 (1919).
61. *Id.*
62. *United States v. Schenck*, 253 F. 212 (E.D. Pa. 1918), *aff'd*, 249 U.S. 47 (1919).
63. Lynskey, Bill, "Reinventing the First Amendment in Wartime Philadelphia," *Pennsylvania Magazine of History and Biography*, Vol. 131, pp. 65-67 (Jan. 2007).
64. *Id.*
65. The First Amendment states:

    Congress shall make no law respecting an establishment of religion, or prohibiting the free exercise thereof; or abridging the freedom of speech, or of the press; or the right of the people peaceably to assemble, and to petition the Government for a redress of grievances.

    Stone, Geoffrey R., *Perilous Times*, p. 192 (W.W. Norton & Co., 2004).
66. *Schenck*, 249 U.S. at 52.
67. *United States v. Schaefer*, 248 F. 290 (E.D. Pa. 1918), *United States v. Schafer*, 254 F. 135 (E.D. Pa. 1918), *aff'd in part, rev'd in part, Schaefer v. United States*, 251 U.S. 466 (1920).
68. Bergdoll purchased the plane from the Wright Brothers in 1912. It is now on display at the Franklin Institute.
69. *Id. The Evening Bulletin*, pp. 1, 32 (January 28, 1966); *The Philadelphia Inquirer*, pp. 1, 10 (January 29, 1966).
70. Dell, Roberta E., *The United States versus Bergdoll*, pp. 35-38 (A.S. Barnes & Co., 1977); *The Evening Bulletin*, p. 32 (Jan. 28, 1966).
71. Dell, Roberta E., *The United States versus Bergdoll*, p. 45 (A.S. Barnes & Co., 1977).
72. *The Philadelphia Inquirer*, pp. 1, 10 (Jan. 29, 1966).
73. "The Flying Dutchman," *Philadelphia Magazine*, pp. 30, 34 (May, June, July 1965).
74. *Ex parte Bergdoll* 274 F. 458 (D. Kan. 1921).
75. *The Philadelphia Record*, p. 1 (Dec. 25, 1933). See letter dated June 16, 1933, from Emma Bergdoll to Mrs. Franklin D. Roosevelt, seeking a pardon for her son Grover.
76. Dell, Roberta E., *The United States versus Bergdoll*, pp. 78-87 (A.S. Barnes & Co., 1977).
77. *Id.* at 88-85, 110.
78. *Id.*, at 116-17.
79. *Id.* at 133-36, 139-41, 176-95.
80. *Id.* at 205-06, 209.

81. *Id.* at 213-14.
82. *Id.* at 211.
83. *Id.* at 214-19.
84. *Id.* at 215.
85. *Id.* at 220-21.
86. *Id.* at 234-35.
87. After conviction at his second-martial, he unsuccessfully sought release through a petition for a writ of habeas corpus. *See United States ex rel Bergdoll v. Drum,* 107 F.2d 897 (2d Cir. 1939), *cert. denied,* 310 U.S. 648 (1940); Dell, Roberta E., *United States versus Bergdoll,* pp. 240-45 (A.S. Barnes & Co., 1977).
88. *Id.* at 249-51.
89. *The Evening Bulletin,* pp. 1, 32 (January 29, 1966); *The Philadelphia Inquirer,* pp. 1, 10 (January 29, 1966).
90. By this time, Charles had changed his surname to Braun, due to the widespread publicity about his brothers. Another brother Louis had changed his surname to Bergson. *See The Philadelphia Inquirer,* p. 3 (Dec. 5, 1944).
91. *The Philadelphia Inquirer,* p. 1 (Sept. 29, 1920).
92. *Id.,* pp. 1, 8 (May 18, 1921); Judgments in *United States v. Bergdoll,* No. 9, June 1920 (E.D. Pa. May 17, 1921) and in *United States v. Bergdoll,* No. 13, June 1920 (E.D. Pa. May 17, 1921).
93. *United States v. Bergdoll,* 272 F. 498 (E.D. Pa. 1921), *appeal dismissed,* 279 F. 404 (3d Cir.), *cert. denied,* 259 U.S. 585 (1922).
94. *The Philadelphia Inquirer,* p. 14 (Feb. 24, 1926).
95. *The Evening Bulletin,* p. E3 (July 27, 1934).
96. *The Philadelphia Inquirer,* pp. 1, 10 (Dec. 5, 1944); *The Evening Bulletin,* p. 3 (Dec. 5, 1944).
97. Docket of *United States v. Bergdoll,* 42 June Term 1918 (E.D. Pa.).
98. Hofstadter, Richard, *The Age of Reform,* pp. 288-93 (Vintage Books, 1955).
99. Heckscher, August, *Woodrow Wilson,* pp. 615-16 (Charles Scribner's Sons, 1991). President Wilson was quite ill at the time of the veto. What role in the veto he played as opposed to that of his wife Edith Bolling Galt Wilson is unknown.
100. Surrency, Edwin C., *History of the Federal Courts,* Second ed., p. 176 (Oceana Publications, Inc., 2002).
101. *United States v. Bergner & Engel Brewing Co.,* 260 F. 764 (E.D. Pa. 1919); *Mellet & Nichter Brewing Co. v. United States,* 296 F. 765 (E.D. Pa. 1923); *United States v. McConnell,* 10 F.2d 977 (E.D. Pa. 1926); *United States v. Liddy,* 2 F.2d 60 (E.D. Pa. 1924); *Quaker Industrial Alcohol Corp. v. Blair,* 19 F.2d 235 (E.D. Pa. 1927); *United States v. Vonski,* 18 F.2d 283 (E.D. Pa. 1927); *United States v. Parzah,* 18 F.2d 1002 (E.D. Pa. 1927); *Daufer-Lieberman Brewing Co. v. Doran,* 38 F.2d 831 (E.D. Pa. 1929).
102. Act of Feb. 25, 1919, Pub. L. No. 65-265, ch. 29, 40 Stat. 1156, § 6; *see Senior Status and Retirement for Article III Judges,* Appendix A (Administrative Office of the U.S. Courts, Sept. 1994).
103. The Act of June 25, 1948, Pub. L. No. 80-773, ch. 17, 62 Stat. 869, pp. 371-72.
104. Pepper, George Wharton, *Philadelphia Lawyer, An Autobiography,* pp. 141-42 (J.B. Lippincott, 1944).
105. Act of September 14, 1922, Pub. L. No. 67-298, ch. 306, 42 Stat. 837, § 1; The law provides that any vacancy occurring after two years would not be filled; *The Philadelphia Inquirer,* p. 4 (Feb. 9, 1923); "In Memoriam - Hon. Charles L. McKeehan," *The Legal Intelligencer,* p. 322 (April 10, 1925).
106. *The Evening Public Ledger,* p. 8 (March 24, 1925); "In Memoriam - Hon. Charles L. McKeehan," *The Legal Intelligencer,* pp. 322-23 (April 10, 1925).
107. Unsigned letter from Special Assistant Attorney General to President, 30 January 1923, January 30 1923-1925 file, Charles McKeehan, Box 751, Applications and Endorsements, 1901-1933, File 25 March 1929, Box 749, Record Group 60 Department of Justice, "Appointment Clerk Applications and Endorsements," 1901-1933, Pennsylvania Eastern, National Archives, College Park, Maryland.
108. *The Evening Public Ledger,* p. 8 (March 24, 1925); "In Memoriam - Hon. Charles L. McKeehan," *The Legal Intelligencer,* pp. 322-23 (April 10, 1925).

109. *The Philadelphia Inquirer*, p. 2 (March 27, 1925).

110. Vare, as it turned out, never took office. After an investigation that dragged on into 1929, the Senate refused to seat him because of what it believed to have been massive voting irregularities in the 1926 primary.

111. The Act of March 3, 1927, Pub. L. No. 69-701, ch. 298, 44 Stat. 1347.

112. Pepper, George Wharton, *Philadelphia Lawyer, An Autobiography*, p. 221 (J.B. Lippincott, 1944).

113. Chidsey, T. McKeen, "Every Inch a Judge," *The Shingle*, pp. 195-96 (Dec. 1944). Lawyer Meeting, Oct. 11, 2007; Oral History of The Honorable Albert Maris, Conducted by Judge Francis Van Dusen, United States District Court for the Eastern District of Pennsylvania (Feb. 19, 1984); Oral History of The Honorable Joseph S. Lord, III, Conducted by Seymour Toll, United States District Court for the Eastern District of Pennsylvania, pp. 43-44 (Apr. 27, 1987); Borneman, Harold B., "More About the Way Things Used to Be: The Federal Court," *The Shingle*, 35, pp. 174, 178 (Nov. 1972); Chidsey, T. McKeen, "Every Inch a Judge," *The Shingle*, 7 pp. 195-96 (Dec. 1944).

114. Recollection of Seymour I. Toll, Esquire.

115. *The Pennsylvania Manual*, Vol. 91, pp. 664, 1086 (1953-1954); *The Philadelphia Inquirer*, p. 14 (Nov. 30, 1970); Chidsey, T. McKeen, "Every Inch a Judge," *The Shingle*, pp. 195-96 (Dec. 1944); Interview by Magistrate Richard A. Powers III with Judge C. William Kraft, pp. 32-33 (Feb. 28, 1995).

# V
# The Depression, World War II, and Beyond: The 1930's and 1940's

As the 1930's began, Herbert Hoover occupied the White House. The country was soon to be in the midst of the Great Depression. Franklin Delano Roosevelt was inaugurated as President in March 1933, and the New Deal and the repeal of Prohibition quickly followed. The Second World War began in Europe in 1939 and for the United States with the bombing of Pearl Harbor on December 7, 1941. Harry S. Truman succeeded Roosevelt in April 1945 before the war ended and surprised the pundits with his election to a four-year term in 1948. After the War, America entered into a period of prosperity. With the Marshall Plan it helped to save Western Europe from Communism and economic devastation. In this period, the role of the federal government in the economic life of the nation expanded and with it the role of the federal courts.

Philadelphia like other cities suffered through the Depression. Yet, throughout the 1930's and 1940's it remained the third largest city in the United States, behind New York and Chicago. It still was a manufacturing, shipping, and railroad center. Strong agricultural output was concentrated in the outlying counties of the Eastern District.

In 1931, as previously noted, President Hoover named J. Whitaker Thompson to the Court of Appeals. This left a vacancy to be filled on the Eastern District. George Wharton Pepper, now the former Senator and more recently the Chancellor of the Philadelphia Bar Association, no longer was picking judges as he had done in the cases of Charles McKeehan and William Kirkpatrick. The process this time did not move as expeditiously as it had in the 1920's. Instead, a prolonged deadlock existed between Republican Senators David A. Reed and James J. Davis who supported Philadelphia Congressman George A. Welsh and Philadelphia Republican organization head William S. Vare who supported a local lawyer, I. Gordon Foster. The newspapers reported on various deals purportedly in the making. The President deferred any nomination while the impasse continued. In April 1932, Vare finally threw his support to Welsh.[1] President Hoover nominated him shortly thereafter, and he was confirmed in May.

George Austin Welsh was an interesting and colorful figure who sat on the Court for thirty-two years. As one of his colleagues recalled, "he had the most charming appearance and manner that you'll ever want to see ... he loved people."[2] Born on a farm in Maryland in 1878, he arrived in Philadelphia at the age of nine. In the late

1890's, he became an amateur featherweight boxing champion who fought matches not only in Philadelphia but also in New York City's Madison Square Garden. In his sixties, Welsh was taking marathon bicycle vacations and often walked the fifteen miles from his home to the courthouse.[3]

He earned his law degree from Temple University in 1905, later became a vice president and trustee of his alma mater, and received an honorary LL.D. in 1939. As a young man, he quickly immersed himself in Republican politics. His career included service as the Secretary to Mayor Samuel H. Ashbridge, as well as stints as an Assistant City Solicitor and an Assistant District Attorney, and for ten years he sat as a member of the Philadelphia Board of Education. He was a Congressman from West Philadelphia from 1923 until his appointment as a federal judge in 1932. Among his other activities, he was a Mason.

Shortly after his appointment, Welsh eyed a return to the political stage. While remaining on the bench, he ran for the Republican nomination for Governor in the spring primary of 1934 but lost decisively to Pennsylvania Attorney General William A. Schnader.[4] It came as no surprise that Welsh believed that a jurist should have a political background, in order to be able to function as a "human judge on the federal courts."[5] He would be the last Republican to be seated on the Court until 1954.

In 1936, Democratic Senator Joseph Guffey, elected in 1934 as an ardent New Dealer, was instrumental in effecting the addition of a temporary judgeship for the Eastern District.[6] On the recommendation of the Senator, President Roosevelt nominated Albert Branson Maris of Delaware County to fill the position. At a testimonial dinner in honor of Maris at the time of his confirmation, one of the speakers was Guffey, who declared, "I have known Albert Maris for sixteen years. He was the chief legal advisor to the Democratic state committee, and we always found his judgment to be good and his advice to be sound, and that was why he was appointed to the judgeship."[7] Guffey then predicted, "You [Maris] are destined to have a fine judicial career, and this is just the first step in your advancement toward great honors." The Senator's words turned out to be prescient.

The family of Albert Maris had been in Pennsylvania since the days of William Penn. One of his ancestors had arrived in 1683, served as a justice in Chester County, and sat as a member of the Provincial Assembly and Provincial Council.[8]

Maris, who was born in 1893, served in the Army in World War I. He first obtained a law degree from Temple University and thereafter an engineering degree from Drexel Institute of Technology. Like all judges up to that time, he had been active in politics. The voters elected him as the auditor of the Borough of Yeadon in the 1920's. In 1928, his try for higher office as the Democratic candidate for the state Senate from Delaware County ended in defeat, but he was a member of the Yeadon Borough council when appointed to the federal bench. In the 1920's, he chaired the County's Democratic Party. He practiced law in Philadelphia and was the presiding clerk of his Monthly Meeting of the Society of Friends.[9] Maris was a "soft-spoken, gentle, thoughtful Quaker with a deep sense of basic fairness in all his judicial dealings."[10]

His time on the District Court, however, was brief. In 1938, President Roosevelt appointed him to the Court of Appeals. Well-versed in the law and procedure, Maris was a member of various Judicial Conference Committees over the years and had a major responsibility in the much needed recodification of both the Criminal and Judicial Codes in 1947 and 1948. He was also selected as the codifier and draftsman of much of the Revised Organic Act of 1954 of the Virgin Islands.[11] Not surprisingly, he was the first recipient of the prestigious Devitt Award for his significant contributions to the administration of justice, the advancement of the rule of law, and the improvement of society as a whole.

President Roosevelt selected Harry Ellis Kalodner to succeed Judge Maris. Born in Philadelphia to Jewish immigrant parents, he was selling newspapers at age thirteen on the ferries between Philadelphia and Camden. Upon being graduated from South Philadelphia High School at age sixteen, he entered the University of Pennsylvania Law School without having attended college. After graduation in 1917, he served in the Army in World War I.

In addition to engaging in private practice, Kalodner was a newspaper reporter, first with the *Philadelphia North American* and then with the *Philadelphia Record* where for a few years he was the Financial and Political Editor. Two Pulitzer Prize Honorable Mentions were awarded to him in the 1930's for stories on corruption in Philadelphia city government and on a fraudulent securities scheme.[12] As a reporter, he was not easily deterred from ferreting out a story. On one occasion, he was eager to attend a "top-secret" meeting of the shareholders of the Philadelphia Rapid Transit Company, the corporation that owned and operated the City's buses and trolleys. Reporters, however, were barred. To circumvent this impediment, Kalodner quickly sought out a broker from whom he purchased two shares of the company's preferred stock. He was admitted to the meeting as a shareholder and then wrote his exclusive story.[13]

When George H. Earle III ran as Democratic candidate for Governor of Pennsylvania in 1934, Kalodner acted as his campaign manager. When Earle was elected over William Schnader, Kalodner joined his cabinet as Secretary of Revenue but resigned after only a few months to become a judge of the Court of Common Pleas of Philadelphia County. After two years in that position, President Roosevelt, on the recommendation of Senator Guffey, chose him for the open seat on the District Court. Kalodner remained on the Court until 1946 when President Truman named him to the Court of Appeals.

Throughout the years, he was active in Jewish service organizations and was a trustee of Yeshiva University. In his political leanings, Kalodner was a fervent supporter of Roosevelt and the New Deal.[14] When time permitted, he enjoyed an outing at the race track.

Following the death in 1939 of the aged Judge Dickinson, a Wilson appointee, President Roosevelt replaced him with Guy Kurtz Bard of Lancaster County, again on the recommendation of Senator Guffey. Bard held an undergraduate degree from Franklin & Marshall College and was a teacher and principal before earning his law degree at the University of Pennsylvania. Like Judges Maris and Kalodner, he was a veteran of World War I and was quite active in Democratic politics. He was the unsuccessful Democratic candidate for Lieutenant Governor in 1930, but two years later was a delegate to the Democratic Convention in Chicago which nominated Franklin Roosevelt. As a member of the Convention's Platform Committee, he drafted the party plank urging the repeal of Prohibition. Upon Roosevelt's election, he became an Assistant United States Attorney and later the United States Attorney for the Eastern District of Pennsylvania. He resigned to become a member of the state Public Service Commission and thereafter was appointed by Governor Earle as the Commonwealth's Attorney General.[15]

Bard received a recess appointment to the federal bench in 1939 and was confirmed in 1940. In 1952, he opted to run for political office, as had Judge Welsh back in 1934. He won the contested Democratic nomination for the United States Senate but did not resign from the bench until July 16, 1952, several months after the primary. Running for office while remaining a federal judge would not be countenanced today under the current Code of Conduct for United States Judges.[16] Bard was defeated in the November general election by the incumbent Senator Edward Martin and died a year later.[17]

Roosevelt's final appointee to the Eastern District was James Cullen Ganey in 1940.[18] He was born in 1899 in Phillipsburg, New Jersey and grew up in Bethlehem, Northampton County, Pennsylvania. After obtaining his undergraduate degree from Lehigh University and his law degree from Harvard, he practiced law in Bethlehem. During this time, he served for six years as the Democratic Party Chairman of Northampton County. A political ally of Senator Joseph P. Guffey, he was named as the United States Attorney for the Eastern District in 1937 to succeed Guy Bard. In his demeanor, he was jovial and featured a broad smile. He was a delightful raconteur. Much of his time off the bench was spent in helping youth as Chairman of the Board of the Sandlot Sports Association.[19] His trademark was a large gold watch chain which he wore across his chest in his vest. Ganey's approach to life was "do the best you can and don't give yourself ulcers over it."[20] He too enjoyed the racetrack and from time to time joined Judge Kalodner at that venue. With Roosevelt's appointments of Judge

Kalodner, who was Jewish, and Judge Ganey, who was a Roman Catholic, the District Court at last became religiously and ethnically diverse.

The Court by the late 1920's had outgrown the Courthouse on Ninth Street which had been its home as well as that of the Post Office since 1884. When that nineteenth century Courthouse was built, it had to provide space for only one Eastern District judge. By 1930, the District Court had three judges: Oliver B. Dickinson, J. Whitaker Thompson, and William H. Kirkpatrick, all of whom needed chambers and courtrooms. Moreover, since 1891, when the Circuit Courts of Appeals were created, appellate judges of the Third Circuit had to be accommodated. Not only had the number of judges increased but so had the size of the judicial staff, the office of the Clerk, and the office of the United States Attorney which were all located in that now outmoded building.

In 1931, Congress approved the construction of a new courthouse in Philadelphia at an estimated cost of $2.9 million, but construction was then delayed. Plans were proposed the next year for an addition to the existing courthouse, but these were soon shelved. Some suggested that a new complex should be located on the Benjamin Franklin Parkway to avoid city congestion. In September 1932, the Treasury Department announced the selection of Harry Sternfeld and the Ballinger Company of Philadelphia as architects for a new courthouse to be constructed on Ninth Street between Market and Chestnut Streets on the same site as the existing 1884 Courthouse.[21]

With the approaching 1932 presidential election and the onset of the Depression, the project was again postponed, this time for several more years. In 1936, Judge Maris corresponded with Senator Guffey in an effort to halt the demolition of the old courthouse and to urge the construction of an annex across the street from Independence Hall on Chestnut Street between Fifth and Sixth Streets. The Senator replied that it was now too late.[22]

Finally, in September 1937, the Treasury Department wrote to Judge Dickinson, the senior active judge, "It is contemplated to begin demolition of the present Post Office and Court House building, Philadelphia, Pennsylvania, on or about December 1, 1937. It will, therefore, be necessary to vacate the building prior to that date."[23] The Court, as a result of this directive, moved to temporary quarters in the Custom House at Second and Chestnut Streets where it remained for over two years.

By this time, the Court also had another venue. In 1930, Congress authorized it to sit in Easton in Northampton County, the home county of Judge Kirkpatrick.[24]

The 1884 Courthouse and Post Office on Ninth Street was demolished in the winter of 1937-1938. The sculpture of "Law, Prosperity, and Power" adorning the edifice was saved from the wrecker's ball and was moved to George's Hill in Fairmount Park where it can be seen today. A new courthouse arose, built as one of the New

Deal's Public Works Projects. It was designed in the Art-Moderne style, with extensive use of pink marble in the interior and an exterior of limestone and granite ornamented with two large rectangular bas-relief sculptures symbolizing justice on both the Market and Chestnut Street sides of the building.[25] On the Ninth Street facade were placed bas-relief medallions representing the seals of the first thirteen states to ratify the Constitution, together with two inscriptions carved in the stone: "The Law is the last result of human wisdom acting upon human experience for the benefit of the public" from Samuel Johnson[26] and "And if a man also strive for masteries, yet is he not crowned, except he strive lawfully" from the Bible.[27] Gone were the fireplaces of the old courthouse, but now air-conditioning would permeate the building.

The post office again occupied the ground floor as in the old courthouse. Above the post office were both the District Court and the Court of Appeals for the Third Circuit. The new courthouse contained twelve judicial chambers on the second floor with six handsome wood-paneled courtrooms with high ceilings and a law library. Although the building was originally planned for ten stories, it was constructed with only six because of a shortage of funds.

The post office part of the building opened in late 1939, and the Court moved into its new quarters on May 6, 1940 with a special en-banc session presided over by Judges Kirkpatrick, Welsh, Kalodner, and Bard.[28] Also housed there were the Internal Revenue Service, the FBI, Postal Inspectors, Bankruptcy referees, the United States Attorney's Office, and the District's United States Marshal and his staff.[29] The new courthouse was soon bustling with activity, and in the long hall outside the courtrooms on the second floor a pall of smoke could be seen from the lawyers gathered during a recess for conversation and a quick cigarette.[30] The designation of courthouses as smoke-free was an idea whose time had not yet come.

Before the new courthouse was erected, the United States went off the gold standard. In 1934, during the Depression, the use of gold as legal tender ended, and the Secretary of the Treasury was authorized to prescribe by regulations the conditions under which persons could hold or acquire this precious metal. Failure to comply subjected persons to monetary penalties including forfeiture. One such action was *United States v. 98 $20 United States Gold Coins.*[31] Government agents seized gold coins from Israel Switt as he was boarding a train from Philadelphia to Baltimore to meet a dealer in gold with whom he had previously done business. Judge Maris found that Switt had been required to deliver the coins to the Federal Reserve Bank for the account of the United States. Because of his failure to do so, the coins were declared forfeited to the Government.[32] Interestingly, many years later in 2006, Switt's name surfaced posthumously in a lawsuit in this Court. His descendants sought to recover ten 1933 Double Eagle $20 gold coins which the Government had seized and which they claimed had properly belonged to Switt and his wife.[33]

The Court, in the 1930's, had on its docket cases involving business insolvencies and bankruptcy reorganizations. Judge Kalodner presided over the reorganization of the Philadelphia and Reading Coal & Iron Company with assets having a book value of $94,219,000.[34] Judge Maris decided an action brought by the Trustees of the General Assembly of the Presbyterian Church as a general creditor of Northwestern National Bank in Philadelphia which had become insolvent and was under a conservatorship.[35]

Matters related to organized labor were beginning to appear in the District Court in the late 1930's and early 1940's. In *Heintz Mfg. Co. v. Local No. 515 of the United Automobile Workers*,[36] the company sought an injunction to limit picketing at its plant during a strike. It claimed that the Mayor of Philadelphia had refused to order the police to impose any limits and that the large number of picketers was intimidating those employees who wanted to enter the plant to work. Judge Kirkpatrick recognized that his power to enter such an injunction was circumscribed by the recently enacted Norris-La Guardia Act. It prohibited a federal court from issuing such an injunction in a labor matter unless the local authorities were unable or unwilling to provide adequate protection to persons and property. He found after a hearing that the police were preserving order, protecting property, and allowing all who wanted to work to do so. The injunction was denied.

The 1930's and 1940's were the era of the radio, which provided information and entertainment for countless listeners. It is not surprising that the use of this medium became the subject of lawsuits. In a case in front of Judge Bard, the National Association of Performing Artists sued the William Penn Broadcasting Co. and its program advertisers for broadcasting phonograph records of Fred Waring and others without the consent of the performers. While Judge Bard agreed that the station may be restrained if a notice of restriction was placed on the record, he concluded that the advertisers were improper defendants since they had no role in determining what records were to be played.[37]

In addition to legal actions concerning new technologies, the court continued to grapple with the age-old questions involving the rights of minorities and unpopular causes. In late 1937, as fascism and communism were on the ascent in parts of Europe, a very significant case came before the District Court. It involved the requirement that public school children salute the flag. Walter Gobitis, a Jehovah's Witness, filed suit on behalf of himself and his two children who had been expelled from the Minersville Public School in Schuylkill County after refusing as a matter of religious conscience to participate in this daily exercise mandated by the local School Board. Gobitis asserted that saluting the flag would cause his children to deny the supremacy of God and to bow down to a graven image in violation of the first two of the Ten Commandments set forth in the Twentieth Chapter of the Book of Exodus. Judge Maris denied a motion to dismiss the complaint. In concluding that a cause of action had been stated, he declared, "In these days when religious intolerance is again rearing its ugly head in other parts of the world, it is of the utmost importance that the liberties guaranteed to our citizens by the fundamental law be preserved from all encroachment."[38]

Judge Maris thereafter granted an injunction compelling school officials to readmit the Gobitis children. He ruled that the students' freedom of religion under the Fourteenth Amendment to the Constitution had been violated. While he conceded that he found "it difficult to understand the plaintiffs' point of view," he explained:

> Upon such a foundation of religious freedom our Commonwealth and Nation were built. We need only glance at the current world scene to realize that the preservation of individual liberty is more important today than ever it was in the past. The safety of our nation largely depends upon the extent to which we foster in each individual citizen that sturdy independence of thought and action which is essential in a democracy. The loyalty of our people is to be judged not so much by their words as by the part they play in the body politic. Our country's safety surely does not depend upon the totalitarian idea of forcing all citizens into one common mold of thinking and acting or requiring them to render a lip service of loyalty in a manner which conflicts with their sincere religious convictions. Such a doctrine seems to me utterly alien to the genius and spirit of our nation and destructive of that personal liberty of which our flag itself is the symbol.[39]

Although the Court of Appeals affirmed,[40] the Supreme Court, speaking through Justice Felix Frankfurter, reversed over the dissent of Justice Harlan F. Stone.[41] The School District's expulsion of the Gobitis children was sustained. The Supreme Court, which ruled shortly before the United States entered World War II, held that compulsory saluting of the flag did not abridge the freedom of religion under the Constitution and was simply an allowable policy decision made by the School Board to promote patriotism. Within several years, however, the Supreme Court thought better of its decision. It reversed itself in *West Virginia State Board of Education v. Barnette*.[42] Judge Maris, at last, was vindicated.

From time to time, a judge is called upon to decide a case where one of the parties belongs to a reviled political group and the court of public opinion has prejudged the matter. One such case was *Reeve v. Howe*, in front of Judge Welsh in 1940 on the eve of America's entry into World War II.[43] A special investigator of the House Un-American Activities Committee headed by Congressman Martin Dies had conducted a search and seizure at the office of the Communist Party in Philadelphia. Various Communist officials brought suit to quash the warrant obtained from a local magistrate and to recover the records and other property seized. The case aroused intense comment from high public officials and widespread discussion in the press.

Judge Welsh noted he had received hundreds of letters at his chambers. Nonetheless, he made it clear he would not be swayed by the passions of the moment which he said had been stirred up "due to existing world conditions." In his Opinion, he asserted, "It just so happens that the aggrieved parties in this case are apparently very much in the minority in our country. But their rights which they claim were invaded are rights that are sacred to all of us."[44] He found that the affidavit in support of the warrant was defective as without probable cause required by the Fourth Amendment to the Constitution. He emphasized that the right to be free of an unreasonable search and seizure stands upon "a parity today with freedom of religion, of speech, of the press and of assembly as guaranteed by the Bill of Rights."[45] He warned, "Let the seal of judicial approval be placed upon such Constitutional violations and liberty of the person, and liberty of religious and political thought and action will have vanished from our land."[46] In Judge Welsh's obituary in *The New York Times* thirty years later, this decision was remembered.[47]

A court, in times of war, sometimes encounters the clash between Presidential or military authority and the claimed constitutional rights of a citizen, often one who is unpopular. Judge Ganey faced such a challenge during World War II when a naturalized United States citizen, Karl Scherzberg, was excluded by a military order from the Eastern Seaboard, including certain counties of the Eastern District of Pennsylvania, even though he had not committed any act subjecting him to prosecution. The case illustrates contrasting attitudes in America at that time between Japanese-Americans as a group and German-Americans as a group.

Scherzberg sought an injunction to prevent his exclusion. The evidence at the hearing showed that he had been born in Germany, maintained close ties to that country, had traveled there several times as late as 1939, had sent his sons there for education, had purchased a home in Bavaria in the 1930's, cheered the British defeat at Dunkirk, was a known Nazi sympathizer, and had sent contributions to German prisoners of war. While recognizing the cogency of the Government's argument, Judge Ganey granted the injunction requested by Scherzberg on the ground that the exclusion order had no rational basis. By this time, the orders removing those of Japanese ancestry from certain areas of the West coast were in effect. In Judge Ganey's view, the treatment of those American citizens resulted from "all the attendant circumstances which were then existent [sic] on the Pacific Coast by reason of the racial problem there involved."[48] In contrast, with respect to Scherzberg, a person of German ancestry, only an "individual exclusion program" was at issue and "every normal phase of civilian life was being engaged in" on the Eastern Seaboard. According to Judge Ganey, the Government had simply not shown "some immediacy of danger to the welfare of the Country" so as to allow the military to exclude Scherzberg.[49]

The reach of the government during the war seemed to penetrate into every facet of the economic life of the nation. Indeed, the government was even concerned about an adequate supply and the equitable distribution of a type of tobacco known as cigar filler type 41. It obtained an injunction from Judge Kalodner to stop violations of an order of the War Food Administrator related to this product. As part of its decision, the Court declared void certain contracts under which Lancaster County tobacco growers agreed to sell their crop to a cigar company which processed and packaged tobacco.[50]

Other cases which came before the Court during World War II raised issues of citizenship and deportation, trading with the enemy, war contracts, rationing, emergency price controls, and housing. There were also numerous lawsuits involving the draft and the decisions of the Selective Service Boards.

As specifically recognized in the Judiciary Act of 1789, courts must have procedural rules to function. In 1938, the new Federal Rules of Civil Procedure took effect. They dramatically changed the way civil cases would be conducted in the federal courts. Among other modifications, notice pleading replaced the more detailed and technical fact pleading, and pretrial discovery was greatly liberalized. Now, a complaint, the paper which initiates a civil lawsuit, need only contain "a short and plain statement of the action showing that the pleader is entitled to relief."[51] Broader discovery allows each side to obtain relevant information about the case from the other side and from third parties so as to facilitate settlements and to reduce if not eliminate trials by surprise.

Probably the most well-known case in legal history involving a discovery dispute under the new Rules of Civil Procedure arose out of this District. In February 1943, five seamen had drowned when the Tug *J.M. Taylor* capsized in the Delaware River near Philadelphia. The widow of one of those seamen filed a lawsuit, *Hickman v. Taylor*, against the tug's owners for damages under the Jones Act for his wrongful death. During discovery, plaintiff served interrogatories asking whether any statements had been made by members of the crew of the sunken tug. If the answer was in the affirmative, plaintiff sought "exact copies of all such statements if in writing" and "the exact provisions of any … oral statements or reports." The defendants through their counsel, Samuel B. Fortenbaugh, Jr. objected on the ground that the interrogatories called for "privileged matter obtained in preparation for litigation."[52]

Fortenbaugh, as counsel for the tug owner, had interviewed and taken written signed statements from four surviving crew members shortly after the incident. He also had conducted and made memoranda of interviews of other individuals who he believed had relevant information.

Plaintiff moved to compel defendants and attorney Fortenbaugh to produce the requested information when they refused to do so voluntarily. Recognizing the precedent-setting nature of the motion, the entire District Court consisting of Judges Kirkpatrick, Welsh, Kalodner, Bard and Ganey, heard the matter. In July 1945, the Court ordered defendants and Fortenbaugh to produce the written statements and other information requested. Judge Kirkpatrick, writing for the Court, reasoned that:

> The guiding principle is the broad conception of the Rules that discovery of all matters relevant to a suit should be allowed to the fullest extent consistent with the orderly and efficient functioning of the judicial process.[53]

Fortenbaugh and the defendants refused to obey the order on the ground that it went beyond the scope of permissible discovery under the new Federal Rules of Civil Procedure. Accordingly, they were found guilty of contempt and sentenced to jail until they complied. Fortenbaugh immediately filed a Notice of Appeal, and the order to report to jail was held in abeyance.[54] This distinguished member of the Bar would not be wearing prison garb, at least not until the matter was finally resolved.

The Court of Appeals, sitting en banc, reversed. It held that the "memoranda of talks with witnesses, signed statements made by witnesses, the lawyer's recollection of talks with witnesses,"[55] were in effect "work product of the lawyer" and protected from discovery.[56] The Supreme Court, after first denying a petition for a writ of certiorari, reconsidered and accepted the case even though it involved the type of question not ordinarily arousing the curiosity or interest of the justices.[57]

The Court characterized the new discovery rules as "one of the most significant innovations of the Federal Rules of Civil Procedure." Now parties were able "to obtain the fullest possible knowledge of the issues and facts before trial" and "civil trials in the federal courts no longer need be carried on in the dark."[58] While the Court acknowledged that the rules needed to be accorded "a broad and liberal treatment," there were limits. It held that the memoranda and other information sought from Samuel Fortenbaugh did not have to be handed over because no "necessity or justification" had been established under the particular circumstances as the witnesses and their testimony were equally available to the plaintiff. In affirming the Court of Appeals, the Supreme Court concluded:

> When Rule 26 and the other discovery rules were adopted, this Court and the members of the bar in general certainly did not believe or contemplate that all the files and mental processes of lawyers were thereby opened to the free scrutiny of their adversaries. And we refuse to interpret the rules at this time so as to reach so harsh and unwarranted a result.[59]

Many a court and trial lawyer in the Eastern District and elsewhere have cited this case during the course of discovery disputes over attorney work product and have had to wrestle with its meaning and implications.

In April 1945, just as World War II was nearing an end, President Roosevelt died, and Vice-President Harry S. Truman succeeded him. During his time in office, Truman named three judges to this Court plus an additional judge who was initially designated to sit in the Eastern, Middle, and Western Districts of Pennsylvania.

President Truman first selected Frederick Voris Follmer, the eleven-year United States Attorney for the Middle District of Pennsylvania to the newly created "floating" judgeship encompassing all three districts within the borders of the Commonwealth. A native of Northumberland County, he was graduated from Bucknell University and Harvard Law School. In 1955, he opted to sit exclusively in the Middle District where he later served as Chief Judge from 1962 to 1967.

In 1946, President Truman chose James Patrick McGranery to fill the vacancy created by the move of Judge Kalodner to the Court of Appeals. Born in South Philadelphia in 1895, McGranery was an observation pilot in the First World War. He worked his way through Temple Law School and became active in Democratic politics in Philadelphia at a time when the party's fortunes were at a low ebb. He was in private practice until he was elected to Congress from Philadelphia's Second Congressional District as a New Deal Democrat in 1936. He remained a Representative until 1943 when President Roosevelt named him an Assistant Attorney General under Attorney General Francis Biddle, a fellow Philadelphian. McGranery helped to streamline the Department of Justice. In early 1946, President Truman awarded him the Medal of Merit in appreciation for his administration of the Selective Service Act. A few months later, the President elevated him to a federal district judgeship. In 1952, in the last months of his administration, Truman selected him to be the Attorney General.[60] How that appointment came about in a phone call from President Truman to McGranery has been recounted by McGranery's son:

| | |
|---|---|
| Truman: | Jim, I just fired McGrath and I want you to come to Washington to be the Attorney General. |
| McGranery: | Boss [as he always called the President] I am flattered, but it's a big decision and I'll have to take some time and talk to Regina [McGranery's wife] about it. |
| Truman: | I want you to take all the time that you and your wife require, but in 20 minutes I'm announcing that you're my Attorney General![61] |

During McGranery's short tenure as Attorney General, the United States filed an amicus curiae brief in the Supreme Court in support of appellants who sought to overturn the "separate but equal" system of public schools in *Brown v. Board of Education.* [62]

McGranery was an active Roman Catholic layman. For his service to the Church, Pope Pius XII honored him as a Knight Commander of the Order of St. Gregory the Great.[63]

Truman's next opportunity for a court appointment did not come until 1949, when he nominated Thomas J. Clary, who had been active for years in Democratic politics in the 22nd Ward in Philadelphia, to fill a new seat on the Court.[64] Born in Seneca Falls, New York in 1899, he earned his undergraduate degree from Cornell University and his law degree from Georgetown University. Following his defeat in 1941 for a judgeship on the Court of Common Pleas in then Republican-dominated Philadelphia, he worked as an Assistant United States Attorney from 1944 until he resigned in 1947 to run unsuccessfully for Philadelphia District Attorney. Richardson Dilworth, who headed the Democratic ticket that year as his party's candidate for Mayor, was also beaten. Clary was a founder of the Lawyers' Reference Service of the Philadelphia Bar Association.[65] While he was "a very dour looking man with a perpetual frown," he was actually "a very soft guy at heart" who was "a very lenient sentencer."[66] He was "firm, at times rough, but always fair."[67]

His portrait is among those hanging in the Ceremonial Courtroom of the present courthouse. It is distinct from all the others. As he wished, it starkly portrays the loneliness of one who has responsibility for sitting in judgment in a court of law.[68]

President Truman's final appointment was Allan K. Grim, who was born in 1904 in Kutztown, Berks County. He was a graduate of Swarthmore College and Harvard Law School. He practiced law in Reading and chaired the Berks County Democratic Party between 1940 and 1944.[69] Upon being confirmed to the bench, he wrote President Truman, "It has always seemed to me that a district court judgeship is about the finest position to which a lawyer can aspire. Naturally, my feeling of gratitude is very great. I hope that I shall fill the position so well that I will be a credit to you and the Democratic Party."[70]

The Court, as always, had before it the usual array of tort, maritime, commercial and antitrust actions. They concerned a wide variety of subject matter. Judge Bard, in one case, refused to dismiss a complaint for unfair competition by one Philadelphia area bubble gum manufacturer against another. The plaintiff, which produced "Blony" bubble gum, sued a competitor that made gum with the name "Bubly," an allegedly inferior product similar in shape and wrapping to the former. According to the complaint, "At least 6,000,000 children in the United States buy and chew Blony, and for the last few years over 100,000,000 pieces have been sold annually."

Plaintiff contended that school-age children were now being unfairly confused when purchasing their bubble gum.[71]

The case was tried non-jury before Judge Ganey who found for the defendant on the ground that no likelihood existed that the public would confuse the defendant's product with the plaintiff's product. He ruled that the color scheme of the wrapping, the ends of the wrapping, and the printing were sufficiently different so as to deny plaintiff any relief. The Court of Appeals affirmed but on a different ground. It held that even if the products were indistinguishable in appearance, plaintiff had not proven that its Blony bubble gum was associated in the public mind with it as the manufacturer or that defendant had claimed its imitating product as being made by plaintiff.[72] As far as is known, millions of happy children, oblivious of the lawsuit, continued to chew their bubble gum as in the past.

Then there was the case of *Stork Restaurant, Inc. v. Marcus*, in which owners of the Stork Club, the famed New York night club patronized by a variety of celebrities, sued the defendant who ran a "Stork Club" in Philadelphia. Plaintiff claimed trademark infringement and unfair competition. After a trial, Judge Bard entered an injunction restraining the operator of the Philadelphia establishment from using that or any similar name.[73] Those in the city who enjoyed frequenting this restaurant because of its fancy appellation now had to find another place to dine.

During the New Deal, Congress had enacted a wide range of other social, economic, and regulatory legislation, including the Securities Exchange Act of 1934.[74] With its passage, the Court began to see lawsuits alleging misrepresentation and fraud in connection with the sale of securities. In *Kardon v. National Gypsum Co.*,[75] plaintiffs claimed that they had been fraudulently induced to sell stock to two of the defendants for less than its true value. The important question presented was whether § 10(b) of the Act and Rule X-10B-5 which implemented it granted a private cause of action to persons claiming injury. In 1946 Judge Kirkpatrick ruled in the affirmative. This landmark decision was widely cited in the years ahead. Another twenty-five years would pass before the Supreme Court finally settled the issue in *Superintendent of Insurance v. Bankers Life and Casualty Co.*,[76] when it reached the same result as had Judge Kirkpatrick.

Agriculture was and is a major part of the economy in the Eastern District. The soil of Lancaster County is some of the most fertile in the United States. Other counties in the District also contributed extensively to food production. Under the circumstances, farmers sometimes found themselves in court.

In one case, Campbell Soup Company, a leading producer of canned soups located in Camden, New Jersey, sued two farmers who grew various crops, including carrots, on their farm in Upper Dublin Township, Montgomery County. Campbell alleged that the farmers had agreed to sell it all "the Chantenay red cored type" carrots that grew on fifteen acres of their land. Instead, according to Campbell, defendants had sold sixty-two tons of these carrots to a third defendant and held the remainder of their crop in storage. Campbell sought a preliminary injunction from Judge Bard to enjoin defendants from delivering such carrots to anyone but it and to order defendants to turn over all such carrots in their possession. The record established that this variety of carrot was an ingredient in fifteen of the twenty-one soups then manufactured by Campbell and had a special blunt shape making it easier to process than other varieties.

After hearing much about carrots and the production of soups, Judge Bard, who was from rural Lancaster County, conditionally denied the preliminary injunction. The Court of Appeals affirmed. It recited the harsh contractual terms Campbell had imposed on the farmers and concluded "that a party who has offered and succeeded in getting an agreement as tough as this one is, should not come to a chancellor and ask court help in the enforcement of its terms."[77]

Several years after the lawsuit about the carrots had been resolved, Judge Welsh, who was born on a farm, had to decide a similar matter involving tomatoes. Campbell Soup again sued a number of farmers who in this case allegedly breached their contracts to sell it tomatoes for canning at fixed prices. Campbell had the capacity to process 250,000 5/8 bushels of tomatoes a day and had a "carefully devised schedule" for receipt of "a steady flow" of "highly perishable" tomatoes during the seven to eight week canning season. To facilitate crop production, Campbell sold the farmers special varieties of tomato plants "most suitable for its canning purposes" and provided free soil analysis and technical advice to farmers who entered contracts with it. Sales of its tomato products to consumers amounted to millions of dollars each year.

Judge Welsh found that defendant farmers had exclusive contracts with Campbell but instead were selling their tomatoes to other buyers in violation of their agreements. In contrast to the case involving the carrots, Judge Welsh determined the contracts here were fair and beneficial to both sides. Because Campbell was suffering irreparable harm and had no adequate remedy at law, he entered a permanent injunction requiring defendants to honor their promises.[78]

Cases involving the draft and the Selective Service Act continued to appear on the Court's docket after the close of World War II. One such action evidenced the early stirring of the civil rights movement in Philadelphia. In 1948, DeVreaux Tomlinson, an African-American, refused to present himself for a physical examination after being directed to do so by his draft board. Thereafter, he was ordered to appear for induction and again refused to comply. He was part of a group of 692 African-Americans and White Americans who had collectively advised the Secretary of Defense and all the Philadelphia Draft Boards that they would not report for induction if they were assigned to segregated military installations. Tomlinson's draft board advised him that it had no jurisdiction over his duty station after he was inducted.

Tomlinson was indicted and found guilty by a jury for failing to appear for induction. In his post-trial motions, he contended that the notice of induction violated his constitutional rights to due process and equal protection. Judge Clary denied the motions.[79] He explained that the draft board had no control over where and under what conditions an inductee serves in the military and that it would be mere speculation for the Court to make any such determination. At this juncture, the issue of discrimination was hypothetical. Judge Clary cited the well-established principle that courts will determine constitutional questions "only on specific and concrete problems presented in the facts of a particular case."[80]

In the background was President Truman's Executive Order to desegregate the military which was still in the process of implementation when the Tomlinson trial took place in January 1950. Although Judge Clary did not mention the Order, Truman had issued it shortly before the November 1948 election. It provided: "There will be equality of treatment and opportunity for all persons in the armed forces." The President directed it to be "put into effect as rapidly as possible, having due regard to the time required to effectuate any necessary changes without impairing efficiency or morale."[81] By 1951, segregation in this sphere of American life had virtually disappeared.[82]

It was at this point that Tomlinson appeared before Judge Clary for sentencing. On January 18, 1951, shortly after filing his opinion denying Tomlinson's post-trial motions, Judge Clary suspended imposition of sentence and placed him on probation "to terminate upon [his] induction into the Armed Forces of the United States."[83] Tomlinson apparently was now prepared to serve as separation of the races in the military had become a thing of the past.

While still on the District Court bench, Judge McGranery confronted an unusual situation in a criminal case before him. Edward Turner, who had been indicted for sending obscene materials through the mails, had engaged Philadelphia Congressman Earl Chudoff as his attorney. Chudoff announced to Judge McGranery that his client would ask to plead not guilty "temporarily" while he, Chudoff, discussed the matter with the Postal Inspectors and the United States Attorney's Office. Judge McGranery chided Chudoff, "Don't you know that in your position as a Congressman you are not permitted to do that?" Chudoff replied that he did not know that. The judge refused to take the plea. According to the judge, himself a former Congressman, it was a criminal offense for a Representative to discuss with any agency of the United States a matter for which he was being separately compensated.[84] Chudoff countered by petitioning the Court of Appeals for a writ of mandamus or in the alternative for a writ of prohibition to permit him to appear and represent Turner.

In the meantime, while the matter was pending in the appellate court, Turner, represented by Chudoff, entered a plea of guilty before Judge Welsh, also a former

Congressman. The Court of Appeals thereupon dismissed the petition as moot without ruling on the merits.[85] History does not record Judge McGranery's reaction to this turn of events.[86]

The 1930's and 1940's saw an increase in the workload and complexity of cases before the District Court. Up until this time, judges researched and wrote their own opinions without the aid of law clerks. In 1922, this began to change when the Congress authorized a law clerk for each Supreme Court justice. It was not until 1936, however, that District Judges were given law clerks but then only if permitted by the senior Circuit Judge of the particular circuit. This benefit was not of widespread value since the number of clerks was limited to thirty-five throughout the country. Finally, in 1945, every District Judge was allowed a law clerk as long as the need was certified by the senior Circuit Judge.[87]

In 1948, as the decade was coming to a close, Congress created the position of Chief Judge for every federal district that had more than one judge.[88] It did so "in view of the great increase of administrative duties" that were being performed informally by the senior District Judge, that is, the judge who was senior in service.[89] The Chief Judge, according to the statute, shall be the judge "senior in commission" and "shall have precedence and preside at any session which he attends."[90]

The Eastern District now had seven authorized judgeships. Other districts had experienced similar increases. Support staff including that of the Clerk's Office was continuing to grow. By the mid-1940's, the Court for the first time was hiring salaried court reporters. It had simply become a necessity that the District Courts become more structured for purposes of administration. Since William Kirkpatrick was the judge senior in commission in 1948, he became the first Chief Judge in the Eastern District of Pennsylvania. He served in that role for ten years, until 1958, when he took senior status.

In the late 1940's, efforts to create racial diversity on the bench were in motion. Raymond Pace Alexander, a prominent Philadelphia lawyer and African-American leader, as well as others were urging President Truman to appoint an African-American to the Eastern District. This goal would not be achieved until the mid-1960's, although President Truman did name William Henry Hastie to the Court of Appeals for the Third Circuit, the first African-American ever selected for a federal appellate judgeship.[91]

## Notes

1. *The Philadelphia Inquirer*, pp. 1, 4 (April 15, 1932). *See also*, *Philadelphia Public Ledger*, pp. 1, 6 (February 17, 1931); Young, John Randolph, *The History of Clark, Ladner, Fortenbaugh and Young, 1903-1983*, p. 11 (Clark, Ladner, Fortenbaugh and Young, 1986); Hinshaw, David to Newton, Walter H., December 7, 1931, Presidential Subject File--Judiciary--Judges--U.S. District Judges, Pennsylvania, Herbert Hoover Papers, Herbert Hoover Presidential Library and Museum, West Branch, Iowa; Mayor Mackey telephone notes, February 13, 1931, Presidential Subject File--Judiciary--Judges--U.S. District Judges, Pennsylvania, Herbert Hoover Papers, Herbert Hoover Presidential Library and Museum, West Branch, Iowa; Rosenwald, Lessing J. to Akerson, George, January 13, 1931; Memo on meeting with Kinter, William, February 20, 1932, Presidential Subject File--Judiciary--Judges--U.S. District Judges, Pennsylvania, Herbert Hoover Papers, Herbert Hoover Presidential Library and Museum, West Branch, Iowa; Attorney General to President Hoover, April 12, 1932, Presidential Subject File--Judiciary--Judges--U.S. District Judges, Pennsylvania, Herbert Hoover Papers, Herbert Hoover Presidential Library and Museum, West Branch, Iowa.
2. Interview by Magistrate Judge Richard A. Powers III with Judge C. William Kraft, p. 31 (Feb. 28, 1995).
3. *The New York Times*, p. 34 (Oct. 24, 1970); *The Philadelphia Inquirer*, p. 12 (Oct. 24, 1970).
4. *The Pennsylvania Manual*, p. 414 (Commw. of Pa., 1935-36).
5. Interview of Judge C. William Kraft by Magistrate Judge Richard A. Powers III, p. 31 (Feb. 28, 1995).
6. Act of June 16, 1936, 74 Pub. L. 689, 49 Stat. 1523. In 1938, this judgeship was made permanent. The District now had four permanent judgeships. Act of June 2, 1938, 52 Stat. 780.
7. *Upper Darby Township Review*, p. 1 (Aug. 8, 1936).
8. *The 69th Street News*, p. 1 (June 25, 1936).
9. Presser, Stephen B., *Studies in the History of the United States Courts of the Third Circuit*, p. 189-91 (Government Printing Office, 1982); *The Pennsylvania Manual*, p. 514 (Commw. of Pa. 1929); Toll, Seymour I., *A Judge Uncommon: A Life of John Biggs, Jr.*, pp. 150-51 (Legal Communications, Ltd., 1993); *The 69th Street News*, p. 1 (June 25, 1936); Sloviter, Dolores K., Brennan, William J., and Pollak, Louis H., "Albert Branson Maris 1893-1989," *Temple Law Review*, Vol. 62, pp. 471-79 (Summer 1989).
10. Toll, Seymour I., *A Judge Uncommon: A Life of John Biggs*, Jr., p. 151 (Legal Communications, Ltd., 1993).
11. "Presentation of the Edward J. Devitt Distinguished Service to Justice Award to Honorable Albert Maris," 699 F.2d at p. LXV (Mar. 23, 1983); Presser, Stephen B., *Studies in the History of the United States Courts of the Third Circuit*, p. 190 (Government Printing Office, 1982).
12. *The Evening Bulletin*, p. 37 (March 16, 1977).
13. *Id.*
14. Presser, Stephen B., *Studies in the History of the United States Courts of the Third Circuit*, p. 192, 246 (Government Printing Office, 1982); Toll, Seymour I., *A Judge Uncommon: A Life of John Biggs, Jr.*, p. 153 (Legal Communications, Ltd., 1993); "Judge Harry E. Kalodner," *The Shingle*, Vol. IX, pp. 155-57 (Philadelphia Bar Ass'n, Oct. 1946).
15. *The Evening Bulletin*, September 19, 1939, December 20, 1939; *Philadelphia Record*, December 21, 1939; *Philadelphia Record*, April 25, 1940; *Penn Gazette*, January 1944, Guy Kurtz Bard Clipping File, Archives of the University of Pennsylvania; Guy K. Bard to President Franklin D. Roosevelt, April 8, 1937, President's Official File 400 "Appointments-Pennsylvania," Franklin D. Roosevelt Presidential Library and Archives, Hyde Park, New York.
16. Canon 5 which is entitled "A Judge Should Refrain from Political Activity" provides in relevant part, "Resignation upon Candidacy. A judge should resign the judicial office if the judge becomes a candidate in a primary or general election for any office." Code of Conduct for United States Judges (July 2009).
17. Presser, Stephen B., *Studies in the History of the United States Courts of the Third Circuit*, p. 246

(Government Printing Office, 1982); *The Pennsylvania Manual*, Vol. 91, pp. 96, 105 (Commw. of Pa. 1954); Biography supplied by the Federal Judicial Center.

18. Congress created another temporary judgeship by Act of May 24, 1940, 76 Pub. L. 521, 54 Stat. 219. It was made permanent by Act of Dec. 7, 1944, 78 Pub. L. 467, 58 Stat. 796.
19. McDevitt, Vincent P., "J. Cullen Ganey, J., A Study in Judicial Temperament," *The Shingle*, pp. 150-51 (October 1961); Interview by Magistrate Judge Richard A. Powers III Judge C. William Kraft, p. 34 (Feb. 28, 1995).
20. Interview by Magistrate Judge Richard A. Powers III with Judge C. William Kraft, p. 34 (Feb. 28, 1995).
21. *The Evening Bulletin*, February 27 and December 18, 1931, September 12, November 22, December 16, 27, 28, 1932; January 17, 20, 26, and February 2, 1933; Peter Graham Fish, *The Politics of Federal Judicial Administration* (Princeton University Press, 1973), 213, 232.
22. Letter from Judge Albert B. Maris to Senator Joseph Guffey, dated December 3, 1936; letter from Senator Joseph Guffey to Judge Albert B. Maris, dated December 17, 1936; U.S. Courthouse, Ninth and Market Street Folder, Courthouse Facilities, Box 32, Honorable Albert B. Maris Collection, Third Circuit Court Library, Philadelphia, Pennsylvania.
23. Letter from J.V. Dreisonstok, Chief Section of Space Control of the Treasury Department, Procurement Division, to The Hon. Oliver B. Dickinson, Senior Judge, U.S. District Court, dated Sept. 18, 1937.
24. Act of June 27, 1930, ch. 634, Pub. L. No. 71-448, 46 Stat. 820; Surrency, Erwin C., "Federal District Judges and the History of their Courts," 40 F.R.D. 139, 274 (1967).
25. National Register of Historic Places, U.S. Dept. of the Interior, National Park Service.
26. *Mrs. Piozzi*, Anecdotes of Samuel Johnson (1786).
27. II Timothy 2:5.
28. *Philadelphia Record*, p. 2 (May 7, 1940).
29. *Id.*
30. Toll, Seymour I., "Lawyers' Philadelphia," *The Shingle*, pp. 9, 24 (January-February 1976).
31. 20 F. Supp. 354 (E.D. Pa. 1937).
32. *Id.* at 355.
33. *Langbord v. United States Department of the Treasury*, No. 06-5315 (E.D. Pa. filed Dec. 5, 2006).
34. *In re Phila. & Reading Coal & Iron Co.*, 27 F. Supp. 256 (E.D. Pa. 1939).
35. *Trustees of Gen. Assembly of Presbyterian Church v. Ward*, 22 F. Supp. 579 (E.D. Pa. 1938).
36. 20 F. Supp. 116 (E.D. Pa. 1937).
37. *Nat'l Ass'n of Performing Artists v. Wm. Penn Broadcasting Co.*, 38 F. Supp. 531 (E.D. Pa. 1941).
38. *Gobitis v. Minersville Sch. Dist.*, 21 F. Supp. 581, 586 (E.D. Pa. 1937).
39. *Gobitis v. Minersville Sch. Dist.*, 24 F. Supp. 271, 274 (E.D. Pa. 1938).
40. 108 F.2d 683 (3d Cir. 1939).
41. 310 U.S. 586 (1940).
42. 319 U.S. 624 (1943).
43. 33 F. Supp. 619 (E.D. Pa. 1940).
44. *Id.* at 621.
45. *Id.* at 623.
46. *Id.* at 624.
47. *The New York Times*, p. 34 (Oct. 24, 1970).
48. *Scherzberg v. Maderia*, 57 F. Supp. 42, 47 (E.D. Pa. 1944).
49. *Id.*
50. *United States v. Gen. Cigar Co.*, 58 F. Supp. 620 (E.D. Pa. 1945).
51. Rule 8(a)(2) of the Federal Rules of Civil Procedure.

52. *Hickman v. Taylor*, 4 F.R.D. 479, 480 (E.D. Pa. 1945).
53. *Id.* at 481.
54. *See* Docket of *Hickman v. Taylor*, Civil Action No. 3511, in the United States District Court for the Eastern District of Pennsylvania.
55. *Hickman v. Taylor*, 153 F.2d 212, 223 (3d Cir. 1945).
56. *Id.*
57. *Hickman v. Taylor*, 327 U.S. 808 (1946); *Hickman v. Taylor*, 328 U.S. 876 (1946).
58. *Hickman v. Taylor*, 329 U.S. 495, 500-01 (1947).
59. *Id.* at 514.
60. "Hon. James P. McGranery," *The Shingle*, pp. 203-04 (December 1946; Bolger, Robert V., "The Honorable Patrick McGranery," *The Shingle*, pp. 180-83 (October 1952).
61. Stiles, Michael R. (United States Attorney), "James P. McGranery," Remarks at the Eleventh Meeting of the Historical Society of the United States District Court for the Eastern District of Pennsylvania, p. 21 (May 15, 1995); "Hon. James P. McGranery," *The Shingle*, pp. 203-04 (December 1946; Bolger, Robert V., "The Honorable Patrick McGranery," *The Shingle*, pp. 180-83 (October 1952).
62. See 1952 WL 82045 (Dec. 2, 1952).
63. Bolger, Robert V., "The Honorable James P. McGranery," *The Shingle*, pp. 180, 182-83 (October 1952).
64. By Act of August 3, 1949, two additional permanent judgeships were added to the Eastern District. Act of Aug. 3, 1949, ch. 387, Pub. L. No. 81-205, 63 Stat. 493.
65. *The Philadelphia Inquirer*, p. 8A (Aug. 2, 1977); Lord, Jos. S. III, "Hon. Thomas J. Clary," *The Shingle*, p. 114, (Philadelphia Bar Ass'n, June 1969).
66. Recollection of Judge Joseph Lord, "Symposium on the Electrical Equipment Antitrust Cases," p. 18 (Oct. 15, 1987).
67. Lord, Jos. S. III, "Hon. Thomas J. Clary," *The Shingle*, p. 116 (Philadelphia Bar Ass'n, June 1969).
68. Recollection of Michael E. Kunz, Clerk of Court.
69. Records of Federal Judicial Center.
70. Grim, Allan K. to President Truman, Oct. 24, 1949 (208-M Eastern District File, Harry S. Truman Presidential Library and Archives, Independence, Missouri).
71. *Gum, Inc. v. Gumakers of Am., Inc.*, 1 F.R.D. 586 (E.D. Pa. 1941).
72. Unpublished Opinion and Order by Judge Ganey, Civil Action No. 1186 (E.D. Pa. May 14, 1942), *aff'd* 136 F.2d 957 (3d Cir. 1943).
73. 36 F. Supp. 90 (E.D. Pa. 1941).
74. 15 U.S.C. § 78a *et seq.*
75. 69 F. Supp. 512 (E.D. Pa. 1946).
76. 404 U.S. 6 (1971).
77. *Campbell Soup Co. v. Wentz*, 75 F. Supp. 952 (E.D. Pa. 1948), *aff'd* 172 F.2d 80, 83 (3d Cir. 1948).
78. *Campbell Soup Co. v. Diehm*, 111 F. Supp. 211 (E.D. Pa. 1952).
79. *United States v. Tomlinson*, 94 F. Supp. 854 (E.D. Pa. 1950).
80. *Id.* at 859
81. Exec. Order No. 9981, 3C.F.R. 722 (1943-1948).
82. Goldman, Eric F., *The Crucial Decade*, pp. 182-86 (Alfred A. Knopf, 1956).
83. *See* Docket of *United States v. Tomlinson*, Criminal Action No. 15385.
84. Title 18 U.S.C. § 281, which has since been repealed, provided in relevant part:

    Whoever, being a Member of ... Congress, ... directly or indirectly receives or agrees to receive, any compensation for any services rendered or to be rendered, either by himself or another, in relation to any proceeding, contract, claim, controversy, charge, accusation, arrest, or other matter in which the United States is a party or directly or indirectly interested, before any department, agency, court martial, officer, or any civil, military, or naval commission, shall be fined not more than $10,000 or imprisoned not more than two years, or both; and shall be incapable of holding any office of honor, trust, or profit under the United States.

85. *Chudoff v. McGranery*, 179 F.2d 869 (3d Cir. 1950).

86. In 1958, Chudoff was to become a judge of the Court of Common Pleas of Philadelphia County.

87. Surrency, Erwin C., *History of the Federal Courts*, Second Ed., pp. 537-38 (Oceana Publications, Inc., 2002).

88. 28 U.S.C. § 136.

89. *Id.*

90. *Id.*

91. Raymond Pace Alexander to Judge James P. McGranery, July 14, 1949, Judge Files 1946-1952, Box 42, James P. McGranery Papers, Library of Congress, Washington, D.C.; Raymond Pace Alexander to David Niles, Sept. 2, 1949, 208-M Eastern District File, Harry S. Truman Presidential Library and Archives, Independence, Missouri; Rep. William A. Barrett to Pres. Harry S. Truman, Aug. 24, 1949, 208-M Eastern District End. Misc. File, Harry S. Truman Presidential Library and Archives, Independence, Missouri; L.B. Schachter to John R. Steelman, Aug. 12, 1949, 208-M Eastern District File, Harry S. Truman Presidential Library and Archives, Independence, Missouri. Goldman, Sheldon, *Picking Federal Judges: Lower Court Selection from Roosevelt through Reagan*, pp. 100-01 (Yale University Press, 1997). In 1959, Alexander would become the first African-American to serve as a judge on the Court of Common Pleas of Philadelphia County.

# VI
# Prosperity and The Cold War: The 1950's

The decade of the 1950's, while a time of widespread prosperity, was also the period of the Cold War, when serious tensions existed between the United States and its Communist rivals, the Soviet Union and Red China. Fresh on everyone's mind was the fact that the Soviets had successfully exploded an atomic bomb in 1949. Senator Joseph McCarthy of Wisconsin was at the peak of his power inveighing against Communists and fellow travelers in the Government and elsewhere. School children throughout the country were engaged in practice drills of hiding under their desks to avoid danger from a foreign attack. The effects of the Cold War reverberated in this Court as they did elsewhere.

During this era, significant strides were also being made in civil rights with the critical assistance of the federal courts. In May 1954, a unanimous Supreme Court handed down its watershed decision in *Brown v. Board of Education*, which held that segregated public schools were unconstitutional under the Equal Protection Clause of the Fourteenth Amendment.[1] The next year it ordered the plaintiff students to be admitted to schools "on a racially nondiscriminatory basis" with "all deliberate speed."[2] As it turned out, "with all deliberate speed" was more deliberate than speedy. In the decades ahead, the District Court would become immersed with civil rights cases.

The presence of a home television, albeit with a black and white picture, was becoming more and more common. The interstate highway system was also being planned and constructed which resulted in increased and faster travel by automobile and truck.

In January 1953, Dwight D. Eisenhower, the victorious World War II General, became the first Republican President in twenty years and held office for two terms. The appointment of a number of Republican judges to the Eastern District was on the horizon.

President Eisenhower's first nomination came about in 1954 when he selected John Whitaker Lord, Jr., to fill the seat previously held by Judge McGranery, who had resigned in 1952 to become President Truman's Attorney General. Lord was supported by Senator Edward Martin,[3] who had recently won re-election by defeating Guy Bard. In less than two months after his name was submitted to the Senate, Lord was confirmed and sitting as a judge. He was an extremely affable individual and during his years on the bench was well-known for his accommodation of lawyers.

Born in 1901 and a native of the Germantown section of Philadelphia, Lord was graduated from Temple Law School in 1928. Thereafter he became a partner at what is now known as White & Williams and taught part-time at his alma mater. He was also active in Republican politics. For a number of years, he held the position of Deputy State Attorney General. He won election as a state senator from the Northwest section of Philadelphia in 1946 but was unsuccessful in his bid for a second term in 1950 as the city was becoming increasingly more Democratic.

In the spring of 1951, the voters of Philadelphia adopted a new Home Rule Charter which guaranteed two of the seven at-large seats on City Council to the minority party. Lord was elected in the fall as one of the two Republican councilmen-at-large as the reformed Democratic ticket was being swept in office. Joseph S. Clark became the first Democratic mayor in sixty-seven years, and Richardson Dilworth won as the District Attorney. Throughout his political career, Lord was greatly aided by his dynamic wife Lilias who was a leader in Republican women's circles and whose trademark was her large hats.

At the same time as John Lord was nominated, President Eisenhower chose Francis Lund Van Dusen of Montgomery County, a Republican, to succeed Judge Bard, who as previously noted had resigned in 1952 to run for the United States Senate.[4] Van Dusen came from a family of prominent attorneys. His father Lewis H. Van Dusen had presided as the President Judge of the Orphans' Court of Philadelphia County, and his brother Lewis was a leading lawyer in the City who served a year as Chancellor of the Philadelphia Bar Association. After Francis Van Dusen was graduated from Princeton University and Harvard Law School, he practiced law in Philadelphia before heading to Washington to work for a variety of war-related boards. During World War II, he became a naval officer. He had returned to his law firm, then known as Barnes, Dechert, Price, Myers, and Rhoads, when he was nominated for the District Court.[5]

Van Dusen's confirmation did not move nearly as quickly or easily as that of John Lord. In fact, it was delayed until mid-1955, more than a year after he was first nominated. While Van Dusen's chief backers were Congressman Hugh Scott of Philadelphia and the American Bar Association, initially he did not have the endorsement of Lloyd Wood, the Montgomery County Republican Chairman and former Lieutenant Governor, or more importantly, the critical support of Senator Martin and Senator James Duff. Not until Martin finally withdrew his opposition was Van Dusen confirmed.[6]

Eisenhower's third appointment went to C. William Kraft, Jr., of Delaware County to fill a new judgeship Congress had created for the Eastern District.[7] He was given a recess appointment in August 1955 and was confirmed in March 1956.

Kraft was born in the Brewerytown neighborhood of Philadelphia in 1903, but his family moved to Delaware County when he was five. He received both his undergraduate and law degrees from the University of Pennsylvania. His leadership ability and political skills developed early in life. At the age of seventeen, when he held a summer job as a marble setter's helper, he was elected vice president of his Union. At the age of twenty-one, having already become involved in Republican politics, he was elected a councilman in the Borough of Clifton Heights where he served two terms.[8]

Kraft was engaged for ten years as an Assistant District Attorney. He moved on to higher office as Delaware County's District Attorney from 1944 to 1952 and then returned to full time private practice.[9] Senator Duff recommended him to President Eisenhower for the position of United States Attorney when the President first took office. Upon consulting with Gerald Gleeson, a former United States Attorney, Kraft decided he would not enjoy having to deal with the bureaucrats in Washington. He also had misgivings about the pay cut he would suffer if he left his law practice. Consequently, he declined the offer.[10]

Several years later, he was approached about accepting a federal judgeship. He agreed to do so only after a candidate supported by Senator Martin and a different candidate supported by Senator Duff both failed to make it through the evaluation process and after being assured that Congress was about to enact a substantial pay raise for judges.[11]

Once on the bench, he and Judge Van Dusen, with the approval of Chief Judge Kirkpatrick, totally revised the Court's local rules which had not been updated since 1913.[12] Judge Kraft also had strong views about opinion writing. In an interview long after he had retired, he reiterated the importance of "very short, well-reasoned opinions," and stressed "the shortness thereof I would commend to the attention of many of the judiciary today whose inclination toward verbosity seems at times to be getting a bit out of hand."[13] By common consent, he was considered one of the best trial judges ever to sit on the Court.

In 1961, *Fortune* magazine carried an article entitled "The Crisis in the Courts."[14] It painted a gloomy picture primarily of state courts because of their large backlog of untried civil cases, their lack of innovation, and their judges who were the product of machine politics and not merit selection. It also mentioned one federal court (not the Eastern District) which had had a huge backlog until decisive action was taken by an out-of-district judge appointed to deal with the situation. Yet, the article noted signs for optimism. It singled out six federal and six state judges for praise, calling them "a Blue-ribbon jury of American judges." Included in this illustrious group was Judge Kraft about whom it was stated, "C. William Kraft, fifty-seven, ex-district attorney, rated a political appointee in 1955, has won the Philadelphia bar's respect for cutting through complex cases."[15]

In 1957 after Judge Welsh took senior status, President Eisenhower chose Thomas C. Egan of Philadelphia, a stalwart organization Republican, to take his place. He was easily confirmed. Born in Shenandoah, Schuylkill County in 1894, he was graduated from Georgetown University in 1917 and thereafter from the University of Pennsylvania Law School. In between, he served in the Army during World War I. Governor Gifford Pinchot appointed him to the Pennsylvania Public Service Commission in 1934, and Governor John Fine named him to its successor, the Public Utility Commission, in 1953. He also was a member and later Chairman of the Philadelphia Gas Commission. In July 1961, Egan collapsed with a stroke in the courtroom as he was leaving the bench after imposing a sentence on a conscientious objector who had refused alternative service. He died hours later after less than four years as a federal judge.[16]

Eisenhower's final nominee was Harold K. Wood of Chester County who succeeded Chief Judge Kirkpatrick when he became a senior judge. After obtaining his undergraduate degree from Colgate University, he came to Philadelphia to attend the University of Pennsylvania Law School. He then worked as an Assistant District Attorney in Chester County and as legal counsel for the Selective Service System during World War II. Subsequently, he was in private practice until the President named him as the United States Attorney for the Eastern District of Pennsylvania in 1957. He moved from that post to his federal judgeship in 1959.[17]

The Eastern District faced several high profile cases in the 1950's against the backdrop of the Cold War. One such case, involving Harry Gold, played out not only here but also in the Southern District of New York. Gold was born in Switzerland but grew up in a poor working class home in Philadelphia. After his graduation from South Philadelphia High School, he attended the University of Pennsylvania for several semesters and then took night courses in chemistry at Drexel Institute of Technology. He was employed at one point as a laboratory chemist for a local sugar company and later as a biochemist at the Philadelphia General Hospital.[18] In 1935, he was recruited into a Soviet front company for industrial espionage and later became part of the Soviet's atomic spy ring for which he was awarded the Red Star medal. As a result of disclosures made by the German-born, British Scientist Klaus Fuchs after his arrest as a Soviet spy, Gold was identified as the courier who carried information to an official at the Soviet embassy.[19]

Gold's arrest in Philadelphia in May 1950 was the top news story that day throughout the United States. A banner headline in *The Philadelphia Inquirer* declared, "Chemist Arrested Here as Atomic Spy, Gave Fuchs' Stolen Secrets to Reds."[20] Thousands later gathered at the courthouse to obtain a brief look at the atomic spy.[21]

Once taken into custody, Gold was totally cooperative with the FBI and implicated Julius and Ethel Rosenberg who were later indicted and convicted in the Southern District of New York of conspiracy to commit espionage for transmitting to the Soviet Union documents related to the national defense of the United States.

They were sentenced to death and executed.[22] Gold was an unindicted co-conspirator in that case.

He also faced his own indictment, which was originally filed in the Eastern District of New York but later transferred to the Eastern District of Pennsylvania. Gold was charged with "conspiring, while the United States was at war, to communicate, deliver or transmit to a foreign government, to wit: The Union of Soviet Socialist Republics, and representatives and agents thereof, documents, writings, etc., relating to the national defense, with intent or reason to believe that it was to be used to the advantage of a foreign nation."[23] The case was assigned to Judge James McGranery.

Gold, who was without economic resources, requested Judge McGranery to appoint an attorney to represent him. Those were the days before an impecunious criminal defendant had a constitutional right to have court-appointed counsel. Recognizing the gravity of the matter, the judge called on John D.M. Hamilton, a distinguished member of the Philadelphia Bar, to serve as Gold's attorney. Hamilton agreed to the representation of this highly unpopular client although many of his law partners at Pepper, Bodine & Stokes were not particularly happy about it.[24] At Hamilton's urging, the judge also named Hamilton's young associate Augustus Ballard to assist him. McGranery issued a statement about his appointment of counsel:

> Because of the gravity of the charge and its possible far reaching international implications, it behooves the court to appoint a lawyer whose patriotism would be above reproach, who has public confidence and the respect of the Court, and a deep understanding of the Anglo-Saxon principles as stated in our Constitution of every defendant having the right to be represented by counsel of his choice. With all these factors in mind, the Court could think of no one at the Philadelphia bar who more fittingly fits into that description than Mr. John D. M. Hamilton, who is a law partner of former Senator George Wharton Pepper, the dean of the Philadelphia bar. Mr. Hamilton has consulted with the defendant, Harry Gold, at my invitation and has agreed to accept this appointment of him as official counsel for Gold in the public interest, for which the court is grateful to Mr. Hamilton. Mr. Hamilton has suggested that I name, together with him, Mr. Augustus S. Ballard as associate counsel. Mr. Ballard is a young man at the bar in whom the Court has explicit confidence and I am delighted to name him as associate counsel as Mr. Hamilton has requested.[25]

Hamilton, a native of the Midwest, had been a friend of Governor Alf Landon of Kansas and the Chairman of the Republican National Committee in the mid-

1930's. He had become acquainted with George Wharton Pepper at this time and had later joined his law firm in Philadelphia.[26] While Hamilton and Ballard were prepared to assist Gold in presenting a vigorous defense, he decided to make a full confession and plead guilty. Gold, however, made it clear he would never enter a plea of guilty to any indictment charging him with intending to injure the United States, and he was not charged with any such crime.[27] Assuring himself that Gold had not been coerced and that his confession was voluntary, Judge McGranery accepted his guilty plea in July 1950.[28]

The Government sought a sentencing delay until early in 1951 to allow for additional investigations to occur, but Judge McGranery, after stating he had spoken to FBI Director J. Edgar Hoover about any need for additional time, refused to postpone the matter that long.[29] Whether by accident or design, he scheduled the sentencing for December 7, 1950, the ninth anniversary of the surprise attack at Pearl Harbor. At the hearing, in a packed courtroom at Ninth and Market Streets, United States Attorney Gerald Gleeson described Gold's life as a spy and his role in passing valuable information to the Russians. The FBI agent in charge of the case also testified. Hamilton's turn was next. He made an extensive argument on Gold's behalf which McGranery characterized as "one of the most brilliant" he had ever heard.[30] In response to the Court's inquiry, Gleeson recommended a twenty-five-year sentence as a fit punishment for Gold's nefarious crime. At that point, McGranery announced he wanted to reflect on the matter and would reconvene the hearing on Saturday morning, December 9.[31] Gold himself addressed the Court at that weekend session. He ended his allocution with these words: "I have tried to make the greatest possible amends by disclosing every phase of my espionage activities, by identifying all of the persons involved, and by revealing every last scrap, shred, and particle of evidence."[32] After noting he had considered the "cogent and analytical statement" of Hamilton, Judge McGranery rejected the Government's recommendation for a twenty-five-year sentence and instead imposed a sentence of thirty years "to deter others in the future from the commission of similar offenses."[33]

Gold thereafter testified as a Government witness at the Rosenberg trial in New York and was then incarcerated at the United States Penitentiary at Lewisburg, Pennsylvania, where he was a model prisoner.[34] He was paroled in May 1966, with the help of Hamilton and Ballard after serving fifteen years of his sentence. Ballard was present to meet him at Lewisburg when he was released.[35] Gold died in Philadelphia in 1972 out of the public eye during an unsuccessful heart operation.[36] Neither Hamilton nor Ballard ever received a penny for representing him.[37]

Several years after Gold's plea and sentencing, in the midst of the Cold War and the tirades of Senator McCarthy, a highly publicized trial of nine admitted Communists took place in this Court in *United States v. Kuzma*.[38] The nine were indicted for conspiracy to advocate the overthrow of the Government of the United States by force and violence in violation of the Smith Act. Recognizing the unpopularity of the defendants, the Philadelphia Bar Association, under the leadership of its Chancellor Bernard G. Segal, passed a resolution that it would support any lawyer who agreed to represent them and would strive to educate the public on the "rights and duties of a lawyer in representing any client regardless of the unpopularity of the client or the cause." No lawyer appeared to be persuaded by the resolution by the time defendants pleaded not guilty without the presence of counsel in September 1953 before Judge Grim.[39]

Thereafter, Thomas McBride, an eminent Philadelphia lawyer and later a justice of the Pennsylvania Supreme Court, stepped forward. With the encouragement of Bernard Segal, other lawyers were recruited to represent the defendants, including Joseph S. Lord III, who subsequently was appointed as a District Judge. Again, as in the case of Harry Gold, lawyers were found who acted courageously and in the best tradition of the bar.

Jury selection before Judge Ganey began on March 22, 1954. The trial lasted for seventy-one days, making it the longest criminal jury trial in the Eastern District of Pennsylvania up to that time. Although the defendants conceded they were Communists, they denied that they had committed any acts which constituted a violation of the Smith Act. Carloads of books, pamphlets, and other publications were brought into the courtroom and read to the jury. There were witnesses who testified about the doctrines espoused by Marx, Engels, Lenin, and Stalin. At the end of the trial, the jury returned a verdict of guilty against all nine defendants.[40] On appeal, the Court of Appeals, speaking through Judge Hastie, explained:

> ... a Smith Act conspiracy is proved only if the government can show a conspiracy to teach people to take concrete action toward the violent overthrow of the existing government as soon as possible. .... Moreover, the [Supreme] Court indicates that an individual defendant cannot be convicted of willful and knowing adherence to such a Smith Act conspiracy unless something said by him or communicated to him shows his understanding that, beyond endorsing the idea and objective of violent overthrow of the existing government, particular action to that end is projected and is to be advocated.[41]

The Government conceded on appeal that it had not proven a crime as to two of the nine defendants under this standard, and the Court of Appeals ordered a judgment of acquittal to be entered as to them. It also ordered judgments of acquittal as to two others because of lack of evidence. With respect to the remaining five defendants, the Court denied their motion for judgment of acquittal but granted each of them a new trial. In doing so, it admonished the Government that its evidence must meet the appropriate legal requirements. When the case returned to the District Court, the Government decided not to proceed with any further prosecutions. The story of this long, highly charged criminal proceeding ended in 1957 without any convictions. No further prosecutions of this kind took place in the Eastern District.

In addition to the *Gold* and *Kuzma* cases, the Court had before it an important civil case, *Reynolds v. United States*,[42] with Cold War implications. It involved significant discovery and privilege issues concerning state secrets and ultimately reached the Supreme Court. In October 1948, three civilian contractors were killed in Georgia in the crash of a B-29 bomber which had been in flight to test secret electronic equipment for the military. The widows of the decedents, represented by Charles Biddle of Drinker Biddle & Reath, brought suit in the Eastern District under the Federal Tort Claims Act for negligence on the part of the Government in causing the wrongful deaths of their husbands.[43]

During the discovery phase of the case, plaintiffs sought production of the statements given shortly after the crash by three soldiers who had survived by bailing out of the aircraft, as well as a government report and investigative findings. The Government refused to produce the documents on the ground that the report and findings were privileged and that good cause did not exist for the production of the statements. Rejecting the arguments, Chief Judge Kirkpatrick ordered the documents to be turned over to the plaintiffs.[44]

Shortly thereafter, the Secretary of the Air Force sent the judge a letter in which he stated, "It has been determined that it would not be in the public interest to furnish this report."[45] Based on the letter, the Court ordered reconsideration of the matter. The Secretary then filed a "claim of privilege" explaining his objection "for the reason that the aircraft in question, together with the personnel on board, were engaged in a highly secret mission of the Air Force."[46] The Government, however, offered to produce the surviving witnesses for deposition who would be allowed to refresh their recollection from any statements they had made and testify except as to classified matters.[47]

Not satisfied, Judge Kirkpatrick ordered the Government to provide the documents for his in-camera inspection so that he could determine for himself whether they contained privileged matter. When the Government refused to do so, he ruled that negligence on the part of the Government in causing the deaths of the decedents would be deemed established. He then held a hearing on damages and entered judgment in the amount of $255,000 for the plaintiffs. The Court of Appeals affirmed his rulings on the discovery issues and on the merits.[48]

The Supreme Court granted certiorari and reversed by a vote of 6 to 3. Chief Justice Fred Vinson, writing for the majority, held that the privilege against the disclosure of military secrets had long been established in the law of evidence. While the Court recognized that the "judicial control over the evidence in a case cannot be abdicated to the caprice of executive officers,"[49] it refused to go as far as to allow the judiciary in every case to review the evidence in order to determine if the privilege applied. The high Court took "judicial notice that this is a time of vigorous preparation for national defense," that "air power is one of the most potent weapons in our scheme of defense, and that newly developing electronic devices have greatly enhanced the effective use of air power."[50] When military secrets are at stake as here, even "the most compelling necessity cannot overcome the claim of privilege."[51] Although reversing the District Court and Court of Appeals, the Supreme Court never reviewed the documents in issue to determine if state secrets were really implicated. It simply took the word of the Government.

Ultimately, the plaintiffs settled with the Government for $170,000.[52] As the seminal Supreme Court decision on state secrets, *Reynolds* is invariably cited by the Government in cases where it seeks to withhold information on the ground of national security.

For the families of the decedents in *Reynolds*, the story did not end with the settlements in 1953. Over four decades later, in February 2000, Judy Palya Loether, the daughter of one of the three civilians who had died in the plane crash, learned from an Internet search that the accident report which Charles Biddle had unsuccessfully sought to obtain was now available to the public. After paying the reproduction charge, she received a copy and, as far as she could ascertain, it contained no state secrets but instead evidence of what appeared to be government negligence.[53]

Ms. Loether contacted Drinker Biddle & Reath. Although Charles Biddle had been dead for almost thirty years, the firm agreed to represent her and the descendants of the other two men who had been killed in the plane crash.[54] Their goal was not to overturn the holding of *United States v. Reynolds,* but simply to obtain the $55,000 which represented the difference between what Judge Kirkpatrick had awarded and the amount for which they had settled. In 2002, after much thought and recognizing the uphill battle faced at that late date, Drinker, Biddle & Reath filed a petition for extraordinary relief in the Supreme Court. Petitioners asserted that the Government had submitted a false affidavit and committed fraud on the Court. The Supreme Court denied the petition without explanation in a short order in June 2003.[55]

Not to be deterred, the firm then filed an independent action in the Eastern District seeking to vacate the dismissals entered in 1953. Judge Legrome Davis of this Court denied relief on the ground that plaintiffs had not shown egregious conduct on the part of the Government or a gross miscarriage of justice, particularly in light of the decisions in 1953 to settle.[56] The Court of Appeals affirmed,[57] and in 2006, the Supreme Court denied a petition for a writ of certiorari. Thus, the *Reynolds* case and its progeny finally came to a close over fifty years after the fatal air crash in Georgia during the Cold War.[58]

The issue of civil rights, which had reared its head in the *Tomlinson* case before Judge Clary, was beginning to stir again ever so slightly in the Eastern District of Pennsylvania in the mid-1950's. Three plaintiffs, who were railroad workers, sued their employer, the Atlantic Coast Line Railroad Company, for personal injuries they had suffered as a result of the derailment of one of defendant's trains near Dillon, South Carolina. One plaintiff resided in Chester, Pennsylvania, and two in Washington, D.C. All three were men of color. The railroad moved to transfer the action to the District of South Carolina where the accident had occurred and where, the railroad argued, it would be more convenient to try the case. In July 1954, Judge Kirkpatrick granted the defendant's motion to transfer based on his interpretation of the change-of-venue statute and the relevant facts. The Court of Appeals denied plaintiffs' petition to set aside his order.

The Supreme Court granted certiorari and by a vote of 5 to 3 affirmed Judge Kirkpatrick's decision.[59] While none of the opinions mentioned race, it was clearly the elephant in the kitchen.[60] Plaintiffs' counsel had one sentence in their brief in the Supreme Court which stated the obvious for that time period, "All three of them [plaintiffs] are Negroes ... who prima facie will fare better in Philadelphia than in Florence, South Carolina."[61]

By the 1950's, television was augmenting, if not superseding, radio as the medium for entertainment. At this time, the Government filed an antitrust action in the Eastern District in which it contended that the contract between the National Football League and its teams restricting television broadcasting of certain games was an illegal restraint of trade in violation of § 1 of the Sherman Act. Defendants raised the argument that football was not interstate commerce so as to subject it to the antitrust laws.

Judge Grim decided that even if defendants were correct about the game of football, restrictions on television broadcasting constituted interstate commerce.[62] Quoting a Supreme Court precedent, he wrote, "If it is interstate commerce that feels the pinch, it does not matter how local the operation which applies the squeeze."[63] He further explained that all contracts in restraint of trade are not illegal, only those that unreasonably restrain trade. In the end, Judge Grim, with one exception, threw out all limitations imposed by the National Football League on the televising of games. He left in place only the prohibition against the televising of out-of-territory games into the territory of a team that was playing a game at home at that same time. He explained that that narrow exception protected weaker teams against the simultaneous broadcasting of games of superior teams.[64]

The business of entertainment further occupied the time of the Court. During the 1950's, as had occurred in the 1940's[65] and would continue into the 1960's, there was continual antitrust litigation in this District over control, distribution, and bookings for theatrical productions and movies in theatres in Philadelphia. Goldlawr, Inc., controlled by magnate William Goldman, was in the general theatrical and amusement business including the presentation of legitimate attractions and motion pictures. In 1956 and 1957, it sued a number of entities and individuals alleging conspiracy in restraint of trade. Judge Kraft presided over the cases for more than ten years. While the defendants ultimately conceded that they had maintained monopolistic control of the legitimate theater business at one time, Judge Kraft found, after a non-jury trial, that it had ended years before in 1950. He entered judgment for the defendants.[66]

The Clause of the First Amendment that "Congress shall make no law ... abridging the right of the people ... to petition the Government for a redress of grievances" became the focus of a hard fought antitrust case in this District. The lawsuit pitted the trucking industry against the railroads over the long distance transportation of heavy freight. In *Noerr Motor Freight, Inc. v. Eastern Railroad Presidents Conference*,[67] forty-one truck operators and their trade association instituted litigation in this Court against twenty-four eastern railroads and related entities for conspiracy to restrain trade under the Sherman Act. Their complaint alleged that the railroads had fostered "fraudulently and corruptly" the adoption and retention of laws favorable to the railroads and had engaged in what in effect was a public relations campaign against the trucking industry designed to create public and customer hostility. Included was a charge that the railroads had persuaded the Governor of Pennsylvania to veto a "Fair Truckers Bill" which would have allowed heavier loads on Pennsylvania highways. The case proceeded to trial before Judge Clary without a jury. He found in favor of the truckers and awarded damages and injunctive relief.

The Court of Appeals affirmed, and the Supreme Court then decided to hear the matter on certiorari. It reversed in a unanimous opinion by Justice Hugo Black. First, he explained that any restraint of trade as a result of valid government action cannot be a violation of the Sherman Act. The Court then turned to the right to petition the Government, which it emphasized was one of the freedoms protected by the Bill of Rights. Upon review of the record, it concluded that the railroads had not directly attempted to persuade anyone not to deal with the truckers. Rather, the railroads had simply directed their efforts in a highly successful manner to persuade governmental bodies to retain and pass legislation favorable to them and unfavorable to the truckers even if, as the Court noted, their ethical standards, and those of the truckers, may have left something to be desired. The Court acknowledged that there may be situations where a group's efforts ostensibly to influence governmental action are a sham for interference with private business relationships in violation of the Sherman Act. Nonetheless, that situation had not existed here.

The railroads' win in *Noerr* turned out to be a pyrrhic victory. With the building of the interstate highway system, the truckers were able to compete vigorously in the years ahead. The railroad industry in turn entered a period of decline, which culminated in bankruptcy proceedings in this Court in the 1970's.

There were, of course, countless other cases passing through the courthouse at Ninth and Market Streets in the 1950's which never made the headlines and had no connection with the momentous national and international issues of the day. Personal injury claims, maritime actions, commercial disputes, patent and trademark matters, selective service issues as well as indictments for federal white collar and other crimes were part of everyday life before those judges who sat for all or part of that period: William Kirkpatrick, George Welsh, Guy Bard, Cullen Ganey, James McGranery, Thomas Clary, Allen Grim, John Lord, Francis Van Dusen, William Kraft, Thomas Egan, and Harold Wood.

Up until 1954, judges were not permitted to retire with pay or take senior status before they had reached the age of seventy. Congress in that year allowed them to do so at age sixty-five as long as they had served on the bench for at least fifteen years.[68]

Near the end of the decade, a noteworthy administrative change took place at the Court. In 1958 Chief Judge Kirkpatrick stepped down as the first Chief Judge of the Eastern District of Pennsylvania when Congress passed a statute prohibiting anyone from holding that position upon attaining the age of seventy.[69] Kirkpatrick at that time was seventy-three and had served as the Chief Judge for ten years. J. Cullen Ganey followed him as the Court's second Chief Judge.

## Notes

1. 347 U.S. 483 (1954).
2. 349 U.S. 294, 301 (1955).
3. *The Evening Bulletin*, p. 1 (March 29, 1954).
4. *Id.*
5. Interview by Lewis Van Dusen with Judge Francis L. Van Dusen (May 23, 1996); William C. Tuttle to James C. Hagerty, April 13, 1954, Mrs. Arthur M. Wilson to President Dwight D. Eisenhower, April 15, 1954, Congressman Ivor D. Fenton to Sherman Adams, April 8 and April 29, 1954, General File 4-D Pennsylvania Eastern District, Box 89, Dwight D. Eisenhower Presidential Library, Abilene, Kansas; Gough, Deborah Mathias, *Christ Church, Philadelphia: The Nation's Church in a Changing City*, p. 324 (University of Pennsylvania Press, 1995).
6. *The Evening Bulletin*, p. 1 (March 29, 1954); *The Evening Bulletin*, p. 3 (May 18, 1954); *The Pittsburgh Post-Gazette*, p. 8 (March 4, 1955); *The Philadelphia Inquirer*, p. 2 (July 29, 1955).
7. Interview by Magistrate Judge Richard A. Powers III with Judge C. William Kraft, pp. 23-27 (Feb. 28, 1995).
8. *Id.* at 5, 9-11; *The Philadelphia Inquirer*, p. B4 (Jan. 28, 2002); *Delaware County Daily Times*, p. 1 (Nov. 4, 1970).

9. Interview by Magistrate Judge Richard A. Powers III with Judge C. William Kraft, pp. 12-13 (Feb. 28, 1995).
10. Interview by Magistrate Judge Richard A. Powers with Judge C. William Kraft (Feb. 28, 1995).
11. *Id.* at 20-27, 30.
12. Interview by Lewis H. Van Dusen with Judge Francis L. Van Dusen, pp. 2-5 (May 23, 1996).
13. Interview by Magistrate Judge Richard A. Powers III with Judge C. William Kraft, pp. 68-69 (Feb. 28, 1995).
14. Banks, Louis, "The Crisis in the Courts," *Fortune*, p. 85 ff. (December 1961).
15. *Id.* at 91.
16. *The Reading Eagle*, pp. 1, 10 (July 6, 1961; *The Philadelphia Daily News*, p. 4 (July 6, 1961); Interview by Magistrate Judge Richard A. Powers III with Judge C. William Kraft (Feb. 28, 1995); David F. Maxwell to Sherman Adams, March 8, 1957, General File 4-D, Pennsylvania Eastern District, Endorsements, Egan, Thomas C., Box 89, Dwight D. Eisenhower Presidential Library, Abilene, Kansas; Senator Edward Martin to Sherman Adams, March 18, 1957, General File 4-D, Pennsylvania Eastern District, Endorsements, Egan, Thomas C., Box 89, Dwight D. Eisenhower Presidential Library, Abilene, Kansas; Roundtable Meeting, Jan. 30, 2008.
17. *The Evening Bulletin*, p. 12 (Dec. 18, 1972).
18. Hornblum, Allen M., *The Invisible Harry Gold*, pp. 5-8, 23-27, 37-38 (Yale University Press, 2010).
19. *Time*, Dec. 18, 1950; Williams, Robert Chadwell, *Klaus Fuchs, Atom Spy*, pp. 5, 61, 64, 70-71, 84 (Harvard University Press, 1987); Haynes, John Earl and Klehr, Harvey, *Venona: Decoding Soviet Espionage in America*, pp. 288-90, 298-99, 304-07 (Yale Nota Bene, 2000); J. Edgar Hoover to Judge James P. McGranery, Dec. 11, 1950, FBI-Hoover File, Box 54, James P. McGranery Papers, Library of Congress, Washington, D.C.; Wolfinger, James, *Philadelphia Divided: Race and Politics in the City of Brotherly Love*, pp. 24, 42, 45 (University of North Carolina Press, 2007); *Philadelphia City Paper*, June 19-25, 2003; Romerstein, Herbert and Breindel, Eric, *The Venona Secrets: Exposing Soviet Espionage and America's Traitors*, pp. 158, 226-29 (Regnery Publishers Inc., 2000).
20. Hornblum, Allen M., *The Invisible Harry Gold*, pp. 219-20 (Yale University Press, 2010).
21. *Id.* at p. 240.
22. *United States v. Rosenberg*, 195 F.2d 583 (2d Cir. 1952); Ambrose, Stephen E., *Eisenhower: The President*, pp. 65, 83-85 (Simon and Schuster, 1984).
23. *See* Docket and Indictment in *United States v. Gold*, Criminal No. 15769 (E.D. Pa., filed July 20, 1950).
24. Hornblum, Allen M., *The Invisible Harry Gold*, pp. 228-29 (Yale University Press, 2010).
25. *Id.* at p. 228.
26. Pepper, George Wharton, *Philadelphia Lawyer: An Autobiography*, p. 284 (J.B. Lippincott Co., 1944); Hornblum, Allen M., *The Invisible Harry Gold*, pp. 225-27 (Yale University Press, 2010).
27. *Id.* at pp. 321-22.
28. *See* Transcript of Hearing before Judge James P. McGranery in *United States v. Gold*, Criminal No. 15769 (E.D. Pa., filed July 20, 1950).
29. *Id.* at pp. 251-53.
30. *Id.* at p. 265.
31. *Id.* at pp. 262-66.
32. *Id.* at p. 267.
33. *Id.*; on December 14, 1950, Judge McGranery reduced his sentence to "29 years, 223 days," undoubtedly to account for the time he had spent in custody between the date of his indictment and the date of his sentencing. *See* Docket, Judgment and Commitment Order, and Transcripts of Guilty Plea and Sentencing in *United States v. Gold*, Criminal No. 15769 (E.D. Pa., filed July 20, 1950); *Time*, Dec. 18, 1950. *See also United States v. Rosenberg*, 109 F. Supp. 108, 114 (S.D.N.Y. 1953).
34. Hornblum, Allen M., *The Invisible Harry Gold*, pp. 268-95 (Yale University Press, 2010).
35. *Id.* at 343-47.
36. *Id.* at 354-55; *The New York Times*, p. 44 (Feb. 14, 1974).

37. Hornblum, Allen M., *The Invisible Harry Gold*, pp. 228, 363 (Yale University Press, 2010).
38. 141 F. Supp. 91 (E.D. Pa. 1954), *rev'd* 249 F.2d 619 (3d Cir. 1957).
39. Lord, Joseph S. III, "Communists' Trial," *The Shingle*, p. 144 (Nov. 1978).
40. *Id.* at 145-46.
41. *United States v. Kuzma*, 249 F.2d at 621-22.
42. *Brauner v. United States* and *Reynolds v. United States*, 10 F.R.D. 468 (E.D. Pa. 1950), *aff'd* 192 F.2d 987 (3d Cir. 1951), *rev'd sub nom.*, *United States v. Reynolds*, 345 U.S. 1 (1953).
43. Siegel, Barry, *Claim of Privilege*, pp. 90-104 (HarperCollins, 2008).
44. *Id.* at 105-19.
45. *Id.* at 119-20.
46. *Id.* at 125.
47. *Id.* at 124-25.
48. *Id.* at 119-56.
49. *United States v. Reynolds*, 345 U.S. at 9-10; Siegel, Barry, *Claim of Privilege*, pp. 171-76 (HarperCollins, 2008).
50. *United States v. Reynolds*, 345 U.S. at 10.
51. *Id.* at 11.
52. Siegel, Barry, *Claim of Privilege*, p. 181 (HarperCollins, 2008).
53. *Id.* at p. 202-11.
54. *Id.* at 217-18, 222-44.
55. *Id.* at 245-67.
56. *Herring v. United States*, No. 03-CV-5500, 2004 WL 2040272 (E.D. Pa. Sept. 10, 2004).
57. *Herring v. United States*, 424 F.3d 384 (3d Cir. 2005).
58. Siegel, Barry, *Claim of Privilege*, pp. 269-305 (HarperCollins, 2008).
59. *Norwood v. Kirkpatrick*, 349 U.S. 29 (1955).
60. Interview by Seymour Toll with The Honorable Joseph S. Lord III, pp. 47-48 (April 27, 1987).
61. Brief for Petitioners-Appellants in U.S. Supreme Court in *Norwood v. Kirkpatrick*, p. 3.
62. *United States v. Nat'l Football League*, 116 F. Supp. 319 (E.D. Pa. 1953).
63. *Id.* at 328 (E.D. Pa. 1953) (quoting *United States v. Women's Sportswear Mfrs. Ass'n*, 336 U.S. 460, 464 (1949)).
64. *United States v. Nat'l Football League*, 116 F. Supp. at 325-26.
65. *See*, e.g. *William Goldman Theatres, Inc. v. Loew's, Inc.*, 54 F. Supp. 1011 (E.D. Pa. 1944), *rev'd* 150 F.2d 738 (3d Cir. 1945).
66. *Goldlawr, Inc. v. Shubert*, 290 F. Supp. 482 (E.D. Pa 1968); *see also* 268 F Supp. 965 (E.D. Pa. 1967); 169 F. Supp. 677 (E.D. Pa. 1958).
67. 155 F. Supp. 768 (E.D. Pa. 1957); 166 F. Supp. 163 (E.D. Pa. 1958), *aff'd* 273 F.2d 218 (3d Cir. 1959), *rev'd* 365 U.S. 127 (1961).
68. Act of Feb. 10, 1954, Ch. 6 § 4, 68 Stat. 8,12.
69. 28 U.S.C. § 136 (a)(3)(c).

# VII
# New Challenges: The 1960's

In January 1961, John F. Kennedy was inaugurated as the thirty-fifth President of the United States. At that time, the Eastern District of Pennsylvania had eight active judges: Cullen Ganey, Thomas Clary, Allan Grim, John Lord, Francis Van Dusen, William Kraft, Thomas Egan, and Harold Wood. William Kirkpatrick, appointed by President Coolidge in 1927, and George Welsh, appointed by President Hoover in 1932, were still sitting as senior judges. Significant changes in the composition of the Court, however, were soon to take place. In 1961, Judge Egan died, Judge Grim took senior status, Judge Ganey moved to the Court of Appeals, and Judge Clary became the Court's Chief Judge to succeed Judge Ganey. That same year, Congress expanded the size of the Court by creating three additional judgeships, which brought the total to eleven.[1] Within a few years, Judge Welsh retired and Judge Grim was deceased. More judgeships would be added before the end of the decade as the work of the Court expanded.

President Kennedy, in his initial year in office, named three new judges. The first was Joseph S. Lord III. Born in 1912 in Philadelphia, he had received his undergraduate degree from the University of Pennsylvania where he had captained the boxing team and later earned his law degree from the same institution. At the time, his uncle, Charles A. Waters, was a judge of the Court of Common Pleas of Philadelphia County. Years later, Lord's brother, Charles A. Lord, would also sit on the Common Pleas bench. After law school, Lord became the law clerk for the Philadelphia Court of Common Pleas No. 4. From 1936 to 1961, he was a highly successful trial lawyer, with time out for his service in the Navy along with his four brothers during World War II. He first was employed as an associate with Schnader and Lewis and later practiced with Richter, Lord and Farage, a firm that represented plaintiffs in personal injury and wrongful death cases. During his career, he was a member of the Board of Governors of the Philadelphia Bar Association and served on the Board of the Philadelphia Port Authority.

President Kennedy appointed him initially as the United States Attorney for the Eastern District in 1961. He held this office for only a few months before being chosen for the federal bench. These appointments in such rapid succession were due to the influence of Congressman William J. Green, Philadelphia's powerful Democratic party leader. Lord had the good fortune to have defended the Congressman successfully in the Middle District of Pennsylvania in connection with his federal indictment and trial for allegedly receiving kickbacks related to the construction of the Tobyhanna Signal Corps Depot near Scranton. As Lord candidly stated, "I was picked [to be a judge] because I was fortunate enough to be in the right place at the right time."[2] He did not suffer fools gladly. His wit and humor were legendary. He quipped that he elevated the bench by becoming a judge and advised his colleagues to learn to sleep with their eyes open.[3]

John Lord and Joseph Lord were not related and had quite different political views. The former was a Republican and the latter a Democrat. Nonetheless, they were often mistaken for one another in the public mind. Whenever they were asked if they were confused with the other Judge Lord, they had a standard retort. Each would note in jest that he was confused without the other Judge Lord. John Lord had an additional response when dealing with the identity issue: 'If someone praises me for an opinion of [Judge Joseph Lord], I just nod and smile .... But if someone tells me I handed down a terrible decision ... I say it must have been the other Judge Lord.'[4]

At about the time of Joseph Lord's nomination, President Kennedy also tapped Abraham L. Freedman for the District Court. He was born in 1904 in Trenton, New Jersey and was a graduate of Temple Law School. Thereafter, he was an associate and later a partner in the law firm of Wolf Block Schorr and Solis-Cohen. He and his brother Maurice coauthored a multi-volume treatise, *Law of Marriage and Divorce in Pennsylvania*. Freedman also taught domestic relations law and Pennsylvania practice at Temple. He was a leader in the Jewish community, where he was the first President of the Federation of Jewish Agencies and served as a member of the Board of the Jewish Publication Society. Included among his other activities was his involvement with the Americans for Democratic Action. Along with William A. Schnader and Robert T. McCracken, Freedman was one of three principal drafters of the Philadelphia Home Rule Charter of 1951.[5] In 1952, reform Mayor Joseph S. Clark named him the City Solicitor of Philadelphia, a post he held until 1956.

Unlike Joseph Lord, Freedman was not a favorite of Congressman Green and the regular Democratic organization. In fact, Green at one point blocked his appointment to a vacancy on the Philadelphia Court of Common Pleas where Freedman at the time would have preferred to sit rather than on the District Court. He believed a seat on a Common Pleas bench would be a stepping-stone to a state appellate judgeship.[6] By the time of Freedman's selection for the District Court, Clark had been elected a United States Senator, and it was Clark's influence that prevailed over Green's. Within several years, again with Clark's sponsorship, President Johnson named him to the Court of Appeals.[7]

The third appointment by President Kennedy in 1961 was Alfred L. Luongo. His commission and that of Judge Freedman were dated the same day. Younger than both Joseph Lord and Abraham Freedman, he was born in 1920 in an Italian neighborhood in South Philadelphia before his family moved to Germantown. He held both his undergraduate and law degrees from the University of Pennsylvania. His law school days were interrupted by service in World War II. Following his completion of law school, he obtained the coveted position as the sole law clerk in the highly respected Philadelphia Court of Common Pleas No. 6 which was then comprised of Judges Curtis Bok, Gerald F. Flood, and Louis E. Levinthal.[8] In 1949, Judge Clary hired him as his law clerk. Luongo remained with Judge Clary until 1952 and then spent several years as an Assistant United States Attorney. Thereafter, he practiced law at the Blank, Rome law firm. In 1959, the voters elected him as a Philadelphia District Councilman, and he was holding that office when appointed to the bench. Because of his independence on City Council, he noted that "the Mayor [Dilworth] insisted that ... I be made a Federal Judge in order to get me out of his hair permanently."[9]

Ralph C. Body was the last Kennedy addition to the Eastern District. He was born in Yellow House, Berks County, in 1903. He earned degrees from Penn State and the University of Pennsylvania Law School. Aside from his service in World War II as an Army officer in the Judge Advocate General Corps, he had engaged continuously in the practice of law in Reading. For a number of years, he was also the Solicitor to the Berks County Recorder of Deeds and the Assistant County Solicitor. Like his father before him, he headed the Berks County Democratic Party for a time. In 1959, he won a seat on the Court of Common Pleas. Body joined the federal bench in 1962[10] where he was always seen wearing a bow tie. He is fondly remembered for his efforts to encourage and arrange social activities for the judges and their spouses and to promote an esprit de corps at the Court.[11]

As a result of President Kennedy's assassination on November 22, 1963, it fell to President Lyndon Johnson to fill vacancies on the federal courts. In January 1964, Johnson gave a recess appointment to A. Leon Higginbotham, Jr., age thirty-five, who had been nominated by Kennedy before his death. Higginbotham was the first African-American to have been chosen as a judge in the Eastern District's history. While white supremacist Mississippi Senator James Eastland, Chair of the Senate Judiciary Committee, for a time put obstacles in his way, Higginbotham was ultimately confirmed and commissioned in March.[12]

He was born and grew up in Trenton, New Jersey. His college career began at Purdue University, but after suffering racial discrimination, he transferred to Antioch College from which he was graduated. He earned his law degree at Yale Law School. Thereafter, he served as a law clerk to Judge Curtis Bok of the Philadelphia Court of Common Pleas No. 6, and then as an Assistant District Attorney under Richardson Dilworth, who had truly integrated the District Attorney's office. Higginbotham subsequently obtained a position with the law firm headed by Austin Norris, the legendary African-American Philadelphia lawyer. This was a time when no white firm would hire a lawyer of his race, no matter how well-qualified. Over the years a number of associates and partners in the Norris firm became federal or state judges. When in private practice, Higginbotham served for a period as the President of the Philadelphia Chapter of the NAACP. President Kennedy appointed Higginbotham to the Federal Trade Commission in 1962. Within a short time, he was sitting on the bench in the Eastern District.[13]

Higginbotham had not lobbied for a federal judgeship and did not have a close relationship with any influential Pennsylvania political figures. One day in 1963, he received a call out of the blue from Congressman Green. As Higginbotham recounted, Green told him, "I've got good news for you .... You've always been my number one candidate for the vacant judgeship." Green made it clear he had been "battling" Senator Clark, for whom Green had some uncomplimentary remarks, to make the appointment happen. Five minutes later, Higginbotham's phone rang again, and this time it was Senator Clark. The Senator stated, "Leon, you can't believe it ... I've finally gotten Bill Green to see the light ... I have always been pushing for you ...." Clark added that Green had "opposed it .... unless you got it, I was going to cause problems on the Judicial Committee." According to Higginbotham, he later learned that the real story was somewhat different than what he had heard on the phone from either of his two prominent callers. Attorney General Robert Kennedy had warned Clark and Green that if they could not agree on a candidate, he was going to recommend to President Kennedy that Higginbotham be nominated.[14] It appears that Green and Clark were hastily jumping aboard the train just as it was pulling out of the station.

Higginbotham chose his law clerks not simply based on their academic achievements but also on their degree of social consciousness. He encouraged his fellow judges to do likewise.[15]

On one occasion, following the assassination of Martin Luther King, Jr., in April 1968, he and Circuit Judge William H. Hastie calmed a crowd gathered outside the courthouse.[16] Judge Higginbotham's stature was such that President Johnson invited him, along with other leaders, to the White House for a conference on how to deal with the turmoil in the country as a result of King's death.[17]

Higginbotham, who was a very tall man with a deep, rich voice, was a renowned advocate for civil rights and authored two award-winning books, *In the Matter of Color* and *Shades of Freedom*. In 1977, President Carter named him to the Court of Appeals for the Third Circuit. He retired from the Court in 1993, then taught at Harvard University's John F. Kennedy School of Government, and died in 1998. A recipient of the Presidential Medal of Freedom, he will always be remembered as a heroic and passionate spokesman for social justice and racial equality.

At the same time that Higginbotham was nominated to the bench, President Johnson chose John Morgan Davis to fill another vacancy. He was born in Shenandoah in Schuylkill County in 1906, spent his formative years in Berks County, and lived most of his adult life in Philadelphia. His undergraduate and law degrees were awarded from the University of Pennsylvania. During his college and law school days, he was a radio announcer, a job for which he was extremely well-suited with his melodious baritone voice. In the 1940's, the National Association of Broadcasters retained him as its General Counsel.

Davis won election as a judge of the Court of Common Pleas of Philadelphia County in 1951 and as Lieutenant Governor of Pennsylvania in 1958. He held the latter office from 1959 to 1963. Thereafter, having failed in his quest to obtain support for the Democratic Party's nomination for Governor or for Mayor of Philadelphia, party leaders, including Congressman Green and former Governor David Lawrence under whom he had served, persuaded President Kennedy to select him for the Eastern District bench. President Kennedy's death intervened before Davis could be confirmed, but President Johnson followed through in early 1964 with what his predecessor had initiated.[18]

During this era, the Supreme Court, under the leadership of Chief Justice Earl Warren, was extremely active handing down a number of significant constitutional pronouncements, particularly in the area of criminal law. In 1961, it decided *Mapp v. Ohio,*[19] which required state courts, like federal courts, to suppress evidence illegally seized. The Supreme Court ruled that suppression was the only effective remedy to enforce the Fourth Amendment which prohibited unreasonable searches and seizures. There was the landmark decision of *Gideon v. Wainwright,*[20] which held that all criminal defendants both in federal and state court were entitled to the assistance of counsel under the Sixth and Fourteenth Amendments to the Constitution. The Court also decided *Miranda v. Arizona.*[21] This earthshaking decision mandated that the police inform those arrested of their rights, including the right to remain silent and the right to counsel, before any interrogation takes place. Failure to do so would result in suppression of any statements made. While these decisions are now all well-established and cause relatively little stir today, *Mapp* and *Miranda* particularly were extremely controversial at the time. The federal courts, including the Eastern District, would be inundated in the years ahead with filings from prisoners who sought to have their prior convictions overturned for alleged constitutional violations.

At the same time these precedent-setting decisions were being handed down, the Cold War was still an ever-present reality. In *MacEwan v. Rusk,*[22] the plaintiffs sought a declaration from the Eastern District to be allowed to travel to Cuba after the State Department had prohibited them from doing so by refusing to provide a special endorsement in their passports. Judge Freedman explained that the President, under the Constitution as well as pursuant to statutory authority, was empowered to conduct foreign policy. As part of that authority, the President could prohibit citizens from traveling to certain parts of the world. Furthermore, Judge Freedman found that the President's power had not been unreasonably exercised given the hostility existing between the Cuban and United States Governments.

Accordingly, he denied the relief plaintiffs had requested. In his opinion, he reminded the reader of Cuba's "avowed ... solidarity with world Communism and its fraternal relations with the Soviet Union and Communist China." He continued:

> Tensions rose to unprecedented dimensions at the confrontation between the United States and the Soviet Union over the presence of missiles hidden in Cuba. For some days following the declaration of an embargo by the President of the United States the world lived in dread of the unleashing of a thermonuclear war in the immediate vicinity of the United States. The United States Government has since announced many times that it considers Cuba a continuing danger spot because of the ever present threat of the clandestine concealment or return of Soviet missiles.... Our Government has joined with the governments of Latin America to devise means of isolating Cuba and dealing with its threat of Communist infiltration and subversion. Among these measures is the restriction of movement between free world countries and Cuba.... Thus the policy of the United States, reflected in congressional and executive action, recognizes the Cuban government, so close to us geographically, as an important and militant link in a movement aimed at the destruction of the influence of this country abroad and of its tranquility at home.[23]

Other areas of the law also consumed the time of the Court. Probably the most significant antitrust matter in the early part of the decade anywhere in the country was what came to be known as the "Electrical Equipment Antitrust Cases," in the Eastern District of Pennsylvania. They surely constituted the most complex litigation the District had encountered in its history.

In 1959, Tennessee Senator Estes Kefauver, after a series of Senate Committee hearings, requested the Justice Department to look into the pricing of heavy electrical equipment purchased by the Tennessee Valley Authority. Out of this request arose a prolonged and intensive investigation by federal grand juries in Philadelphia. When word leaked out that a significant grand jury witness had disclosed critical information about the conspiracy, the dam of resistance broke and others came forward. The conspiracy, it turned out, operated at the pinnacle of corporate power. By October 1960, indictments had been handed down in this Court against twenty-nine manufacturers of heavy electrical equipment, including General Electric and Westinghouse, and forty-five of their executives.[24] The indictments charged the defendants with a massive conspiracy to fix prices and allocate markets in twenty separate product lines in violation of the Sherman Act.

All except one executive whose case was dismissed promptly pleaded guilty or nolo contendere, and in February 1961, Chief Judge Ganey imposed sentence. He ordered heavy fines to be paid by all the corporations and forty-four executives. What was even more shocking and unprecedented, he sentenced seven executives to thirty days in jail, and twenty-one others to suspended prison sentences with five years' probation at a time when the law deemed the crime to be only a misdemeanor with a maximum jail term of a year.[25] It was reported that when the executives were serving their prison sentences at the Montgomery County Prison Farm, the President of the International Brotherhood of Electrical Workers sent each of them the game of Monopoly as a gift.[26]

Once the criminal cases concluded, the deluge of related civil antitrust actions inundated the courts. The plaintiffs ranged from large investor-owned utilities to small rural public-power operators and cooperatives. Ultimately, over 1,900 civil cases were filed in thirty-five federal districts.[27] The Judicial Conference of the United States under the leadership of Chief Justice Earl Warren appointed a nine-member committee of federal judges to coordinate the discovery and processing of the cases.[28] Judge Kirkpatrick, then a senior judge, had agreed to manage the consolidated discovery occurring in the Eastern District of Pennsylvania. This included presiding over depositions at the courthouse. Soon thereafter, he was hospitalized, and Chief Judge Clary assigned the discovery oversight and any trials to Judge Joseph Lord.[29]

Ultimately, of nearly 2,000 cases nationwide, only one, *Philadelphia Electric Co. v. Westinghouse Electric Corp.*,[30] involving a single electrical product, went to trial in the Eastern District. Most of the trial, which lasted over three months, consisted of the reading of depositions. The jury returned a verdict in June 1964 of more than $9 million in favor of plaintiffs, which the Court trebled to almost $29 million as provided under the Sherman Act.[31] Recognizing that their position was untenable due to the criminal convictions and admissions of conspiracy, the defendants soon undertook to settle the remaining cases. They ended up paying out many millions of dollars.[32]

Because of these Electrical Equipment Antitrust cases, and with the strong support of Chief Justice Warren, Congress passed legislation allowing for the transfer to one district "for coordinated or consolidated pretrial proceedings" civil actions pending in different districts which involved "one or more common questions of fact" if it is determined to be "for the convenience of parties and witnesses and will promote the just and efficient conduct of such actions."[33] This multi-district litigation statute authorized the Chief Justice to designate a panel of judges to make pretrial transfers in appropriate circumstances. Judge Joseph Lord served for a number of years as one of the original panel members.[34] Former Supreme Court Justice Tom Clark, as Director of the Federal Judicial Center, later named Judge Clary to be editor-in-chief of the *Handbook for Protracted and Multidistrict Litigation*.[35] As time went on, the Eastern District was to see many more treble damage antitrust cases and an abundance of multi-district litigation.

Another noteworthy antitrust action came before Chief Judge Clary in 1961. The Government filed a civil suit to prevent the merger of the Philadelphia National Bank and the Girard Trust Corn Exchange Bank, two venerable Philadelphia institutions. The wider business and banking community both inside and outside the District exhibited great interest in this case. After a non-jury trial, Judge Clary found that the merger would not substantially lessen competition or tend toward monopoly or restrain trade in violation of the Clayton and Sherman Acts. Based on the evidence, he concluded "that all indications are that competition will be even more vigorous after the merger than before" and that "the Court can see no reasonable probability that competition among commercial banks in the four-county area will be substantially lessened."[36]

On appeal, the Supreme Court, over the dissent of two justices, reversed and ordered the District Court to enter judgment enjoining the proposed merger. Viewing the facts differently than had Judge Clary, the Supreme Court decided that the merger was anti-competitive in the relevant geographic market and would substantially lessen competition whether or not "on some ultimate reckoning of social or economic debits and credits, it may be deemed beneficial."[37] The Supreme Court's decision doomed the efforts in Philadelphia to create a larger bank to compete at the level of those in New York.[38] Years later, both the Philadelphia National Bank and the Girard Trust Corn Exchange Bank were absorbed into other banking institutions, and their names, which were once familiar to all Philadelphians, are now but a memory.

At approximately the same time as the Government was pursuing these major antitrust actions in the Eastern District, Edward Schempp and his wife Sidney Schempp, who were Unitarians, sued the School District of Abington Township, Montgomery County where their children attended school. They sought to enjoin as unconstitutional the daily reading of ten verses of the Bible by a teacher or student as required by Pennsylvania law.

The case was heard by a three-judge panel consisting of District Judges Kirkpatrick and Kraft and Circuit Court Chief Judge John Biggs. At that time, the law mandated that two District Judges and one Circuit Judge preside over an action where the constitutionality of a state statute was challenged.[39] The Court unanimously agreed that the statute violated both the Establishment of Religion Clause and the Free Exercise of Religion Clause of the First Amendment as applied to the States by the Fourteenth Amendment.[40] As Chief Judge Biggs stated in the Court's opinion, "Whether or not mere reading of the Bible, without comment, is a religious ceremony, a state supported practice of daily reading from that essentially religious text in the public schools is, we believe, within the proscription of the First Amendment."[41]

Pennsylvania, however, did not give up easily. The General Assembly proceeded to amend the law. It continued to require that ten verses of the Bible be read daily without comment but now allowed any student to be excused from attending Bible readings upon the written request of a parent or guardian. After further legal maneuvering by the parties, the three judges unanimously struck down the amended statute on the ground that it too violated the constitutional prohibition against the establishment of religion. The Court reasoned:

> The fact that some pupils, or theoretically all pupils, might be excused from attendance at the exercises does not mitigate the obligatory nature of the ceremony for the 'new' [statute], as did the statute prior to its 1959 amendment, unequivocally requires the exercises to be held every school day in every school in the Commonwealth.[42]

The defendants appealed to the Supreme Court. On June 17, 1963, the same day the Supreme Court decided *United States v. Philadelphia National Bank*, it handed down its ruling affirming the District Court. In the words of Justice Tom Clark:

> The place of religion in our society is an exalted one, achieved through a long tradition of reliance on the home, the church and the inviolable citadel of the individual heart and mind. We have come to recognize through bitter experience that it is not within the power of government to invade that citadel, whether its purpose or effect be to aid or oppose, to advance or retard. In the relationship between man and religion, the State is firmly committed to a position of neutrality. Though the application of that rule requires interpretation of a delicate sort, the rule itself is clearly and concisely stated in the words of the First Amendment.[43]

From that point forward, Bible reading in the public schools of the Commonwealth was a thing of the past. But in the process, as often happens in controversial cases, the Court in Philadelphia received a plethora of hate mail. Incongruously, some of those who professed to favor the nurturing of school children with a message from the Scriptures filled their correspondence with obscenities.[44]

While this Court was faced with lofty matters of religion in *Schempp*, it also encountered the less sublime matter of obscenity in the highly publicized case of

*United States v. Ralph Ginzburg*. The Government indicted Ginzburg under a federal law making it a crime to send obscene material through the mail.[45] Ginzburg, the editor and publisher of *Eros Magazine*, had mailed copies of it along with books such as *Housewife's Handbook in Selective Promiscuity* and another similar publication from the post office in Middlesex, New Jersey. This site for the mailings was selected after he was denied advantageous mailing privileges at the post offices at Blue Ball and Intercourse, Pennsylvania, in Lancaster County in the Eastern District. Having waived his right to a jury, Ginzburg was tried for five days before Judge Ralph Body who found him guilty on all counts. He was sentenced to five years in prison.

In his post-trial opinion, Judge Body explained that "the material to be obscene must appeal ... to the prurient interest of the average person, applying contemporary community standards."[46] He found that all the publications easily met this threshold. With respect to one of them, he wrote:

> The Handbook, standing bare of any socially redeeming value, is a patent offense to the most liberal morality. The descriptions leave nothing to the imagination, and in detail, in a clearly prurient manner offend, degrade and sicken anyone however healthy his mind was before exposure to this material. It is a gross shock to the mind and chore to read. Pruriency and disgust coalesce here creating a perfect example of hardcore pornography.[47]

Judge Body concluded, "This Court has the power and the right as a fact finder and as one who is aware of all types of material sold, tolerated and not tolerated by the community as a whole, to find, as it has found, that the material in question exceeds the standard. It does so unequivocally."[48]

The Court of Appeals, after emphasizing it had carefully reviewed the record, affirmed. The Supreme Court, granting a writ of certiorari, had to contend with the applicability of the First Amendment's guarantee of freedom of speech to matter found to be obscene. With Justice William Brennan writing the majority opinion, the Supreme Court affirmed by a vote of five to four over the vigorous dissents of Justices Hugo Black, William Douglas, John Marshall Harlan, and Potter Stewart. The latter declared:

> Censorship reflects a society's lack of confidence in itself. It is a hallmark of an authoritarian regime. Long ago those who wrote our First Amendment charted a different course. They believed a society can be truly strong only when it is truly free. In the realm of expression they put their faith, for better or for worse, in the enlightened choice of the people, free from the interference of a policeman's intrusive thumb or a judge's heavy hand.[49]

And so, after having lost in the Supreme Court by one vote, Ralph Ginzburg went to prison. Of all Judge Body's cases, this was the one that was mentioned years later in his obituary.[50]

On the civil side of the Court's docket, there was a precedent-setting case involving the issue of venue, that is, the proper district where a lawsuit is to be heard. On October 4, 1960, an Eastern Airlines plane on a flight from Boston to Philadelphia crashed into Boston Harbor shortly after take-off from Logan Airport. Over 150 passengers were killed or injured. Fifty-five diversity cases were brought in the Eastern District of Pennsylvania while others were instituted in the District of Massachusetts. The defendants moved to transfer to the federal court in Massachusetts the cases filed here under the widely used federal change-of-venue statute. Judge Van Dusen granted the motion as to the wrongful death cases "for the convenience of parties and witnesses, in the interest of justice."[51] Since the decision was not immediately appealable, the plaintiffs sought a writ of mandamus or prohibition against Judge Van Dusen in the Court of Appeals to compel him to vacate his order. Underlying this heated legal struggle over the location of the trials was a much more consequential practical issue. Massachusetts law at the time capped the damages in a wrongful death action at $20,000 while Pennsylvania law had no such arbitrary limitation.

The Court of Appeals held that Judge Van Dusen had erred in transferring these cases. The Supreme Court thereupon granted the defendants' petition for a writ of certiorari. The high Court reversed the Court of Appeals and remanded to the District Court for further consideration in light of its construction of the venue statute. This, however, was not the most noteworthy aspect of its decision. In this case known as *Van Dusen v. Barrack*, the Supreme Court ruled that even if the cases were ultimately transferred, the substantive law of the state of the transferor court, here the law of Pennsylvania with no cap on damages, would be applicable rather than that of Massachusetts.[52] This decision had broad ramifications, for now the law of the state where any diversity action was originally filed would apply even if a change of venue was later granted.

The mid-and-late 1960's was also a time of political tumult as a result of the civil rights struggle. In 1963, the centennial year of President Lincoln's Emancipation Proclamation, The Rev. Martin Luther King, Jr. gave his eloquent "I have a Dream" speech at the Lincoln Memorial in Washington. He would be assassinated in Memphis on April 4, 1968.

Congress was finally enacting significant civil rights legislation. The Civil Rights Act of 1964 outlawed discrimination in places of public accommodation as well as in employment.[53] The Voting Rights Act of 1965 was also enacted.[54]

The courts, primarily in the South, were dealing with the desegregation of schools and lunch counters and facing massive resistance in some localities. The Civil Rights movement, however, was also taking place in the North. In the Eastern District, Judge Joseph Lord presided over the most important and closely followed civil rights case in this region. It concerned Girard College, a well-known Philadelphia secondary school, which had been established under the will of Stephen Girard before the Civil War.

Girard was born in Bordeaux, France, in 1750. At the age of fourteen he went to sea, became a ship captain, and ultimately settled in Philadelphia where he prospered as a merchant, shipowner, and banker. He was also a generous philanthropist who, among other good works, provided funds to fight the several yellow fever epidemics in the City in the 1790's. At the time of his death in 1831, he was said to be the richest man in America.[55] Orphaned at twelve, he left a large portion of his fortune in trust to the City of Philadelphia to establish a school for "poor male white orphan children ... to provide them a better education as well as a more comfortable maintenance than they usually receive from the application of the public funds."[56] Girard College opened in 1848 in a then sparsely populated area on land designated by Girard in Penn Township, Philadelphia County just north of the city.[57]

Over the years as the City expanded, Girard College eventually found itself in the midst of a densely populated row house neighborhood of North Philadelphia. By the 1950's and 1960's, the residents in the area were largely African-American. Girard College with its stately Founders Hall in the Greek revival style[58] and its other marble buildings, a high stone wall around the circumference of the campus, and an all white student body stood out in sharp contrast to its surroundings. This incongruity did not go unnoticed. The Local NAACP, led by the flamboyant attorney and ex-Marine Cecil B. Moore, as well as other civil rights activists, began to turn their attention to Girard College with frequent marches outside its gates to protest the racial discrimination taking place within. Even Martin Luther King added his voice and presence on one occasion.[59]

Not surprisingly, various parties also turned to the courts for relief. In the mid-1950's two African-American children petitioned the Orphans' Court of Philadelphia County for admission to Girard College.[60] Defending Girard's will was the Board of Directors of City Trusts which managed all charitable bequests to the City of Philadelphia and which had responsibility to oversee the operation of the school. The Court rejected the children's constitutional claim and turned down their request for admission on the ground that to do otherwise would violate the clear language of Girard's will. The Pennsylvania Supreme Court, in an opinion by Chief Justice Horace Stern, agreed with the Orphans' Court, although he described the result as "unfortunate."[61] The lawsuit reached the United States Supreme Court, which in a short per curiam opinion, summarily reversed. It stated:

> The Board which operates Girard College is an agency of the State of Pennsylvania. Therefore, even though the Board was acting

> as a trustee, its refusal to admit Foust and Felder to the college because they were Negroes was discrimination by the State. Such discrimination is forbidden by the Fourteenth Amendment. Brown v. Board of Education, .... Accordingly, the judgment of the Supreme Court of Pennsylvania is reversed and the cause is remanded for further proceedings not inconsistent with this opinion.[62]

When the matter returned to the Orphans' Court, it promptly removed the Board of City Trusts as the trustee with oversight of Girard College. In place of the Board it appointed a group of "private" trustees, who were not associated with the City. The Court reasoned that its primary obligation was to uphold the terms of Girard's will and that its selection of private trustees would insulate the trust and Girard College from claims of state sponsored discrimination.

The Commonwealth of Pennsylvania, with the support of Governor William Scranton, and the City of Philadelphia as well as a number of African-American children, filed a lawsuit in the Eastern District of Pennsylvania in which they alleged Girard College's race-based admission policy not only was unconstitutional but also contravened Pennsylvania law. Judge Joseph Lord, after a hearing, ruled that the exclusion of African-American boys from the education offered at the school violated the Pennsylvania Public Accommodations Act.[63] He did not decide the constitutional issues raised. Reversing the District Court's order, the Court of Appeals held that Pennsylvania law had not been broken and remanded for Judge Lord to resolve the federal constitutional questions involved.[64]

With the case back in District Court, Judge Lord ruled that the exclusion of non-white applicants to Girard College violated the Equal Protection Clause of the Fourteenth Amendment to the United States Constitution. While recognizing that private discrimination, however invidious, does not infringe the Constitution, he wrote that "the transfer of immediate supervisory control to private trustees by the Orphans' Court failed to effectively disassociate the State from the discriminatory policies and purposes which the State operation of the school had come to embody." He found, "the College has not purged itself of critical State involvement nor has the State erased the impression of public approval which long attached to the school's racial policies." Accordingly, "Since the strictures of the Fourteenth Amendment apply to the administration of the institution, it may no longer deny admission to applicants simply because they are not 'white.'"[65]

This time, the Court of Appeals, sitting en banc, unanimously affirmed his decision, and the Supreme Court denied certiorari.[66] Now, for the first time in its history, Girard College would be admitting not only poor male white orphan children but also poor male non-white orphan children.

As often occurs with court decisions, the matter at issue, in this case the integration of Girard College, caused widespread discussion and debate among Philadelphians. Many saw Judge Lord's ruling as advancing the promise of America. Others viewed it as undermining the sanctity of wills and wrongfully depriving persons of the right to dispose of their property as they see fit. Emotions ran high on both sides. However, as the years passed, the passions of the day abated, and Girard College quietly goes about its worthy educational mission unvexed, now with female as well as male students of all colors.[67]

The civil rights actions were not the only cases which sought to bring about widespread social change through the courts. Organizations such as Community Legal Services and the Public Interest Law Center of Philadelphia were also busy instituting and winning lawsuits on behalf of the economically disadvantaged.

In the mid-1960's, one of the first successful poverty law cases decided by the Supreme Court arose out of the Eastern District. A class action challenged the constitutionality of the Pennsylvania law requiring welfare recipients to have resided in the Commonwealth for a year immediately preceding their application for benefits. A three-judge court consisting of District Judge Joseph Lord, District Judge Michael Sheridan of the Middle District of Pennsylvania, and Circuit Judge Harry Kalodner heard the matter.[68]

The Court, over the dissent of Judge Kalodner, held that the one-year waiting period had no legitimate purpose and violated the Equal Protection Clause of the Constitution. Although noting that there is no constitutional right to receive public welfare, it decided that it was arbitrary to draw a distinction between those who had been residents in the state for at least a year and those who had lived in the state for a shorter time. The Court also concluded that the statute had the prohibited effect of inhibiting the movement of indigent persons from other states into Pennsylvania. In the Court's opinion, Judge Lord declared, "The right to travel freely without deterrence is inherent in the notion of a unified nation, and no State may exclude citizens migrating from other States, whatever the reason for the migration."[69]

The Supreme Court affirmed. It agreed that the Equal Protection Clause and the fundamental right to travel voided the Pennsylvania law as well as similar laws of Connecticut and the District of Columbia.[70]

Years later, Judge Lord singled out this and the *Girard College* case as two of his decisions that made a real difference. As to the former, he remarked, "I felt that I had done a good thing in that and I felt gratified that I had the opportunity."[71]

The rights of prisoners were also beginning to be litigated in the federal courts in the 1960's. One early case involved Richard J. Mayberry, who had been convicted in the Philadelphia Court of Common Pleas of armed robbery of a dry cleaning establishment and sentenced to state prison. In order to aid him with his appeals, Mayberry bought a copy of the Rules of the Supreme and Superior Courts of Pennsylvania. After the prison authorities confiscated these materials as contraband, he brought a civil rights action in this Court. Judge Grim ruled in Mayberry's favor. The judge wrote that reasonable access to the court is guaranteed by the due process clause of the Fourteenth Amendment and that the right at least included reasonable access to the Rules of Procedure.[72] As events turned out, Mayberry would have extensive need of the Rules and other law-related tomes.

In the ensuing years, Mayberry became a notorious figure in the courts of the Commonwealth. He was convicted of prison breach and holding hostages in a state penal institution in Western Pennsylvania. At his trial in the Common Pleas Court of Allegheny County, while representing himself, he continually insulted the judge and at times had to be gagged and removed from the courtroom because of his disruptive behavior. The judge sentenced him to eleven years to twenty-two years for criminal contempt, in addition to his lengthy sentences on the underlying charges. His case ended up in the United States Supreme Court, which vacated his contempt sentence and remanded for further proceedings.[73]

In another instance, he was convicted of perjury in the Court of Common Pleas of Philadelphia County. At that trial, again representing himself, he acted in a contumacious and insulting manner, which included hurling a book at Judge Leo Weinrott. His five-year sentence for contempt was upheld by the Pennsylvania Supreme Court.[74] In addition to his activity in the state criminal courts, he litigated in the federal courts the issue of his state prison conditions.[75]

As always, most of the cases before the Court did not generate newspaper headlines and did not become storied legal precedents. A variety of such cases were heard and decided on the Court's civil docket. They included antitrust, securities, patent, copyright, trademark, and labor disputes as well as common law contract and defamation claims, to name a few. Lawsuits under the Federal Employer's Liability Act were also common. This statute allowed railroad workers to sue their employers for negligence for injuries suffered on the job.[76] As had been happening since 1789, the Court had before it many maritime cases, now including those under the Jones Act and other statutes[77] which provide remedies for seamen injured aboard vessels and longshoremen injured unloading cargo. These were the days before the reduction in the large number of longshoremen due to the containerization of cargo at the Port of Philadelphia.

There were many non-maritime personal injury and wrongful death actions, involving state law, where the parties were of diverse citizenship, that is, the plaintiff and defendant were citizens of different states. Not infrequently, diversity was "manufactured" with an out-of-state plaintiff so that a Pennsylvania defendant could be sued in federal court. It was then thought that damage awards were higher and cases moved more quickly in the District Court than in the Common Pleas Court of Philadelphia County.

The personal injury and death cases where diversity was manufactured were often filed by a plaintiff named Stella McSparran. She was a New Jersey citizen, who was a secretary at a successful Philadelphia law firm, headed by B. Nathaniel Richter, which represented plaintiffs in tort cases. Before a personal injury or wrongful death action was brought in the federal court on behalf of a client who was a Pennsylvania minor, a Pennsylvania incompetent, or the estate of a Pennsylvania decedent, the firm secured her appointment by the Orphans' Court as the person's guardian or the estate's administratrix. In this way, federal court jurisdiction was obtained because it was the citizenship of the legal representative that was relevant in determining diversity rather than the citizenship of the minor, incompetent or decedent.

In late 1968, in a case originally before Judge Clary,[78] the Court of Appeals, sitting en banc, overturned prior precedent with its ruling that the practice of manufacturing diversity with non-resident plaintiffs was forbidden under a federal statute which states that "a district court shall not have jurisdiction in which a party has been improperly or collusively ... joined to invoke the jurisdiction of such court."[79] Thus, the citizenship of the child or incompetent who was injured or the person who had died would now be determinative. Henceforth, the name of the omnipresent Stella McSparran was seen no more on the caption of newly filed complaints.[80]

In the last half of the 1960's, four more judges were added to the roster of the Eastern District. First, in 1966, John P. Fullam joined the Court with the endorsement of Senator Joseph Clark, but only after about a year's delay caused by fellow Senator Hugh Scott, who was urging President Johnson to nominate a Republican to the Court.[81] Fullam, a native of Bucks County, was a graduate of Villanova University and Harvard Law School. During his deployment as a Naval officer on a tanker in the Pacific during World War II, the ship had occasion to fuel the *U.S.S. J. William Ditter*, a destroyer-mine sweeper named for J. William Ditter, a Pennsylvania Congressman from Montgomery County. As fate would have it, Fullam and the Congressman's son, J. William Ditter, Jr., were destined to be colleagues on the federal bench many years later.

In the 1950's, Fullam served as Chair of the Delaware River Joint Toll Bridge Commission and twice ran unsuccessfully for Congress on the Democratic ticket. In 1960, Governor David Lawrence appointed him to fill a vacancy on the Bucks County Court of Common Pleas, as Fullam put it, to get him out of the hair of the politicians.[82] He was then elected with the endorsement of both parties to a ten-year term and became the first Democrat to have won election to the Bucks County Court since the memory of man runneth not to the contrary. Six years after he joined the state bench, he was sitting on the Eastern District where he was destined to hear cases for almost forty-five years before his retirement. His tenure in this regard was longer than that of any other judge in the Court's history, surpassing by over a year the previous record set by Judge Kirkpatrick.

In addition to sharing his legal acumen, he acted as the District Court's grammarian and resident Latin scholar. He never hesitated to flag both grammatical and spelling errors in his colleagues' opinions. His own opinions he kept extremely short, often unencumbered by legal citations. When singing was required at court functions, it was he who took the lead with his fine tenor voice.

In 1967, with the creation of three temporary judgeships,[83] President Johnson had the opportunity to augment the ranks of the Eastern District of Pennsylvania. In the process, Senator Scott achieved his goal of obtaining the appointment of one Republican, E. Mac Troutman of Schuylkill County, to the District Court as well as that of District Judge Francis Van Dusen, a Republican, to the Court of Appeals. The other two District Court nominees were Thomas A. Masterson and Charles R. Weiner, both of Philadelphia and both Democrats.

E. Mac Troutman, born in 1915 and a graduate of Dickinson College and Dickinson Law School, was a longtime resident of the rural community of Orwigsburg, Schuylkill County. He practiced law in Pottsville after serving in the Army in World War II, and for many years was also associated with the Philadelphia and Reading Coal and Iron Company where for a time he held the position of its general counsel. Troutman was an inveterate cigar smoker and avid outdoorsman and hunter. His storytelling skill was a potent catalyst in helping him to settle countless cases. It was largely through his efforts, and those of Senator Scott, that court stations were established in Reading and Allentown, which were much nearer his home than was Philadelphia.[84]

Masterson, age thirty-nine, had an undergraduate degree from Harvard and a law degree from the University of Pennsylvania. He practiced law with Morgan, Lewis & Bockius, and had ties with the Democratic organization in Philadelphia. After only a few years on the Court, he resigned to return to his former law firm in order to be able to support his large family.

Charles Weiner, a World War II Navy veteran, obtained his college degree from the University of Pennsylvania and his law degree from Temple Law School. Unique among his colleagues before or since, he also earned a Ph.D. in Political Science from the University of Pennsylvania. He was a longtime Democratic State Senator representing a district in North Philadelphia. His legislative colleagues chose him at different times as either the Senate's majority or minority leader, depending on whether his party had control of the chamber. The NAACP strongly supported his appointment to the bench. A man of boundless energy, he always seemed to be able to do a dozen things at once and was second to none in his ability to settle or otherwise dispose of cases. Like Joseph Lord, he served on the Judicial Panel for Multidistrict Litigation.

In January 1969, as the decade was coming to a close, President Richard Nixon took office after eight years of the Kennedy and Johnson administrations. Scott, the senior senator from Pennsylvania and soon to be the Senate's minority leader, was now the person whose influence was decisive in the appointment of new judges to this Court. While recommending only Republicans, Scott insured that the Court would have not only more racial diversity but also judges from counties in the district not currently represented.

President Nixon announced John Berne Hannum as his first nominee a few months after his inauguration. Hannum's father had been the Orphans' Court Judge in Delaware County for sixteen years in the 1920's and 1930's. Although Hannum, a World War II Navy veteran, practiced law in Philadelphia at Pepper, Hamilton & Scheetz, he resided in the horse country of rural southwestern Chester County. He was active in that community as a member of the Boards of the Unionville-Chadds Ford School District, the Chester County Hospital, and Lincoln University. His resume also included membership on the Board of Dickinson Law School. For two years, he chaired the Republican Party in Chester County and was elected as a delegate to the 1967-1968 Pennsylvania Constitutional Convention. He was an accomplished equestrian and enjoyed fox hunting. Before joining the District Court, Governor Raymond Shafer had appointed him to an interim term on the Pennsylvania Superior Court. Hannum was confirmed to the District Court without difficulty.

The number of criminal actions in the Eastern District in the 1960's was small compared to later years. It was an era before the avalanche of drugs and gun cases. The bulk of the criminal indictments consisted of interstate transportation of stolen goods, postal thefts, and the occasional bank robbery.

Then came the selective service cases. At a time when opposition to the Vietnam War was escalating, the court docket contained not only civil cases involving student, occupational, and hardship deferments but also indictments against those who were alleged to have engaged in draft evasion. Conscientious objector cases were frequent. Among the latter were criminal actions against Amish young men from Lancaster County who refused to serve for religious reasons. Although conscientious objector status was not new or unusual in America, the Amish would not undertake non-combatant service which the law required of conscientious objectors who refused to join the Armed Forces. The Eastern District grappled with many heart wrenching cases of Amish young men who appeared before the bar of the federal court in Philadelphia, with their German accents and in the distinct garb of the "plain people," to voice their religious objections and then face jail sentences. Many Jehovah's Witnesses, who were pacifists like the Amish, also came before the Court in these years and encountered the same fate.[85] These cases were decided by judges who, for the most part, had served in World War II.

Most judges in the 1960's still had a staff consisting of one law clerk, a secretary, and a bailiff, who more often than not was a political appointee. As time went on and as their workload increased, judges did not replace their bailiffs when they died or retired and instead added a second law clerk. The law clerks, like the judges, were always male, except when Judges Van Dusen, Wood, and Higginbotham as real pioneers each hired a female law clerk for one year. In what was probably unique in the federal system in the 1960's, both Judge Kirkpatrick and Judge Welsh employed blind law clerks. The wife of each of these law clerks was the judge's secretary and was able to read cases and briefs to her husband.

Each judge had an assigned court reporter when needed. Some of them still recorded trial testimony and other proceedings the old-fashioned way by means of shorthand, with many fountain pens, bottles of ink, and sheets of paper at hand.

Court security at Ninth and Market Streets was not of great concern. The post office occupied the main floor of the courthouse. The public had easy access to the courtrooms and judges' chambers on the upper floors by simply taking an elevator. The judges, lawyers, parties, witnesses, jurors, court personnel, and visitors rode the same elevators. Prisoners were marched through the halls in handcuffs. Although deputy federal marshals were present in the building, there were no other security officers and no monitors or cameras, and no metal detectors. The doors to the chambers were not locked during business hours with court personnel, lawyers, and outsiders coming and going at will.

The Court was still using the time-honored master calendar system in the 1960's. Under it, each judge was scheduled for certain weeks of the year for criminal trials, civil trials, discovery and other pretrial motions, settlement conferences, and time in chambers. The trial periods for each judge did not usually extend more than two or three weeks at a time. The same judge would not be responsible for a case from beginning to end. Instead, one judge might decide a discovery dispute or a motion to suppress evidence, another the motion to dismiss or for summary judgment, still another would preside over any settlement conference, and finally a different judge would try the case, depending on when a particular event in the life of a case occurred and what judge happened to be assigned to deal with such matters. There was no overarching scheduling order setting deadlines for the various phases of a case, and cases sometimes languished for want of judicial oversight.

In the late 1960's, the Federal Judicial Center persuaded Chief Judge Clary to experiment with an individual calendar system for both criminal and civil cases. In contrast to the then current practice, the proposed system called for a case to be assigned to a judge at random when it was first filed with that same judge presiding over the matter for all purposes until its conclusion. The judge would set deadlines, resolve all motions, have responsibility for case management, and try the case if necessary. Those advocating this change argued that cases would move toward trial and be resolved much more expeditiously than under the master calendar system. Two of the newer judges, John Fullam and Charles Weiner, agreed to participate in a pilot program. In due course, it was apparent that efficiency and backlog reduction were the clear result.

Making the conversion applicable to all judges, however, was hotly contested. By the time the matter was ripe for decision, John Lord had succeeded Thomas Clary as Chief Judge. Following a vigorous discussion at a judges' meeting on June 25, 1969, in Courtroom #11 in the Courthouse at Ninth and Market Streets, Chief Judge John Lord cast the tie-breaking vote in favor of a court-wide individual calendar system. It took effect on January 1, 1970.[86] As a result, the Eastern District of Pennsylvania became one of the first of the District Courts throughout the country to make this monumental shift. It remains in effect today and constitutes one of the most important administrative reforms in the history of the Court.

## Notes

1. Act of May 19, 1961, Pub. L. No. 87-36, 75 Stat. 81.
2. Interview by Seymour I. Toll with Joseph S. Lord III, p. 61 (April 27, 1987).
3. *Id.*; *The Philadelphia Inquirer*, p. 11-D (April 25, 1991); "Memorial Ceremony for The Honorable Joseph S. Lord III," United States District Court for the Eastern District of Pennsylvania, pp. 11, 13, 27 (June 28, 1991).
4. *The Philadelphia Inquirer*, p. 31 (April 28, 1969).
5. Kranzel, Isador & Klinek, Eric, "Political Influence in Philadelphia Judicial Appointments: Abraham L. Freedman's Account." *The Pennsylvania Magazine of History and Biography*, Vol. CXXXIII, No. 4, pp. 348, 351 (Oct. 2009).
6. *Id.* at pp. 352-86.
7. *The Philadelphia Inquirer*, p. 1 (March 15, 1971).
8. Interview by Marvin Comisky, Esquire with Judge Alfred L. Luongo, pp. 11-14 (July 11, 1986).
9. Interview by Marvin Comisky, Esquire with Judge Alfred L. Luongo, pp. 19-21 (July 11, 1986). The Mayor at the time was Richardson Dilworth.
10. *The Philadelphia Inquirer*, p. 6B (June 4, 1973).
11. Interview by Magistrate Judge Richard A. Powers with Judge C. William Kraft, p. 71 (Feb. 28, 1995).
12. Interview by Seymour I. Toll with Judge A. Leon Higginbotham, Jr., pp. 76-78 (Sept. 1, 1995).
13. *Id.* at pp. 41-54, 58-62; Ogletree, Charles J., "In Memoriam: A. Leon Higginbotham, Jr.," 112 Harvard Law Review, 1804 (June 1999); Becker, Edward R., "In Memoriam: A. Leon Higginbotham, Jr.," 112 Harvard Law Review, 1814-16 (June 1999).
14. Interview by Seymour I. Toll with Judge A. Leon Higginbotham, Jr., pp. 65-67 (Sept. 1, 1995).
15. Remarks by Judge Clifford Scott Green at the Presentation of the Portrait of the late Chief Judge A.

Leon Higginbotham, Jr. in the Ceremonial Courtroom (Oct. 26, 2000).

16. Interview by Jason S. Lantzer with Judge John P. Fullam (Jan. 31, 2008).
17. Remarks of Judge Nathaniel R. Jones at the Presentation of the Portrait of the late Chief Judge A. Leon Higginbotham, Jr. in the Ceremonial Courtroom (Oct. 26, 2000).
18. *The Philadelphia Inquirer*, p. 10 (Sept. 4, 1963); *The Philadelphia Inquirer*, p. 3 (Jan. 8, 1964); *Reading Eagle*, p. 8 (Mar. 10, 1964).
19. 367 U.S. 643 (1961).
20. 372 U.S. 335 (1963).
21. 384 U.S. 436 (1966).
22. 228 F. Supp. 306 (E.D. Pa. 1964).
23. *Id.* at 309-10.
24. Record of Symposium presented by The Historical Society of the United States District Court for the Eastern District of Pennsylvania on the Electrical Equipment Antitrust Cases, pp. 7-12 (Oct. 15, 1987).
25. *Id.* at pp. 12, 14-15.
26. *Id.* at p. 15.
27. *Id.* at pp. 15, 18, 51.
28. *Id.* at p. 4.
29. *Id.* at pp. 16-17.
30. The United Gas Improvement Co. and Conowingo Power Co. were also plaintiffs. The other defendants, in addition to Westinghouse, were Allis-Chalmers Mfg. Co., General Electric Co., McGraw-Edison Co., Moloney Electric Co., and Wagner Electric Co. No. 30015 (E.D. Pa.).
31. *See* Docket No. 30015, Item #318, dated June 2, 1964 (E.D. Pa.); Record of Symposium presented by The Historical Society of the United States District Court for the Eastern District of Pennsylvania on the Electrical Equipment Antitrust Cases, p. 22 (Oct. 15, 1987).
32. Record of Symposium presented by The Historical Society of the United States District Court for the Eastern District of Pennsylvania on the Electrical Equipment Antitrust Cases, pp. 50-53 (Oct. 15, 1987).
33. 28 U.S.C. § 1407; Record of Symposium presented by The Historical Society of the United States District Court for the Eastern District of Pennsylvania on the Electrical Equipment Antitrust Cases, p. 73 (Oct. 15, 1987).
34. Interview by Seymour I. Toll with Joseph S. Lord III, pp. 75-76 (April 27, 1987).
35. Lord, Jos. S. III, "Hon. Thomas J. Clary," *The Shingle*, p. 116 (June 1969).
36. *United States v. Phila. Nat'l Bank*, 201 F. Supp. 348, 368 (E.D. Pa. 1962).
37. *United States v. Phila. Nat'l Bank*, 374 U.S. 321, 371 (1963).
38. *Time Magazine*, p. 88 (Jan. 26, 1962); Lord, Jos. S. III, "Hon. Thomas J. Clary," *The Shingle*, p. 115 (Philadelphia Bar Ass'n, June 1969).
39. The three-judge panel was required under the then existing 28 U.S.C. § 2284.
40. The First Amendment provides in relevant part: "Congress shall make no law respecting an establishment of religion, or prohibiting the free exercise thereof; ...." The Supreme Court has applied this amendment to the states through the due process clause of the Fourteenth Amendment. *Cantwell v. Connecticut*, 310 U.S. 296 (1940).
41. *Schempp v. School Dist. of Abington Twp.*, 177 F. Supp. 398, 406 (E.D. Pa. 1959), 184 F. Supp. 381 (E.D. Pa.), *vacated*, 364 U.S. 298 (1960). The Supreme Court *vacated* the decision and remanded the case for further consideration in light of the amended statute the Pennsylvania General Assembly had enacted in the meantime. *See also* Toll, Seymour I., *A Judge Uncommon*, pp. 253-54, 290-97 (Legal Communications, Ltd., 1993).
42. *Schempp v. School Dist. of Abington Twp.*, 201 F. Supp. 815, 819 (E.D. Pa. 1962).
43. *School Dist. of Abington Twp. v. Schempp*, 374 U.S. 203, 226 (1963).
44. Toll, Seymour I., *A Judge Uncommon*, pp. 296-97 (Legal Communications, Ltd., 1993).

45. 18 U.S.C. § 1461.
46. *United States v. Ginzburg*, 224 F. Supp. 129, 133 (E.D. Pa. 1963).
47. *Id.* at 136.
48. *Id.* at 137.
49. *Ginzburg v. United States*, 383 U.S. 463, 498 (1966).
50. *The Philadelphia Inquirer*, p. 6B, June 4, 1973.
51. 28 U.S.C. § 1404(a).
52. *Popkin v. Eastern Air Lines*, 204 F. Supp. 426 (E.D. Pa. 1962); *Barrack v. Van Dusen*, 309 F.2d 953 (3d Cir. 1962) as amended (3d Cir. 1963); rev'd *sub nom. Van Dusen v. Barrack*, 376 U.S. 612 (1964).
53. 42 U.S.C. § § 2000e et seq.
54. 42 U.S.C. § § 1973 et seq.
55. Weigley, Russell F., ed., *Philadelphia: A 300-Year History*, pp. 186-87, 215 (W.W. Norton and Company, 1982).
56. *Girard Will Case*, 386 Pa. 548, 551 (1956); Johnson, Allen & Malone, Dumas, eds., *Dictionary of American Biography*, Vol. IV, pp. 319-22 (Charles Scribner's Sons, 1932).
57. *Girard Will Case*, 386 Pa. at 551, 553.
58. Moss, Roger W. (Tom Crane, Photographer), *Historic Landmarks of Philadelphia*, pp. 110-15 (University of Pennsylvania Press, 2008).
59. Weigley, Russell F., ed., *Philadelphia: A 300-Year History*, pp. 662, 679 (W.W. Norton and Company, 1982).
60. The Orphans' Courts of the various counties of Pennsylvania were separate courts at that time. They had jurisdiction over the administration of decedent's estates, including testamentary trusts.
61. *Girard Will Case*, 386 Pa. 548, 550 (1956).
62. *Pennsylvania v. Bd. of Directors of City Trusts*, 353 U.S. 230, 231 (1957).
63. Pa. Stat. Ann. tit. 18 § 4654; *Pennsylvania v. Brown*, 260 F. Supp. 358 (E.D. Pa. 1966).
64. *Pennsylvania v. Brown*, 373 F.2d 771 (3d Cir. 1967).
65. *Pennsylvania v. Brown*, 270 F. Supp. 782, 790-92 (E.D. Pa. 1967).
66. *Pennsylvania v. Brown*, 392 F.2d 120 (3d Cir.), *cert. denied*, 391 U.S. 921 (1968).
67. Moss, Roger W. (Tom Crane, Photographer), *Historic Landmarks of Philadelphia*, p. 115 (University of Pennsylvania Press, 2008).
68. *Smith v. Reynolds*, 277 F. Supp. 65 (E.D. Pa. 1967).
69. *Id.* at 68.
70. *Shapiro v. Thompson*, 394 U.S. 618 (1969).
71. Interview by Seymour I. Toll with Joseph S. Lord III, p. 69 (April 27, 1987).
72. *United States ex rel. Mayberry v. Prasse*, 225 F. Supp. 752 (E.D. Pa. 1963). *See The Philadelphia Inquirer*, p. K01 (Oct. 2, 1988).
73. *Mayberry Appeal*, 255 A.2d 131 (Pa. 1969), *vacated and remanded, Mayberry v. Pennsylvania*, 400 U.S. 455 (1971).
74. *Commonwealth v. Mayberry*, 255 A.2d 548 (Pa. 1969).
75. *Mayberry v. Maroney*, 529 F.2d 332 (3d Cir. 1976).
76. 45 U.S.C. §§ 51 et seq.
77. 46 U.S.C. §§ 12101 et seq. and prior history; 33 U.S.C. §§ 901 et seq. and prior history.
78. *McSparran v. Weist*, 270 F. Supp. 421 (E.D. Pa. 1967).
79. *McSparran v. Weist*, 402 F.2d 867 (3d Cir. 1968); *see also* 28 U.S.C. § 1359.
80. Even though the Court decided the case on jurisdictional grounds, it applied its ruling prospectively. In 1988, Congress added 28 U.S.C. § 1332(c)(2) which provides:

    [T]he legal representative of the estate of a decedent shall be deemed to be a citizen only of the same State as the decedent, and the legal representative of an infant or incompetent shall be deemed to be a citizen only of the same State as the infant or incompetent.

81. Interview by Nancy Fullam, Esquire with Judge John P. Fullam, pp. 14-15 (Aug. 8, 1999); Interview by Jason S. Lantzer with Judge John P. Fullam (Jan. 31, 2008); Interview by Jason S. Lantzer with Seymour I. Toll, Esquire (Mar. 27, 2008).

82. Interview by Jason S. Lantzer with Judge John P. Fullam (Jan. 31, 2008).

83. Act of March 18, 1966, Pub. L. No. 89-372, 80 Stat. 75.

84. Act of June 2, 1970, Pub. L. No. 91-272, 84 Stat. 294, 297.

85. *E.g.*, *United States v. Rubino*, 294 F. Supp. 1161 (E.D. Pa. 1969); *United States v. Heljenek*, 275 F. Supp. 579 (E.D. Pa. 1967); *United States v. Kovalchick*, 255 F. Supp. 826 (E.D. Pa. 1966).

86. Minutes of Judges' Meeting on June 25, 1969; Interview by Seymour I. Toll with Judge A. Leon Higginbotham, Jr., pp. 70-73, 81-82 (Sept. 1, 1995); Recollection of Michael E. Kunz, Clerk of the United States District Court for the Eastern District of Pennsylvania.

John B. McPherson (1846 – 1919)
District Judge: 1899 – 1912

James B. Holland (1857 – 1914)
District Judge: 1904 – 1914

J. Whitaker Thompson (1861 – 1946)
District Judge: 1912 – 1931

Oliver B. Dickinson (1857 – 1939)
District Judge: 1914 – 1939

Charles L. McKeehan (1876 – 1925)
District Judge: 1923 – 1925

Albert Branson Maris (1893 – 1989)
District Judge: 1936 – 1938

Frederick V. Follmer (1885 – 1971)
Eastern District Judge: 1946 – 1955

Thomas C. Egan (1894 – 1961)
District Judge: 1957 – 1961

Samuel Caldwell
Clerk
1789 – 1798

David Caldwell
Clerk
1798 – 1831

Francis Hopkinson
Clerk
1831 – 1847

Thomas Leiper Kane
Clerk
1847 – 1858

George Brodbeck
Clerk
1918 – 1951

Leo A. Lilly
Clerk
1951 – 1956

Gilbert W. Ludwig
Clerk
1956 – 1962

W. Halton Spann
Clerk
1962 – 1963

John J. Harding
Clerk
1964 – 1979

Michael E. Kunz
Clerk
1979 –

Federal Building
Second & Ferry Streets
Easton

The Court sat here from
time to time from the 1930's to 1990.

The Holmes Building
101 Larry Holmes Drive
Easton

This has been the Court's location
in Easton since 1990.

American Bank Building
Sixth & Court Streets
Reading

The Court held sessions here
starting in the 1970's.

The Madison Building
400 Washington Street
Reading

The Court has heard cases here since 1988.

Old Lehigh County Courthouse
445 Hamilton Street, Allentown

The Court occupied a courtroom and chambers in this Courthouse in Allentown from the mid-1970's until the mid-1990's.

The Edward N. Cahn U.S. Courthouse
504 Hamilton Street, Allentown

This Courthouse opened in 1995.

Courtroom 6
Ninth & Market Streets
Philadelphia

Ceremonial Courtroom
601 Market Street
Philadelphia

**1941**

**Front Row L to R:** George A. Welsh, William H. Kirkpatrick, Harry E. Kalodner **Back Row:** Guy K. Bard, J. Cullen Ganey

**1949**

**Seated L to R:** Thomas J. Clary, J. Cullen Ganey, George A. Welsh, William H. Kirkpatrick, Guy K. Bard, James P. McGranery, Allan K. Grim

**1962**

**Front Row L to R:** Allan K. Grim, William H. Kirkpatrick, Thomas J. Clary, George A. Welsh, John W. Lord Jr.
**Second Row:** Alfred L. Luongo, Joseph S. Lord III, C. William Kraft Jr., Francis L. Van Dusen, Harold K. Wood, Abraham L. Freedman, Ralph C. Body

**1968**

**Front Row L to R:** C. William Kraft Jr., William H. Kirkpatrick, Thomas J. Clary, John W. Lord Jr., Harold K. Wood
**Second Row:** Thomas A. Masterson, John P. Fullam, John Morgan Davis, Alfred L. Luongo, Joseph S. Lord III, Ralph C. Body, A. Leon Higginbotham Jr., Charles R. Weiner, E. Mac Troutman

**1972**

**Front Row L to R:** John P. Fullam, John Morgan Davis, Alfred L. Luongo, C. William Kraft Jr., Joseph S. Lord III, Harold K. Wood, Ralph C. Body, A. Leon Higginbotham Jr., Charles R. Weiner **Second Row:** Louis C. Bechtle, Clarence C. Newcomer, James H. Gorbey, Daniel H. Huyett 3rd, Edward R. Becker, E. Mac Troutman, Thomas A. Masterson, John B. Hannum, Donald W. VanArtsdalen, J. William Ditter Jr., Raymond J. Broderick, Clifford Scott Green

**1980**

**Front Row L to R:** Norma L. Shapiro, Alfred L. Luongo, Joseph S. Lord III, John Morgan Davis **Second Row:** Joseph L. McGlynn Jr., James T. Giles, E. Mac Troutman, John B. Hannum, Edward N. Cahn, Raymond J. Broderick, Louis C. Bechtle **Third Row:** J. William Ditter Jr., John P. Fullam, Edward R. Becker, Daniel H. Huyett 3rd, Charles R. Weiner, Louis H. Pollak, Donald W. VanArtsdalen, Clarence C. Newcomer, Clifford Scott Green

**1986**

**Front Row L to R:** John B. Hannum, E. Mac Troutman, Joseph S. Lord III, Alfred L. Luongo, John P. Fullam, Charles R. Weiner, Donald W. VanArtsdalen **Second Row:** Louis C. Bechtle, Clarence C. Newcomer, J. William Ditter Jr., Daniel H. Huyett 3rd, Raymond J. Broderick, Clifford Scott Green, Joseph L. McGlynn Jr. **Back Row:** Anthony J. Scirica, James McGirr Kelly, James T. Giles, Louis H. Pollak, Edward N. Cahn, Norma L. Shapiro, Thomas N. O'Neill Jr., Marvin Katz, Edmund V. Ludwig

**1989**

**Front Row L to R:** J. William Ditter Jr., Donald W. VanArtsdalen, John B. Hannum, Joseph S. Lord III, John P. Fullam, Charles R. Weiner, E. Mac Troutman, Daniel H. Huyett 3rd, Raymond J. Broderick **Second Row:** James T. Giles, Louis H. Pollak, Joseph L. McGlynn Jr., Clifford Scott Green, Clarence C. Newcomer, Louis C. Bechtle, Edward N. Cahn, Norma L. Shapiro, Thomas N. O'Neill, Jr. **Back Row:** Herbert J. Hutton, Jan E. DuBois, Robert S. Gawthrop III, Robert F. Kelly, Marvin Katz, James McGirr Kelly, Edmund V. Ludwig, Franklin S. Van Antwerpen, Lowell A. Reed Jr., Jay C. Waldman

**1991**

**Front Row L to R:** Raymond J. Broderick, E. Mac Troutman, John P. Fullam, Louis C. Bechtle, Charles R. Weiner, Donald W. VanArtsdalen, J. William Ditter Jr. **Second Row:** Thomas N. O'Neill Jr., Norma L. Shapiro, Edward N. Cahn, Clifford Scott Green, Clarence C. Newcomer, Joseph L. McGlynn Jr., Louis H. Pollak, James T. Giles **Third Row:** Jan E. DuBois, Robert S. Gawthrop III, Robert F. Kelly, Marvin Katz, James McGirr Kelly, Edmund V. Ludwig, Franklin S. Van Antwerpen, Lowell A. Reed Jr., Herbert J. Hutton **Back Row:** Harvey Bartle III, Ronald L. Buckwalter, Jay C. Waldman, William H. Yohn Jr., Stewart Dalzell

**1994**

**Front Row L to R:** J. William Ditter Jr., E. Mac Troutman, John P. Fullam, Edward N. Cahn, Charles R. Weiner, Donald W. VanArtsdalen, Raymond J. Broderick **Second Row:** Marvin Katz, Thomas N. O'Neill, Jr., Norma L. Shapiro, Joseph L. McGlynn Jr., Clifford Scott Green, Clarence C. Newcomer, Louis C. Bechtle, Louis H. Pollak, James T. Giles, James McGirr Kelly **Third Row:** Jay C. Waldman, Jan E. DuBois, Robert S. Gawthrop III, Robert F. Kelly, Edmund V. Ludwig, Franklin S. Van Antwerpen, Lowell A. Reed, Jr., Herbert J. Hutton **Back Row:** Anita B. Brody, J. Curtis Joyner, Stewart Dalzell, William H. Yohn Jr., Ronald L. Buckwalter, Harvey Bartle III, John R. Padova, Eduardo C. Robreno, Marjorie O. Rendell

**2000**

**Front Row L to R:** Raymond J. Broderick, Donald W. VanArtsdalen, John P. Fullam, James T. Giles, Charles R. Weiner, J. William Ditter Jr., Clarence C. Newcomer **Second Row:** Thomas N. O'Neill Jr., Norma L. Shapiro, Louis C. Bechtle, Clifford Scott Green, Louis H. Pollak, James McGirr Kelly **Third Row:** Marvin Katz, Jay C. Waldman, Jan E. DuBois, Franklin S. Van Antwerpen, Robert F. Kelly, Lowell A. Reed Jr., Herbert J. Hutton, Ronald L. Buckwalter, Edmund V. Ludwig **Back Row:** Bruce W. Kauffman, Eduardo C. Robreno, John R. Padova, Harvey Bartle III, William H. Yohn Jr., Stewart Dalzell, J. Curtis Joyner, Anita B. Brody

**2004**

**Front Row L to R:** Norma L. Shapiro, Clifford Scott Green, J. William Ditter Jr., John P. Fullam, James T. Giles, Charles R. Weiner, Clarence C. Newcomer, Louis H. Pollak, Thomas N. O'Neill Jr. **Second Row:** Stewart Dalzell, William H. Yohn Jr., Lowell A. Reed Jr., Edmund V. Ludwig, James McGirr Kelly, Marvin Katz, Robert F. Kelly, Jan E. DuBois, Ronald L. Buckwalter, Harvey Bartle III **Third Row:** Berle M. Schiller, Mary A. McLaughlin, Anita B. Brody, J. Curtis Joyner, John R. Padova, Eduardo C. Robreno, Bruce W. Kauffman, Petrese B. Tucker, R. Barclay Surrick, Legrome D. Davis **Back Row:** Paul S. Diamond, Gene E. K. Pratter, Timothy J. Savage, Cynthia M. Rufe, Michael M. Baylson, James Knoll Gardner, Lawrence F. Stengel, Juan R. Sanchez

**2006**

**Front Row L to R:** James T. Giles, Louis H. Pollak, J. William Ditter Jr., John P. Fullam, Harvey Bartle III, Donald W. VanArtsdalen, Clifford Scott Green, Norma L. Shapiro, Thomas N. O'Neill Jr. **Second Row:** William H. Yohn Jr., Jan E. DuBois, Robert F. Kelly, Marvin Katz, Edmund V. Ludwig, Lowell A. Reed Jr., Ronald L. Buckwalter, Stewart Dalzell **Third Row:** Berle M. Schiller, Mary A. McLaughlin, Anita B. Brody, J. Curtis Joyner, John R. Padova, Eduardo C. Robreno, Bruce W. Kauffman, Petrese B. Tucker, R. Barclay Surrick
**Back Row:** Thomas M. Golden, Paul S. Diamond, Gene E. K. Pratter, Timothy J. Savage, Cynthia M. Rufe, Legrome D. Davis, Michael M. Baylson, James Knoll Gardner, Lawrence F. Stengel, Juan R. Sánchez

**2009**

**Front Row L to R:** Robert F. Kelly, Thomas N. O'Neill Jr., J. William Ditter Jr., John P. Fullam, Harvey Bartle III, Donald W. VanArtsdalen, Louis H. Pollak, Edmund V. Ludwig, Lowell A. Reed Jr. **Second Row:** Eduardo C. Robreno, John R. Padova, William H. Yohn Jr., Jan E. DuBois, Norma L. Shapiro, Ronald L. Buckwalter, Stewart Dalzell, J. Curtis Joyner. **Third Row:** Michael M. Baylson, Legrome D. Davis, Berle M. Schiller, Mary A. McLaughlin, Anita B. Brody, Petrese B. Tucker, R. Barclay Surrick, Cynthia M. Rufe, Timothy J. Savage. **Back Row:** C. Darnell Jones II, Thomas M. Golden, Paul S. Diamond, Gene E. K. Pratter, James Knoll Gardner, Lawrence F. Stengel, Juan R. Sánchez, Joel H. Slomsky, Mitchell S. Goldberg

# VIII
# Growth and Change: The 1970's and 1980's

The decades of the 1970's and 1980's saw the continued growth not only in the number of judges in the Eastern District of Pennsylvania but also in the number, complexity, and variety of the cases coming before the Court. The docket contained more and more filings raising constitutional issues as well as claims under an ever-increasing array of federal statutes. Maritime actions and cases where jurisdiction was based on diversity of citizenship played a lesser role than in the past.

While most criminal prosecutions continued to be brought in the state courts, the federal courts were now focusing as never before on "street crime" indictments usually involving drugs and guns as the public and the powers that be in Washington became greatly concerned about the rise of violence throughout the country. There was also focus on organized crime and political corruption as had not been seen previously.

By the late 1960's, it was quite evident that the courthouse built in the late 1930's at Ninth and Market Streets was no longer adequate. A proposal in the 1950's to add four additional floors never came to fruition. Chief Judge Clary became the leading advocate for a new judicial home, and Senator Scott lent his strong support. A site was ultimately selected on the north side of Market Street between Sixth and Seventh Streets, which was at one time part of "skid row" but now adjoined Independence National Historical Park. The construction of the twenty-two story courthouse was not without problems or controversy. It clearly lacked the architectural grandeur or the fine appointments of its predecessor. Of more practical concern, it was erected over an old creek bed with foundation pylons that were later determined to be only forty-five feet deep rather than the required ninety feet to bedrock. As a result of this miscalculation, the new building began to tilt shortly after occupancy. The matter was rectified, but to this day the foundation level is regularly monitored. Finally, there was distress among the judges that the courthouse was being named for James A. Byrne, an obscure former Congressman from the Kensington section of Philadelphia who had served as the U.S. Marshal for the District in the 1940's. Known to his friends and acquaintances as "Digger," Byrne was not a lawyer but rather, as his nickname suggests, an undertaker. Making the best of the situation, most have generally continued to refer to the edifice simply as the United States Courthouse.

The courthouse opened in 1975 and has remained the home of both the District Court and the Court of Appeals to the present. It was designed with a plaza and main entrance fronting on Sixth Street. Near that entrance on the inside of the building is a sculpture by Louise Nevelson called "Bicentennial Dawn." The design notwithstanding, most use the more easily accessible Market Street doors. The address of the courthouse, recognizing reality, is 601 Market Street.

Unlike all previous places of holding court, the judges designated this one in March 1987 as smoke-free except for certain limited areas including chambers.[1] Today, smoking is off limits throughout the courthouse.

Despite other deficiencies in the building, most District Judges have a large courtroom and a spacious chambers. The chambers have floor-to-ceiling windows with a panoramic eastward view not only of the Benjamin Franklin Bridge and the Delaware River, but also of Independence Hall and the Christ Church burial ground where Francis Hopkinson, the Court's first judge, is interred. Out the windows can be seen the many tourists in Independence National Historical Park and the not infrequent commemorations, rallies, and protests that take place there. Just west of the courthouse on the southwest corner of Seventh and Market Streets is a reconstruction of the Graff House where Thomas Jefferson drafted the Declaration of Independence in 1776.

This time no post office occupies the first floor of the courthouse. Instead, there is a vast lobby which initially had inadequate lighting. The first floor also includes a large display case and a spacious law library. On the north side of the lobby is a corridor connecting to a large Ceremonial Courtroom which has a bench that seats twenty-two judges. On the walls hang the portraits of the early judges starting with Francis Hopkinson and of later judges who have presided as Chief Judge of the Eastern District of Pennsylvania.

The lobby is usually a place of calm where people enter and exit the courthouse in an orderly manner and where quiet conversation often transpires. From time to time, judges, lawyers, and guests gather there for receptions held after sessions in the nearby Ceremonial Courtroom to induct a new judge, to memorialize a deceased colleague, or to unveil a judicial portrait. In the early part of 1979, the tranquility normally experienced in the lobby was disturbed. It became the site of a controversy over the exhibition of art which eventually resulted in a lawsuit. Under a federal program to encourage the use of public buildings for cultural and educational purposes and to stimulate pedestrian traffic, the works of local artists were displayed in the lobby. Some of the paintings featured females whose countenance left nothing to the imagination. Other artwork contained purportedly offensive political content.

Chief Judge Joseph Lord, acting in his administrative capacity, directed that ten paintings of nudes be removed forthwith by the General Services Administration ("GSA") which administered the federal program. Leaving no doubt about his feelings on the matter, he declared emphatically that the subject matter was not fit for viewing by priests, nuns, or school children.[2]

The publicity and stir over the removal of the nude paintings had barely subsided when artwork allegedly critical of the FBI appeared in the lobby. Chief Judge Lord promptly banished it from the courthouse. He was quoted as having said, 'I order it out and I don't care who takes it out as long as it's out.'[3]

At that point, eminent Philadelphia lawyer Henry Sawyer filed a lawsuit in this Court for an injunction to overturn Judge Lord's directive and its execution by GSA.[4] The matter was assigned to Judge Fullam. After Sawyer presented the case and made an impassioned argument in support of liberty and freedom of speech, Judge Fullam, ruling from the bench, ordered the politically offensive art to be restored to the lobby.[5]

During the time the early plans were being discussed for the current courthouse and before incidents over artwork were making headlines, additional judges were being appointed. In 1970, President Nixon named four judges, all Republicans, to fill newly authorized seats for the Eastern District. They were Edward R. Becker, Donald W. VanArtsdalen, Daniel H. Huyett 3rd, and J. William Ditter Jr., each of whom resided in a different county. They progressed through confirmation in lockstep. Had the President signed their commissions on the same day, their seniority on the court would have been determined by age, with Becker, the youngest of the four, having the least seniority. Instead, Becker's commission was signed by the President a day ahead of the others so that he had precedence over his three older colleagues.

Becker, age thirty-seven, lived in the Northwood neighborhood of Northeast Philadelphia in the house where he grew up and usually rode the Market-Frankford elevated line to the courthouse. He had served as counsel to the Republican City Committee, was close to William Austin Meehan, the city's Republican leader, and had run unsuccessfully for City Council and the State Senate. He had practiced law with his father and brother-in-law in a small firm. As a judge, he wrote long erudite opinions with a plethora of footnotes, and in 1981 was appointed to the Court of Appeals for the Third Circuit where he eventually became the Chief Judge. Becker, a hard worker with enormous energy, was rarely seen without a brief in his hand. One of his most notable and oft-repeated comments was his description of the Eastern District as Valhalla for Philadelphia Republicans who had been defeated for elective office.[6]

Becker was actively involved in countless efforts for judicial, administrative, and civic improvement. The prestigious Devitt Award was presented to him in 2001. His leadership and persistence resulted in the opening of Chestnut Street between Fifth and Sixth Streets after it had been closed to pedestrian and vehicular traffic purportedly to protect Independence Hall after the terrorist attacks of September 11, 2001.

Donald W. VanArtsdalen was an experienced trial lawyer who resided and practiced in Bucks County. He had enlisted in the Canadian Army in 1940 before the United States entered World War II and participated in the Battle of Britain. After the United States declared war, he joined the American Army, became a Ranger, and saw heavy action in North Africa and Italy. From 1954 to 1958, he was the elected District Attorney of Bucks County.

Daniel H. Huyett 3rd was a lawyer in Berks County whose ancestors had settled there before the Revolution. He had a very gracious demeanor. During most of the Second World War he was stationed as an Army Officer in Panama. Some years later, he was appointed the Solicitor of the City of Reading and headed the Berks County Republican Party. In 1968, Governor Raymond P. Shafer named him to the state Public Utility Commission. He was an early and strong proponent of electronic sound recording of court proceedings in place of a court reporter who would take down testimony manually. He persuaded most of his judicial colleagues to follow his lead.

The last of the four 1970 appointees by President Nixon was J. William Ditter Jr. of Montgomery County. His father had represented the County in Congress from 1933 until his death in a navy plane crash in 1943. Ditter served in the Navy during World War II and again during the Korean conflict. Later during his legal career, he was the County's First Assistant District Attorney and a named partner in an Ambler law firm. In 1963, the voters elected him as a judge of the Court of Common Pleas of Montgomery County where he had been one of the court's two law clerks in his younger days.

Ditter, who lives on a farm, has long engaged in a variety of agricultural activities. Emulating Sherlock Holmes, he was an avid keeper of bees for many years. He is also a gifted speaker and writer. Each December, his colleagues and friends eagerly await his Christmas letter in which he describes with dry humor the holiday visit of his "Cousin Misty." Only the skeptics of this world believe her to be an apocryphal figure.

At five-year intervals after their appointments to the federal bench in 1970, Judges Becker, VanArtsdalen, Huyett, and Ditter hosted a luncheon for all their district court colleagues at the nearby Down Town Club. Forty years later, the two surviving judges, Donald VanArtsdalen and William Ditter, have continued this congenial quinquennial tradition.

During his time in office, President Nixon was to add seven more judges to the District Court. In December 1970, James H. Gorbey, of Delaware County, was named to the bench. Previously, Gorbey had served as the Mayor of the City of Chester and as a judge of the Court of Common Pleas of Delaware County. He died of cancer only six years after his confirmation.

In 1971, the President nominated Raymond J. Broderick, Clarence C. Newcomer, and Clifford Scott Green to the Court. Broderick, a Philadelphian who had been a Naval Officer during World War II, was Lieutenant Governor of Pennsylvania between 1967 and 1971 under Governor Raymond P. Shafer. During his tenure, Broderick was the president of the 1967-1968 Pennsylvania Constitutional Convention which reformed the state Constitution's Judiciary Article and provided for a unified court system for the Commonwealth. After he was defeated for Governor in 1970, Senator Scott and other Republican leaders endorsed him to fill a vacancy on the District Court. While on the federal bench, Broderick successfully persuaded Congress to allow compulsory arbitration of smaller damage cases before a panel of court appointed lawyers with the right of a trial *de novo* in the District Court if any party is not satisfied with the arbitration result. He had a memorable Irish wit, and there was no better storyteller.

For many years Broderick and his lovely wife Marjorie graciously hosted a summer outing for the judges and their spouses at their beachfront home in Ocean City, New Jersey. The event always included swimming in the ocean, a sumptuous meal featuring steaks cooked on their outdoor grill, and an abundance of good fellowship. On June 25, 1999, about a year before his death, Broderick wrote a poignant letter to his fellow judges and their spouses:

> Marjorie and I are finding it difficult to tell you that there will not be a beach party on the Broderick sand dunes this summer. Recently Marjorie and I have been experiencing some health problems.
>
> . . .
>
> For more than twenty years, our Judges' day on the beach on the Broderick dunes has been the focal point of our love for you and your family. We are saddened by this interruption.
>
> Marjorie and I look forward to seeing you soon.
>
> Sincerely,
> Ray

Later in 1971, in accordance with Senator Scott's goal of geographic diversity, the President chose Clarence C. Newcomer, only the second nominee in the Court's history from Lancaster County. Newcomer had served in the Navy in the South Pacific during the Second World War and like Judge VanArtsdalen had been elected to a term as his county's District Attorney. At the time of his nomination, he was a partner in a law firm in Lancaster.

President Nixon's last appointment in 1971 was Clifford Scott Green from Philadelphia. He was the second African-American to be selected for the Eastern District. After his time in the Army Air Corps during World War II, he matriculated to Temple University where he obtained a B.S. degree in economics, the first member of his family to attend college. His original plan was to become a certified public accountant, but he was told there were no such jobs in Philadelphia for African-

Americans. He then decided to pursue a career in law and was graduated near the top of his class at Temple Law School. Like Leon Higginbotham, he secured a position with the law firm headed by Austin Norris and later became a partner. Again, this was at a time when other employment opportunities for African-American lawyers in Philadelphia, even ones of his ability, were virtually non-existent.

After law school, Green became involved in politics and was the Republican Leader in the 44th Ward in West Philadelphia for a number of years. He ran unsuccessfully for City Council and the Municipal Court but ultimately was appointed and then elected to the old County Court of Philadelphia (later merged into the Court of Common Pleas) with the strong support of Governor William Scranton. He was a judge of the Court of Common Pleas when named to the federal bench. Citing the "joy his district court job provided him and the numerous friendships he enjoyed there," he subsequently declined an appointment to the Court of Appeals.[7]

Judge Broderick told an amusing story about his friend Clifford Green, which he repeated often and which Judge Green continued to recount after Judge Broderick's death. When Broderick was running for state-wide office, he noticed in reviewing the election returns that he had received only one vote in the home division of Clifford and Mable Green in West Philadelphia. When Broderick asked Clifford Green about it, Green insisted that he had indeed voted for Broderick. When Broderick inquired of Mable Green, she responded emphatically that she was the one who had cast the ballot for him. The matter, of course, was never resolved, but the story always generated laughter among the judges.

In 1972, President Nixon appointed to the Court Louis C. Bechtle, the United States Attorney since 1969. Bechtle traveled the same path to the District Court as eight of his predecessors: Judges Lewis, Holland, Thompson, Bard, Ganey, Follmer, Wood, and Joseph Lord, all of whom had held the office of United States Attorney. Bechtle resided in Montgomery County and had previously practiced law there at the Wisler Pearlstine firm. Chief Justice William Rehnquist designated him as a member of the Judicial Panel on Multidistrict Litigation. He also served as the Chief Judge of the Eastern District for several years in the early 1990's.

Bechtle's appointment was followed by those of Herbert A. Fogel in 1973 and Joseph L. McGlynn, Jr., in 1974. They were both Philadelphians. Before he became a District Judge, Fogel was a partner at Obermayer Rebmann Maxwell & Hippel and a close friend of Senator Scott, who was also affiliated with the same firm. Fogel resigned from the bench in 1978.

Joseph McGlynn had served in the Navy in World War II and later as an Assistant United States Attorney. In 1959, toward the end of the Eisenhower administration, he was named the United States Attorney. He was sitting on the Court of Common Pleas of Philadelphia County at the time when he was nominated to the federal court.

McGlynn, like Judge Becker, lived in Northeast Philadelphia and was close to Bill Meehan and the Philadelphia Republican organization. He often quipped that a judge was simply a lawyer who knew a politician.

Edward N. Cahn, a young lawyer in private practice in Allentown, Lehigh County, was the next appointee to the District Court who took office in January 1975. He was the only judge named by President Gerald R. Ford to the Eastern District. In the 1990's, he was to serve as Chief Judge of the Court, succeeding Louis Bechtle. For three years he was the District Court representative from the Third Circuit on the Judicial Conference of the United States, the policymaking body for the federal courts presided over by the Chief Justice.

President Jimmy Carter, Ford's successor, was strongly committed to the appointment of more women and minorities to the federal bench.[8] During his time in office, he filled three vacancies on the Eastern District with Louis H. Pollak, Norma L. Shapiro, and James T. Giles. Each had the endorsement of Pennsylvania's two Republican Senators, Richard Schweiker and John Heinz.

Louis Pollak was an academician and a fervent advocate for civil rights. After completing his undergraduate studies, he entered the Army during World War II. Upon completing law school, he was hired by Supreme Court Justice Wiley Rutledge as his law clerk. During his time in private practice as a young lawyer, he helped the NAACP Legal Defense Fund in writing a Supreme Court brief in support of school desegregation in the landmark case of *Brown v. Board of Education*.[9] Beginning in 1951, he served two years in the State Department as a special assistant to Ambassador-at-Large Philip C. Jessup. He then was employed as assistant counsel to the Amalgamated Clothing Workers of America. Teaching followed. After serving on the faculty and as Dean of Yale Law School, he moved to Philadelphia in 1975 to become Dean of the University of Pennsylvania Law School. With the support of the NAACP Legal Defense Fund and a number of influential lawyers such as William T. Coleman, he was seated as a federal judge in 1978. Chief Justice Warren Burger later appointed him to the Multidistrict Litigation Panel.

Norma Shapiro was the first woman ever confirmed to the Eastern District. Following her completion of law school, Justice Horace Stern of the Pennsylvania Supreme Court chose her as his only female law clerk. Sometime later, she temporarily put her legal career on hold when her three sons were young and then returned to practice to become the first woman partner at Dechert Price & Rhoads. She was also elected to the Lower Merion School Board and served as its President for several years. Her interests have included both the Philadelphia Bar Association where she chaired the Board of Governors and the American Bar Association where she presided over the Judicial Division of the House of Delegates. Recently, the President of the American Bar Association has named her to head its prestigious

Standing Committee on Federal Judicial Improvements. Throughout her career, she has remained a strong advocate for women in the legal profession. Although she was a Republican, President Carter in her case transcended partisan politics when he selected her to be a judge.

Her arrival on the Court in 1978 was greeted at first with less than enthusiasm by some of her male colleagues who had not been accustomed to associating with professional women in the workplace. As time passed and they came to know her, these gender-related feelings ultimately disappeared.

In that era when a new judge joined the Eastern District, it was the custom for each of the other judges to select a certain number of cases from his docket and transfer them to the new member of the Court. Not uncommonly, there was a tendency to pick for transfer what were characterized as "dog" cases, that is, those which in the transferor judge's view were either uninteresting or otherwise unappetizing. When Judge Shapiro received her bundle of assignments and then questioned the fairness of the selection process, the Court approved, albeit prospectively, a more equitable arrangement whereby cases for transfer from each judge's calendar are chosen at random, with the transferor judge having only a veto on the reassignment of any particular case.[10] Each succeeding judge has owed her a lasting debt of gratitude for this change in practice.

Judge Shapiro soon instituted a gracious and generous custom of her own which continues to this day and which is undoubtedly unique among courts anywhere. She writes lyrics and provides a cake for each of her colleagues on that colleague's birthday. These celebrations now occur over thirty times a year during lunch in the judges' dining room. With the assistance of Judge Fullam until his retirement and now that of Judge Dalzell, she leads all judges in attendance in singing the lyrics to some known tune of her choosing, and the cake is then cut and eagerly consumed. A good time is always had by all. As a result of the countless cakes she has purchased over more than three decades, it is believed that she has single-handedly kept the local baking industry in the black.

The judges have reciprocated by holding a birthday celebration for Judge Shapiro each year. As long as the summer outings at the Brodericks in Ocean City took place, the festivities were held there, with John Fullam always singing in her honor a solo, with modified English lyrics, from Vincenzo Bellini's opera, *Norma*. Since that time, the tradition has endured, generally taking place in the judges' dining room at the Courthouse.

James T. Giles, at age thirty-six, was the third African-American named to the Eastern District and the last judge named by President Carter. His appointment came in 1979. He grew up in segregated southwestern Virginia but went to college at Amherst and then on to Yale Law School. Following his employment as a field attorney with the National Labor Relations Board, he became an associate and then a partner at Pepper, Hamilton & Scheetz in Philadelphia. He followed Edward Cahn as the Chief Judge of the Court, a position he held for seven years.

President Carter was defeated in his re-election bid, and Ronald Reagan was sworn in as President in January 1981. At that point, Pennsylvania's two Senators were John Heinz and Arlen Specter, both Republicans. Specter had become the Commonwealth's junior senator when he was elected in 1980 to replace Senator Richard Schweiker who had opted not to run for a third term. Prior to his election, Specter was a partner at Dechert Price & Rhoads. With a Republican President and two Republican Senators, the process for the appointment of new judges was less complicated than it might have been otherwise. Specter, an experienced trial lawyer and former Philadelphia District Attorney, and Heinz, who had an M.B.A., worked together to recommend for the federal bench qualified individuals with diverse backgrounds from the different counties within the District.

President Reagan named twelve judges, all Republicans, to the Eastern District during his eight years in office: Thomas N. O'Neill Jr., James McGirr Kelly, Marvin Katz, Anthony J. Scirica, Edmund V. Ludwig, Robert F. Kelly, Franklin S. Van Antwerpen, Robert S. Gawthrop III, Lowell A. Reed Jr., Jan E. DuBois, Herbert J. Hutton, and Jay C. Waldman. Of the twelve, Judges Scirica, Ludwig, Robert Kelly, Van Antwerpen, and Gawthrop were sitting state Common Pleas Judges at the time of their appointments.

Judge Ludwig, as a state court judge and thereafter, taught and lectured extensively on a myriad of legal subjects. He also authored a number of articles on law-related topics, including the law as it impacts on the mentally ill and on sentencing.

Judges Scirica and Gawthrop were not the first jurists in their families. Judge Scirica's father had been President Judge of the Court of Common Pleas of Montgomery County while Judge Gawthrop's grandfather had sat on the Superior Court of Pennsylvania and his uncle on the Court of Common Pleas of Chester County. Off the bench, Gawthrop had another judicial career of sorts. He was well known for singing leading roles in various Gilbert & Sullivan operettas including the learned judge in *Trial by Jury*.

After law school, Gawthrop had clerked for Common Pleas Judge Lee F. Swope of Dauphin County. Scirica and he had also been Assistant District Attorneys in their respective home counties, and Van Antwerpen had served as Chief Counsel to the Northampton County Legal Aid Society.

The other seven Reagan appointees had been in private practice when named to the federal bench. Many had served in the military. Some had engaged in significant public service other than elected office during their legal careers.

Thomas O'Neill, who had clerked for Circuit Judge Herbert F. Goodrich and then Supreme Court Justice Harold Burton, participated extensively in bar activities. He served as Chancellor of the Philadelphia Bar Association, a member of the Board of Governors of the Pennsylvania Bar Association, and a member of the House of Delegates of the America Bar Association. He practiced law as a partner with Montgomery, McCracken, Walker & Rhoads and was twice counsel to the Pennsylvania Legislative Reapportionment Commission. Upon joining the Court, Judge O'Neill, an angler by avocation, placed on the bench facing him a small plaque which reads, "By the mouth the fish is caught." This piscatorial aphorism acts as a reminder that peril often awaits those including lawyers and judges who fail to weigh their words carefully.

Judge James McGirr Kelly had been the law clerk to Judge Edward J. Griffiths of the Philadelphia Court of Common Pleas and later served as an Assistant District Attorney, an Assistant United States Attorney, and a Special Assistant Pennsylvania Attorney General. For several years he was engaged as the Master of the Jury Selection Board for the Philadelphia Common Pleas Court. Governor Shafer appointed him in 1967 to a ten-year term on the state Public Utility Commission.

Judge Katz, a close college friend and one time law partner of Senator Specter, had worked for a year as the law clerk of Philadelphia Common Pleas Judge Francis X. McClanaghan. From 1977 to 1981, he held the position of Special Assistant to the Commissioner of the Internal Revenue Service. A strong friendship developed among Katz, Thomas O'Neill, and James Kelly, all of whom joined the Court at the same time. They regularly took walks together after lunch before returning to their judicial duties.

Similar to a number of his colleagues, Judge Waldman had also spent time as a judicial clerk, in his case with Pennsylvania Superior Court Judge Gwilym A. Price, Jr. His career continued as an Assistant United States Attorney in the Western District of Pennsylvania and then as a Deputy Assistant Attorney General in the Justice Department in Washington, both under Dick Thornburgh. After acting as Thornburgh's campaign manager for his successful bid for Governor in 1978, Waldman became General Counsel in the Thornburgh Administration. Waldman, prior to his appointment to the court, was a partner at Dilworth, Paxson, Kalish & Kauffman. Those who knew him remembered his fondness of fine cigars from which he was seldom parted except when in the courtroom.

Judge Hutton, like his African-American colleagues, Judges Higginbotham and Green, was an alumnus of the Norris law firm. His career also included time as a Hearing Officer for the Philadelphia Board of Revision of Taxes.

Judge Reed had been a law clerk for Philadelphia Common Pleas Judge Ethan Allen Doty and was a partner at Rawle & Henderson. He had been a director of the Abington Memorial Health Care Corporation and was active in the Temple Law School Alumni Association.

As a young lawyer, Judge DuBois had worked as the law clerk for Circuit Judge Harry Kalodner and ultimately became a partner at White & Williams. DuBois, like

Marvin Katz, was a close friend of Arlen Specter. And like his new colleagues, Thomas O'Neill and Lowell Reed, DuBois had appeared frequently as a trial lawyer in the Eastern District before he became a judge.

In contrast to many Eastern District judges in the past, only three of the Reagan appointees, Judges Scirica, Reed, and Robert Kelly, had ever been elected by the voters to a non-judicial office. Scirica served as a Representative in the Pennsylvania General Assembly from the Norristown area of Montgomery County for eight years before his days as a Common Pleas Judge. Kelly had won a term as the Prothonotary of the Delaware County Common Pleas Court, and Reed had been elected to the Abington-Rockledge School Board.

Scirica would later have a distinguished career as the Chief Judge of the Court of Appeals for the Third Circuit. Among his many notable achievements, he would chair the Executive Committee of the Judicial Conference of the United States on appointment of Chief Justice Roberts and like Judges Maris and Becker before him would receive the Devitt Award.

Two of Reagan's appointees, Robert Gawthrop and Jay Waldman, both of whom enlivened the Court with their vibrant personalities, suffered premature deaths. Each succumbed to cancer while still in his fifties.

The marked increase in the number of judges in the Eastern District in the 1970's and 1980's reflected the Court's increasing caseload. In the early 1970's as the Vietnam War persisted, that caseload included criminal draft evasion cases. Judges grappled with them in different ways.[11] In a case before Judge Luongo, a person who made a belated claim for conscientious objector status was convicted for failure to submit to induction. Judge Luongo had announced to counsel before trial his standing policy to sentence to thirty-months imprisonment all selective service violators "if they are good people" whether or not they pleaded guilty or were found guilty after trial. His goal was uniformity in sentencing, a principle that was to become one of the cornerstones of the Sentencing Guidelines which went into effect years later. The Court of Appeals, however, reversed the conviction due to Judge Luongo's failure to recuse himself. It read his stated policy of imposing uniform thirty-month sentences as indicating a bent of mind that may prevent or impede impartiality of judgment.[12]

Several months later, the Court of Appeals again reversed him for his policy of imposing a thirty-month sentence on a person convicted of violations of the Selective Service Act. It concluded that he had exhibited personal bias against this class of defendants. In the Court's opinion, Chief Judge Collins Seitz explained that a defendant has the right to make his own statement before sentencing and to present other evidence in mitigation. A fixed sentence determined in advance is "inconsistent" with the "mandate to tailor the sentence imposed to the circumstances surrounding each individual defendant" and "frustrates" those rules designed for that purpose.[13]

Judge Luongo took the unusual step of engaging his old law firm to file on his behalf in the Supreme Court a motion for leave to file a petition for writ of prohibition and/or mandamus directed against the United States Court of Appeals for the Third Circuit. When the Supreme Court denied his motion,[14] he ceased presiding over Selective Service cases.[15]

In an interview over a decade later and only a few days before his death, he spoke of those Court of Appeals' rulings. They still rankled him. While recognizing that reasonable minds could differ on whether he had abused his discretion in imposing a uniform sentencing policy, he vehemently rejected any notion of personal bias.[16] Most of his colleagues agreed that the Court of Appeals had treated him, a well-respected judge, unfairly.[17]

One selective service lawsuit filed in the Eastern District in 1972 had potentially widespread consequences. It dealt with the issue of gender discrimination. Robert Goldberg challenged the constitutionality of the Military Selective Service Act on the ground that only males were subject to registration and conscription. A three-judge court consisting of District Judges James Gorbey and Joseph Lord and Circuit Judge Max Rosenn was convened. Shortly thereafter, the draft ended and the case lay dormant for a number of years. Ultimately, the matter was reactivated, and Judge Cahn replaced the late Judge Gorbey on the three-judge panel.[18]

In 1980, President Jimmy Carter asked Congress to reinstitute the registration process in order to facilitate a draft if one should ever be reinstated. He proposed that women as well as men register as a matter of equity. Congress authorized the President to require registration of males but rejected his request with respect to women.[19]

The question now before the three-judge panel was whether the Military Selective Service Act was constitutional when it compelled men, but not women, to register. The panel ruled unanimously that the law violated the due process clause of the Constitution and enjoined enforcement of registration on the ground that it did not treat men and women equally. In an opinion by Judge Cahn, the Court stated:

> It is undisputed that the MSSA [Military Selective Service Act] creates a gender-based classification and that the government has the burden of justifying that classification .... We ... hold that the complete exclusion of women from the pool of registrants does not serve "important governmental objectives" and is not "substantially related" ... to any alleged government interest. Thus, the MSSA unconstitutionally discriminates between males and females.[20]

The Court's order was stayed by Justice William Brennan to give the Supreme Court an opportunity to consider the matter. After argument, the Supreme Court reversed. Chief Justice William Rehnquist wrote for the majority that the District

Court must defer to Congress which has the exclusive power under the Constitution to raise and maintain an Army and a Navy and to make rules and regulations for the land and naval forces.[21] According to the high Court, Congress had made a valid policy decision that women in the military were not to engage in combat and therefore should not be required to register for a possible draft. Consequently, men and women were not similarly situated for purposes of a draft or registration for a draft and the Military Selective Service Act did not violate due process.[22]

Because of the civil rights legislation passed in the 1960's, the Court's docket in the 1970's and 1980's was filled with cases alleging race and gender discrimination, primarily but not exclusively discrimination in the work place. Most were actions brought by individuals who sought damages or other relief only for themselves.

Other lawsuits, in contrast, sought systemic change. Judge Green had before him a class action in *Bolden v. Pennsylvania State Police*[23] in which the named plaintiff claimed that the Pennsylvania State Police were engaged in racially discriminatory policies in the hiring and promotion of state troopers. In 1974, Judge Green approved a Consent Decree which mandated the hiring and promotion of more minorities. At the time it was entered, total minority representation among the employees of the Pennsylvania State Police was only 1.48% compared with 10.8% for all Pennsylvania state agencies[24] and a minority population in the Commonwealth of 9.2%.[25] The Decree, which Judge Green monitored, remained in effect for twenty-five years.

Judge Higginbotham dealt with claims of racial discrimination against Local 542 of the International Union of Operating Engineers and several contractor associations because of the failure to hire African-Americans for construction jobs. These defendants moved to disqualify him from the case due to a speech he had delivered before the Association for the Study of Afro-American Life and History. Judge Higginbotham forcefully rejected the effort as meritless:

> I concede that I am black. I do not apologize for that obvious fact. I take rational pride in my heritage, just as most other ethnics take pride in theirs. However, that one is black does not mean, ipso facto, that he is anti-white; no more than being Jewish implies being anti-Catholic, or being Catholic implies being anti-Protestant. As do most blacks, I believe that the corridors of history in this country have been lined with countless instances of racial injustice. This is evident by the plain historical fact that for more than two and a half centuries, millions of blacks were slaves under the rule and sanction of law - a fate which confronted no other major minority in this country .... To suggest that black judges should be so disqualified would be analogous to suggesting that the slave masters were right when, during tragic

> hours for this nation, they argued that only they, but not the slaves, could evaluate the harshness or justness of the system.[26]

This case was hotly contested for a number of years, but eventually a Consent Decree was entered. The Court to this day continues to monitor compliance with it.[27]

This was not the only case of its kind before the Eastern District. Judge Newcomer presided over a similar protracted race discrimination class action and related individual actions filed against United States Steel Corporation by African-American production and maintenance employees at the corporation's Fairless Works.[28]

Housing integration was another volatile matter in the 1970's. The placement of low income public housing into a white neighborhood in Philadelphia became a highly contentious political issue which ultimately resulted in a lawsuit in this Court. In the late 1950's, the Philadelphia Housing Authority condemned and then cleared for low income public housing several deteriorated blocks in the predominantly white Whitman Park section in South Philadelphia. Federal funds were committed for a high-rise housing project. Fierce local opposition was aroused, and in 1964, a special Act of Congress was passed at the initiation of veteran Philadelphia Congressman William Barrett to change the design from high-rise to low-rise construction. With the neighborhood uproar persisting unabated, the Philadelphia Housing Authority procrastinated until 1970 before it finally chose a developer for the project. In the spring of 1971, when construction was about to begin, thirty neighborhood women gathered at the site and blocked the developer's operation of heavy equipment. Various injunctions were obtained from the Common Pleas Court to little effect. Construction did not go forward.

In 1971, Frank Rizzo, the former Philadelphia Police Commissioner, was running for mayor. He publicly announced during the campaign that within the framework of the law, he would support communities in their resistance to public housing. Elected mayor in November 1971 and taking office in January 1972, he accelerated his vociferous opposition to the Whitman Park Project. He declared he would not allow public housing to ruin neighborhoods or to be placed in white neighborhoods where whites did not want African-Americans moving near them.

In the meantime, with the project stalled with the complicity of City officials, a group of plaintiffs filed a class action in the federal court in June 1971, claiming violations of their rights under the Constitution and various federal civil rights laws. The lawsuit was hotly contested and hard fought. It was finally tried by Judge Broderick for fifty-seven days in 1976. In ruling in favor of the plaintiffs, he found that the City had acted with racially discriminatory intent in opposing and obstructing the Whitman Park Project to prevent African-Americans from living in that neighborhood. He ordered the City and various local and federal agencies to "take all necessary steps for the construction of the Whitman Park Townhouse Project as planned." He also enjoined interference "in any manner" with its construction. The Court of Appeals affirmed Judge Broderick's findings of discriminatory intent and modified only slightly the injunctive relief he had granted.[29]

Other major litigation occurred in the 1970's with respect to gender discrimination in the Philadelphia Police Department. In 1974, the United States as well as Philadelphia police officer Penelope Brace filed actions against the City of Philadelphia, its Police Commissioner Joseph O'Neill and others in which they alleged systematic discrimination against females in violation of Title VII of the Civil Rights Act of 1964 and the Equal Protection Clause of the Constitution's Fourteenth Amendment in connection with recruiting, hiring, promotion, transfer, and assignment practices of the City's Police Department. The City did not dispute that its policy of hiring women only as Juvenile Aid Officers was discriminatory. Instead, relying on the statutory bona-fide occupational defense, it argued that only men could function effectively as police officers in other situations.

In the middle of the trial in front of Judge Weiner, the parties agreed to the entry of an interim order in which the Court enjoined certain discriminatory practices and required an increase in the number of women to be hired on the force. Further hearings ensued in which Judge Weiner had to deal with the City's violations of his orders to remedy discrimination as well as with the exception under the Civil Rights Act for a bona-fide occupational need.[30] Today, women serve in all types of roles within the Philadelphia Police Department, and no one appears to give it much thought.

Civil rights actions filed by state and local prisoners acting pro se were becoming more frequent. They pleaded a variety of violations of their constitutional rights by prison guards and other prison officials. In 1982, several inmates incarcerated in Holmesburg Prison in Philadelphia filed a pro se class action complaint on behalf of themselves and others similarly situated, in which they sought damages as well as injunctive relief. They claimed they were suffering cruel and unusual punishment because of prison overcrowding in violation of the Eighth and Fourteenth Amendments.[31] The action landed on the docket of Judge Shapiro. She initially dismissed it on the ground that relief could be obtained under the terms of a judgment handed down in a case in the Court of Common Pleas of Philadelphia County. The Court of Appeals disagreed and returned it to her for further proceedings.[32] She was destined to preside over this action for almost twenty years.

An amended complaint was subsequently filed to expand the scope of the class action to include the conditions at the Detention Center and the House of Correction, the other two Philadelphia County jails. In 1986, the parties reached a settlement, approved by Judge Shapiro, which included a number of conditions such as a cap on the inmate population, a mechanism for reducing the inmate population if and when the cap was exceeded, and the construction of a new prison with 650 beds and a downtown detention facility of 440 beds.[33] This, however, did not end the lawsuit. Over the years, the cap was exceeded. Judge Shapiro, along with a Special Master she had appointed, had to contend with that issue to insure that unconstitutional prison conditions did not occur. Before her were difficult questions concerning what categories of detainees, how many, and under what conditions they would be released pending trial. This was a highly controversial matter, with the District Attorney and the newspapers often vituperative and abusive in their unfair criticism.

The Decree was modified from time to time to allow for an increase in the prison population due, among other circumstances, to the growth of illegal drug trafficking in the City. The two prisons to be built under that Consent Decree were never constructed, but the City ultimately increased the number of beds for its inmate population. In 1991, by agreement of the parties and approval of the Court, the 1986 Decree was replaced by a new Decree. It included, among other provisions, a requirement that the City construct a new prison and expand by 1,250 the number of inmate beds and that it build a new courthouse. A new release mechanism to reduce any overcrowding was also included. Finally, the City committed to develop a long-range plan to alleviate this critical problem. A new prison facility and a new criminal justice center for the trial of state criminal cases were constructed in the 1990's under the watchful eye of Judge Shapiro. She ended her years of oversight of the Philadelphia prisons in 2000.

The perennial issue of separation of church and state continued to confront the District Court. In 1969, an African-American parent of a student attending a public school in Pennsylvania as well as the National Association for the Advancement of Colored People and several Jewish and Protestant groups among others brought suit in *Lemon v. Kurtzman* in which they challenged the constitutionality of the Pennsylvania Nonpublic Elementary and Secondary Education Act. That law provided public funds to sectarian and private schools for "secular educational services," that is, for actual expenditures for teachers' salaries, textbooks, and instructional materials. It prohibited reimbursement for any course or materials relating to religion.

A three-judge panel consisting of District Judges Alfred Luongo and Mac Troutman and Circuit Judge William H. Hastie was convened to hear the case since the constitutionality of a state statute was at issue.[34] The Court, in an opinion by Judge Troutman, dismissed the complaint over the dissent of Judge Hastie. Judge Troutman wrote for himself and Judge Luongo:

> The mandate of the First Amendment is neutrality with respect to religious teachings, beliefs and practices. The Education Act does not employ religion as its standard.
>
> ...

> Admittedly, the line is not an easy one to draw. However, we believe the Education Act is consistent with neutrality towards religion and comes within the permissible limits and spirit of the non-establishment principle. Consequently, we will dismiss the plaintiffs' complaint under the establishment clause.[35]

The plaintiffs appealed the dismissal to the Supreme Court which unanimously reversed. Chief Justice Warren Burger, speaking for the high Court, enunciated what has come to be known as the *Lemon* test. To pass constitutional muster, "... the statute must have a secular legislative purpose; ... its principal or primary effect must be one that neither advances nor inhibits religion; ... [and] the statute must not foster 'an excessive government entanglement with religion.'"[36] Finding that the Pennsylvania law created "excessive entanglement between government and religion," the Court struck it down as a violation of the Establishment of Religion Clause of the First Amendment.[37] It explained that "political fragmentation and divisiveness on religious lines" are likely to be intensified as a result of regular legislative appropriations that benefit only a small number of religious groups. Among the Court's other concerns was the fact that the state governments and religious schools would necessarily become entangled by government oversight and auditing of these payments. The Chief Justice concluded:

> The sole question is whether state aid to these schools can be squared with the dictates of the Religion Clauses. Under our system the choice has been made that government is to be entirely excluded from the area of religious instruction and churches excluded from the affairs of government. The Constitution decrees that religion must be a private matter for the individual, the family, and the institutions of private choice, and that while some involvement and entanglement are inevitable, lines must be drawn.[38]

The *Lemon* test came into play a few years later in *Gilfillan v. City of Philadelphia.* On October 3, 1979, Pope John Paul II was scheduled to visit Philadelphia and celebrate a Roman Catholic Mass before an estimated one million people. The City of Philadelphia was in the process of designing and constructing a large platform at Logan Circle above the Swann Fountain to accommodate the Pope, Bishops, and other clergy for the Mass. The platform was to contain an altar and a thirty-six-foot cross supplied by the Archdiocese of Philadelphia.

A group of plaintiffs brought suit to enjoin the City from using public funds for the platform on the ground that such an expenditure violated the Establishment of Religion Clause of the First Amendment. Before the hearing, in return for the plaintiffs' agreeing not to seek an injunction, the Archdiocese consented to reimburse the City for its construction and design costs should the plaintiffs prevail. The case was randomly assigned to Judge Broderick, a staunch Roman Catholic. After reviewing the history and purpose of the First Amendment, he ruled that the actions of the City were unconstitutional under the *Lemon* test in that they had no secular purpose or effect and caused excessive entanglement between government and religion by promoting divisiveness between and among religious groups. Judge Broderick explained:

> We find that, under the facts presented in this case, the actions of the City of Philadelphia in constructing and decorating the platform amount to public sponsorship of a religious service. The secular purposes expressed by the City are incidental to this non-secular purpose. The beauty of the service, and its appeal to millions of people, Catholics and non-Catholics alike, cannot overcome the fact that the expenditure of public funds for items necessary to the service crossed the "wall of separation" mandated by the Constitution.[39]

The Court of Appeals affirmed,[40] and the Archdiocese thereafter reimbursed the City in the amount of $204,569.

The District Court was also busy with other cases of public interest. The Supreme Court handed down its controversial abortion decision, *Roe v. Wade*, in January 1973.[41] It held that because of the right of privacy under the Due Process clause of the Fourteenth Amendment, a state may not interfere with a woman's abortion decision and the medical judgment of her physician during the first trimester of her pregnancy. However, as the pregnancy progresses beyond that point, the state has an increasingly greater interest as against the woman's right of privacy and may "regulate the abortion procedure in ways that are reasonably related to maternal health." At the stage "subsequent to viability," the state may prohibit abortion "except where it is necessary, in appropriate medical judgment, for the preservation of the life or health of the mother."[42]

While Justice Blackmun stated that "Our task, of course, is to resolve the issue by constitutional measurement, free of emotion and predilection," the public's reaction was anything but free of emotion or predilection. The decision created a firestorm. The reverberations have been felt throughout the nation including the Eastern District of Pennsylvania.

As a result of *Roe v. Wade*, the Pennsylvania General Assembly quickly passed the Abortion Control Act of 1974, but it was not long before a three-judge panel comprised of Judge Green, Judge Newcomer, and Circuit Judge Arlin Adams declared portions of the Act unconstitutional, including provisions requiring parental consent for a minor to have an abortion and the provision requiring spousal consent in all cases.[43] Several years later Judge Bechtle held that Pennsylvania's prohibition against

Medicaid funding for abortions other than those necessary to save the life of the mother violated federal law.[44]

But it was Judge Huyett who was faced for well over a decade with the complexities of the abortion issue, with the clash between a woman's right to privacy and the interest of the state in placing limitations and imposing regulations on that right. It began in the early 1980's with a lawsuit claiming the Pennsylvania Abortion Control Act of 1982 was unconstitutional in light of *Roe v. Wade*. The Act and the subsequent amendments were continually challenged as placing undue burdens on a woman's right to choose an abortion. At various times, Judge Huyett enjoined the enforcement of certain provisions of the Act including: (1) the twenty-four hour waiting period between the time the woman was provided certain information and the time the abortion was performed; (2) certain public disclosure requirements; (3) certain rules related to the judicial bypass procedures for minors seeking abortions; (4) the informed parental consent provision; (5) the husband notification requirement; and (6) the mandate that certain information required to be disclosed to a woman must be imparted by a physician.

These several cases, captioned *American College of Obstetricians v. Thornburgh*, and *Planned Parenthood v. Casey*, moved back and forth between the District Court, Court of Appeals and, on several occasions, the Supreme Court. There were close to twenty reported court opinions in the cases originating before Judge Huyett alone. Some of his rulings were affirmed and others were reversed. The last decision, which concerned fees for plaintiffs' counsel, was handed down in 1995.[45]

While Judge Huyett was dealing with the abortion litigation, Judge Broderick had before him in *Halderman v. Pennhurst State School & Hospital*[46] a significant case involving the rights of developmentally disabled individuals. The Commonwealth of Pennsylvania owned and operated Pennhurst State School and Hospital in Chester County. It housed approximately 1,200 residents of whom approximately 75% were either severely or profoundly retarded. Many were also physically handicapped. Plaintiff, a resident of Pennhurst, claimed in her lawsuit that unsanitary, inhumane, and dangerous conditions prevailed there. She asserted that these conditions violated her rights to due process and equal protection under the Fourteenth Amendment and her rights under various federal and state statutes, including the Developmentally Disabled Assistance and Bill of Rights Act of 1975.

Judge Broderick, after a thirty-two-day non-jury trial, found not only that conditions at Pennhurst were dangerous but that it was totally inadequate for the education and training of the mentally retarded and others who were not ill. Some residents had even been physically abused and improperly drugged. Judge Broderick ruled that the residents had a constitutional right to "minimally adequate" and "non-discriminatory habilitation" and "in the least restrictive" environment, and that they had a constitutional right "to be free from harm" under the Eighth Amendment. He ordered that Pennhurst eventually be closed, that appropriate "community living arrangements" be provided, and that individual treatment plans be developed.

The Court of Appeals affirmed but rested its decision on statutory rather than on constitutional grounds.[47] However, it overturned the order that Pennhurst be closed.[48] The case then reached the Supreme Court. According to the high Court, there was nothing in federal law which required Pennsylvania to "assume the high cost of providing 'appropriate treatment' in the 'least restrictive environment' to their mentally retarded citizens." Congress was simply encouraging, not mandating, that states improve services to the developmentally disabled. The Court remanded the action to the Court of Appeals to consider plaintiffs' constitutional and other statutory claims.[49] Not surprisingly, further legal proceedings ensued.[50] Fortunately for all concerned, the entire matter was ultimately settled, and Pennhurst closed in 1986.

Cases attacking long-accepted legal procedures and practices joined the many other constitutional cases in the Eastern District. For centuries, something known as a writ of replevin existed in the English common law. It had undergone changes over time, but in some form it was deeply entrenched in the law of Pennsylvania and other states. In the Commonwealth, a party without any prior notice or hearing could summarily obtain from the prothonotary (clerk) of the Court of Common Pleas a writ of replevin authorizing the seizure of certain goods or chattels in another person's possession simply by filing an affidavit swearing to the value of the goods or chattels and by filing a bond in double that amount. The Sheriff, upon the issuance of the writ, would then seize the described property, again, without any prior notice to the opposing party and without a hearing to determine who actually was entitled to possession or ownership.

Under Pennsylvania procedure, the party from whom the property was seized was then permitted to file a bond within three days in the same amount as the bond of the party seeking seizure of the property and in this way trump the seizure. If no bond was filed, the Sheriff would turn over the property to the person who had obtained the writ of replevin.

This legal procedure was most commonly used to take back consumer goods when the buyer allegedly fell behind in payments under an installment contract. Usually, the consumer did not have the sophistication or money to challenge any taking.

A three-judge Court was convened in the Eastern District to decide a case brought by consumers who alleged that a Pennsylvania statute and the procedure authorizing replevin were in conflict with the Due Process Clause of the Fourteenth Amendment to the Constitution. The panel, made up of District Judges Mac Troutman and John Hannum as well as Circuit Judge Cullen Ganey, denied relief on the ground the procedure on its face was not "fundamentally unfair."

On appeal, the Supreme Court reversed. It held that due process under the circumstances presented required prior notice and an opportunity to be heard, before a creditor, with the help of the state, could seize the consumer goods in issue. The Court concluded that the Pennsylvania law served no important governmental or general public interest and improperly involved the state in a summary action where only private gain was at stake.[51]

The practice of law was also changing as a result of litigation. For as long as anyone could remember, lawyer advertising and soliciting of cases was strictly forbidden by the various professional Codes of Conduct in effect throughout the country. In 1977, the Supreme Court held lawyer advertising to be a form of protected commercial speech and overturned the blanket ban on such activity.[52]

Despite this ruling, many questions remained as to what limitations could still be imposed. A significant loosening in the restrictions in Pennsylvania was mandated by the decision of Judge Joseph Lord in *Spencer v. The Honorable Justices of the Supreme Court of Pennsylvania* in 1984.[53] The plaintiff, a lawyer who wished to advertise by direct mail his credentials in the areas of computer and aviation law, challenged certain sections of the Pennsylvania Code of Professional Responsibility which in his view unconstitutionally curtailed the right of a lawyer to advertise. While recognizing that some limits on lawyer advertising were permissible to prevent deception and to protect a substantial state interest, Judge Lord declared the Pennsylvania Code prohibition against direct mail advertising to be unconstitutional. He also struck down the Code requirement that lawyers who state that their practice was limited to a particular field of law must also state affirmatively that they are not recognized or certified as a specialist in that field.

Not all cases, of course, involved constitutional issues. Judge Becker presided over what came to be known as the Japanese Electronics case, formally *Zenith Radio Corp. v. Matsushita Electric Industrial Co., Ltd.*[54] Plaintiffs were two American corporations that manufactured and sold television sets. They claimed that defendants, twenty-one Japanese and American companies that also manufactured and sold televisions, conspired to fix and maintain high prices in Japan while fixing and maintaining low prices in the United States. After reviewing the massive record, Judge Becker granted summary judgment in favor of defendants. Considering only what would be admissible evidence, he concluded that there were no genuine issues of material fact and that defendants were entitled to judgment as a matter of law, without the necessity of a trial. Judge Becker explained that the evidence established that defendants conspired but not in ways that injured plaintiffs.

Perhaps what was most remarkable was the length of Judge Becker's opinion. It consumes 217 printed pages in Volume 513 of the Federal Supplement - if not a record, probably close to it. The Court of Appeals reversed with a sixty-nine-page opinion, but that reversal was short-lived. The Supreme Court, granting certiorari, held 5 to 4 that Judge Becker had it right. In the opening section of the Court's opinion, Justice Lewis Powell wrote, "Stating the facts of this case is a daunting task" and, undoubtedly much relieved, found it "unnecessary to state the facts in great detail" since the Court's sole role was to decide whether Judge Becker had applied the correct standard in ruling that summary judgment was appropriate and that no trial would be needed. The Court concluded:

> In sum, in light of the absence of any rational motive to conspire, neither petitioners' pricing practices, nor their conduct in the Japanese market, nor their agreements respecting prices and distribution in the American market, suffice to create a "genuine issue for trial."

Judge Higginbotham had on his docket a group of related antitrust cases, although involving a far different activity than the sale of television sets. His concerned professional hockey. In *Philadelphia World Hockey Club, Inc. v. Philadelphia Hockey Club, Inc.*,[55] and other related cases, the basic issue was "whether through their reserve clause, affiliation agreements, and market power dominance, the National Hockey League has violated the federal antitrust laws."[56] Under a reserve clause in a contract, a player or coach is not permitted to play or work for a competing organization without specific approval of that player's or coach's employer. The National Hockey League had grown from a small Canadian organization in 1917 to what Judge Higginbotham characterized as a "position of substantial wealth, power, broad spectator interest, international recognition and many superstars, all crescendoing into huge profits for both its owners and players" in the 1970's. Judge Higginbotham wrote memorably at the outset of his opinion, "Despite the thousands of words uttered on this record by all parties about the glory of the sport of hockey and the grandeur of its superstars, the basic factors here are not the sheer exhilaration from observing the speeding puck, but rather the desire to maximize the available buck."[57]

Judge Higginbotham held that professional hockey operated in interstate commerce and was subject to the antitrust laws. He refused to extend to professional hockey the Supreme Court's holding, articulated by Justice Oliver Wendell Holmes in 1922, that baseball was exempt from the antitrust laws because it did not engage in interstate commerce.[58] After a hearing and making extensive findings of fact and conclusions of law, he granted a preliminary injunction restraining the National Hockey League from enforcing the reserve clause in any contract against a player or coach. The Court found that there was a clear and substantial likelihood the National Hockey League exercised monopoly power in violation of § 2 of the Sherman Act through their interlocking agreements with the various National Hockey League teams, the reserve clause in players' contracts, and the agreements between the National Hockey League and minor and amateur hockey organizations. Ultimately, all these actions were either settled or dismissed.

There were other substantial antitrust actions in the District at this time. Judge Cahn was assigned a Multidistrict Litigation ("MDL") involving allegations that major sugar refiners and others East of the Mississippi River had conspired to fix prices of refined sugar in violation of § 1 of the Sherman Act.[59] Judge McGlynn presided over an MDL consisting of thirty-seven class actions charging a conspiracy to fix the prices of fine paper. His opinion awarding counsel fees and costs consumed 171 printed pages in the Federal Rules Decisions, coming close but not exceeding Judge Becker's record of 217 pages in the Japanese Electronics case.[60] Judge McGlynn is supposed to have wrapped a copy of his opinion with a ribbon and bow and presented it to his friend Judge Becker with a note, "We're like Avis, we try harder."[61]

The Pennsylvania Railroad and the Reading Company, as previously noted, were two venerable institutions headquartered in Philadelphia. The Pennsylvania Railroad, incorporated by special Act of the Pennsylvania General Assembly in 1846, ultimately became one of the largest privately owned railroads and one of the most powerful corporations in the United States. Its passenger and freight lines ran from Boston to Washington and as far west as Chicago and St. Louis. It also operated six commuter lines ridden by thousands each day into its Suburban Station in downtown Philadelphia. The Pennsylvania Railroad was so much a part of the life of the Philadelphia region that the Western Suburbs were called the "Main Line" because of the railroad's main track line to Pittsburgh and Chicago that intersected the area. The glory of the railroad can still be seen in its 30th-Street Station in Philadelphia which was completed just before the onslaught of the Great Depression.

The Reading Company was a much smaller railroad centered in eastern Pennsylvania and New Jersey, but it too in its heyday was formidable. At the beginning of the twentieth Century, its President, George F. Baer, a confidant of J.P. Morgan, made headlines as a vocal opponent of the United Mine Workers Union and of the efforts of President Theodore Roosevelt to settle a 1902 strike on terms favorable to the coal miners.[62] The Reading's main source of revenue came from the transportation of coal from the anthracite region of northeastern Pennsylvania into Philadelphia.[63] It also had six important commuter lines reaching from the Philadelphia suburbs into the landmark Reading Terminal with its expansive train shed at Twelfth and Market Streets where the railroad had its main offices.

By the 1970's, the golden era of the railroads had come to an end. In an effort to solve their financial woes, the Pennsylvania Railroad and the New York Central Railroad Company had merged in 1968 to form the Penn Central Transportation Company with over 20,000 miles of track in sixteen states, two Canadian provinces, and the District of Columbia, close to $7 billion in assets, and more than 100,000 employees. This merger, however, did not bring about the profits and cost savings for which the two railroads had hoped. By late June 1970, in the words of a Penn Central spokesman, it was suffering "a severe cash squeeze" and was "unable to acquire from any source additional working capital."[64]

The unthinkable happened on Sunday, June 21, 1970. The railroad's law firm, Dechert Price & Rhoads, had drafted a petition to place the Penn Central in reorganization under the Bankruptcy Act. Judge Hannum, the emergency judge that weekend, was alerted but deferred to his colleague Judge Kraft. After approval of the Penn Central's Board of Directors at an emergency meeting that Sunday afternoon, H. Francis De Lone, a partner at the Dechert firm, and Lawrence Turner, a Dechert associate, rushed the petition to Judge Kraft at his farm in Edgmont, Delaware County, where Kraft signed the fateful Order placing the railroad in reorganization at 5:40 p.m.[65]

At a meeting of the judges of the Court the next day, all in attendance realized that this bankruptcy would be a massive undertaking and would not be resolved anytime soon. It was quickly decided that it should be assigned to a younger judge. Due to the fact that some judges owned Penn Central stock or had other reasons to recuse, there remained just four available contenders. Their names were placed into the fedora of Chief Judge John Lord. Judge Fullam's name was drawn, and he received the assignment.[66]

The case thereafter proceeded under the Regional Rail Reorganization Act of 1973 after the Supreme Court rebuffed a challenge to the Act's constitutionality.[67] A phalanx of lawyers appeared before Judge Fullam, and endless hearings and arguments took place. He could become exasperated when a lawyer did not meet his high expectations. On one occasion, an issue arose involving the disappearance of 352 Penn Central boxcars. When a lawyer kept pressing a meritless argument, Fullam exclaimed, "Did it ever occur to you that the reason you are having such a difficult time with this case is that you don't have a case to present?"[68]

Judge Fullam signed the order consummating the plans of reorganization of the Penn Central Transportation Company in August 1978. The adjudication of the reorganization continued thereafter, and a few subsidiary issues remain open even today. It was one of the most complex cases the Eastern District had ever seen, with over 4,300 court orders issued to date.[69]

In November 1971, the Reading Company, because of its grave financial condition, took the same track as the Penn Central and filed for bankruptcy and then reorganization under the Regional Rail Reorganization Act. Again, the assignment of a judge had to be accomplished. In a similar fashion as with the Penn Central, the names of the judges were placed into a hat at a judges' meeting, and a name was drawn. The winner was J. William Ditter Jr., who happened to have been absent from the meeting that day. After this turn of events, it has been said that Judge Ditter has had perfect attendance at all subsequent gatherings of judges where Court business is conducted. The Reading Reorganization was likewise a protracted undertaking which also took years and over 3,500 orders to resolve. Ultimately, the Reading's rail properties were transferred to Conrail for approximately $186,000,000 from the Government. All the Reading creditors were paid as were its stockholders. The reorganization was ultimately resolved in 1980.[70]

The commuter railroad system as well as the bus, trolley, and subway lines in Philadelphia and its suburbs are now operated by the Southeastern Pennsylvania Transportation Authority ("SEPTA"), a state agency. In the 1970's and 1980's, while the sale and distribution of illegal drugs were becoming an increasingly large part of the criminal docket of this and other courts, use of drugs in the workplace was also arousing public concern. The Transport Workers' Union and several other unions filed suit against SEPTA to prevent it from implementing a program for the random testing of employees for alcohol and drug use.[71]

With certain limitations, Judge Ludwig held that random drug testing without any suspicion of illegal usage did not violate any constitutional right of workers against unreasonable searches, particularly those who were operating equipment which put the public at risk. However, before allowing any program to take effect, he ordered SEPTA and the unions to bargain in good faith under the Railway Labor Act. In his view, the Act required such bargaining because random drug testing was a clear departure from the collective bargaining agreements then in effect.

The Court of Appeals affirmed, but the Supreme Court summarily remanded to the Court of Appeals. The District Court's stay order was vacated and the testing program was put into effect.[72]

Political corruption was a focus of the Justice Department in the 1970's and 1980's, and many well-known political figures in the region were successfully prosecuted in the Eastern District. They included: Congressman Joshua Eilberg; State Senator Henry J. "Buddy" Cianfrani; the Speaker of the State House of Representatives Herbert Fineman; State Representative Matthew Cianciulli; Philadelphia City Councilmen Leland Beloff, Harry Jannotti, George X. Schwartz, and James Tayoun; Philadelphia City Commissioner Maurice Osser; the Mayor of the City of Chester John Nacrelli; and Chester County Republican Party leader Theodore Rubino.

The case against George Schwartz and Harry Jannotti is perhaps the most memorable. In the late 1970's, the FBI undertook an undercover sting operation known as ABSCAM. In 1980, the Government indicted Schwartz, the powerful President of Philadelphia's City Council, and Jannotti, the Majority Leader, under the Racketeer Influenced and Corrupt Organizations Act and the Hobbs Act.[73] FBI agents had posed as representatives of Arab sheiks from Abu Dhabi who were interested in building a hotel in Philadelphia. Ultimately, Schwartz agreed to meet with a corrupt attorney, Howard Criden, and an undercover FBI agent posing as an intermediary for the Arab sheiks at a suite in the Barclay Hotel on Rittenhouse Square. After discussion about local politics, Schwartz's power, and the need for his help to smooth the way for the construction of the hotel, the undercover agent opened a briefcase and without comment handed Schwartz an envelope which contained $30,000 in cash. Schwartz then placed it in his jacket without counting it. Unbeknown to Schwartz, the entire meeting was videotaped.

The next evening, the lawyer and undercover agent met with Councilman Jannotti in the same suite at the Barclay. Again, after a conversation similar to what had occurred the previous evening, the undercover agent gave Jannotti an envelope containing $10,000 in cash. As with Schwartz, this event was videotaped.

A jury convicted both councilmen of conspiracy to violate the Hobbs Act which makes it a criminal offense to conspire to affect interstate commerce by extortion. Schwartz was also found guilty of conspiracy to commit racketeering. Judge Fullam, before whom the case was tried, reluctantly overturned the jury verdicts on the ground that the Government had overreached and had improperly entrapped Schwartz and Jannotti. He wrote:

> These conclusions have been reached with great reluctance. No-one who has viewed the videotape evidence in this case could avoid feelings of distress and disgust at the crass behavior the tapes reveal. The jury's verdict represents a natural human reaction to that evidence. But, in the long run, the rights of all citizens not to be led into criminal activity by governmental overreaching will remain secure only so long as the courts stand ready to vindicate those rights in every case.[74]

The Government appealed. Initially, the three judge appellate panel affirmed Judge Fullam by a vote of 2 to 1. Nonetheless, after hearing argument en banc, the Court of Appeals reversed and reinstated the verdicts.[75] The political careers of Schwartz and Jannotti came to an end, and they went to prison.[76]

Judge Katz had before him what was known as the "Roofers case,"[77] another significant multi-defendant and multi-count criminal action focused on political corruption. Stephen Traitz, Jr., the head of the local Roofers' Union and a number of his associates, were charged with racketeering and other offenses involving violence, intimidation, kickbacks from contractors, embezzlement of union funds, and bribery of federal, state, and local officials. In December 1985, at Traitz's directions, one of his lieutenants delivered nineteen envelopes containing cash gifts to public officials including a number of state judges. As a result of electronic surveillance of the Business Manager's Office and Business Agent Meeting Room of the Roofers Union and other evidence, Traitz and a dozen others were convicted and imprisoned.

Organized crime was likewise the subject of government prosecutions. The most prominent target was Nicodemo Scarfo, the powerful and feared head of the Mafia in Philadelphia and Southern New Jersey. In one trial in the Eastern District before Judge O'Neill in 1987, where the Government's main witnesses were convicted murderers, Scarfo was acquitted.[78]

The Government had more success with two other indictments against him. Scarfo was convicted of conspiracy and extortion before Judge Fullam and an anonymous jury, that is, one with jurors whose identities were unknown to either the Government or the defense. The conspirators, who included Philadelphia Councilman Leland Beloff, sought to extort $1 million from real estate developer Rouse & Co. in connection with a project to develop the waterfront at Penn's Landing in Philadelphia. After the initial contact by one of Scarfo's lieutenants, Willard Rouse reported the extortion attempt to the FBI. Due to the FBI's effective infiltration into the Scarfo organization and the extortion plot, two of the codefendants who were members of the Scarfo crime family pleaded guilty and testified for the Government. The conviction of Scarfo was affirmed on appeal.[79]

In 1988, Scarfo and sixteen of his confederates were again convicted, this time before Judge Franklin Van Antwerpen, for racketeering activities which included multiple acts of murder, attempted murder, extortion, collection of unlawful debts, illegal lotteries, and distribution of controlled substances. The trial lasted ten weeks, again with an anonymous jury. In an extremely rare move for the Eastern District, the judge also sequestered the jury for the duration of the trial. The defendants were all convicted and the Court of Appeals affirmed. Scarfo is currently serving a life sentence in a maximum security federal prison.[80]

Skyjacking has now become a matter of great concern after the tragic events of September 11, 2001. However, it is not a new phenomenon. In 1972, Michael Stanley Green and other persons boarded a plane in Philadelphia before its scheduled flight to New York. As it approached Kennedy Airport, the defendant and his companion pulled a pistol and a shotgun on the flight attendants and demanded $600,000 as well as parachutes. They warned they had a bomb that would explode in ninety minutes and demanded that the plane return to Philadelphia. The pilot, as instructed, returned to Philadelphia, but running low on fuel landed contrary to the order of the hijackers. After the members of the crew were tied up and passengers held hostage for a prolonged period while the temperature in the plane rose to over 100°F, the hijackers finally exited this plane and transferred to another on which had been placed $500,000 and three parachutes. The plane headed south toward Jamaica but, after some harrowing experiences, it finally landed on a small field in Texas where the hijackers finally surrendered after negotiation with the FBI. After a guilty verdict was handed down by a jury before Judge Ditter, Green received a sixty-year prison sentence.[81]

While the court is always busy trying civil and criminal cases, lawsuits are sometimes filed which a judge must dismiss without reaching the merits because the party filing the lawsuit did not have what is called standing to sue. Under Article III of the Constitution, the federal courts may only adjudicate certain enumerated categories of "Cases" and "Controversies." For a matter to be a case or controversy, the party bringing a lawsuit must have standing, that is, the party must have suffered some actual injury or be threatened with actual injury, whether it is economic or non-economic, in order to obtain relief from a federal court. Simply because a person seeks to have a federal court rectify or prevent a violation of law is alone not enough to confer standing. What is actual injury or threat of an actual injury to a party, however, is not always easy to discern and will depend on the circumstances.

In *Americans United for Separation of Church and State, Inc. v. United States Department of Health, Education and Welfare*,[82] the government conveyed seventy-seven acres of land in Chester County to the Valley Forge Christian College, operated by the Assemblies of God. The land was transferred under a federal law which authorized the sale or lease of surplus government property to tax-exempt institutions for health and educational purposes. The law also allowed a certain discount known as a public benefit allowance. Although the total value of the property was some $577,500,[83] the government granted a 100% public benefit allowance so that the property was turned over without any payment by the College.

The Americans United for Separation of Church and State, Inc. and a number of individuals sued on the ground that the transfer violated the clause of the First Amendment which prohibits Congress from making any law respecting an establishment of religion. Judge Ditter dismissed the action because the plaintiffs lacked standing. The Court of Appeals reversed. The Supreme Court took the case and by a vote of 5 to 4 reversed the judgment of the Court of Appeals. It concluded that Judge Ditter was correct. Chief Justice Rehnquist wrote that merely being a taxpayer was not sufficient in and of itself to constitute standing to enforce the Establishment Clause. The plaintiffs themselves, according to the majority of the Court, were not suffering any actual or threatened injury from the conveyance of the property to the College. The Chief Justice emphasized that "Article III [of the Constitution] ... is every bit as important in its circumscription of the judicial power of the United States as in its granting of that power ...."

Judge Ditter took to heart the advice, often ignored, of his judicial predecessors Francis Hopkinson and William Kraft that judges should avoid verbosity and keep their written opinions short and concise. His decision in this case consisted of one and a half pages of double-spaced type.[84] In contrast, the Court of Appeals' majority and dissenting opinions ran for twenty-one printed pages of smaller type in the Federal Reporter 2d, and the Supreme Court opinions consumed forty-nine printed pages in the official United States Reports.[85]

In addition to presiding over their dockets, the judges approved a number of administrative changes in the 1970's and 1980's. Ending an age-old custom, the Court gave notice to the Bar in January 1980 that as of September 1, pleadings and other documents were no longer to be filed on legal-size paper measuring 8 ½" x 13." From that point forward, documents were to be submitted on standard 8 ½" x 11" paper for ease of handling and storage. According to Michael Kunz, the Court Clerk, it took several years before full compliance was achieved. Traditions often die hard, or maybe some lawyers simply possessed stockpiles of the larger paper that they did not want to waste.

To conserve space, the Court also directed that discovery documents such as interrogatories and interrogatory answers, requests for production, any objections thereto, and deposition transcripts were no longer to be filed unless needed for the Court's review to resolve a dispute. Another change occurred with the advent of credit cards. The Eastern District was one of the first courts to authorize their use in payment of fees to the Clerk's Office.

During the 1970's and 1980's, the Court had several Chief Judges. John Lord stepped down on his seventieth birthday in December 1971, after two years in that position. He died shortly thereafter in May 1972. Judge Kraft would have been next in line to succeed him but in 1970 had taken senior status. He soon began to spend most of his time in Key Biscayne and heard cases in the Southern District of Florida for a number of years. Judge Wood, the last Eisenhower appointee, had assumed senior status for health reasons in mid-1971, and the mantle passed from John Lord to Joseph Lord who presided until 1982, the longest tenure of any Chief Judge of the Eastern District.

In 1958, as noted previously, Congress had changed the law so that no judge may serve as Chief Judge after attaining the age of seventy. In 1982, it again amended the statute to impose additional time and age limitations. While retaining the existing age restriction, Congress for the first time prohibited a judge from assuming that position unless he or she is under the age of sixty-five. It also now limited the term of a Chief Judge to a maximum of seven years.[86] Before this latter provision took effect, Chief Judge Joseph Lord reached the age of seventy and relinquished his post. He was followed by Alfred L. Luongo, his colleague with the greatest seniority under age sixty five.

It was under Chief Judge Luongo's leadership that the Historical Society of the United States District Court for the Eastern District of Pennsylvania was established in 1984. Others who were instrumental in its formation were Judge Ditter, Patrick T.

Ryan, Esquire, and the Court Clerk Michael E. Kunz.

The Society is a non-profit organization whose purpose is to heighten the public's awareness of the Court's many contributions to American history. Included among its various activities are legal symposia and lectures as well as an annual black-tie dinner. Judge Ditter is largely responsible for the Society's nationally heralded calendar, complete with historical themes and accompanying sketches, which has been published each year since 1985. The Society also commissions portraits of judges to hang in the Courthouse.

It was also during Chief Judge Luongo's tenure that Congress enacted in 1984 what is known as the Rule of 80. It allows a judge to take senior status when his or her age and years of service total eighty, provided that the judge has reached the age of sixty-five and has completed ten years of judicial service. [87]

Chief Judge Luongo died two years later. John Fullam took the helm and remained as Chief Judge into 1990.

## Notes

1. *See* Order of March 16, 1987, signed by Chief Judge John P. Fullam, adopting Policy to Implement Federal Smoking Regulations in the United States Courthouse.
2. *The Evening Bulletin*, p. 11 (March 30, 1979).
3. *Id.*
4. *Foundation for Today's Art-Nexus v. General Services Admin.*, Civil Action No. 79-1260 (E.D. Pa.).
5. Letter from Joseph A. Dworetzky, Esquire to Patrick W. Kittredge, Esquire (Nov. 4, 2009).
6. Roberts, John C., "In Memoriam: Tribute to Judge Edward R. Becker, 155 *University of Pennsylvania Law Review*, p. 3 (Nov. 2006); Burbank, Stephen B., "Tribute: Making Progress the Old-Fashioned Way," 149 *University of Pennsylvania Law Review*, p. 1231 (May 2001); Hamilton, Marci A., "Tribute: Chief Judge Edward R. Becker: A Truly Remarkable Judge," 149 *University of Pennsylvania Law Review*, p. 1237 (May 2001).
7. *The Philadelphia Tribune*, p. 4-A (June 3, 2007).
8. Goldman, Sheldon, *Picking Federal Judges: Lower Court Selection from Roosevelt Through Reagan*, p. 238 (Yale University Press, 1997).
9. 347 U.S. 483 (1954).
10. Transcript of Presentation of Portrait of The Honorable Norma L. Shapiro, United States District Court for the Eastern District of Pennsylvania (Oct. 24, 2003).
11. Interview by Nancy Fullam, Esquire with Judge John P. Fullam, pp. 46-50 (Aug. 8, 1999); *see e.g.*, *United States v. Marshall*, 340 F. Supp. 117 (E.D. Pa. 1972); *Eleey v. Volatile*, 339 F. Supp. 57 (E.D. Pa. 1971); *United States v. Khan*, 336 F. Supp. 354 (E.D. Pa. 1971); *Spiewak v. Selective Service Board*, 327 F. Supp. 422 (E.D. Pa. 1971).
12. *United States v. Townsend*, 335 F. Supp. 425 (E.D. Pa. 1971), *rev'd*, 478 F.2d 1072 (3d Cir. 1973).
13. *United States v. Thompson*, 483 F.2d 527, 529 (3d Cir. 1973).

14. *Luongo v. United States Court of Appeals for the Third Circuit*, 415 U.S. 911 (1974).
15. Interview by Marvin Comisky, Esquire with Judge Alfred L. Luongo, p. 50 (July 11, 1986).
16. *Id.* at 48-51.
17. Interview by Nancy Fullam, Esquire with John P. Fullam, p. 49 (Aug. 8, 1999).
18. *Rowland v. Tarr*, 341 F. Supp. 339 (E.D. Pa. 1972) *aff'd in part and vacated in part*, 480 F.2d 545 (3d Cir. 1973); *Goldberg v. Rostker*, 509 F. Supp. 586 (E.D. Pa. 1980), *rev'd* 453 U.S. 57 (1981).
19. *Rostker v. Goldberg*, 453 U.S. 57, 60-62 (1981).
20. *Goldberg v. Rostker*, 509 F. Supp. 586, 605 (E.D. Pa. 1980).
21. Article I, § 8, cl. 12-14.
22. *Rostker v. Goldberg*, 453 U.S. 57, 64, 78-79 (1981).
23. 371 F. Supp. 1096 (E.D. Pa. 1974), 73 F.R.D. 370 (E.D. Pa. 1976), *aff'd in part and vacated in part* 578 F.2d 912 (3d Cir. 1978).
24. *Oburn v. Shapp*, 393 F. Supp. 561, 567 (E.D. Pa. 1975).
25. *Bolden v. Pa. State Police*, 578 F.2d 912, 921 (3d Cir. 1978).
26. *Pennsylvania v. Local Union 542, Int'l Union of Operating Eng'rs*, 388 F. Supp. 155, 163-65 (E.D. Pa. 1974).
27. *See Pennsylvania v. Local Union 542, Int'l Union of Operating Eng'rs*, 469 F. Supp. 329 (E.D. Pa. 1978); 488 F. Supp. 988 (E.D. Pa. 1979), 502 F. Supp. 7 (E.D. Pa. 1979), *aff'd*, 648 F.2d 922 (3d Cir. 1981); 507 F. Supp. 1146 (E.D. Pa. 1980), *aff'd*, 648 F.2d 923 (3d Cir. 1981); *Pennsylvania v. Local Union 542, Int'l Union of Operating Eng'rs*, 90 F.R.D. 589 (E.D. Pa. 1981), *rev'd General Bldg. Contractors Ass'n v. Pennsylvania*,458 U.S. 375 (1982).
28. *See, e.g., Dickerson v. United States Steel Corp.*, 472 F. Supp. 1304 (E.D. Pa. 1978).
29. *Resident Advisory Bd. v. Rizzo*, 425 F. Supp. 987, 1029 (E.D. Pa. 1976) *aff'd* with modifications, 564 F.2d 126 (3d Cir. 1977).
30. *See Brace v. O'Neill*, 567 F.2d 237 (3d Cir. 1977); *United States v. City of Philadelphia*, 573 F.2d 802 (3d Cir.), *cert. denied*, 439 U.S. 830 (1978); *Sanford v. O'Neill*, 616 F.2d 92 (3d Cir. 1980); Dockets of the United States District Court for the Eastern District of Pennsylvania in said cases.
31. The Eighth Amendment provides in part: "Excessive bail shall not be required, nor excessive fines imposed, nor cruel and unusual punishments inflicted." U.S. Const. amend. VIII.
32. *Harris v. Pernsley*, 755 F.2d 338 (3d Cir. 1985).
33. *Harris v. Pernsley*, 654 F. Supp. 1057 (E.D. Pa. 1987); *Harris v. Reeves*, 761 F. Supp. 382 (E.D. Pa. 1991).
34. 28 U.S.C. §§ 2281 (repealed 1976), 2284.
35. *Lemon v. Kurtzman*, 310 F. Supp. 35, 48 (E.D. Pa. 1969).
36. *Lemon v. Kurtzman*, 403 U.S. 602, 612-13 (1971) (quoting *Walz v. Tax Comm'n of N.Y.*, 397 U.S. 664, 674 (1970)).
37. *Id.* at 614. The First Amendment provides in relevant part: "Congress shall make no law respecting an establishment of religion, or prohibiting the free exercise thereof; ..." U.S. Const. amend. I.
38. *Lemon*, 403 U.S. at 625.
39. *Gilfillan v. City of Philadelphia*, 480 F. Supp. 1161, 1166 (E.D. Pa. 1979).
40. *Gilfillan v. City of Philadelphia*, 637 F.2d 924 (3d Cir. 1980).
41. 410 U.S. 113 (1973).
42. *Id.* at 164-65.
43. *Planned Parenthood v. Fitzpatrick*, 401 F. Supp. 554 (E.D. Pa. 1975).
44. *Roe v. Casey*, 464 F. Supp. 487 (E.D. Pa. 1978), *aff'd*, 623 F.2d 829 (3d Cir. 1980).
45. *See, e.g., American College of Obstetricians v. Thornburgh*, 552 F. Supp. 791 (E.D. Pa. 1982), *aff'd in part and rev'd in part*, 737 F.2d 283 (3d Cir. 1984), *aff'd*, 476 U.S. 747 (1986) *overruled by Planned Parenthood of Southeastern Pennsylvania v. Casey*, 505 U.S. 833 (1992), 613 F. Supp. 656 (E.D. Pa. 1985), 656 F. Supp. 879 (E.D. Pa. 1987). *Planned Parenthood v. Casey*, 686 F. Supp. 1089 (E.D.

Pa. 1988); 736 F. Supp. 633 (E.D. Pa. 1990), 744 F. Supp. 1323 (E.D. Pa. 1990), *aff'd in part and rev'd in part*, 947 F.2d 682 (3d Cir. 1991), *aff'd in part and rev'd in part*, 505 U.S. 833 (1992), *remanded to*, 978 F.2d 74 (3d Cir. 1992), 812 F. Supp. 541 (E.D. Pa. 1993), 822 F. Supp. 227 (E.D. Pa. 1993), *rev'd*, 14 F.3d 848 (3d Cir. 1994), *stay of mandate denied*, 510 U.S. 1309 (1994) (Souter, Circuit Justice); 869 F. Supp. 1190 (E.D. Pa. 1994), *adopting in part*, 60 F.3d 816 (3d Cir. 1995).

46. 446 F. Supp. 1295 (E.D. Pa. 1977 and 1978).
47. 42 U.S.C. § 6010.
48. 612 F.2d 84 (3d Cir. 1979).
49. 451 U.S. 1 (1981).
50. The case made its way to the Supreme Court a second time. On this occasion, the Court ruled that the Eleventh Amendment barred a District Court from ordering state officials to conform their conduct to state law. 673 F.2d 647 (3d Cir. 1982) *rev'd*, 465 U.S. 89 (1984).
51. *Epps v. Cortese*, 326 F. Supp. 127 (E.D. Pa. 1971), *rev'd sub nom. Fuentes v. Shevin*, 407 U.S. 67 (1972).
52. *Bates v. State Bar of Arizona*, 433 U.S. 350 (1977).
53. 579 F. Supp. 880 (E.D. Pa. 1984), *aff'd*, 760 F.2d 261 (3d Cir. 1985).
54. 513 F. Supp. 1100 (E.D. Pa. 1981), *rev'd*, 723 F.2d 238 (3d Cir. 1983), *rev'd and remanded*, 475 U.S. 574 (1986).
55. 351 F. Supp. 462, 465-66 (E.D. Pa. 1972).
56. *Id.* at 467.
57. *Id.* at 466.
58. *Fed. Baseball Club of Baltimore, Inc. v. Nat'l League of Prof. Baseball Clubs*, 259 U.S. 200 (1922).
59. *In re Sugar Indus. Antitrust Litig.*, 399 F. Supp. 1397 (E.D. Pa. 1975).
60. *In re Fine Paper Antitrust Litig.*, 98 F.R.D. 48 (E.D. Pa. 1983), *aff'd in part and rev'd in part*, 751 F.2d 562 (3d Cir. 1984).
61. Recollection of Judge Thomas N. O'Neill, Jr.
62. Morris, Edmund, *Theodore Rex*, pp. 133-69 (Random House, 2001).
63. *See* Weigley, Russell F., ed., *Philadelphia: A 300-year History*, pp. 272-73, 322-23, 430, 477-78, 739 (W.W. Norton & Co., 1982).
64. Daughen, Joseph R. and Binzen, Peter, *The Wreck of the Penn Central*, pp. 4, 206-08, 219, 306-07 (Beard Books, 1999).
65. *Id.* at 300-07. *See* Docket and Records, *Penn Central Transportation Co.*, No. 70-347 (Bankr. E.D. Pa., filed June 21, 1970); Recollection of George J. Miller, Esquire and Michael E. Kunz, Court Clerk; *The Delaware County Times*, p. 1 (June 22, 1970).
66. Recollection of Judge John P. Fullam and Michael E. Kunz.
67. *Blanchette v. Connecticut Gen. Ins. Corp.*, 419 U.S. 102 (1974).
68. *The Wall Street Journal*, pp. 1, 18 (Jan. 3, 1972).
69. Interview by Jason Lantzer with Judge John P. Fullam (Jan. 31, 2008).
70. *See* Docket and Records, *Reading Co.*, Bankruptcy No. 71-828 (E.D. Pa.).
71. *Transp. 543 Workers' Union v. Southeastern Pa. Transp. Auth.*, 678 F. Supp. 543 (E.D. Pa.); *aff'd*, 863 F.2d 1110 (3d Cir. 1988), *vacated*, 492 U.S. 902 (1989), *on remand at*, 884 F.2d 709 (3d Cir. 1989).
72. *Transp. 543 Workers' Union*, 884 F.2d at 713.
73. *United States v, Jannotti*, 501 F. Supp. 1182 (E.D. Pa. 1980), *rev'd* 673 F.2d 578 (3d Cir. 1982); Interview by Jason Lantzer with Peter Vaira and Joseph Fioravanti (March 28, 2008); Reppetto, Thomas A., *Bringing Down the Mob: The War Against the American Mafia*, pp. 136-44 (Henry Holt and Co., 2006).
74. *United States v. Jannotti*, 501 F. Supp. 1182, 1205 (E.D. Pa. 1980).
75. 673 F.2d 578 (3d Cir. 1982).
76. Two Philadelphia Congressmen and another Philadelphia councilman were convicted of crimes

arising out of this ABSCAM investigation in the Southern District of New York.

77. *United States v. Traitz*, 646 F. Supp. 1086 (E.D. Pa. 1986), *aff'd*, 807 F.2d 322 (3d Cir. 1986); 871 F.2d 368 (3d Cir. 1989).

78. *United States v. Scarfo*, Criminal Action No. 87-258 (E.D. Pa.).

79. *United States v. Scarfo*, 850 F.2d 1015 (3d Cir.); *cert. denied*, 488 U.S. 910 (1988). The trial of Beloff was severed from that of Scarfo. He too was imprisoned.

80. *United States v. Scarfo*, 711 F. Supp. 1315 (E.D. Pa. 1989), *aff'd sub nom. United States v. Pungitore*, 910 F.2d 1084 (3d Cir. 1990); *cert. denied sub nom. Scarfo v. United States*, 500 U.S. 915 (1991). *See also* Dockets of United States District Court for the Eastern District of Pennsylvania in these cases.

81. *United States v. Green*, 373 F. Supp. 149 (E.D. Pa. 1974); Interview by Jason Lantzer with Judge J. William Ditter (March 10, 2009).

82. 619 F.2d 252 (3d Cir. 1980), *rev'd sub nom. Valley Forge Christian College v. Americans United for Separation of Church and State*, 454 U.S. 464 (1982).

83. This was the appraised value stated in the Supreme Court's opinion. *Valley Forge Christian College v. Americans United for Separation of Church and State*, 454 U.S. at 468. The Court of Appeals opinion states the "total fair value" to have been $1,303,730. *Americans United for Separation of Church and State, Inc. v. United States Dep't of Health, Education and Welfare*, 619 F.2d at 253.

84. *Americans United for Separation of Church and State, Inc. v. U.S. Dep't of Health, Education and Welfare*, Civil Action No. 77-1321 (E.D. Pa. filed Dec. 15, 1978).

85. *Americans United for Separation of Church and State, Inc. v. United States Dept. of Health, Education and Welfare*, 619 F. 2d 252 (3d Cir 1980), *rev'd sub nom. Valley Forge Christian College v. Americans United for Separation of Church and State*, 454 U.S. 464 (1982).

86. 28 U.S.C. § 136.

87 *See* Bankruptcy Amendments and Federal Judgeship Act of 1984, P.L98-353, § 204(A), 98 Stat. 333, 350; 28 U.S.C. § 371; *see* Senior Status and Retirement of Article III Judges, Appendix A (Administrative Office of the U.S. Courts, Sept. 1994).

# IX
# The Current Court: The 1990's to the Present

In September 1989, the Court quietly passed a notable milestone as it entered its third century since it was "ordained and established" by the first Congress. At the beginning in September 1789, it had one judge, Francis Hopkinson, with a staff of one, the Clerk Samuel Caldwell. The civil and criminal jurisdiction of the Court was then quite limited with the small number of cases before it concerning mostly maritime or admiralty matters. It did not have its own courthouse but borrowed space in the Pennsylvania State House, now known as Independence Hall. In fact, the Court did not have a home specifically erected by the federal government for its use until the Civil War. Up until that time it had sat in no fewer than six different locations. While Congress reduced the geographic size of the District in 1818 and again in 1901, it was not until 1904 that it considered the Court busy enough for a second judgeship.

Today, the Eastern District is one of the largest and busiest of the ninety-four federal districts throughout the United States. It has twenty-two authorized judgeships presently augmented by eleven senior judges who ably assist with the Court's workload.[1] The diversity of the bench in race, gender, ethnicity, religion, and background contrasts sharply with the similarity of the male judges during the Court's first century and a half. Until 1949, all the judges of the Court had either been born or had grown up in Pennsylvania. With the appointment of Thomas J. Clary in that year, the Court would always have one or more judges who had first come to the Philadelphia area to attend college or law school or had arrived later as an adult. Currently, fewer than two-thirds of the members of the Court are native sons or daughters of the Commonwealth.

Each active judge and most senior judges now have either two or three law clerks, plus a secretary and an assigned deputy court clerk. The Clerk has a staff of over 200. The Court occupies a high-rise courthouse in Philadelphia devoted solely to Court business as well as a courthouse in Allentown where one district judge is stationed. Several judges also hear cases in leased space in Reading. All other judges sit only in Philadelphia.

Time has wrought dramatic changes to the confirmation process for district judges. In the more intimate world of the late eighteenth century, the President was well acquainted with his judicial nominees at least in the District of Pennsylvania. Francis Hopkinson, William Lewis, and Richard Peters, who were all leading citizens of Philadelphia, were personally known to George Washington and were seated on the bench in short order and without debate. Even well into the twentieth century, nominations often moved rapidly and on occasion with lightning speed as in the case of William Kirkpatrick in 1927.

The path toward confirmation has now become more complicated and protracted as the role of the federal courts has dramatically increased, the partisanship of the Senate has escalated, and the nominees are no longer personally known to the President or even in many cases to the home-state Senators. In Pennsylvania, beginning with John Heinz and Arlen Specter, the senators have established committees of lawyers and laypersons in each of the Commonwealth's three judicial districts to screen those interested in federal district judgeships. Applicants must fill out a form and appear for an interview. Once the White House and a state's senators tentatively agree on a judicial candidate, he or she must fill out a lengthy questionnaire. The FBI then interviews and fingerprints the candidate and proceeds to do an in-depth investigation, including contact with the candidate's friends, neighbors, and acquaintances. Tax and health records are checked. The prospective judge is also interviewed by lawyers at the Justice Department or at the White House.

In addition to the review by the FBI, the Department of Justice, and the White House, another layer of scrutiny is imposed. Since the time of President Eisenhower, almost all the Administrations have asked the American Bar Association to evaluate the integrity, professional competence, and judicial temperament of the candidate. This involves yet another interview, this time by a member of the ABA's Standing Committee on the Federal Judiciary, and calls are made by that ABA Committee member to persons who may have relevant information. The Committee, however, refrains from considering the candidate's politics or judicial philosophy. Ultimately, it prepares a report in which it rates the candidate as well-qualified, qualified, or not qualified for the district judgeship.[2]

If no impediments are uncovered, the President sends the nomination to the Senate. The nominee fills out another questionnaire for that body. In due course, the nominee will be invited to appear, often with other nominees, for a hearing in Washington before two Senators, one of each party, who serve on the Judiciary Committee. Thereafter, assuming all has gone well, the full Committee will transmit the nomination to the Senate for consideration. The nominee is then confirmed, rejected, or never calendared for a vote. If a favorable vote occurs, the President will sign the judge's commission. Only at that point may the judge take the oath of office and begin to sit. This odyssey can consume many months in the best of circumstances even if the President moves quickly and the Senate does not engage in delay for political or other reasons.

As the 1990's began, George H.W. Bush was President of the United States. During his one term in office, he appointed eight judges to the Eastern District of Pennsylvania, all of whom went through this onerous confirmation process. Each was a Republican. The first four, Ronald L. Buckwalter, William H. Yohn, Jr., Harvey Bartle III, and Stewart Dalzell, were named on the joint recommendation of Senators Heinz and Specter. The nominations of Yohn, Bartle, and Dalzell were still in progress in April 1991 when Senator Heinz was killed in a helicopter crash in a schoolyard in suburban Philadelphia. Governor Robert P. Casey shortly thereafter appointed Harris Wofford, a Democrat, the former President of Bryn Mawr College and the then current state Secretary of Labor and Industry, to fill the vacancy. While senators have a de facto veto over District Court nominees from their home state, Senator Wofford supported all three when they came up for a confirmation vote in September of 1991. This occurred shortly before the Senate became totally consumed by the bitter battle over the nomination of Clarence Thomas to the Supreme Court.

Thereafter, the confirmations of John R. Padova, J. Curtis Joyner, Eduardo C. Robreno, and Anita B. Brody were delayed as an outgrowth of the Thomas confrontation. The Senate majority simply postponed consideration of all of President Bush's judicial nominations for a number of months due to the hard feelings left in the wake of the Senate's approval of Thomas, by the close vote of 52 to 48. Ultimately, in 1992, after tempers had cooled, these four remaining nominees successfully navigated the process and were inducted as federal judges in what turned out to be the waning months of the Bush administration. Again, Senator Wofford gave them his approval. This unfortunate practice of holding up judicial confirmations would recur with greater frequency in the years ahead.

Similar to the pattern with the Reagan appointees, four of the eight Bush judges, Ronald Buckwalter, William Yohn, Curtis Joyner, and Anita Brody arrived from the state Common Pleas bench. Judge Brody was only the second woman to sit on the Eastern District. The other new judges had been partners in Philadelphia law firms: Harvey Bartle with Dechert Price & Rhoads; Stewart Dalzell with Drinker Biddle & Reath; John Padova with Padova & Hinman; and Eduardo Robreno with Fox, Rothschild, O'Brien & Frankel. Bartle, Dalzell, and Padova were trial lawyers while Robreno had focused his practice in the Bankruptcy Court.

Most of the Bush appointees had had periods of public service other than or in addition to a state court judgeship. Judge Buckwalter at one time had been an Assistant District Attorney and then held the office of District Attorney of Lancaster County, having been chosen by the Common Pleas Court to fill an unexpired term. Previously, he had clerked for President Judge John Bowman and Judge Anthony Appel in Lancaster County. Judge Yohn had prosecuted cases as an Assistant District Attorney in Montgomery County. Judge Bartle had served as the Insurance Commissioner and then as the Attorney General of Pennsylvania in the administration of Governor Dick Thornburgh. In the mid-1960's, Bartle clerked for Judge John Morgan Davis in the old Courthouse at Ninth and Market Streets. Judge Padova was the former Vice-

Chairperson of the Disciplinary Board of the Supreme Court of Pennsylvania while Judge Joyner had been the First Assistant District Attorney in Chester County.

In the past, the resumes of many federal judges included election to political office. Judge Yohn was the only Bush nominee who fit this mold. The voters had elected him to six terms as a Representative in the Pennsylvania General Assembly from the Pottstown area of Montgomery County before he became a Common Pleas judge.

Most of these new judges had been active at some point in politics, and one had sought higher state judicial office. Judge Dalzell, before his induction, had significantly aided John Heinz as the Treasurer and General Counsel of his successful campaigns for the United States Senate in 1976, 1982, and 1988. Judge Bartle had been a Presidential Elector for the Reagan-Bush ticket in 1984.[3] Judge Brody had run unsuccessfully for the Pennsylvania Supreme Court while on the Common Pleas bench.

The appointment of Judge Robreno was another significant milestone in diversity in the Eastern District. He was the first Hispanic judge on this Court and the first Cuban-American judge in United States history. He had fled Cuba as a boy to escape the Castro regime and grew up and was educated in the United States.

William J. Clinton, who followed George H.W. Bush as President in 1993, had the opportunity to choose six new judges during his two terms: Marjorie O. Rendell, Bruce W. Kauffman, Mary A. McLaughlin, Petrese B. Tucker, Berle M. Schiller, and R. Barclay Surrick. All but Judges Kauffman and Surrick were Democrats.

Three of the Clinton appointees moved from private practice to the bench. Judge Rendell, the spouse of Philadelphia Mayor Edward G. Rendell, was a partner at Duane, Morris & Heckscher where she concentrated her work in the field of bankruptcy law.

Judge Kauffman was a trial lawyer and partner at Dilworth, Paxson, Kalish & Kauffman. For several years in the 1980's, he had sat as a Justice of the Pennsylvania Supreme Court as a result of an interim appointment by Governor Thornburgh.

Judge McLaughlin was a trial partner at Dechert Price & Rhoads. Her resume included a clerkship with Judge Stanley S. Brotman of the District of New Jersey and time as an Assistant United States Attorney and an assistant professor of law at Vanderbilt. On the recommendation of Senator Specter, she was appointed in 1995 as Special Counsel to the Senate Judiciary Subcommittee on Terrorism, Technology and Government Information that was charged with investigating the confrontation at Ruby Ridge, Idaho, where a deputy marshal and several civilians had been killed.

Judge Tucker was serving as the Administrative Judge of the Orphans' Court Division of the Philadelphia County Court of Common Pleas at the time of her confirmation to the Eastern District. Earlier in her career, she had clerked for Common Pleas Judge Lawrence Prattis and tried cases as an Assistant District Attorney. Her appointment as the first African-American woman on the Eastern District was a major advance in furthering judicial diversity but did not come about until thirty-one years after Norma Shapiro was sworn in as this Court's first female judge. A number of years after Judge Tucker joined the federal bench, her husband was elected a judge of the Philadelphia Common Pleas Court.

Judge Schiller had held several public positions: Deputy Director of Personnel in the Administration of his uncle, Governor Milton Shapp; Chief Counsel to the Federal Transit Administration; and interim appointments as a Pennsylvania Superior Court Judge. Off the bench, Schiller is an enthusiastic bow hunter whose trophies, large and small, fill his chambers. Each fall, his colleagues look forward to a delicious meal of venison stew which he provides at the courthouse.

Of all the Clinton appointees, Judge Surrick had the longest tenure as a state judge. He had been sitting on the Delaware County Common Pleas Court for over twenty years.

Only two of the six Clinton judges had ever been elected to office other than to the state bench. Bruce Kauffman, like John Hannum, had been sent to Harrisburg by the voters in his state senatorial district as a delegate to the 1967-68 Pennsylvania Constitutional Convention, and Barclay Surrick had won a term as a Commissioner of Nether Providence Township in Delaware County.

A little more than a year after the last of the Clinton appointees had been sworn in and a few months after George W. Bush had assumed the Presidency, the tragic events of September 11, 2001 befell America. On that fateful day, over 2,900 innocent people died when al Qaeda members hijacked and crashed two commercial airliners into the Twin Towers in New York City, flew a third hijacked airliner into the Pentagon, and seized a fourth which the heroic passengers brought down over Western Pennsylvania before it too could strike an occupied structure. When word reached Philadelphia that morning as to what had occurred in New York City, judicial business ceased and the courthouse closed for the remainder of the day as no one was able to focus on the work at hand, and no one was certain what would happen next. It was the first time in anyone's memory that the doors of the courthouse were shut during the day other than on weekends, holidays, or snow days.

Over four years later, in the first part of 2006, a highly publicized trial arising out of the horror of that day was broadcast by closed circuit television into the courthouse in Philadelphia. Zacarias Moussaoui, one of the conspirators alleged to have been involved in the hijackings, was indicted in Alexandria in the Eastern District of Virginia. He ultimately pleaded guilty, and a lengthy jury trial was then held to determine whether the death penalty should be imposed.[4]

Congress had enacted legislation requiring the trial to be broadcast to other courthouses for the convenience of family members of victims so that they, but not the public, could observe the proceedings nearer their homes.[5] Judge Leonie Brinkema of the Eastern District of Virginia designated the United States Courthouse in Philadelphia as one of those venues.[6] Special passes were provided to the distraught viewers, and enhanced security was put in place. Many family members of those who died attended every day, and their emotions were palpable.

The rules for the trial directed that a judge preside in any courtroom into which the broadcast was to be transmitted. Here, Judges VanArtsdalen, Ditter, and Reed as well as Magistrate Judge Peter Scuderi took turns doing so for approximately seven weeks during the opening statements of counsel, the presentation of evidence and arguments, the taking of the verdict, and the imposition of sentence. The jury declined to inflict the death penalty, and Moussaoui was imprisoned for life without the possibility of release.[7]

While life was not quite the same after September 11, 2001, the work of the Court continued unabated, and judicial vacancies were filled although often after extended delay. During his two terms in office, President George W. Bush named thirteen new judges, the most ever appointed to the Eastern District by any one Chief Executive. They were Legrome D. Davis, Cynthia M. Rufe, Michael M. Baylson, Timothy J. Savage, James Knoll Gardner, Gene E.K. Pratter, Lawrence F. Stengel, Paul S. Diamond, Juan R. Sanchez, Thomas M. Golden, Joel H. Slomsky, C. Darnell Jones II, and Mitchell S. Goldberg. They comprised a geographically diverse group representing seven different counties in the District. Ten were Republicans and three, Judges Davis, Savage, and Jones, were Democrats. All thirteen had the endorsement of Senator Specter and either Senator Rick Santorum, who had defeated Senator Wofford in 1994, or Senator Robert P. Casey, Jr., who took office in 2007 after defeating Senator Santorum. In contrast to times past, none of this group of judges had ever been elected to non-judicial office.

Consistent with the recent pattern, President Bush selected seven of his nominees from the ranks of the Common Pleas bench: Judges Davis, Rufe, Gardner, Stengel, Sanchez, Jones, and Goldberg. Legrome Davis had been the Supervising Judge of the Criminal Division of the Philadelphia Court of Common Pleas while Darnell Jones at the time of his appointment was the President Judge of that large Court by election of his peers.

Not unusual for the Eastern District, two of these nominees had other family members who were or had been state court jurists. Judge Rufe's husband was serving as a Bucks County Common Pleas Judge, and Judge Gardner's father had presided as a Lehigh County Common Pleas Judge for several years in the 1950's by appointment of Governor John S. Fine.

Earlier in their careers, Judge Davis had been Chief of the Rape Unit in the Philadelphia District Attorney's Office, and Judge Gardner had practiced law with his father and sister and had held the position of first Assistant District Attorney of Lehigh

County. Judge Rufe had taught secondary school, later became the Deputy Public Defender in Bucks County, and then had gone into private practice. Two others, namely Judges Sanchez and Jones, had served as public defenders in Chester and Philadelphia Counties, respectively. Judge Goldberg had been an Assistant District Attorney in Philadelphia, after which he moved on to the law firm of Cozen O'Connor and thereafter prosecuted cases as an Assistant United States Attorney. Before beginning his state judicial service, Judge Stengel had practiced law in Lancaster. He has also been the President of the Lancaster Bar Association and taught as an adjunct professor at Franklin & Marshall College and Millersville University.

The remainder of the Bush appointees had been in private practice immediately before they were inducted. Their resumes also included public service or other professional or civic activities.

Judge Baylson, at the time of his confirmation, was a partner at Duane, Morris & Heckscher. He had clerked for Philadelphia Common Pleas Judge Joseph Sloane, was hired as an Assistant District Attorney by Arlen Specter, and had been the United States Attorney in the Eastern District under Presidents Ronald Reagan and George H.W. Bush. He was the eleventh judge of this Court to have held the office of United States Attorney.

Judge Savage practiced as an attorney in Northeast Philadelphia where he served as the Democratic Party Leader in the 23rd Ward for over twenty-eight years. For several decades, he had also sat as a Hearing Examiner for the Pennsylvania Liquor Control Board.

Like Judge Baylson, Judge Pratter was a partner at Duane, Morris. Her many professional, civic, and charitable endeavors included six years as a member of the Board of Overseers of the University of Pennsylvania Law School.

Judge Diamond, a partner at Obermayer, Rebmann, Maxwell & Hippel, was an Assistant District Attorney in Philadelphia for a number of years. He interrupted his time as a prosecutor to become a law clerk to Justice Bruce Kauffman of the Pennsylvania Supreme Court. Kauffman and he were later to be law partners and then colleagues on this Court.

Judge Golden was the managing partner at Golden, Masano, Bradley in Wyomissing, Berks County for twenty-five years. Among his other professional accomplishments, he served as President of the Berks County Bar Association and then as President of the Pennsylvania Bar Association.

When he was named to the bench, Judge Slomsky was a sole practitioner and criminal defense lawyer who was a member of the House of Delegates of the Pennsylvania Bar Association. Previously in his professional life, he was an attorney with the Department of Justice and was assigned to the Philadelphia Strike Force which concentrated its efforts in combating illegal gambling, public corruption, and organized crime.

In recent years, it was becoming more and more common throughout the federal judicial system for judges to resign to return to more lucrative private practice. In the first 200 years of this Court's history, such resignations had only happened three times: William Lewis in 1792, Thomas Masterson in 1973, and Herbert Fogel in 1978. In contrast, between 1994 and 2009, a span of just fifteen years, four judges, Louis Bechtle, Edward Cahn, James Giles, and Bruce Kauffman relinquished their black robes to become once again lawyers representing clients.

Other judges, of course, had resigned over the years when seeking or appointed to other public positions. In 1952 Judge Bard departed to run for the United States Senate, and Judge McGranery went to Washington to become the Attorney General of the United States. Then there were the twelve members of the Eastern District bench who were subsequently confirmed for the Court of Appeals: Judges McPherson (1912), Thompson (1931), Maris (1938), Kalodner (1946), Ganey (1961), Freedman (1964), Van Dusen (1967), Higginbotham (1977), Becker (1981), Scirica (1987), Rendell (1997), and Van Antwerpen (2004).

In the 1990's and up to the present, several members of the Court have held the position of Chief Judge. Louis Bechtle succeeded John Fullam in 1990 to be followed by Edward Cahn in 1993. When Chief Judge Cahn resigned from the bench at the end of 1998, James Giles headed the Court for seven years until the end of 2005. Harvey Bartle became the Eastern District's eleventh Chief Judge on January 1, 2006. Curtis Joyner succeeded him in that post on June 7, 2011.

The current size of the Court's caseload would not have been imaginable in the eighteenth or even the nineteenth century. Congress has enacted in the last few decades an ever increasing number of laws with which this Court must contend. In addition to an expanded array of federal question cases, the Court continues to have jurisdiction over lawsuits involving state law where the parties are of diverse citizenship and the amount in controversy exceeds $75,000 exclusive of interest and costs.[8] The Court's criminal jurisdiction has also grown dramatically.

In 1990, there were 7,419 civil actions, excluding multidistrict litigation, filed in the Eastern District and 586 civil jury and non-jury trials conducted. The volume of civil filings in 2010 was slightly over 6,800, although the number of civil trials following a recent trend had dropped that year to 153. On the criminal docket, 1990 saw 507 felony indictments and informations initiated charging 918 defendants and 105 criminal trials. In 2010 the Government filed 691 felony indictments and informations naming 1,057 defendants, most of whom pleaded guilty. Only 104 criminal trials took place. Complicating some criminal actions is the inclusion of as many as twenty-five to thirty defendants in one indictment.

The docket of civil and criminal cases differs markedly from those of yesteryear. Maritime and admiralty cases are now insignificant in number. A multitude of different kinds of lawsuits under federal law, unforeseen in bygone generations, have taken their place. On a daily basis judges contend with civil rights actions, generally involving claims of race, gender, religious, national origin, or age discrimination in employment. Disability discrimination lawsuits involving employment, public accommodation, and education as well as those under the Family and Medical Leave Act[9] are common. Some plaintiffs allege that police and law enforcement have used excessive force or otherwise infringed their constitutional rights. Voting rights and election issues appear from time to time. The Court encounters lawsuits involving antitrust, securities, labor, patent, copyright, trademark, unfair competition, and environmental laws among others. There are individuals seeking social security benefits allegedly wrongfully denied and cases involving pensions and other benefits purportedly withheld in violation of Employee Retirement Income Security Act ("ERISA").[10]

Other actions are brought under the Federal Tort Claims Act,[11] which allows a person to sue the Government under certain circumstances for personal injuries, such as a slip and fall in a Post Office. More obscure federal statutes surface on occasion such as the Perishable Agricultural Commodities Act.[12]

Further, the Court often has to decide whether a case may properly proceed as a class action, where the named plaintiffs sue not only on behalf of themselves but also as representatives of those similarly situated.[13] The class may consist from several dozen members up to tens of thousands.

The Court regularly hears suits under state statutes and the common law, such as those involving negligence, product liability, medical malpractice, defamation, and breach of contract, when the opposing parties are citizens of different states or there is a related federal claim.

Another major focus on the time of District Judges are the actions brought by both state and federal prisoners who sue under federal habeas corpus statutes seeking release from custody or a new trial on the ground that they had ineffective assistance of counsel at trial or that other constitutional rights were violated.[14] Some involve prisoners under sentence of death. In 2010, habeas corpus cases comprised 9% of the Court's civil docket. Other lawsuits under the federal civil rights laws challenge prison conditions.

The Court in the 1990's and beyond continued to be a favored venue for significant multidistrict civil litigation. In 1991, the Judicial Panel on Multidistrict Litigation transferred Asbestos MDL No. 875, the largest MDL in history, to the Eastern District of Pennsylvania for coordinated pretrial proceedings before Judge Weiner. This MDL involved tens of thousands of lawsuits involving millions of claimants who had sued thousands of manufacturers and sellers of asbestos and asbestos products for personal injuries and wrongful death resulting from various forms of cancer. To complicate matters, over a hundred of the defendants are now in bankruptcy or otherwise out of business. After Judge Weiner died in 2005, Chief Judge Giles assumed his responsibilities. When Judge Giles resigned from the bench in 2008, the torch passed to Judge Robreno under whose able management this MDL is presently moving toward a foreseeable conclusion.

The Court has had on its docket dozens of other MDLs with subject matter as varied as breast implants, orthopedic bone screw implants, diabetic drugs, latex gloves, processed egg products, insurance and marketing sales practices, patents, securities, and antitrust claims. MDL No. 1203, involving the diet drugs known as fen-phen, was assigned to Judge Bechtle and then Judge Bartle. It also had a class action component. This litigation has entailed tens of thousands of claimants and over seven billion dollars in compensation, counsel fees, and costs.

As always, some of the cases before the Court have significance far beyond their relevance to the particular parties involved. Occasionally, such a case reaches the Supreme Court. Perhaps one of the most important actions arising out of this District in the last two decades in terms of its nationwide impact was *Markman v. Westview Instruments, Inc.*[15] in front of Judge Katz. The plaintiff Herbert Markman sued for infringement of his patent encompassing a system which keeps track of clothing going through the dry cleaning process. Every issued patent contains claims which specifically define the scope of the invention. The jury returned a verdict for the plaintiff. Thereafter, Judge Katz, overturning the verdict, ruled that claim interpretation was a matter for the Court and construed the claims in a manner that precluded any finding of infringement.

The key question on appeal was whether the Seventh Amendment to the Constitution, which guarantees the right to a jury trial in certain types of civil cases,[16] requires the Court or the jury to construe, that is, interpret, the claims of a patent. Both the Court of Appeals for the Federal Circuit and the Supreme Court agreed with Judge Katz that it was the sole province of the Court to do so. Since that time, District Courts throughout the country hold what are known as Markman hearings to construe the meaning of claims before the issue of patent infringement is submitted to a jury.

The criminal caseload, as previously noted, has increased far beyond what anyone could have envisioned in the days of Francis Hopkinson. In more recent times, numerous statutes have been enacted which have criminalized certain conduct affecting interstate commerce. The criminal docket in this Court today consists largely of drug and firearms offenses, mail and wire fraud, extortion, bank robberies and other robberies affecting interstate commerce, interstate transportation of stolen goods, tax evasion, and immigration offenses. The Government also continues to concentrate a significant portion of its resources in prosecuting cases involving health care fraud and political corruption. The Court is constrained by the Speedy Trial Act, which sets deadlines, with certain exceptions, by which criminal cases must be called for trial.[17]

During the course of criminal cases, defendants sometimes file motions to suppress evidence in which they challenge the constitutionality of a government search or seizure under the Fourth Amendment or the lack of appropriate warnings before law enforcement elicited an incriminating statement.[18] Hearings before the Court are generally required to sort out the facts.

Sentencing is undoubtedly the weightiest and loneliest responsibility of any judge. Up until November 1, 1987, a District Judge had absolute discretion in meting out punishment as long as it did not exceed the statutory maximum set by Congress or fall below any mandatory minimum. On that date, a striking transformation took effect as a result of legislation imposing mandatory sentencing guidelines on the courts. Congress did so in response to two concerns. It sought to eliminate what were believed to be lenient sentencing practices by some judges and to prevent wide disparity in sentences for similarly situated defendants.

A Sentencing Commission was established to prepare guidelines, which judges were bound to follow. It also was charged with gathering statistics and recommending changes to the guidelines from time to time. What resulted was a guideline manual of over 500 pages, which is updated annually. It contains a grid with thirty-six offense levels and six criminal history categories. A judge was required to calculate where each defendant fit on the grid after obtaining a presentence report from the Probation Office and holding a sentencing hearing. Each intersection on the grid contained but a narrow range within which the Court was compelled to impose sentence. For crimes where Congress had passed mandatory minimum sentences, those sentences superseded any lower guideline term of imprisonment. Every sentence was subject to review by the Court of Appeals. Judges were permitted to depart from the guidelines in only very limited circumstances. If a defendant provided substantial assistance to authorities about criminal activity, judges were released from the guideline constraints altogether and any mandatory minimum sentence. However, the Court was permitted to reduce a sentence for substantial assistance only upon motion by the Government.

In 2005, the Supreme Court dramatically changed the landscape in *United States v. Booker*[19] when it invalidated the compulsory guidelines on constitutional grounds and made them advisory. While judges must still calculate a guideline sentence, they are not now bound by the result if they adequately explain on the record why they are imposing a different sentence. Any punishment must be sufficient but not greater than necessary, after taking into account certain statutory factors.[20] The District Court's decision is subject to the standard of reasonableness on appellate review.[21] The courts, however, are still bound by the Congressionally mandated minimum sentences for certain crimes and, of course, may not exceed the maximum term set by Congress. Generally, judges had considered the mandatory guidelines as unjustly draconian for drug offenses and unduly constraining their judgment in many other cases. Thus, the *Booker* decision was warmly received by most judges who are pleased that their discretion may now play a role in fashioning a just sentence based on the particular circumstances of the case.

The Constitution guarantees the right of trial by jury in all criminal cases except impeachment.[22] In the Eastern District, the right is rarely waived so that the decision on the guilt of a defendant in virtually all criminal trials is made by a jury rather than a judge sitting alone. The Constitution also guarantees the right to a jury trial in certain types of civil cases.[23] Until 1968, the Eastern District utilized a "key man" system under which the Clerk would call men and women who volunteered to serve, including those recommended by public officials and community leaders. Since 1968, the law has required the jury pool to be selected at random from a cross-section of the community in the district where the Court sits without regard to race, color, religion, sex, national origin, or economic status.[24] Consistent with the statutory mandate, the Eastern District now chooses prospective jurors at random from the voter registration lists of each county of the District in the same ratio as the number of registered voters in that county is to the total number of registered voters in the District.

In 2010, over 13,000 citizens of this District reported for jury duty and over 2,000 actually served as petit or grand jurors. Since time immemorial, civil and criminal juries have consisted of twelve jurors. The various federal courts in the early 1970's began to reduce the number of jurors in civil cases to eight at the outset of a trial, with the trial continuing to proceed as long as the count does not fall below six. The Eastern District was one of the first courts to make this change resulting in a reduction in the number of citizens called to serve as jurors and in a significant cost savings to the taxpayers.[25] In the past, jury service extended for two weeks, plus the time for any trial which extended beyond that period. Now, to lessen the burden, those summoned serve for two days or one trial. Currently jurors are paid $40 per day, but after ten days of testimony, the daily rate increases to $50.

The role of the judge in recent years has expanded significantly into the area of case management. Before the adoption of the individual calendar system, a judge would generally try a case only when the parties decided they were ready to do so. Today, the size and complexity of the Court's docket does not permit this more leisurely way of conducting judicial business. Judges, in addition to adjudicating cases, must also act as case supervisors or managers to insure there is no undue delay in the progress of an action. The judge normally will hold a status conference with counsel early in the life of a civil case and set deadlines for the completion of discovery, the filing of motions, and a date some months hence for trial if the case is not settled.[26] The judge often plays an active part in helping the parties resolve the matter amicably at some point in the process. Status conferences in criminal cases are also becoming common. However, a judge may not participate in any plea negotiations in such cases.

Thanks to the valiant efforts of Judge Broderick, this Court was in the forefront in adopting an innovative compulsory arbitration program, initially approved by Congress in 1988, whereby certain smaller cases are tried in the first instance by a panel of three lawyers who volunteer to participate in the program and are approved by the Court. Only cases seeking money damages in the amount of $150,000 or less where no constitutional claim is involved are eligible. The arbitration is less formal than the courtroom setting and usually lasts no more than a few hours at most. A party unhappy with a decision is entitled to a trial de novo before a District Judge, with a jury if one has been demanded.[27]

District Judges have other official responsibilities beyond those of managing and deciding the cases before them. In every district throughout the country, they appoint Magistrate Judges for eight year terms to perform various judicial duties designated by law. The candidates are selected from recommendations made by a merit selection panel appointed by the particular Court. The panels consist of both lawyers and lay persons. The number of Magistrate Judges in any district is determined by the Judicial Conference of the United States. [28]

At present this Court has twelve sitting Magistrate Judges, including two who have been recalled from retirement. Ten are stationed in Philadelphia and two in Allentown. Among other responsibilities, Magistrate Judges approve arrest and search warrants, preside over arraignments and preliminary hearings, and set bail. They try misdemeanor offenses including those that occur in Independence National Historical Park and Valley Forge National Park. Their duties encompass making reports and recommendations to the assigned District Judge in social security cases and on habeas corpus motions filed by state prisoners. With the consent of the parties, Magistrate Judges may also try civil cases. One of their most important responsibilities in the Eastern District is to hold settlement conferences in civil cases pending before District Judges.[29] Every Magistrate Judge in the Eastern District is paired with several District Judges for this and other purposes.

The Eastern District in 2008 established an innovative program known as a reentry court under the leadership of Magistrate Judges Timothy Rice and L. Felipe Restrepo. As a result of the efforts of Judge Brody and the Court's Criminal Business Committee, together with those of the United States Attorney's Office, the Federal Defenders, and the Court's Probation Office, a program was developed to work intensively with selected defendants who have committed serious crimes, have completed their prison terms, and are now on supervised release. The goal of the program is to reduce recidivism and integrate the participants into society as useful and productive citizens. Extra efforts are made to aid them in dealing with personal and family issues, coping in the wider world, and obtaining training and employment. The reentry court meets once a month with the participants appearing before one of the two Magistrate Judges for a progress report, guidance, encouragement and, if necessary, admonishment. For those defendants who successfully complete the program, the sentencing judge will reduce their term of supervised release by one year. The reentry court program not only has been a success but also a model for other district courts.

In addition to the Magistrate Judges, the Eastern District currently has six Bankruptcy Judges who constitute "a unit of the district court to be known as the bankruptcy court for that district." They are appointed by the Court of Appeals for a term of fourteen years. The District Court hears appeals from the decisions of the Bankruptcy Judges.[30]

One of the most pleasant duties of a judge of this Court is presiding over naturalization ceremonies which are held regularly at the courthouse or the nearby National Constitution Center. The administration of the oath of allegiance to new citizens from all parts of the world, often with family and friends present, is always a very moving experience and brings home the reality that we are a nation of immigrants. Presiding over the admission of new attorneys to the bar of the Court is another happy occasion. This continues a custom begun by Judge Francis Hopkinson at the first session of the District Court in Independence Hall in November 1789.

The tradition of judges of this Court being assigned to cases outside the District, which started with Judge Butler in the 1880's, has endured. Chief Justice John Roberts named Judge Mary McLaughlin in 2008 to the seven member Foreign Intelligence Surveillance Court which takes her to Washington several weeks a year.[31] The Chief Judge of the Circuit from time to time has requested that the judges of this Court assist other courts within the Circuit with their workload. In the late 1980's, the Eastern District for a time accepted cases from the District of New Jersey.[32] In the middle 1990's, Circuit Chief Judge Becker designated several judges to try cases in Pittsburgh in the Western District of Pennsylvania.

The Virgin Islands have been a part of the Third Circuit since they were purchased from the Kingdom of Denmark in 1917. Going back to the days of Chief Judge Clary, judges of the Eastern District have sat regularly in St. Thomas and St. Croix in order to assist with the heavy caseload there and to handle cases when the local district judges must recuse themselves because of a conflict of interest.

The District of Delaware, which has only four authorized judgeships, has had a growing backlog due to a long-standing vacancy. To remedy the situation, Circuit Chief Judge Scirica, beginning in 2008, designated Judges of the Eastern District as well as the District of New Jersey to take assignments from that Court. He has also named Judges from this District to sit when needed as a member of three-judge panels to hear appeals from districts in the Circuit other than the Eastern District.[33] These assignments have continued under Circuit Chief Judge Theodore A. McKee.

A number of Judges in the Eastern District, by appointment of the Chief Justice, have been members of various committees of the Judicial Conference of the United States, the policymaking body of the federal court system.[34] They have served over the years on the Advisory Committees on Civil Rules, Criminal Rules, Evidence Rules, and Bankruptcy Rules as well as on the Committees on Codes of Conduct, Court Administration and Case Management, Defender Services, Financial Disclosure, the Judicial Branch, Judicial Resources, and Judicial Security.

The Judicial Conference of the United States elected Judge Yohn to a term on the Board of the Federal Judicial Center, which has the responsibility for continuing legal education for judges and the development of improved judicial administration for the federal courts. Judge Yohn also chairs a special committee established by the Court of Appeals which has drafted model jury instructions for criminal cases. Those on the committee include Judges Buckwalter and Baylson. Judges Pollak and McLaughlin are members of a similar committee which has prepared model civil jury instructions. Judge Bartle currently serves as the District Court representative of the Third Circuit on the Judicial Conference of the United States and was named in 2010 by Chief Justice Roberts to the seven-member Executive Committee of the Conference.

The District Court also has a number of committees appointed by the Chief Judge to aid with court administration and governance. Every judge serves on at least two committees. Business meetings of the entire Court are held at the call of the Chief Judge, usually at 1:15 p.m. on a Monday, in the Judges' Conference Room on the third floor of the courthouse in Philadelphia. The room contains a long table that can accommodate over thirty judges. Hanging on its walls are fifteen court photographs, the earliest of which dates back to 1941 when the Eastern District had only five judges (Kirkpatrick, Welsh, Kalodner, Bard, and Ganey). At the end of any judges' meeting, it has long been the custom for the Chief Judge to call on the next most senior active judge in attendance to make the motion to adjourn.

In the early 1990's, Chief Judge Bechtle organized a court retreat, a several-day event away from the courthouse. The judges found the retreat to be very helpful, and one has been held in most subsequent years. The topics vary from "nuts and bolts" issues with which judges must contend in their everyday work to discussions on matters of broader interest. Sometimes the judges themselves conduct the program on a particular subject while on other occasions they engage outside speakers. Judge Padova heads the Committee which plans the retreat.

The Court recognizes the need for the public to be better informed about the significant role of the federal courts in our constitutional system of government. The Court's Outreach Committee chaired by Judge Rufe has worked assiduously to promote the education of high school students in this regard. Among other efforts, each year the Committee organizes a number of mock trials over which the judges of the Court preside in Philadelphia, Reading, and Allentown, and in which high school students participate with the help of volunteer lawyers. At the conclusion of these trials during which the students act as lawyers, witnesses and jurors, the judges and lawyers talk to the students about the federal courts and answer their many questions.

Each year the Court looks forward to hosting judges and lawyers from foreign countries. The guests observe trials and other Court proceedings, speak and lunch with judges, and learn about the newest technology used in the courtroom and the Clerk's Office. It is a splendid opportunity to showcase the federal judicial system and to teach the importance of judicial independence and the rule of law.

Today, several statutes as well as a Code of Conduct for United States Judges require those on the federal bench to avoid not only conflicts of interest but also the appearance of conflicts of interest. They may not hear cases involving parties or lawyers who are related to them or cases in which they have any financial interest, however slight. They must recuse themselves even if they own only one share of stock of a corporation that is before them. In sum, whenever the impartiality of a judge might reasonably be questioned in a matter, the judge must step aside. It is also improper for a judge to communicate with one side in a case without the presence of the other side, except in certain special circumstances. There are also limitations on the extrajudicial activities of a judge. For example, participation in politics is forbidden, and contributions to political parties or candidates may not be made. If a judge decides to run for office, he or she must resign from the bench. Further, a judge may not belong to a club that discriminates or solicit funds for a charitable organization. All of these rules governing in-court and out-of-court conduct help to maintain the integrity of the federal judicial system and the public's confidence in it.[35]

A further requirement imposed on every federal judge by Congress is the annual filing of a completed financial disclosure form with the Administrative Office of the United States Courts. On one occasion, Judge Ditter received an inquiry requesting an explanation of his farm income of $171.50, which had resulted from the sale of "one-half a hog, a few dozen eggs, and some honey." He responded in his customary thorough and straightforward manner:

> Actually we grew both sides of the hog and sold what I believe was the starboard side -- although when one tries to figure whether scrapple and sausage came from the right or the left, it may be difficult to be precise. In any event, the hog grew on the same property at which my family and I reside although not at our actual place of residence. We kept the hog in a hog pen and we occupied the house. This seemed

> to work out satisfactorily from the standpoint of all concerned. At least there were no complaints from the people and if the hog was unhappy, he did not let on.
>
> Part of the farm income came from the sale of eggs. The eggs came from chickens which, although they were on our property, did not live in our place of residence. We provided a hen house for them. From what little I know of the physiology of a chicken I would believe that an egg grows. To hear the chickens discuss it, post-event, one could only conclude that each egg had been manufactured with a great deal of skill and care.
>
> The remaining part of the farm income came from the sale of honey. Once again, the bees that produced the honey did not live in our actual place of residence. They had their own quarters which we call beehives and while one or two from time to time may have gotten into the house (a problem we did not have with either the hog or the chickens) we did not make them feel welcome and tried to make reasonable efforts to exclude them. Honey comes from nectar. I think that much of the nectar gathered by our bees was found on other persons' properties although I must admit I have made no real effort to trace it. In my judgment honey does not grow at all nor is it manufactured. Therefore, it must come under the heading "etc."
>
> I hope this clears up any questions the committee may have about our farm income but I will be happy to furnish further explanation if you feel it necessary for me to do so.[36]

Judge Ditter's response apparently satisfied the inquirer as no follow-up occurred.

Since 1789, the Court has had a Clerk whom it has appointed. As the Court has become larger, the filings more numerous, and the court administration more structured, the work of the Clerk and his staff has become more critical to the smooth operation of the Court and the expeditious and economical administration of justice. In 1976, the Court selected Michael E. Kunz, as the Chief Deputy Clerk when the Clerk, John Harding, became ill. When Harding retired in 1979, the Court named Kunz as its fifteenth Clerk of Court. He has now served with distinction in that position for over thirty years during the terms of eight Chief Judges, one of the longest tenures of any Clerk in the Court's history. The Clerk's Office under the leadership of Michael Kunz has been at the forefront of administrative and technological innovation and has ably handled an ever increasing and more complex caseload. The Administrative

Office of the United States Courts has called upon him on frequent occasions for his knowledge and expertise.

The Court also has a Pretrial Services Office and a Probation Office. The former, headed by Donna M. Makowiecki, has fifteen pretrial services officers who supervise those on bail before trial. The latter, under the leadership previously of Daniel W. Blahusch and now Ronald DeCastro, employs over eighty probation officers who prepare detailed presentence reports on each defendant and monitor defendants sentenced to probation and those on supervised release after having completed terms of imprisonment. Both these offices do their difficult work with professionalism and in a timely and efficient fashion.

Technological advances have been occurring at an ever accelerating rate. The year 1955 saw the end of handwritten docket entries by the Clerk's Office to record the filings in cases and the beginning of the use of the typewriter to do so. More recently, the Court docket entries have been computerized, and all Court filings, including orders and opinions, other than filings by pro se parties, are now done electronically. The judges, lawyers, and others can view on the internet the dockets of all cases as well as the content of the documents filed, except when the Court, for security or other compelling reasons, orders that a document be sealed from public examination.

As a result of the efforts of Judge Huyett mentioned previously, most judges have opted to use electronic sound recording for Court proceedings rather than an individual court reporter taking down testimony. Some courtrooms are now equipped with real time reporting so that the transcripts are immediately available and with screens for the Court and each juror to view exhibits.

Heavy security in the courthouse has been a fact of life since 1983 with the engagement of a cadre of court security officers to augment the protection ably provided by the United States Marshal for the Eastern District and the assigned deputy marshals. All lawyers, court employees, and other visitors, together with their brief cases, bags, and purses, must pass through a metal detector as they enter the building. For some criminal trials, additional security is provided with a metal detector at the entrance of the courtroom. Special elevators bring prisoners directly from the courthouse cellblock to the courtroom. There is no automatic public access to judges' chambers as had existed in the old courthouse at Ninth and Market Streets. Each chambers entrance is equipped with a camera, buzzer, and intercom system. Mail is also thoroughly screened before it is delivered.

In the summer of 1998, a major problem arose with the exterior walls of the courthouse in Philadelphia. Several bricks fell onto the sidewalk below after a violent storm. Upon inspection, it was soon discovered that the facade of the twenty-two story structure was in danger of collapse because the original contractors had not properly fastened the bricks to the exterior frame. The Government had no choice but to rectify this dire safety hazard by recladding the entire edifice. It took more than a year at a cost to the taxpayers of over $25 million. The courthouse now has an exterior with a million new bricks, together with a wide horizontal granite band, far above the street, inscribed in large letters with the words "Justice the Guardian of Liberty," the same legend as is emblazoned on the East pediment of the Supreme Court building in Washington. These words are also carved into the new granite segment of the exterior wall adjacent to the Market Street entrance of the courthouse.

Other changes took place during this period in the appearance of the interior of the courthouse. Through the efforts of Circuit Chief Judge Becker and Senator Specter, an appropriation was obtained from Congress to refurbish the expansive lobby to make it more inviting. The lighting was vastly improved, and three transparent floor-to-ceiling panels were installed containing quotations referencing due process of law, the right of trial by jury, and justice. One was authored by Daniel Webster: "Justice is the great interest of man on earth. It is the ligament which holds civilized beings and civilized nations together." Another originated with Martin Luther King, Jr.: "True peace is not merely the absence of tension; it is the presence of justice." Since these renovations, the first floor of the courthouse has been designated as the Edward R. Becker Lobby.

The lobby of the courthouse was not handicapped-accessible from the Market Street entrance when it was constructed in the mid-1970's. A set of interior steps existed as a barrier from the lower part of the lobby to its main upper area. In the last decade, a small elevator was installed to travel the short distance from one level to the other. As a result, those in wheelchairs or who are otherwise unable to climb stairs can enter and exit the building without difficulty.

The present courthouse was built with space to accommodate future growth. While originally the United States Attorney's Office, the Pretrial and Probation Offices, and other federal agencies were located there, they have long since departed to other nearby venues due to the expanded needs of both the District Court and the Court of Appeals. The two Courts, their Clerk's Offices and support staffs, the U.S. Marshals Service, and the Law Library, now fill the courthouse to capacity.

Until 2000, the trials in the courthouse in Philadelphia of criminal defendants who were in custody were somewhat constrained by the absence of a nearby facility to house them. In the 1980's and 1990's, the closest federal prison was at Fairton, in Cumberland County, New Jersey, some forty miles southeast of Philadelphia. Trials were often delayed because of the distance and frequent traffic problems in bringing defendants to court, and judges would often have to adjourn earlier in the day than they preferred in order to allow the defendants to be returned to Fairton in time for their evening meals. It was also difficult for defense attorneys to meet with their clients and prepare for trial when they were so far away. In short, the need for a detention facility close to the courthouse was acute. Through the efforts of Senator Specter, land was acquired, and a high-rise detention facility was built at Seventh and Arch Streets, across the street from the courthouse. A tunnel under Seventh Street to transport prisoners between the two buildings was also part of the project. The detention facility has a capacity for about 1,200 inmates. Unfortunately, it no longer is sufficient to accommodate all inmates scheduled for trial or hearings, and some must be housed at distant locations. Thus, the problem that it was designed to solve has begun to recur.

With the induction of Edward Cahn in 1975, the Court had a judge sitting in Allentown for the first time since that city was designated by Congress as a court station in 1968. The Commissioners of Lehigh County kindly permitted him to use the old Lehigh County Courthouse with its vintage courtroom since there was no adequate federal facility nearby. In the early 1990's, a federal courthouse was built in Allentown where both civil and criminal cases arising out of that geographic area are now tried. It is situated on Hamilton Street across from the old county courthouse and a block from Zion's Reformed Church where the Liberty Bell was hidden during the Revolution after it was removed from Independence Hall to keep it out of the grasp of the British Army about to occupy Philadelphia. The courthouse contains the portraits of Judges William Kirkpatrick and J. Cullen Ganey, who were from neighboring Northampton County, as well as that of Judge Edward Cahn, who is a native of Lehigh County. All three served as Chief Judge of this Court. Following Judge Cahn's resignation from the bench, Congress named the building the Edward N. Cahn Courthouse. Judge Gardner along with two Magistrate Judges currently have their chambers there.

The Court has had a station in Reading, Berks County since 1968. At first it was housed in leased space in the American Bank Building, where a courtroom and chambers were constructed for Judge Troutman and then for Judge Huyett. The Court moved to space rented in the Madison Building in 1988. After the death of Judge Huyett and the decision of Judge Troutman no longer to sit, no judge regularly had chambers in Reading until the appointment of Judge Golden in 2006. Judge Stengel and Judge Sanchez hear civil cases there as well as in Philadelphia. Since Judge Van Antwerpen was appointed to the Court of Appeals in 2004, no District Judge has sat in Easton, and no judge has ever been stationed in Lancaster, both of which places Congress has authorized for holding court.

The Court still occupies part of the old courthouse at Ninth and Market Streets in Philadelphia including its paneled courtrooms. The Bankruptcy Judges and Bankruptcy Clerk are located there as are several Magistrate Judges. Judge Hutton during his last years on the bench moved his chambers to that site.

The Eastern District, as previously noted, was reduced in size to encompass only ten counties of southeastern Pennsylvania when the Middle District of Pennsylvania was created in 1901. Over the years, some residents of Schuylkill County complained about both the distance and difficulty in coming to Philadelphia for jury duty, and considered it more convenient if they would be allowed to travel instead to Harrisburg, Lewisburg, Scranton, or Wilkes-Barre, the places where the federal court in the Middle District is held. In 1998, their Congressman achieved the passage of a bill to transfer Schuylkill County out of the Eastern District.[37] No secessionist movement has arisen since that time, and the Eastern District continues to include the nine loyal counties of Berks, Bucks, Chester, Delaware, Lancaster, Lehigh, Montgomery, Northampton, and Philadelphia.

The law clerks, most of whom are recent law school graduates, play an important role in the life of each judge's chambers doing legal research and assisting with the crafting of opinions. Judge Pratter has organized an in-depth and well-received orientation program for the new clerks which takes place each fall.

Many judges also take on law students as summer interns. In 2010, the Court began to participate in the Judicial Intern Opportunity Program sponsored by the American Bar Association Section of Litigation. Its purpose is to provide economically disadvantaged law students with an opportunity to work with judges during the summer months.

All, however, is not work. There is an annual softball game between the judges and law clerks each July. Judge Robreno is now the organizer of the event, and has been designated as the Captain and Playing Manager of the Judges' team. Age and maturity sometimes prevail in this hard-fought contest, while at other times youth and exuberance carry the day.

Every December, the Court holds a holiday luncheon at the neighboring Federal Reserve Bank. The event includes not only the District Judges and the Court's alumni on the Court of Appeals but also the Magistrate Judges, the Bankruptcy Judges, the Clerks of the District Court and the Bankruptcy Court, the United States Marshal, the Chief Probation Officer, and the Chief Pretrial Services Officer. One of the judges is always invited to give a ten to fifteen-minute talk on what everyone hopes is a topic of interest. Academic legal subjects are off limits. The program concludes with the singing of familiar holiday tunes.

From time to time, the Court organizes a dinner to fete newly appointed judges and those who have recently assumed senior status. It is always a festive occasion and has been known at times to take on the character of a roast.

Any chronicle of the Eastern District of Pennsylvania would not be complete without a few words about the daily gathering of judges for lunch. In the 1960's, Chief Judge Clary initiated the custom of a weekly judges' luncheon at the dining room of Gimbels or Strawbridge & Clothier, two nearby department stores. Court business was often transacted. A judges' dining room was designated in the present courthouse in Philadelphia when it was constructed in the mid-1970's so that what was a weekly occasion off-site became a more convenient everyday event for those who wished to participate. The room contains a long table where judges eat their lunches purchased from the courthouse cafeteria or bought elsewhere.

The conversation which takes place is always lively and spontaneous. It varies from day to day and even minute to minute. The dialogue ranges from current or historical events to sports to light banter to fond remembrances of departed colleagues to repetition of often-told stories. Sometimes the talk turns to legal subjects such as recent Supreme Court or Court of Appeals decisions or to a knotty issue that a judge faces or some noteworthy encounter that may have occurred that morning in the courtroom. At other times, of course, the main happening is the celebration of a judge's birthday. One thing that is not done at lunch is the transaction of Court business. Above all, the noontime repast in the judges' dining room for those in attendance is a welcomed interlude for fellowship and relaxation during the busy day. Indeed, it is the catalyst for a collegial Court.

---

As of this writing, ninety-three men and women of diverse backgrounds have raised their right hands and have solemnly sworn or affirmed to support and defend the Constitution as Judges of either the United States District Court for the District of Pennsylvania or the United States District Court for the Eastern District of Pennsylvania. The duty imposed is a formidable one.

The decisions these Judges have handed down over more than two centuries in the cases and controversies before them have affected the lives of countless individuals as well as the actions of private entities and governments. Some of these rulings have been courageous. Some have been unpopular. Frequently, the judges of this Court have had to grapple with difficult factual or legal issues. All proceedings before them are important to the parties involved, and many of those proceedings have significant consequences for the public-at-large. In criminal cases particularly, matters of the utmost gravity are often at stake.

There is no country in the world where the courts play a more significant role in society than in the United States. This is all the more remarkable when one considers, as Alexander Hamilton wrote in No. 78 of *The Federalist*, that they possess neither the power of the purse nor the power of the sword. Each era has presented its special challenges to the judiciary and will undoubtedly continue to do so in the future. Those who enter or pass the United States Courthouse in Philadelphia are reminded of the words, "Justice the Guardian of Liberty," chiseled in stone on its exterior. Daily the judges of this Court, free of political or other improper pressures with their lifetime appointments, play an essential part in striving to make these words a reality.

As Judge Kraft aptly observed years ago, a judge is "a mortal charged with tremendous responsibilities. You're dealing with other people's rights, not your own ...."[38] The story of this Court is essentially that story.

## Notes

1. In 1990, the Court also had one temporary judgeship in addition to the twenty-two authorized permanent judgeships. That judgeship has now expired.
2. In some administrations, the ABA evaluations have occurred after the President has made his District Court nominations.
3. U.S. Const. art. II, § 1, cl. 2; U.S. Const. amend. XII.
4. *United States v. Moussaoui*, 333 F. 3d 509 (4th Cir. 2003).
5. Pub. L. No. 107-206 § 203, 116 Stat. 832-33 (2002).
6. *The Third Branch*, Vol. 38, No. 9 (Sept. 2006).
7. *Id.*
8. 28 U.S.C. § 1332.
9. 29 U.S.C. §§ 2601 et seq.
10. 29 U.S.C. §§ 1001 et seq.
11. 28 U.S.C. §§ 2671 et seq.
12. 7 U.S.C. §§ 499a et seq.
13. *See* Rule 23 of the Federal Rules of Civil Procedure.
14. *See* 28 U.S.C. §§ 2254 and 2255.
15. 772 F. Supp. 1535 (E.D. Pa. 1991), *aff'd*, 52 F.3d 967 (Fed. Cir. 1995), *aff'd*, 517 U.S. 370 (1996).
16. The Seventh Amendment provides:

    In Suits at common law, where the controversy shall exceed twenty dollars, the right of trial by jury shall be preserved, and no fact tried by jury shall be otherwise reexamined in any Court of the United States, than according to the rules of the common law.
17. U.S. Const. amend. VI; 18 U.S.C. §§ 3161 et seq.
18. The Fourth Amendment provides:

    The right of the people to be secure in their persons, houses, papers, and effects, against unreasonable searches and seizures, shall not be violated, and no Warrants shall issue, but upon probable cause, supported by Oath or affirmation, and particularly describing the place to be searched, and the persons or things to be seized.
19. 543 U.S. 220 (2005).
20. 18 U.S.C. § 3553(a).
21. *Booker*, 543 U.S. at 260-62. *See also Kimbrough v. United States*, 552 U.S. 85 (2007); *Gall v. United States*, 552 U.S. 38 (2007).
22. Article III, § 2, cL. 2 provides in relevant part: "The Trial of all Crimes, except in Cases of Impeachment; shall be by Jury ..."

    The Sixth Amendment reads in relevant part: "In all criminal procedures, the accused shall enjoy the right to a speedy and public trial, by an impartial jury of the State and district wherein the crime shall have been committed..."

23. *See* fn. 14 *supra.*
24. 28 U.S.C. §§ 1861-62.
25. Rule 48.1 of the Local Rules of the United States District Court for the Eastern District of Pennsylvania. *See* "District Court Adopts Rule Permitting Eight-Member Juries in Civil Cases," *The Legal Intelligencer*, p. 1 (April 14, 1971).
26. *See* Rule 16 of the Federal Rules of Civil Procedure.
27. 28 U.S.C. § 651 et seq.; Local Civil Rule 53.2.
28. 28 U.S.C. §§ 631-33.
29. *Id.* at § 636.
30. 28 U.S.C. §§ 151-52, 157-58.
31. 50 U.S.C. § 1803.
32. Interview by Nancy Fullam, Esquire with Judge John Fullam, p. 66 (Aug. 8, 1999).
33. 28 U.S.C. § 292.
34. 28 U.S.C. § 331. The Chief Justice presides over the Judicial Conference. The Chief Judge of every circuit, the Chief Judge of the International Court of Trade, and a District Judge from every circuit are members of the Conference.
35. 28 U.S.C. §§ 144, 455; Code of Conduct for United States Judges (July 2009).
36. Letter from J. William Ditter, Jr., to The Honorable Edward A. Tamm (July 6, 1981).
37. 28 U.S.C. § 118; *see also* Pub. L. 105-277 § 624(a), 112 Stat. 2681-116 (1998).
38. Interview by Magistrate Judge Richard A. Powers III with Judge C. William Kraft, pp. 66-67 (Feb. 28, 1995).

# APPENDICES

# Appendix I
# District Judges

| Name | Appointing President | Home County at Time of Appointment |
|---|---|---|
| Francis Hopkinson | George Washington | Philadelphia |
| William Lewis | George Washington | Philadelphia |
| Richard Peters | George Washington | Philadelphia |
| Joseph Hopkinson | John Quincy Adams | Philadelphia |
| Archibald Randall | John Tyler | Philadelphia |
| John K. Kane | James K. Polk | Philadelphia |
| John Cadwalader | James Buchanan | Philadelphia |
| William Butler | Rutherford B. Hayes | Chester |
| John B. McPherson | William McKinley | Dauphin |
| James B. Holland | Theodore Roosevelt | Montgomery |
| J. Whitaker Thompson | William H. Taft | Montgomery |

| College | Law School | Years Hearing Cases |
|---|---|---|
| College of Philadelphia[1] | | 1789–1791 |
| | | 1791–1792 |
| College of Philadelphia[1] | | 1792–1828 |
| University of the State of Pennsylvania[1] | | 1828–1842 |
| | | 1842–1846 |
| Yale College | | 1846–1858 |
| University of Pennsylvania | | 1858–1879 |
| | | 1879–1899 |
| College of New Jersey[2] | | 1899–1912 |
| | | 1904–1914 |
| University of Pennsylvania | University of Pennsylvania | 1912–1931 |

| Name | Appointing President | Home County at Time of Appointment |
|---|---|---|
| Oliver B. Dickinson | Woodrow Wilson | Delaware |
| Charles L. McKeehan | Warren G. Harding | Philadelphia |
| William H. Kirkpatrick | Calvin Coolidge | Northampton |
| George A. Welsh | Herbert Hoover | Philadelphia |
| Albert Branson Maris | Franklin D. Roosevelt | Delaware |
| Harry E. Kalodner | Franklin D. Roosevelt | Philadelphia |
| Guy K. Bard | Franklin D. Roosevelt | Lancaster |
| J. Cullen Ganey | Franklin D. Roosevelt | Northampton |
| Frederick V. Follmer[5] | Harry S. Truman | Northumberland |
| James P. McGranery | Harry S. Truman | Philadelphia |
| Thomas J. Clary | Harry S. Truman | Philadelphia |
| Allan K. Grim | Harry S. Truman | Berks |
| John W. Lord Jr. | Dwight D. Eisenhower | Philadelphia |

| College | Law School | Years Hearing Cases |
|---|---|---|
| Lewisburg College[3] | | 1914–1939 |
| University of Pennsylvania | University of Pennsylvania | 1923–1925 |
| Lafayette College | University of Pennsylvania[4] | 1927–1970 |
| | Temple University | 1932–1964 |
| Drexel Institute of Technology | Temple University | 1936–1938 |
| | University of Pennsylvania | 1938–1946 |
| Franklin & Marshall College | University of Pennsylvania | 1939–1952 |
| Lehigh University | Harvard University | 1940–1961 |
| Bucknell University | Harvard University | 1946–1955 |
| Temple University | Temple University | 1946–1952 |
| Cornell University | Georgetown University | 1949–1977 |
| Swarthmore College | Harvard University | 1949–1965 |
| | Temple University | 1954–1972 |

| Name | Appointing President | Home County at Time of Appointment |
|---|---|---|
| Francis L. Van Dusen | Dwight D. Eisenhower | Montgomery |
| C. William Kraft Jr. | Dwight D. Eisenhower | Delaware |
| Thomas C. Egan | Dwight D. Eisenhower | Philadelphia |
| Harold K. Wood | Dwight D. Eisenhower | Chester |
| Joseph S. Lord III | John F. Kennedy | Philadelphia |
| Abraham L. Freedman | John F. Kennedy | Philadelphia |
| Alfred L. Luongo | John F. Kennedy | Philadelphia |
| Ralph C. Body | John F. Kennedy | Berks |
| A. Leon Higginbotham Jr. | Lyndon B. Johnson | Philadelphia |
| John Morgan Davis | Lyndon B. Johnson | Philadelphia |
| John P. Fullam | Lyndon B. Johnson | Bucks |
| Charles R. Weiner | Lyndon B. Johnson | Philadelphia |
| Thomas A. Masterson | Lyndon B. Johnson | Philadelphia |

| College | Law School | Years Hearing Cases |
|---|---|---|
| Princeton University | Harvard University | 1955–1967 |
| University of Pennsylvania | University of Pennsylvania | 1955–1982 |
| Georgetown University | University of Pennsylvania | 1957–1961 |
| Colgate University | University of Pennsylvania | 1959–1972 |
| University of Pennsyvania | University of Pennsylvania | 1961–1990 |
| | Temple University | 1961–1964 |
| University of Pennsyvania | University of Pennsylvania | 1961–1986 |
| Pennsylvania State University | University of Pennsylvania | 1962–1973 |
| Antioch College | Yale University | 1964–1977 |
| University of Pennsyvania | University of Pennsylvania | 1964–1984 |
| Villanova University | Harvard University | 1966–2011 |
| University of Pennsylvania | Temple University | 1967–2005 |
| Harvard University | University of Pennsylvania | 1967–1973 |

| Name | Appointing President | Home County at Time of Appointment |
|---|---|---|
| E. Mac Troutman | Lyndon B. Johnson | Schuylkill |
| John B. Hannum | Richard M. Nixon | Chester |
| Edward R. Becker | Richard M. Nixon | Philadelphia |
| Donald W. VanArtsdalen | Richard M. Nixon | Bucks |
| Daniel H. Huyett 3rd | Richard M. Nixon | Berks |
| J. William Ditter Jr. | Richard M. Nixon | Montgomery |
| James H. Gorbey | Richard M. Nixon | Delaware |
| Raymond J. Broderick | Richard M. Nixon | Philadelphia |
| Clarence C. Newcomer | Richard M. Nixon | Lancaster |
| Clifford Scott Green | Richard M. Nixon | Philadelphia |
| Louis C. Bechtle | Richard M. Nixon | Montgomery |
| Herbert A. Fogel | Richard M. Nixon | Philadelphia |

| College | Law School | Years Hearing Cases |
|---|---|---|
| Dickinson College | Dickinson School of Law | 1967–1998 |
| Franklin & Marshall College | Dickinson School of Law | 1969–1990 |
| University of Pennsylvania | Yale University | 1970–1981 |
| Williams College | University of Pennsylvania | 1970–1999 |
| University of Michigan | University of Pennsylvania | 1970–1998 |
| Ursinus College | University of Pennsylvania | 1970– |
| Bowling Green State University | Temple University | 1970–1977 |
| University of Notre Dame | University of Pennsylvania | 1971–2000 |
| Franklin & Marshall College | Dickinson School of Law | 1971–2005 |
| Temple University | Temple University | 1971–2007 |
| Temple University | Temple University | 1972–2001 |
| University of Pennsyvania | University of Pennsylvania | 1973–1978 |

| Name | Appointing President | Home County at Time of Appointment |
|---|---|---|
| Joseph L. McGlynn Jr. | Richard M. Nixon | Philadelphia |
| Edward N. Cahn | Gerald R. Ford | Lehigh |
| Louis H. Pollak | Jimmy Carter | Philadelphia |
| Norma L. Shapiro | Jimmy Carter | Montgomery |
| James T. Giles | Jimmy Carter | Philadelphia |
| Thomas N. O'Neill Jr. | Ronald Reagan | Montgomery |
| James McGirr Kelly | Ronald Reagan | Philadelphia |
| Marvin Katz | Ronald Reagan | Philadelphia |
| Anthony J. Scirica | Ronald Reagan | Montgomery |
| Edmund V. Ludwig | Ronald Reagan | Bucks |
| Robert F. Kelly | Ronald Reagan | Delaware |
| Franklin S. Van Antwerpen | Ronald Reagan | Northampton |
| Robert S. Gawthrop III | Ronald Reagan | Chester |

| College | Law School | Years Hearing Cases |
|---|---|---|
| Mount St. Mary's College | University of Pennsylvania | 1974–1999 |
| Lehigh University | Yale University | 1975–1998 |
| Harvard University | Yale University | 1978– |
| University of Michigan | University of Pennsylvania | 1978– |
| Amherst College | Yale University | 1979–2008 |
| Catholic University | University of Pennsylvania | 1983– |
| University of Pennsylvania | Temple University | 1983–2005 |
| University of Pennsylvania | Yale University | 1983–2008 |
| Wesleyan University | University of Michigan | 1984–1987 |
| Harvard University | Harvard University | 1985– |
| Villanova University | Temple University | 1987– |
| University of Maine | Temple University | 1987–2004 |
| Amherst College | Dickinson School of Law | 1987–1999 |

| Name | Appointing President | Home County at Time of Appointment |
| --- | --- | --- |
| Lowell A. Reed Jr. | Ronald Reagan | Montgomery |
| Jan E. DuBois | Ronald Reagan | Montgomery |
| Herbert J. Hutton | Ronald Reagan | Philadelphia |
| Jay C. Waldman | Ronald Reagan | Philadelphia |
| Ronald L. Buckwalter | George H.W. Bush | Lancaster |
| William H. Yohn Jr. | George H.W. Bush | Montgomery |
| Harvey Bartle III | George H.W. Bush | Philadelphia |
| Stewart Dalzell | George H.W. Bush | Philadelphia |
| John R. Padova | George H.W. Bush | Philadelphia |
| J. Curtis Joyner | George H.W. Bush | Chester |
| Eduardo C. Robreno | George H.W. Bush | Philadelphia |
| Anita B. Brody | George H.W. Bush | Montgomery |

| College | Law School | Years Hearing Cases |
|---|---|---|
| University of Wisconsin | Temple University | 1988–2011 |
| University of Pennsylvania | Yale University | 1988– |
| Lincoln University | Temple University | 1988–2007 |
| University of Wisconsin | University of Pennsylvania | 1988–2003 |
| Franklin & Marshall College | William & Mary School of Law | 1990– |
| Princeton University | Yale University | 1991– |
| Princeton University | University of Pennsylvania | 1991– |
| University of Pennsylvania | University of Pennsylvania | 1991– |
| Villanova University | Temple University | 1992– |
| Central State University | Howard University | 1992- |
| Westfield State University<br><br>University of Massachusetts (M.S.) | Rutgers University | 1992- |
| Wellesley College | Columbia University | 1992- |

| Name | Appointing President | Home County at Time of Appointment |
|---|---|---|
| **Marjorie O. Rendell** | William J. Clinton | Philadelphia |
| **Bruce W. Kauffman** | William J. Clinton | Montgomery |
| **Mary A. McLaughlin** | William J. Clinton | Philadelphia |
| **Petrese B. Tucker** | William J. Clinton | Philadelphia |
| **Berle M. Schiller** | William J. Clinton | Montgomery |
| **R. Barclay Surrick** | William J. Clinton | Delaware |
| **Legrome D. Davis** | George W. Bush | Philadelphia |
| **Cynthia M. Rufe** | George W. Bush | Bucks |
| **Michael M. Baylson** | George W. Bush | Philadelphia |
| **Timothy J. Savage** | George W. Bush | Philadelphia |
| **James Knoll Gardner** | George W. Bush | Lehigh |
| **Gene E.K. Pratter** | George W. Bush | Montgomery |

| College | Law School | Years Hearing Cases |
|---|---|---|
| University of Pennsylvania | Villanova University | 1994–1997 |
| University of Pennsylvania | Yale University | 1998–2009 |
| Gwynedd-Mercy College<br>Bryn Mawr College (M.A.) | University of Pennsylvania | 2000– |
| Temple University | Temple University | 2000– |
| Bowdoin College | New York University | 2000– |
| Dickinson College<br>University of Virginia (LL.M.) | Dickinson School of Law | 2000– |
| Princeton University | Rutgers University | 2002– |
| Adelphi University | Buffalo School of Law | 2002– |
| University of Pennsylvania | University of Pennsylvania | 2002– |
| Assumption College | Temple University | 2002– |
| Yale University | Harvard University | 2002– |
| Stanford University | University of Pennsylvania | 2004– |

| Name | Appointing President | Home County at Time of Appointment |
|---|---|---|
| Lawrence F. Stengel | George W. Bush | Lancaster |
| Paul S. Diamond | George W. Bush | Philadelphia |
| Juan R. Sanchez | George W. Bush | Chester |
| Thomas M. Golden | George W. Bush | Berks |
| Joel H. Slomsky | George W. Bush | Montgomery |
| C. Darnell Jones II | George W. Bush | Philadelphia |
| Mitchell S. Goldberg | George W. Bush | Bucks |

## Notes

1. Now the University of Pennsylvania.
2. Now Princeton University.
3. Now Bucknell University. He attended into his junior year.
4. Attended Law School for one year.
5. Appointed as a judge of the Eastern, Middle and Western Districts of Pennsylvania.

| College | Law School | Years Hearing Cases |
| --- | --- | --- |
| Saint Joseph's University | University of Pittsburgh | 2004– |
| Columbia University | University of Pennsylvania | 2004– |
| City College of New York | University of Pennsylvania | 2004– |
| Pennsylvania State University | Dickinson School of Law | 2006–2010 |
| Brooklyn College | New York Law School | 2008– |
| Southwestern College | American University | 2008– |
| Ithaca College | Temple University | 2008– |

# Appendix II
# Chief Judges

(Congress first used the designation "Chief Judge" in the 1948 recodification of Title 28 of the United States Code.)

William H. Kirkpatrick. . . . . . . . . . . . 1948–1958
J. Cullen Ganey. . . . . . . . . . . . . . . . . . 1958–1961
Thomas J. Clary . . . . . . . . . . . . . . . . . 1961–1969
John W. Lord Jr. . . . . . . . . . . . . . . . . . 1969–1971
Joseph S. Lord III . . . . . . . . . . . . . . . . 1971–1982
Alfred L. Luongo. . . . . . . . . . . . . . . . . 1982–1986
John P. Fullam. . . . . . . . . . . . . . . . . . . 1986–1990
Louis C. Bechtle . . . . . . . . . . . . . . . . . 1990–1993
Edward N. Cahn. . . . . . . . . . . . . . . . . 1993–1998
James T. Giles . . . . . . . . . . . . . . . . . . . 1999–2005
Harvey Bartle III. . . . . . . . . . . . . . . . . 2006–2011
J. Curtis Joyner . . . . . . . . . . . . . . . . . . 2011–

# Appendix III
# Magistrate Judges

(Congress changed the title of United States Magistrate to United States Magistrate Judge in 1990.)

Tulio Gene Leomporra . . . . . . . . . . . . 1971–2006
Richard A. Powers III . . . . . . . . . . . . . 1971–1997
Edward W. Furia . . . . . . . . . . . . . . . . . . . . . 1971
Edwin E. Naythons . . . . . . . . . . . . . . 1971–1995
Peter B. Scuderi . . . . . . . . . . . . . . . . . 1974–2008
William F. Hall Jr. . . . . . . . . . . . . . . . . 1979–2001
James R. Melinson . . . . . . . . . . . . . . . 1990–2004
M. Faith Angell . . . . . . . . . . . . . . . . . 1990–
Arnold C. Rapoport . . . . . . . . . . . . . . 1992–
Charles B. Smith. . . . . . . . . . . . . . . . . 1992–2007
Diane M. Welsh . . . . . . . . . . . . . . . . . 1994–2005
Thomas J. Rueter . . . . . . . . . . . . . . . . 1994–
Carol Sandra Moore Wells . . . . . . . . . 1996–
Jacob P. Hart . . . . . . . . . . . . . . . . . . . 1997–
Linda K. Caracappa . . . . . . . . . . . . . . 2000–
Timothy R. Rice . . . . . . . . . . . . . . . . 2005–
David R. Strawbridge . . . . . . . . . . . . . 2005–
L. Felipe Restrepo . . . . . . . . . . . . . . . 2006–
Henry S. Perkin . . . . . . . . . . . . . . . . . 2007–
Elizabeth T. Hey . . . . . . . . . . . . . . . . . 2007–
Lynne A. Sitarski . . . . . . . . . . . . . . . . 2007–

# Appendix IV
# Bankruptcy Judges

(Prior to the 1978 change in the law, the Bankruptcy Judges were known as Referees.)

| | |
|---|---|
| Russell L. Hiller | 1948–1974 |
| Thomas J. Curtin | 1953–1975 |
| Bertram K. Wolfe | 1954–1966 |
| Emil F. Goldhaber | 1966–1986 |
| Thomas M. Twardowski | 1975–2006 |
| William A. King Jr. | 1975–1986 |
| David A. Scholl | 1986–2000 |
| Bruce I. Fox | 1986– |
| Diane Weiss Sigmund | 1993–2008 |
| Stephen Raslavich | 1993– |
| Kevin J. Carey | 2001–2005 |
| Richard E. Fehling | 2006– |
| Eric L. Frank | 2006– |
| Jean K. FitzSimon | 2006– |
| Magdeline D. Coleman | 2010– |

# Appendix V
# Clerks of Court

Samuel Caldwell . . . . . . . . . . . . . . . . . . 1789–1798
David Caldwell . . . . . . . . . . . . . . . . . . 1798–1831
Francis Hopkinson . . . . . . . . . . . . . . . 1831–1847
Thomas Leiper Kane . . . . . . . . . . . . . . 1847–1858
Charles Ferris Heazlitt . . . . . . . . . . . . . . . . . . 1858
John M. Jones . . . . . . . . . . . . . . . . . . . 1858–1860
Gilbert Rodman Fox . . . . . . . . . . . . . . 1860–1875
Charles Shippen Lincoln . . . . . . . . . . . 1875–1901
William Wright Craig . . . . . . . . . . . . . 1901–1918
George Brodbeck . . . . . . . . . . . . . . . . 1918–1951
Leo A. Lilly . . . . . . . . . . . . . . . . . . . . . 1951–1956
Gilbert W. Ludwig . . . . . . . . . . . . . . . 1956–1962
W. Halton Spann . . . . . . . . . . . . . . . . 1962–1963
John J. Harding . . . . . . . . . . . . . . . . . . 1964–1979
Michael E. Kunz . . . . . . . . . . . . . . . . . 1979–

# Index of Cited Cases

## W



## Z

# General Index